# An Interdisciplinary Journey from Non-Discrimination to Collective Rights

Jessika Eichler

# An Interdisciplinary Journey from Non-Discrimination to Collective Rights

## A Critique of Equality

Springer

Jessika Eichler
Law & Anthropology Department
Max Planck Institute for Social
Anthropology
Halle/Saale, Germany

ISBN 978-3-031-54617-4 ISBN 978-3-031-54618-1 (eBook)
https://doi.org/10.1007/978-3-031-54618-1



This Springer imprint is published by the registered company Springer Nature Switzerland AG
The registered company address is: Gewerbestrasse 11, 6330 Cham, Switzerland

Paper in this product is recyclable.

*While I still regret the loss of two beings*
*that were so dear to me,*
*my cat Leni and my grandfather Nick,*
*I am deeply indebted to a living being,*
*Adrián,*
*for his genuine support in very difficult*
*moments and times.*
*God put them by my side,*
*and I only wish I was able to return only a*
*tiny bit of this*
*to my (social) environment*

*Thank you, Christoph,*
*for having accepted to assume such a big*
*and special space in my life,*
*there are so few things I do not enjoy*
*sharing and realising with you,*
*you attract me in ways I hadn't imagined*
*before*

*My special thanks go to*
*the Members of the Habilitation Committee*
*at Sciences Po Paris in June 2023*
*who provided invaluable comments on my thesis*
*Miodrag Jovanović, Will Kymlicka, Magali Bessone, Astrid von Busekist*
*and my 'garant' Ariel Colonomos.*

# Contents

# Chapter 1
# Introductory Remarks

When discussing justifications attached to rights, very generically speaking, Elizabeth Wolgast remarks the following:

> In discussing our demands for justifications, Wittgenstein observed that 'it is so difficult to find the beginning'. Or, better: it is difficult to begin at the beginning. And not try to go further back. We may distort our subject if we try to always find something deeper, always look for another and another reason. There has to be an end to justification and with wrongs like murder we have hit bedrock.[1]

Our explorations of the equality principle resemble such almost infinite search for the beginning of the debate which may resemble the '*chicken or egg problem*'; it is indeed this very starting point of the debate which this piece attempts to critically approach. Collective rights theorists[2] and proponents of group-differentiated rights[3] would possibly overlook its relevance, probably owing to, inter-alia, the very focus placed on relevant groups and their specific demands, the necessity of developing a pro-active response to the persisting rationale of individualism in human rights orders, or as reflecting a critique on the common understanding of equality being constrained to its formal manifestation (rather than its de facto, outcome-oriented meaning). Anti-discrimination scholarship,[4] by contrast, commonly works with specific discrimination grounds, or the wider context of anti-discrimination law such as institutional developments or procedural successes, commonly failing to address underlying inequalities while non-discrimination and equality principles usually do go hand in hand, at least if we were to trace them in virtually any legal document.

---

[1] Wolgast (2020), p. 41.

[2] See, prominently, Jovanović (2012).

[3] Kymlicka (1995).

[4] See, for instance, Belavusau and Henrard (2018). For an overview or conceptual approximation, see Lippert-Rasmussen (2018).



J. Eichler, *An Interdisciplinary Journey from Non-Discrimination to Collective Rights*, https://doi.org/10.1007/978-3-031-54618-1_1

What remains or is being relegated to the margins of the debate concerns majoritarian tendencies that continuously embrace and or may lead to legally codifying the equality principle, representing not only a predominant principle in contemporary constitutionalism but also one that operates as an underlying rationale, a leading premise or a raison d'être of many legal codes including human rights orders. The present piece critically approaches much of the common sense built around this classical principle through a multi-level—domestic, regional, international—framework analysis, understanding its way of operating but also possible responses given by competing paradigms, including collective rights, difference-based reasoning generally, positive discrimination and other human rights-based approaches. The work shall hence present a nuanced idea of equality's main claims, its diverse manifestations or meanings, it shall further problematise the principle, both theoretically and as it relates to socio-political context. We may however also spend time on finding alternative approaches that promise to do justice to the demands raised by affected groups, indigenous peoples and ethnic, cultural, religious or linguistic minorities principally. This shall also give rise to entire principles and theoretical approaches, based on the author's own imaginations and reflections; these are discussed in depth (see Chaps. 5 and 7 in particular), establishing an important counterbalance to predominant equality rule, at least in theory. To put it in other words, the piece opted for a particular legal politics that tends to normalise forms of collectivisation, and to provide an overview of various routes of a particular legal politics—or various legal-political (de ferenda) strategies—that tends to normalise the collective rights talk within the dominant equality human rights regime, be it international or constitutional, following Jovanović's observations on my habilitation thesis this book is built on.

The book's major contribution would certainly lie in its legal theoretical dimension with its critique on equality and non-discrimination and the claim for a shifted focus residing on collective rights principally. In some way, the book would qualify as a contribution to critical theory, in the sense that it proposes norms for criticism and also realisable objectives for social transformation, hence living up to Horkheimian criteria of critical theory[5]—what it refrains from doing is a too detailed account of societal malaise, instead, the focus is clearly placed on juridification and other dimensions of the law. It only peripherally addresses societal tendencies in the context of recognition politics[6] and the move to the political right which it however majorly discusses in the institutional context. Indeed, one of its key points certainly is to be found in its embracement of identity and recognition politics, spelling out in detail what form this could take, what processes and procedures could be introduced respectively. It thereby clearly assumes a political theoretical identity, examining more closely what power relations underlie the law,[7] how minority rights fit into an

[5] Bohman (2005) and Horkheimer (1993).

[6] See, prominently, Taylor (1992) and Honneth and Fraser (2003).

[7] See, for instance, de Sousa Santos (2013).

order dominated by (a) majority(ies),[8] and engaging more closely with the idea of justice from the perspective of minorities. What the piece certainly builds on concerns group-differentiated rights as well as State theoretical approaches on the construction of the State and its proneness and aptitude to live up to the expectations and claims made by minority groups, often framed as multicultural or plurinational approaches.[9] Indeed, we are not constraining ourselves to examining equality principles in a punctual, ad-hoc manner, but also in terms of their immediate institutional, commonly constitutional, environment.

In that sense, domestic constitutionalism provides one among other venues for equality paradigms to be further understood and critically examined. Indeed, equality principles may be found as founding provisions in virtually any domestic constitutional framework but they also find further articulation in ordinary legislation and they find expression in virtually universally adopted international human rights treaties but also regional ius commune. These attempts at constitutional level (emblematic being the Bolivian and Ecuadorian constitutions)[10] may hence be considered one possible venue for reform, considering a reorientation of the value attributable to collective subjects of rights, and with the way equality is positioned or not, provoking indeed systemic transformations where a progressive understanding of equality becomes the yardstick of the constitutional reform process. The struggle for a more substantive idea of equality rights necessarily correlates with a more pluralist constitutional conception, both reflecting a certain consensus to systemic transformation in the sense of embracing an outcome-oriented vision of equality[11] with the potential to introduce group rights into the State's founding structure. For those familiar with international law and regional ius commune, it may easily become apparent that respective changes would need to be mirrored at international level, in the sense of providing yet another important safeguard, disciplining States where needed. Indeed, international legal instruments are commonly vested with a binding force (e.g. treaties),[12] at EU level counting with '*direct effect*' and '*supremacy*',[13] which would require States to make respective changes in any type of domestic law to live up to a State's international commitments. Very clearly then, equality paradigms would not be considered a proper legal order, but a transversal principle with instructive potential for these legal orders to be built around it. For that very reason, equality in its conservative shape may carry wide-reaching consequences for juridification processes, for these to hold on to a de facto understanding of equality. In real life, equality may be found in a given, often constitutional, order alongside more far reaching provisions such as entire catalogues or chapters of group-differentiated rights. A few reasons speak in favour of examining the

[8] Kymlicka (2013).

[9] See, notably, Yrigoyen Fajardo (2016).

[10] Ibid. See also Sieder (2016).

[11] See, for instance, Arneson (2015).

[12] For further insights, see Shaw (2008).

[13] For further insights, see Craig and de Búrca (2015).

multiplicity of legal orders, not least to mention questions of the application and effectiveness of the law but also if we think of the sheer diversity of approaches in terms of lessons learnt or best practice cases that may inspire developments elsewhere through judicial dialogue.

More questions may be raised as to the discipline-specific identity of the book, given that it certainly combines theoretical work on the one hand and political science and the law on the other. Questions would legitimately be raised as to the overall orientation or outlook of the work which may be torn between a more philosophical approach establishing an account on the normative foundations of collectivisation, and a socio-political answer rooted in the actual sites of legal politics or legal strategies proposed here. The book provides an in-depth view on the legal strategies or processes that constitute the principles of recognition (Chap. 5) and the processes and scales of collectivisation (Chap. 7) and in that sense clearly adopts a theoretical approach on the matter which it contextualises through socio-political analysis, by identifying dominant political trends, the actual realisation of identity and recognition politics, or through assimilating and integrationist agendas. Without going as far as informing the design of the present work, socio-political realities do play a role as these importantly contextualise the findings, and provide further insights on the relevance of the principles presented here, including current institutional failures but also highlighting opportunities lying with progressive trends in jurisprudence or daily politics.

Instead, a main focus is indeed placed on what the author imagines to be 'principles of recognition' (*principlisation, proceduralisation, specialisation, pluralisation*) and 'processes and scales of collectivisation' (*juridification/ standardisation, establishing sui generis orders, constitutionalisation, institutional mainstreaming, integration/standardisation*) which the author proposes here as possible strategies, processes and procedures that shall allow firstly, recognition to be further 'regulated' in a way, to be further spelt out, and secondly, for collectivisation processes, that is, the process of integrating collective rights into existing orders or creating new orders altogether, to become identifiable, in turn, measurable and also to be further articulated. In principle, these processes are to be imagined as distinct steps, one following the other, without needing to follow any specific sequence, that is, processes may start at different phases, depending on the existing state of the art or level of juridification principally. In some cases, the predominant framework provides facilitating entry points, demonstrating a certain human rights proneness, or a general open spirit reflecting an institutional or societal consensus on spurring progressive developments in the fields. The same could be said about possible hierarchies or priorities guiding the process—this would need to be decided on an ad-hoc, case-by-case basis, with each phase or process bearing the potential of being more pertinent than another at a specific time or situation. These processes are rather to be considered technical, allowing for all sorts of claims to enter into sophisticated juridification processes which may concern the multiplicity of rights in their integrity (see Sect. 7.9), including classical discriminatory grounds such as ethnic background or broader social justice claims being raised by groups suffering such ethnic discrimination; we may indeed want to be attentive to potential cumulative effects, also called intersectional forms of discrimination.

The conceptualisation and the putting in place of principles inevitably brings up methodological challenges that relate to rights holder categories and distinct claims made—it could legitimately be asked to what extent such categorisation lives up to the realities and true needs of the rights holders which could easily be attacked for following the top-down logics of (neo)colonialism including its epistemological assumptions.[14] It needs to be maintained here though that rather than suggesting what group categories or claims are to be collectivised, emphasis is placed on the processes and principles which shall render collectivisation processes realisable, operational and effective. To contextualise these theoretical imaginations, emblematic cases, commonly drawn from indigenous or minority studies, are taken serving illustrative purposes, and also being of inspiration to other group rights that could potentially undergo processes of juridification and follow the steps and phases pictured here. The very opening of existing legal frames to legal pluralism and new categorisations does in itself represent a decolonising effort proving especially crucial where indigenous rights are at stake but also seen from a meta level in drawing our attention to power relations underlying the law. In that sense, decoloniality assumes the role of a transversal and re-occurring variable throughout the book.

Beyond the law and many social science disciplines, categorising or classifying exercise has been subjected to criticism reaching back to Borgès who discourages us from reducing the world to scientific classification into ambiguous and redundant categories, as remarqued by Bessone during the defence of my thesis. Another pertinent objection to the classification(s) made however concerns the self-determined element—to what extent are self-determination and recognition being derived from self-recognition[15] and respectively, represent an affirmation of a specific imagination or proper subjectivity. While the book engages in certain deconstructing exercises, it inevitably needs to build on some variables or premises, the demand for recognising collective rights being one of them. In that sense, it is not further examined to what extent collective rights represent the most appropriate frame, method or strategy to translate rights into a State-dominated scenery, also placing trust in indigenous long-lasting struggles, locally and globally,[16] to make their collective claims heard. For the purpose of the present work, subject-holdership of collective rights proves indeed to be quintessential, if not existential, to establish solid categories of protection, for collective claims to be channelled into the scope of recognised legal orders, or for broader questions of recognition to be heard.

---

[14] Such colonial epistemological assumptions merit a debate on their own terms, see, for instance, Smith (2012).

[15] On indigenous proper collective decisions on responsibilities but also self-identification, see Gover's work, for instance: Gover (2011).

[16] See, for instance, Charters and Stavenhagen (2012).

Particular regard shall further be paid to those categories receiving our particular attention throughout the book, that is, indigenous peoples and 'national', ethnic, cultural, linguistic and religious minorities; it is usually assumed here for them to represent emblematic groups in terms of levels of marginalisation, in assuming a dedicated group character, in the sense of the inequalities suffered, or regarding discrimination against them.[17] Indeed, in a legal sense, indigenous peoples and said minorities alike have been claiming rights in a collective sense, both substantively and procedurally, hence turning them into important objects of analysis in view of the collective claims raised. Indigenous peoples are regularly portrayed as disproportionately vulnerable, especially in extractive contexts.[18] Other than that, both groups certainly occupy the position of being in a minority situation, especially against the background of majority-dominated legal orders or daily politics. In most cases, we can speak of a situation of historical injustice, including intergenerational trauma, affecting indigenous peoples and minorities until the current day, with its multifaceted impacts on life and livelihoods. In both cases, we may also pay particular regard to the relations maintained with externals, including the State and its institutions, being a very delicate question, especially for indigenous groups choosing to live in complete isolation from society at large. This inevitably brings up questions of dependencies, on the natural environment as a source of subsistence, spiritual practice and other (cultural) aspects related to their collective identity. Ultimately, encounters with externals and notably the State bring up questions on representation, autonomies, self-determination and also legal pluralism,[19] that is, recognition of indigenous proper instances of representation but also legal, political, economic, cultural, or religious pluralism. Collective rights naturally come to play a crucial role in all these contexts, either as referring to forms of autonomies, proper customs and practices that are exercised in complete independence from the State, or when interacting with the State, including its educational or health institutions. A special focus is hence placed on the different judicial and institutional regimes without delving too much into historical or other detail, instead, placing emphasis on the abstract level with the objective of generating broader findings, allowing for meta-analysis in the field of collective rights.

We shall also reflect on the broader debates this books tries adding to, leaving equality and non-discrimination aside for a moment which undoubtedly constitute important subjects to debate in their own terms. One of the most known debates in the field of human rights which is of pertinence here concerns the distinction

[17] For an overview of on-the-ground realities including respective human rights challenges, see reports issued by the Special Rapporteur on the Rights of Indigenous Peoples, the Expert Mechanism on the Rights of Indigenous Peoples (EMRIP), the Permanent Forum on Indigenous Issues (PFII), or the annual reports edited by the International Work Group for Indigenous Affairs (IWGIA).

[18] Permanent Forum on Indigenous Issues (2005) *Study on the Treatment of Traditional Knowledge in the Framework of the United Nations Declaration on the Rights of Indigenous Peoples and the Post-2015 Development Agenda.*

[19] See, for instance, Gover (2020) and von Benda-Beckmann and Turner (2020).

between universalism[20] and cultural relativism;[21] a way out is sought by seeing human rights as globally driven but ultimately adaptable to local contexts,[22] that way, regarding human rights as processes rather than static constructs. Such debates prove particularly fitting given the classical orientation of human rights universalism on the individual and her/his/x's rights,[23] often viewed as standing in contradiction with other approaches such as the collective idea of rights. As it may be imagined, collective rights are relegated to specific rights holder groups only, usually falling under soft law, and hence lacking any true enforcement value. The widest conception of collective rights may have been introduced with the idea of the community, as in '*humanity*', having found recognition ever since the foundation of the United Nations, or the idea of the 'community' having found first mentioning in the Universal Declaration of Human Rights, notably in the context of obligations towards the community (art. 29) and the individual right to participate in the cultural life of the community (art. 27). Indeed, the right to take part in a community's cultural life has often arisen in the context of group-specific rights, albeit adopting a restricted view on the community's proper rights, being largely shaped by an individualistic conception of human rights as it has been the case in international law (UN Covenant on Economic, Social and Cultural Rights, art. 15) and the Council of Europe's Framework Convention for the Protection of National Minorities (art. 3 and Explanatory Report to Framework Convention). More insights in that regard may be derived from the African Human and Peoples' Rights order, placing dedicated emphasis on the community and peoples' rights, as in African peoples, a State's population, indigenous peoples, or colonised and oppressed peoples generally.[24]

Further thought shall be spent on the divide between person-specific and person-unspecific rights which is commonly drawn in the human rights literature, especially as to concern international human rights law, distinguishing those rights applicable to all such as CAT, ICCPR or ICESCR from those reserved for specific groups, exercising a form of positive discrimination, materialising, notably, with the adoption of CEDAW, CRC, CRPD or ICERD. As explained above, collective rights have not reached the level of protection granted by treaty law (ILO C169 excepted), often considered under what has become known as '*3rd generation rights*'[25] with its difficulties in terms of causal nexus between violation and perpetrator, regarding definitional questions that concern the rights holder and duty bearer, or the broader recognition of these collective rights to form a proper category. While person-unspecific rights would certainly be of pertinence to the groups discussed here, our focus shall be placed on person-specific rights while these commonly do not depart

[20] Grewal (1998).

[21] Donnelly (2003).

[22] See, for instance, Goodale and Engle Merry (2003).

[23] See, for instance, Freeman (1995).

[24] See, for instance, Dersso (2006). See also: Baldwin and Morel (2009).

[25] See, for instance, Tomuschat (2014).

from the classical individual rights jargon. In recent years however, governments have shown more willing to adopt procedures that would allow for rights to be claimed collectively, that way allowing for group-differentiated rights to be realised procedurally. Emblematically, the optional protocol to ICESCR allows for communications to be submitted not only by individuals but also by "*groups of individuals*" (art. 2). A sort of group-differentiated approach may be identified here, also given that communications may be submitted "*on behalf of individuals or groups of individuals*", hence vesting an individual with important powers of representation which is often demanded from the perspective of indigenous communities and minority groups. It is to be distinguished between '*dual-standing rights*' which indeed allow collective rights to be claimed by individuals or representative instances on the one hand, and "*jointly exercised individual rights*",[26] the latter being the case for most contemporary human rights treaties, including the ICCPR 'minority provision' (art. 27). Conversely, the book clearly assumes a collective stance, substantively, but also for rights to be claimed collectively or in representation of an affected group.

A debate meriting particular attention, an often forgotten element in fact, concerns the postcolonial heritage embedded in legal regimes that remain in force until today, also carrying consequences for equality and non-discrimination principles as a typical manifestation of the ignorance of difference. Considerable epistemological-legal transformations may be required as a result, allowing to develop a certain sensitivity towards colonial manifestations of hierarchies that keep permeating justice orders, typical also being monolingualism or the missed opportunities of paying due regard to collective memory including past injustices. In turn, supposedly universal forms of knowledge and knowledge systems have commenced to be disentangled by scholars.[27] As a consequence, such inherited asymmetries have been termed "*epistemological tyranny*",[28] the "*reach of imperialism into our heads*",[29] or a "*fatal (universalising) convergence and missed occasion*"[30] to decolonise States and minds. Indeed, we are witnessing a form of adherence to 'classical' legal principles, portraying a specific common sense of the law, building on unquestioned patterns of dominance which may become apparent in rather intangible forms, including, prominently, the largely accepted principle of equality. Similar observations may be made in relation to 'property' which has been going hand in hand with 'race', understanding race as a technology of property-making and dispossession, also through extractive colonisation, racialised capitalism.[31] These trends have been subsumed under what has been understood as the "*law's race towards eternal global*

[26] Buchanan (1993).
[27] Smith (2012).
[28] Aveling (2013).
[29] Smith (2012).
[30] Badie (2018).
[31] Adébísí (2023b).

*apartheid*".[32] Epistemological (and beyond!) transformations have been demanded in turn, often taken up in post-colonial discourse, or to put it differently, in what has been termed "*the empire writes back and/or writing from the margins*"[33] approaches with objective of "*decolonis[ing] the mind*" or "*despensar*"[34] (un-think/re-think) predominant patterns of thinking, ultimately hegemony. What this implies in our everyday practice may concern entire new logics of the sense of life—in a way responding to colonial practice that would require the colonised to change their reason of existence, and in that sense change such reason altogether with the process of decolonisation.[35] Indigeneity naturally finds a place in these debates, as one of the most emblematic manifestations of decolonial struggle, also as we consider indigenous intergenerational ties; the decolonised community defines itself with a view to the future and thereby establishes a new connection with humanity.[36] Indeed, an important novelty arising with collective rights concerns indigenous environmental rights channelling intergenerational concerns into the ambit of the law, thereby breaking up old established ideas on rights holdership and responsibilities. It may not come as a surprise then that epistemological changes have been contextualised through the field of indigenous scholarship, including by means of methodological reconsiderations.[37]

Yet another consideration worthy further exploration concerns the positioning of the equality principle in relation to ordinary human rights terminology and resultantly, specific obligations arising therewith. What immediately becomes apparent lies with the triadic human rights obligation, *to respect, to protect and to fulfil*, or, relatedly, the negative vs. positive obligations approach in human rights law.[38] Equality—in its de facto manifestation in particular—clearly qualifies as a negative approach to human rights, that is, for States as main rights holders not to interfere with the exercise of a certain right. Following a classical reading of human rights obligations, the '*duty to respect*' does not entail further reaching steps to be taken, that is, measures to be adopted to contribute to the realisation of a right. At least traditionally, civil and political rights were understood as requiring negative obligations to be put in place while economic, social and cultural rights were originally associated with positive duties.[39]

The field of equality principles in particular seems to reopen the debate on positive obligations, namely through positive action or positive discrimination[40]

---

[32] Ibid. See also: Adébísí (2023a).

[33] Smith (2012).

[34] de Sousa Santos (2013).

[35] Mbembe (2010).

[36] Fanon (2002).

[37] Smith (2012).

[38] See, for instance, Tomuschat (2014).

[39] Ibid.

[40] '*Positive discrimination*' refers to "*actively favouring one category of people over others because they are considered to be disadvantaged and thereby discriminating against those others*" (Law

devoted to mitigating inequalities by explicitly recognising difference and, based on such recognition, to adopt special measures. Collective rights may be taken as one possible venue to operationalise positive discrimination, as argued throughout the book, by embarking on an interdisciplinary journey from (de facto) equality to collective rights. To return to equality for a moment, it may be stated here that the equality principle alludes at its finest to the classical notion of freedom from interference, building on a Berlinian conception of negative freedom.[41] Conversely, positive discrimination would be promoting a positive freedom, a 'freedom to' be or do.[42] Following this line of reasoning, positive discrimination has been portrayed as laying the structural grounds and to permit "*radical, transformative change towards equality*"[43] to be realised. Interestingly, the predominant liberal approach to equality law has been approached from yet another critical angle, notably its supposed limitation to rights holders as abstract individuals without "*extraneous identity categories (...) and some common core*"[44] which inevitably prevents any group-differentiated perspective from being further examined, let alone juridified at the ending. This makes any formation of collective identity and respective rights unthinkable in principle.

A few final observations may be made here as relating to the fundaments of the equality principle, and essentially, its implications for individuals and groups in society, demanding, in turn, a rethinking of the concept and other, arguably complementary, routes to be explored. A first constraint that comes to mind concerns its protective realm that commonly concerns citizenship holders only rather than protecting all those subjected to a given territorial jurisdiction.[45] Unrecognised minorities in particular such as those with a migrant background or stateless persons that way do not benefit from the protection by the law through equality before the law, equal treatment and the like. A second concern relates to certain arbitrariness when it comes to relevant grounds of discrimination which are largely defined at domestic legislative level: while EU law, for instance, needs to be observed, the level of regulatory detail and institutionalisation does not apply to any discriminatory ground equally which may very well exclude certain grounds from the scope of protection or apply to specific sectors (such as education or employment). What may not be forgotten here relates to cumulative grounds, or the intersectional effects of discrimination,[46] requiring us to look beyond the "*single-axis models of*

2018) The concept has also been defined as "*a key instrument of a 'politics of catching up' between different groups as it finds articulation in international law and numerous states where it is being practices. It strives to promote a greater de facto equality among groups or at least to guarantee those members of disadvantaged groups a real equality of opportunities*" (Calvès 2010).

[41] Berlin (1969).

[42] Treiger-Bar-Am (2019).

[43] Noon (2010).

[44] Smith (2016).

[45] See, for instance, Kochenov (2019) and Kymlicka (1995).

[46] Intersectionality was "*introduced in the late 1980s as a heuristic term to focus attention on the vexed dynamics of difference and the solidarities of sameness in the context of antidiscrimination*

*discrimination law*",[47] and instead focus on "*discrete, sequential and severable identity factors*".[48] Resembling the dilemmas we encounter with collective rights, intersectional rights, as we shall call them, may not easily enjoy what juridification commonly provides for; to put this otherwise, intersectional violations may face additional obstacles, such as requiring separate proofs for each ground or the fact that these forms of violations find their roots in structural conditions that may need further exploration beyond the legal discipline.[49] As a response, we may witness the adoption of integrated approaches and novel forms of institution-building; indeed, equality regimes in Europe with specialised mechanisms have come to be absorbed by integrated equality bodies, better equipped to address intersecting violations and their social complexity.[50]

As it becomes apparent here, the very blurriness of the equality principle lends itself for further contextualisation, requiring a detailed analysis of political context, which at the ending qualifies equality further, defines its potential and related challenges in practice. An interdisciplinary exploration thereby becomes a sheer necessity, allowing us to delve deeper into the logics and conditions defined by institutionalism in domestic politics, regional mechanisms and international bodies. This similarly applies to the procedures, principles, processes and scales that are proposed throughout the present piece as they relate to recognition and collective rights which necessarily build on while needing to become embedded in socio-political realities and decisions. Equality hence constitutes a useful starting point for debating difference-oriented human rights work in theory and practice which may be seen as a somewhat incomplete legal construct requiring accompanying positive measures, or, alternatively, it may be critically approached for establishing wrongful premises and rationales of a systemic nature, disguising groups' needs owing to its exclusively individualistic orientation.

## References

Adébísí FI (2023a) Decolonisation and legal knowledge: reflections on power and possibility. Bristol University Press, Bristol

Adébísí FI (2023b) Law and the colonial afterlives of property: (un)creating the sacrifice zones of colonialism. One day hybrid SLS supported conference at the University of Greenwich, 'A decolonial and anti-racist approach to legal education and pedagogy – sharing good practices'

Arneson R (2015) Equality of opportunity. In: The Stanford encyclopedia of philosophy. https://plato.stanford.edu/cgi-bin/encyclopedia/archinfo.cgi?entry=equal-opportunity

---

*and social movement politics. It exposed how single-axis thinking undermines legal thinking, disciplinary knowledge production, and struggles for social justice*" (Cho et al. 2013).

[47] Smith (2016). See also: Xinidis (2019).

[48] Bourke Martignoni (2018).

[49] Solanka (2017).

[50] Krizsan et al. (2012).

Aveling N (2013) 'Don't talk about what you don't know': on (not) conducting research with/in Indigenous contexts. Crit Stud Educ 54(2)
Badie B (2018) Quand le Sud réinvente le monde: Essai sur la puissance de la faiblesse. La Découverte, Paris
Baldwin C, Morel C (2009) Group rights. In: Evans M, Murray R (eds) The African Charter on Human and Peoples' Rights: the system in practice, 1986-2006. Cambridge University Press, Cambridge
Belavusau U, Henrard K (2018) EU anti-discrimination law beyond gender. Hart Publishing, Oxford
Berlin I (1969) Four essays on liberty. Oxford University Press, Oxford
Bohman J (2005) Critical theory. In: Stanford encyclopedia of philosophy
Bourke Martignoni J (2018) Sexual and reproductive rights at the crossroads: intersectionality and the UN Treaty Monitoring Bodies. In: Bribosia E, Rorive I (eds) Human rights tectonics: global dynamics of integration and fragmentation. Intersentia, Cambridge
Buchanan A (1993) The role of collective rights in the theory of indigenous peoples' rights. Transnatl Law Contemp Probl 3(1)
Calvès G (2010) La discrimination positive. Presses Universitaires de France, Paris
Charters C, Stavenhagen R (2012) Making the declaration work: the United Nations Declaration on the Rights of Indigenous Peoples. International Work Group for Indigenous Affairs, Copenhagen
Cho S, Williams Crenshaw K, McCall L (2013) Toward a field of intersectionality studies: theory, applications, and praxis. Signs: J Women Cult Soc 38(4)
Craig PP, de Búrca G (2015) EU law: text, cases, and materials. Oxford University Press, Oxford
de Sousa Santos B (2013) Descolonizar el saber, reinventar el poder. LOM ediciones, Santiago de Chile
Dersso SA (2006) The jurisprudence of the African Commission on Human and Peoples' Rights with respect to peoples' rights. Afr Hum Rights Law J 6
Donnelly J (2003) Universal human rights in theory and practice. Cornell University Press, Ithaca
Fanon F (2002) Les damnés de la terre. La Découverte, Paris
Freeman M (1995) Are there collective human rights? Polit Stud XLIII
Goodale M, Engle Merry S (2003) The practice of human rights: tracking law between the global and the local. Cambridge University Press, Cambridge
Gover K (2011) Tribal constitutionalism – states, tribes and the governance of membership. Oxford University Press, Oxford
Gover K (2020) Legal pluralism and indigenous legal traditions. In: Schiff Berman P (ed) The Oxford handbook of global legal pluralism. Oxford University Press, Oxford
Grewal I (1998) On the new global feminism and the family of nations: dilemmas of transnational feminist practice. In: Shohat EH (ed) Talking visions: multicultural feminism in a transnational age. New Museum of Contemporary Art, New York
Honneth A, Fraser N (2003) Redistribution or recognition? A political philosophical exchange. Verso, New York
Horkheimer M (1993) Between philosophy and social science. MIT Press, Cambridge
Jovanović M (2012) Collective rights: a legal theory. Cambridge University Press, Cambridge
Kochenov D (2019) Citizenship. MIT Press, Cambridge
Krizsan A, Skjeie H, Squires J (2012) Institutionalizing intersectionality: a theoretical framework. In: Krizsan A, Skjeie H, Squires J (eds) Institutionalising intersectionality: the changing nature of European regimes. Palgrave Macmillan, London
Kymlicka W (1995) Multicultural citizenship: a liberal theory of minority rights. Oxford University Press, Oxford
Kymlicka W (2013) Multicultural odysseys: navigating the new international politics of diversity. Oxford University Press, Oxford
Law J (2018) Positive discrimination. A dictionary of law. Oxford University Press, Oxford

Lippert-Rasmussen K (2018) The Routledge handbook of ethics of discrimination. Routledge, London
Mbembe A (2010) Sortir de la grande nuit: Essay sur l'Afrique décolonisée. La Découverte, Paris
Noon M (2010) The Shackled Runner: time to rethink positive discrimination? Work Employ Soc 24(4)
Shaw MN (2008) International law, 6th edn. Cambridge University Press, Cambridge
Sieder R (2016) Indigenous peoples' rights and the law in Latin America. In: Rodríguez-Garavito C (ed) Law and society in Latin America: a new map. Routledge, Abingdon
Smith LT (2012) Decolonizing methodologies. Zed Books, London
Smith B (2016) Intersectional discrimination and substantive equality: a comparative and theoretical perspective. Equal Rights Rev 16
Solanka I (2017) Discrimination as stigma: a theory of anti-discrimination law. Hart Publishing, Oxford
Taylor C (1992) Multiculturalism and the 'politics of recognition'. Princeton University Press, Princeton
Tomuschat C (2014) Human rights: between idealism and realism. Oxford University Press, Oxford
Treiger-Bar-Am K (2019) Positive freedom and the law. Routledge, London
von Benda-Beckmann K, Turner B (2020) Anthropological roots of global legal pluralism. In: Schiff Berman P (ed) The Oxford handbook of global legal pluralism. Oxford University Press, Oxford
Wolgast E (2020) Wrong rights. Hypatia: J Femin Philos 2(1)
Xinidis R (2019) Multiple discrimination in EU anti-discrimination law: towards redressing complex inequality? In: Belavusau U, Henrard K (eds) EU anti-discrimination law beyond gender. Hart Publishing, Oxford
Yrigoyen Fajardo R (2016) The panorama of pluralist constitutionalism: from multiculturalism to decolonisation. In: Rodríguez-Garavito C (ed) Law and society in Latin America: a new map. Routledge, Abingdon

# Part I
# On Equality

Other than what we would possibly expect when it is referred to 'equality' in contemporary legal debates, equality is understood in a broad sense here, as a paradigm that may indeed take the form of an ordinary equality and non-discrimination provision, it may however also very well capture any mediating measure with the objective of creating a level playing field for minorities to gain voice under the umbrella of the State or in strengthening their proper forms of governance. Even if we followed a strict legal interpretation, we are confronted with a wide range of—often incommensurable—meanings and varying effects for those holding the rights protected therewith. This may concern, classically speaking, de jure and de facto manifestations of equality being tantamount to equality of opportunity or formal equality and equality of result or outcome. It may similarly address technical detail such as direct and indirect forms of discrimination. As it may easily become apparent, the most ambitious non-discrimination provisions may not allow for systemic change, permeating the State's very structure, including decision-making capacities or levels of representation. In that sense, the present endeavour seeks to explore 'equality' understood as a paradigm or approach that bears genuine transformative potential, hence distancing itself from the idea of treating rights violations as isolated occurrences or being limited in nature. Instead, it is examined to what extent equality as a predominant paradigm articulates itself in the law, in State-minority relations or any other encounter minorities or indigenous peoples experience without ignoring their proper orders of governance, justice or education to name a few.

Another thought meriting further elaboration in that regard concerns the question of legal orders being responsive (or not) to human rights violations on the ground. As the above debate suggests, classical non-discrimination and equality provisions are to be found in legal codes, commonly domestic constitutions; in fact, equality is enshrined as founding principle in virtually any constitutional framework ever since its embracement by early human rights codes such as the *Déclaration des Droits de l'Homme et du Citoyen*. While some may think of international human rights law as progressive standards establishing guarantees beyond equality, this may not be true for especially generic treaties, that is, those establishing person-unspecific rights. As a corollary, we may not transpose our theoretical frame to those treaties stipulating rights reserved to, inter-alia, women, the child, persons of disabilities, migrated persons or disappeared persons. In any event, our analysis must reach beyond the domestic constitutional realm for the evident reason that the idea of the State as a sovereign—we may say 'absolute'—entity is deeply ingrained in domestic and international instruments alike. We easily derive at such conclusion when considering the intergovernmental setting of the treaty drafting process or when drawing our attention to limiting clauses in those treaties, introducing exceptions where human rights conflict with the State's integrity or sovereignty. As a result, it seems inevitable to understand equality as it materialises in different legal orders, including domestic constitutionalism, regional *ius commune* and international law, and also the way it is being negotiated amongst those orders and competent institutions. Interesting dynamics and forms of dialogue may be observed relatedly, not least to mention legal hierarchies requiring a certain interpretation to predominate throughout different legal orders, or, contrarily, for common constitutional traditions to determine how equality is to be understood.

As it may become apparent from the above, the most vehement critique on equality bases itself in its unresponsiveness and inadequateness in dealing with groups rather than the individual. Again, we are to refer to classical human rights codes but also contemporary treaties that only rarely establish group rights, becoming relegated to isolated provisions instead. Progressive interpretative endeavours become a sheer necessity as a result which comes with certain dependencies that are created for monitoring committees to show a particular group or minority-proneness or for courts to render progressive judgements—otherwise, group rights indeed remain confined to specialised treaties, UNDRIPS, ILO C169 or FCNM. Equality paradigms built on individual rights indeed represent a predominant strand in international and domestic standards alike. This unequivocally comes with certain consequences for rendering rights enforceable, for claiming them in the collective sense despite a persisting insensitivity involved for substantial issues, that is, the particular nature of collective rights. As discussed further below, collective rights stand out, among other aspects, on grounds of their systemic nature, by considering, inter-alia, intergenerational injustices, socio-economic vulnerability, a general background of discrimination and disempowerment, or any infringements that may take a particularly pronounced form. Even for those not studying collective rights, it may easily become clear that the predominant order hardly shows responsive to these particularities, starting with collectivising individual claims such as the individual freedom of expression to be extended to protest action, while showing sensitive for proper procedures and customs of those groups affected, manifesting groups' very autonomies and self-determination.

Relatedly, we may want to argue that equality's generality may not suffice to establish the necessary regulatory detail and rigour that proves crucial to live up to the very particular demands and needs related to specific rights, such as civil and political rights or social, economic or cultural rights to name the most known human rights regimes. This may, of course, concern individuals and groups alike. Importantly, it vests the legislator with considerable discretionary powers to develop (or not) progressive laws, often limited to specific sectors as famously demonstrated by the field of gender equality. This also concerns the case of positive measures as will be discussed further below which only rarely find their way into classical non-discrimination and equality provisions. Similar arguments may be raised in relation to the surrounding socio-political contexts which may easily escape the law and its application, especially when applied in a strict sense. While certainly representing a common ill of judicial practice, equality seems particularly affected by a narrow reading, often limiting itself to its de jure manifestations. Especially group-specific violations necessarily demand wider contexts to be taken into account, given an often long established history of marginalisation, stereotypisation and discrimination, requiring measures to be adopted beyond the immediate damage incurred, or rather the immediate damage visible.

Indeed, the implications of violations unforeseen by equality provisions prove to be manifold, especially in group contexts. Particularly emblematic in that regard would be those violations relating, directly or indirectly, to colonial, neo-colonial and postcolonial contexts respectively. These, it could be argued, bring our attention, at its finest, to the complexities inherent to violations (which equality fails to accommodate for) and resultantly, collective claims, often raised by indigenous communities. While the question of reparations represents an ever present claim having been sidelined for centuries, the colonial condition stands out due to its multidimensionality, that is, a multiplicity of spheres of life that continue being affected, requiring indeed some profound transformations beyond the justice systems and isolated claims made. Equality paradigms in that sense, could be understood as particularly ill-suited to meet the specific needs arising amongst those suffering colonialism-specific violations, often occurring in what has been termed intergenerational trauma context. It needs to be stated here, colonial heritage reaches beyond what the law might be able to respond to, permeating knowledge structures, education systems including a wide panoply of societal factors which may escape the legal realm and institutionality. For good reasons, scholars have referred to epistemologies of the South or indigenous methodologies to provide alternative answers of a systemic nature, requiring, in turn, large-scale transformations from society to the institutions of the State, to constitutional frameworks, and also relevant international legal orders. Much remains little tangible, little identifiable from the perspective of those operating or putting into effect predominant principles, often having grown up in specific educations traditions and circles. Asymmetries may be reproduced throughout a multiplicity of situations and sectors, famously, materialising in the context of resource extraction which may affect indigenous negotiating position, sheer awareness of relevant technical knowledge, and not least to mention their very shaping powers and consent where decisions affect them and indigenous livelihoods. Another context worthy highlighting here concerns land rights and their fit, or rather, incommensurability with equality paradigms. Ever since the embracement of the terra nullius doctrine in colonial times and the accompanying notion of private property including lands, more far-reaching laws were needed to mediate not only the damage incurred but in opening our minds to an entirely different understanding of land management. Illustrative may be the jurisprudence developed by the Inter-

American Court of Human Rights having re-interpreted classical legal concepts to assume a community dimension. Again, equality needs to be rethought, necessarily to be understood in its most de facto sense, to accommodate indigenous cosmovisions, customs, procedures, ultimately legal understanding in order to truly live up to its mitigating promises.

On a final note, we may want to refer to the notion of pluralism and legal pluralism in particular that seem to conflict with the basic preconditions of equality paradigms, especially the somewhat unambitious objective of applying the law in a non-discriminatory manner. Addressing indigenous rights in terms of the detrimental impacts measures may exert on their lives may not be enough—indeed, such minimalistic function of the law mirrors the very technical approach that is being taken, addressing, sporadically, in an ad-hoc manner, specific violations committed. Group-specific rights however demand a detailed analysis of the particularities and constituency of group identity, and therewith, proper collective needs that hardly find articulation in classical legal codes. This commences with indigenous or minority self-governance systems, it also relates to proper justice orders, education and language rights, or the needs related to freedom of religion or spirituality. Yet also more transversally, indigenous proper procedures, practices, customs and legal traditions are to be respected whenever a law is being applied or appropriated. The question of legal (and beyond) pluralism needs to be asked in the procedural sense, as far as, for instance, State law is concerned, but also, importantly, as a manifestation of indigenous or minorities' self-determination and collective autonomy. All this takes us back to the beginning, raising the question of efficiency as far as equality is concerned: equality paradigms hardly bear the capacity to juridify forms of pluralism, being usually relegated to dedicated human rights catalogues that refer to pluralisms in specific contexts only. As it becomes easily observable here, equality is generically understood in a strict, non-discriminatory, negative sense, without carrying any implications for a legal order in its entirety, that is, without mainstreaming equality throughout its decision-making organs, or its constitutive functions.

# Chapter 2
# Equality Paradigms and Non-discrimination: Theoretical Approximations

## 2.1 Equality Paradigms: How to Accommodate Difference?

Equality principles arguably lay the foundations for contemporary human rights orders, often framed as equality in law or de jure manifestations (being obviously highly problematic for prospective victims), referring to rights applicable to all (without discrimination),[1] being person-unspecific in most of the cases.[2] Different manifestations of equality, equality paradigms or principles are to be distinguished from the outset, differing immensely as to their very impact, or overall outcome, on those affected. In other words, equality may be understood as a starting position for individuals and groups born into society; conversely, emphasis may be placed on equality as a process or result, alluding to, for instance, the Rawlsian veil of ignorance[3] and its focus on redistributive social justice principles that shall ultimately mitigate persisting inequalities. A common misconception in that regard lies with how a given person shall be treated: it is often maintained that equality would

[1] The *Universal Declaration of Human Rights* (1948) is certainly emblematic of these developments which explicitly states '*the equal and inalienable rights of all members of the human family*' (preamble) or '*all human beings are born free and equal in dignity and rights*' (art. 1), finding its roots (among other founding documents) in the *Déclaration des Droits de l'Homme et du Citoyen* (1789) maintaining that '*les hommes naissent et demeurent libres et égaux en droits*' (art. 1). Hard law documents seemingly follow and actively embrace such rationale, including but not limited to the *International Covenant on Civil and Political Rights* (ICCPR), being calling upon States to '*undertake to respect and to ensure to all individuals within its territory and subject to its jurisdiction the rights recognised in the present Covenant, without distinction of any kind*...' (art. 2(1)) and the *International Covenant on Economic, Social and Cultural Rights* (ICESCR) which '*undertakes to guarantee the rights enunciated in the present Covenant exercised without discrimination of any kind*...' (arts. 2(2)).

[2] A contrasting view is developed by group rights and collective regimes; person-specific rights may include inter-alia women's rights, the rights of the child, rights of persons with disabilities, indigenous peoples' and (ethnic, cultural, religious and linguistic) minority rights or migrant rights.

[3] Rawls (1999a).



J. Eichler, *An Interdisciplinary Journey from Non-Discrimination to Collective Rights*, https://doi.org/10.1007/978-3-031-54618-1_2

imply treatment of people as equals,[4] which is not to be confused with equal treatment.[5] Indeed, it is maintained that '*recognising that human beings are all equally individual does not mean treating them uniformly in any respects other than those in which they clearly have a moral claim to be treated alike*'.[6] In that sense, it appears virtually natural to consider those very respects or dimensions of difference that merit dedicated attention. This shines through inter-alia, different social justice and (re)distribution theories at different levels,[7] steered towards equal access of opportunities and equality of outcomes,[8] including Sen's capability approach[9] focussing on satisfying inherent needs such as health or nourishment. In fact, our attention shall be directed towards a person's social position, her/his/x's position in society at large,[10] without showing ignorant of humans' natural condition. Following this line of reasoning, we shall be attentive to difference as a decisive starting point to examine equality, alluding to the well-known '*politics of difference*'[11] and its leaning towards such due consideration of difference in unequal societies.

In that sense, the present work differs from accounts on relevant material requirements and precise materialisation of equality,[12] in other words, how would equality materialise in substance? This may concern, for instance, political equality or equal political status,[13] it may refer to socio-economic dimensions[14] or any other form. Rather, we seek to approach equality in a transcendental manner, through principles that shall help us to examine its overall challenges, its deficit in allowing for inclusiveness in terms of access and outcome, its cross-fertilization throughout a multiplicity of institutional orders, and the potential lying in 'beyond equality' articulations such as positive discrimination, positive measures, and collective rights to name a few. We shall also take the opportunity to situate the present equality critique within the predominant equality jargon here. In that sense, it is to be distinguished between '*formal*' and '*substantive*' equality, the former referring to identical treatment[15] irrespective of difference or circumstances while the latter explicitly calls for differential treatment and a contextual approach on the matter.[16] Indeed, equality in the former sense is to be questioned on the basis of its market-driven, meritocratic orientation, proving ignorant of socio-economic inequalities,

---

[4] Dworkin (1977).

[5] Gosepath (2021).

[6] Ibid., para. 19.

[7] Fraser (1998), Stiglitz (2016) and Badie and Vidal (2017).

[8] Clapham (2015).

[9] Sen (1992). See also: Liao (2015)

[10] See e.g. Hobbes (1588-1679).

[11] Taylor (1992) and Honneth and Fraser (2003).

[12] Gosepath (2021).

[13] Besson (2015).

[14] See above, Stiglitz' or Badie's work on socio-economic inequalities (at global scale).

[15] Also known as '*numerical*' treatment, for further reference, see above Gosepath (2021).

[16] Henrard (2008).

unequal access to education and our overall shaping social environment. A common point of departure lies in '*proportional*' equality as in allocating goods to persons based on and commensurate with their unequal positions, hence situating the principle in a distributive context, which reaches back to Aristotle's concept of equality.[17] We would find equality untenable given its prioritisation of 'marketable merit and skill' and 'adequate native talents',[18] played out to the detriment of those left behind. We may further want to distinguish between the underlying rationale as in equality of persons in 'fundamental worth or moral status',[19] predominant in egalitarian doctrines which, however, does not in itself constitute identical treatment.

Yet another key dimension not to be missed includes '*equality of opportunity*' which is commonly contrasted with '*equality of result/outcome*' approaches, the former remaining rather difficult to grasp, showing considerable variance in the extent to which we would attempt to equalise someone's or a group's starting position.[20] Similarly, it has been argued elsewhere that "*different conceptions of equality of opportunity construe this idea of competing on equal terms variously*",[21] finding yet another sub-categorisation relevant to the concept in question. In that sense, it is distinguished between '*formal equality of opportunity*' and '*substantive equality of opportunity*' (see debate above on formal and substantive equality). While the former generally embraces the slogan "*careers open to talents*" to be viewed in the context of a liberal market economy and principally operates in the public space, the latter offers "*genuine opportunities to become qualified*", that is, opportunities that allow to "*develop the needed (...) skills*".[22] Famously, '*substantive*' or '*fair equality of opportunity*' derives its rationale from the Rawlsian, imaginary social justice idea of equality that departs from an identical starting position in the sense of natural assets: "*those who are at the same level of talent and ability, and have the same willingness to use them, should have the same prospects of success regardless of their initial place in the social system*".[23] We may, of course, take this further, understanding the very inequalities in such natural assets as decisive factors to be considered when making sense of persisting inequalities, such as those related to educational failures in successfully addressing and ultimately mitigating these.

Another common differentiation is drawn between '*direct*' and '*indirect discrimination*'. Direct discrimination materialises in a context in which a prohibited criterion of differentiation is being operationalised whereas indirect discrimination places a dedicated focus on the final result; this may include the discriminatory

[17] Aristotle (1984).

[18] Arneson (2013).

[19] Ibid.

[20] Henrard (2008).

[21] Arneson (2015), para. 1.

[22] Ibid.

[23] Rawls (1999a), p. 63.

effects of legal acts that, by their very intention, do not make any distinction.[24] In short, direct discrimination involves the intent of a measure, suggesting explicitness while indirect discrimination rather refers to its effects.[25] The difference between the two legal constructs may be explained by distinguishing between the different traits a person possesses in relation to the treatment received:

> . . .cases of direct discrimination identify cases where disadvantageous treatment is based on the belief that a person possesses some trait P, while in cases of indirect discrimination, a facially neutral action discriminates on the basis of some trait Q, but the fact that a person possesses trait P is causally linked to that person being treated in a disadvantageous manner under Q[26]

Indeed, a distinguishing characteristic is to be found in the "*disparate impact that correlates with such a proscribed ground*"[27] which does not absolve the State or private actor from basic human rights duties to be upheld; this becomes yet more salient where discriminate impacts are known to the infringing entity. Others have hence established a direct relation between indirect discrimination and substantive equality,[28] being actively supported by, for instance, the European Court of Justice which embraces substantive discrimination through its jurisprudence on indirect discrimination;[29] the European Court of Human Rights (ECtHR) also recognised the concept in its case-law.[30] Indeed, the ECtHR addressed indirect discrimination as it exerts de facto impacts, it ruled out the necessity "*to prove any discriminatory intent on the part of the relevant authorities*" and also, importantly, pronounced itself on the burden of proof which would "*lay with the Government to show that the difference in the impact of the legislation was the result of objective factors unrelated to ethnic origin*".[31]

Albeit relatedly, indirect discrimination also enjoys specific mentioning in the context of group rights, of special relevance to the present book. In that sense, it may gain particular relevance as it relates to '*distributive inequalities between groups*',[32] hence alluding to minority situations. Notably, indirect discrimination has been understood in relation to measures that may cause disproportionate impacts on particular groups,[33] or as being intrinsically connected and influenced by group justice ideals.[34] Critical voices also examined the conceptual difficulties in drawing

---

[24] Kasım (2022).

[25] Baldwin and Morel (2009).

[26] Cossette-Lefebvre (2020), p. 340.

[27] Doyle (2007), p. 537.

[28] Henrard (2011).

[29] Belavusau and Henrard (2019). See e.g. *Werner Mangold vs. Rudiger Helm*, Court of Justice of the European Union in 2005.

[30] See e.g. *D.H. and Others vs. The Czech Republic*, European Court of Human Rights in 2007.

[31] Ibid., para. 'Presumption of indirect discrimination'.

[32] Cossette-Lefebvre (2020), p. 340.

[33] Henrard (2011) and Craig (2007).

[34] Henrard (2011).

dividing lines between indirect and direct discrimination in practice: Roma people and other discriminated groups have come to be adversely affected by the grey zones as a result of such dichotomy, especially with societal attitudes constituting or adding to systemic discriminatory practices in those cases.[35]

At the end, equality accounts differ in the extent to which difference is dealt with or to which it is genuinely or holistically addressed. Rather than rejecting difference as such, quite a few approaches adopt an albeit contextual, ad-hoc method in dealing with difference. More precisely, equality-based theories of rights identify the need to "*take into account morally relevant aspects of people's circumstances and to ignore morally irrelevant aspects*",[36] it is argued—hence suggesting we all depart from the same sense of relevance, by way of extracting presumably decisive factors or determining criteria of selection. We may legitimately ask if and to what extent difference actually finds accommodation under such paradigm, or alternatively, escapes the defining filter of equality theory instead. Vulnerability experience often remains undervalued, it goes unperceived under the invisibilising umbrella of other categories, for instance, or other policy objectives defined by majorities. We may also wonder if self-determined group identities actually escape existing categories as predetermined by the law: this may concern those minorities not falling under the conceptual umbrella of e.g. 'national minority groups'.[37] Are these to be considered inferior in legal status and hence group rights protection as a consequence? We easily think of double standards when taking account (or not) of inter-alia ethnic, cultural, linguistic or religious grounds of discrimination. Equality frameworks certainly prove somewhat ill-suited to accommodate difference on grounds of its high threshold of inclusiveness, that is its all-encompassing nature. Further systemic ills may lie in the failure or in its blurriness when addressing de jure and de facto difference, or direct and indirect discrimination—in other words, equality paradigms may prove little sensitive towards the multiplicity of manifestations. Finally and relatedly, internal difference among minority groups may find little accommodation under equality frameworks that limit themselves to (if at all) only a few grounds of discrimination.

## 2.2 Equality and Its Impacts on Majority-Minority Relations

To start with, we may want to contextualise the observations made: equality protection hardly represents a neutral undertaking, rather it is to be understood in the light of persistent patterns of domination and underlying questions of power

---

[35] Belavusau and Henrard (2019).

[36] Letsas (2015), p. 340.

[37] See e.g. Kochenov (2015) and Kymlicka (2013). Also see the following work for a comparative overview of 'national minority' recognition in European frameworks: Ringelheim (2008).

(lessness).[38] This may come with certain complexities, if we were to bear in mind changes in minority-majority relations, resulting in so-called '*minoritised majorities*',[39] for instance, or different layers of minority and majority communities common among language groups in Canada, for example. Such relations may thus easily be understood in a reverse sense, where minority situations change in the course of time, where minorities come to power without losing in (self-perceived) vulnerability status.[40] The influence of external support in such context shall not be disregarded as it may become apparent in the genocidal context of Rwanda in the 1990s, for instance, where old-established colonial relations proved decisive in not only drawing dividing lines between ethnic groups but also in establishing power relations between such groups. Similar conclusions can be reached in contemporary Europe[41] where citizenship holders residing outside their 'jurisdiction of origin' benefit from special treatment granted by their State of 'origin' or 'direct affiliation'. In that sense, minority status remains flexible in some cases, it may be altered (in practice) and hence needs to be situated within its wider political context. This opens up questions on their alliances with States and ties beyond a strict view on jurisdictions as closed entities in a world in which freedom of movement has become a lived reality. It further discloses the relevance of inter-community ties across borders including the formation of global movements.[42] Finally, we may not forget about historical developments such as colonialism assuming a shaping role until today,[43] which demonstrably perpetuate oppressive logics vis-à-vis minorities in the current socio-political scenery.

Answers may also be sought in the way equality has come to operate in (representative) democratic systems in which 'all votes count equally and majority rule prevails'.[44] We will further engage with this issue for a moment, simply because the question of quota as the predominant form of minority representation has predominantly been discussed in relation to education and the labour market so far,[45] and secondly, since electoral rights[46] represent an overarching form in which equality principles operate, involving a convincing majority of people. Some countertendencies may exist or naturally appear where regional and local district level elections take place, allowing minority members to be elected where these happen

---

[38] Gaventa (1980).

[39] Kymlicka (2013).

[40] Ibid.

[41] See e.g. Vizi (2022).

[42] See e.g. art. 36, UN Declaration on the Rights of Indigenous Peoples. Corntassel (2007), Mukhayer (forthcoming) and Charters and Stavenhagen (2012).

[43] Consider, for instance, the case of debt-bondage systems, contemporary forms of slavery maintained by elites, subjecting indigenous communities to forced labour until today: Inter-American Commission on Human Rights (2009) *Captive Communities: Situation of the Guaraní Indigenous People and Contemporary Forms of Slavery in the Bolivian Chaco.*

[44] Arneson (2013), para. 21.

[45] Stojanović (2013) and Belavusau and Henrard (2018).

[46] See also: Weller and Nobbs (2010).

to be territorially concentrated.[47] In that sense, different scenarios may exist, firstly, minorities may benefit from specific dividing lines defining electoral districts (hence: not declared, implicit) as just shown, and secondly, specific policies may be adopted (hence: purposely, declared, explicit) in order to enhance representation of these minorities.[48] We may also want to revisit the underlying rationale of most State theoretical theories, based on the Hobbsian premise of a unifying all-encompassing State, or to put it differently, an idea based on single peoplehood, a people with its single will (*volonté générale*) following the Rousseauian paradigm.[49] Indeed, a people in the European context hardly represents unity, which may be attributable to the plurality and changeability of its constituent individuals.[50] Accordingly, it has been maintained that a people's representation as a unifying force demarcates a clear contrast with (the aspiration for) diversity.[51]

Related thinking similarly finds its roots in postcolonial debates[52] which have been placing a dedicated focus on, firstly, boundary drawing exercise and with it, the exclusionary effects of representational practice, and secondly, on incapacitation through speaking and acting in the name of others, that is, specific groups.[53] Of particular relevance here is the situation of indigenous peoples, considered those most affected by (neo)colonial developments until today. On the bright side, respective standards have proven far-reaching, especially as they are viewed from the normative side (rather than empirically). Other than other ethnic, cultural, religious or linguistic minorities, indigenous peoples' participatory rights are to be considered as fairly developed. Indeed, rights have come to be articulated beyond the participation in cultural life[54] as it is common among other minorities: instead, these are deeply entrenched in land and territorial regimes, emblematic being the right to prior consultation and consent. Broadly speaking, indigenous participation is understood

---

[47] Stojanović (2013).

[48] Ibid.

[49] Voigt (2019).

[50] Rosanvallon (1998).

[51] Voigt (2019).

[52] Postcolonialism and de-colonialism are not to be used interchangeably, with postcolonialism denoting "*perspectives critical of or resistant to colonialism or colonial attitudes. (...) Postcolonialism too is about changing one's mind-set and values. In a comparable way, 'postcolonial theory' involves a conceptual reorientation towards the perspectives of knowledges, as well as needs, developed outside the West*" (p. 1) while de-colonialism refers to "*decolonizing yourself: alongside seeking the expulsion of the colonizer, it was important to undo all the ways that colonization had affected people's modes of seeing themselves and their own cultural assumptions and values. Intellectual decolonization had to accompany any attempts at political decolonization.*" Young (2020), p. 34.

[53] Sauer (2019).

[54] See e.g. UN Committee on Economic, Social and Cultural Rights (2009) *General Comment No. 21: Right of Everyone to Take Part in Cultural Life*. Advisory Committee on the Framework Convention for the Protection of National Minorities (2008) *Commentary No. 2 The Effective Participation of Persons Belonging to National Minorities in Cultural, Social and Economic Life and in Public Affairs*.

from two sides, internal self-governance and autonomies on the one hand, and taking part in the State's decision-making mechanisms on the other.[55] Especially globally, indigenous peoples have demonstrably managed to gain voice,[56] their specific mandates being recognised by the UN alongside ordinary NGO advisory status with ECOSOC, and for their collective rights to become codified in the albeit non-legally binding Declaration on the Rights of Indigenous Peoples.[57] Others have remained rather cautious in understanding these international legal developments as a success,[58] being ultimately the result of long lasting struggle and compromise and with State sovereignty remaining a lasting obstacle to fully recognising indigenous rights.

A final consideration shall relate to a key definitional concern, that of numerical minorities and the relevance of numbers or populational ratios in contemporary orders. Before reaching any conclusions on the substance of rights and legal orders, it may be noted that equality principles may easily ignore the complexities inherent to group-related vulnerabilities, ultimately unequal positions in society and in the State. Very commonly, international legal orders refer to specific grounds of discrimination rather than numerical criteria. We may legitimately ask to what extent any missed reference to numbers would run the risk of turning minority group status redundant, limiting the application of the law to a case-by-case examination beyond anything systemic. In fact, numerical criteria tend to be applied in domestic jurisdictions, for instance, when recognising 'national minorities' under constitutional law, whereby small minorities clearly face a disproportionate burden.[59] Numerical criteria may also simply represent a normality of common governance models, based on clearly demarcated administrative boundaries. In that sense, territorial points of reference become crucial for minority recognition in, for instance, contemporary European constitutional frameworks; in some cases these resemble those adopted by (officially proclaimed) multinational States.[60] Others have pleaded for a combination of qualitative and quantitative elements to find consideration when defining minorities: accordingly, a few defining criteria have come to be established, including a '*shared and single feature of reference*', '*relations with another group*', and a '*largely (but not solely) quantitative criterion*' defining such relations.[61]

[55] Rodríguez-Piñero Royo (2010). Expert Mechanism on the Rights of Indigenous Peoples (2010) *Progress Report on the Study on Indigenous Peoples and the Right to Participate in Decision-Making.*

[56] Charters and Stavenhagen (2012).

[57] Eichler et al. (forthcoming) and Hohmann and Weller (2018).

[58] Watson (2018a).

[59] Crowley (2001).

[60] Palermo (2011).

[61] Ibid. Toniatti (1996).

Resembling the case of indigenous peoples, minority participation[62] may be realised at different levels and in assuming different positions vis-à-vis the majority group. This can include self-governance systems and autonomies or power-sharing arrangements which may be paritarian in format, including the same ratio of representatives, or being of proportional nature, corresponding to the actual group in numbers and without having to meet a specific (numerical) threshold for the group in question.[63] The different scales of (co-)decision are decisive in that matter: (collective) self-determination in that sense has been regarded as more progressive than territorial autonomy, understanding the former as a right and the latter as simply (optionally) granted by the State.[64] It is in relation to governance-related questions, self-determination and autonomies that we need to explore the minority-majority nexus. This also becomes apparent in the context of other minority rights that ought to be realised such as cultural security which appears intrinsically related to minorities' institutional integrity[65] as shown by case studies on French-speaking minorities in Canada,[66] the French Basque people[67] or Lusatian Sorbs.[68] More broadly speaking, the reader is invited to examine minority powers as they become articulated either throughout the institutional apparatus of the State and in the form of parallel institutions, in other words, autonomies exercised through justice mechanisms, cultural institutions, territorial bodies or decision-making instances. Indeed, we may want to explore further how minorities have been made active participants in the State- building process, including dedicated powers reserved to minorities, indigenous peoples and comparable vulnerable groups.

## 2.3 Equality and Institutional Contexts: Inter-Group Relations

Initiating with the twenty-first century, newly founded States have shown particularly eager to accommodate, formalise and institutionalise minority demands. Rather than being re-affirming of equality orders, such experience may be reflective of a contestation of the former, with autonomous institutions enjoying recognition, as defined by the highest ranking law of the State. Instead, 'equality' may gain new

---

[62] Also consult specific instruments adopted in this field, namely the OSCE *Lund Recommendations on the Effective Participation of National Minorities in Public Life* or the OSCE Warsaw *Guidelines to Assist National Minority Participation in the Electoral Process* and a relevant reading on the issue: Verstichel (2011).

[63] Palermo (2011).

[64] Corntassel (2007) and Thornberry (2000).

[65] Carbonneau et al. (2017).

[66] Ibid. Breton (1985).

[67] Carbonneau et al. (2017) and Itçaina (2017).

[68] Carbonneau et al. (2017) and Carbonneau (2017).

meaning, notably it may refer to minority institutionalism that eventually becomes established at eye level with the State. These in-built forms of recognition represent a complex picture, ranging from successfully established co-governance and proper sovereignty to mere pro forma procedures, remaining far from strengthening minority positions through the law.

We may think of what has been dubbed the '*Indigenous State*',[69] an attempt to decolonise the State in Bolivia, a way of "*enacting indigenous alternatives to the liberal state*"[70] while retaining some of its overall architecture. Late twentieth century developments and the 'pink tide' of leftist politics in Latin America have been paving the way for indigenous peoples to gradually enjoy recognition as new social and political actors, also by co-shaping and constructing a wider institutional and societal consciousness.[71] The proclamation of 'plurinational' States[72] in Ecuador and Bolivia may be seen as the result of indigenous marches and other public manifestations pressing for social change. Numerous scholars have hence understood these new forms of constitutionalism, with indigenous peoples playing a key role, as something particular to the region, its post-authoritarian setting and democratic transition, sometimes called New Latin American Constitutionalism[73] or Transformative Constitutionalism in Latin America.[74] As it is often the case, however, indigenous peoples hardly fit into a collective whole which becomes very visible in the Amazon where the State remains largely absent, institutionally and politically speaking,[75] and as a consequence, indigenous communities in the Amazon were less involved, if at all, in the State-building processes in Bolivia and Ecuador.[76] Conflicts and contradictions naturally emerge, given the complexities of interests at stake and dynamics at work when forming the State: ethno-political difference and respective group membership may prove decisive where sensitive issues such as resource extraction by transnational companies comes into play.[77] In such contexts, participation as a mere pro forma arrangement[78] could be considered common place, in the worst case, this may imply divide and rule tactics,[79] or the

[69] This is not to be confused with indigenous or native nation building, defined as "*the process by which a Native nation strengthens its own capacity for effective and culturally relevant self-government and for self-determined and sustainable community development*" (Native Nations Institute, The University of Arizona).

[70] Postero (2017), p. 184.

[71] Stavenhagen (2002). On indigenous movements in the region, see also: Van Cott (2005).

[72] See also Yrigoyen Fajardo (2016).

[73] Barrios Suvelza (2018).

[74] von Bogdandy et al. (2017b).

[75] Yashar (2012).

[76] Ibid.

[77] Merino (2018).

[78] See the following work for gaining deeper insights into prior consultation and consent processes, underlying logics and principles as well as the overall extractive context in which they take place: Rodríguez-Garavito (2011), Fontana and Grugel (2016) and Szablowski (2010).

[79] Sawyer (2004) and Schilling-Vacaflor and Eichler (2017).

sowing of distrust and bribing practices,[80] which naturally also weakens indigenous institutions in the long run. It may also be maintained that such manifestations of dominance can be traced back to the colonial era,[81] again, revealing the long term impacts on indigenous peoples' possibilities in the shaping and making of the State. Indeed, current realities reflect how the power of hope and its future- orientation has been operating on the ground as a colonial force, namely by diminishing the urgency of current concerns in indigenous-State relations.[82] Bad practice strategies are far-reaching and could be considered a key obstacle in any question of implementation, also where indigenous peoples actually did take an active part in the building of the State and the conscious mainstreaming of indigenous representation throughout its institutions.

Similarly, minority regimes, it is argued, have been set in place to work preventively against coercive assimilation or targeting practices against minority groups when building the State or placed in the broader context—while operating contrarily to—of a State's nationalisation strategy, to put it bluntly.[83] So-called 'national' minorities have almost naturally become respected as part of a State's collective memory, especially in Europe, which was, in turn, explicitly taken up when designing the State's overall architecture. In that sense, we could distinguish between and hence classify different positionalities that are being attributed to minorities in European State-building processes: those frameworks establishing special rights reserved for linguistic minorities and also allowing for territorial autonomy (Belgian and Spanish cases), those orders referring to 'national' or ethnic minorities and stipulating some (specific) rights respectively (Central and Eastern European States), and finally those attributing special status to specific ethnic groups (Norway, Finland, Cyprus, Hungary, Slovenia, and Italy).[84] We may want to recall that minority rights, in their breadth and depths, constitute an exceptionalism. Oftentimes, minorities are included, if only peripherally, to avoid stereotypisation or derogative labelling that would portray minorities as '*second-class-citizens*' as was the case between "*ruling Macedonians and the structurally excluded Albanians*",[85] eventually leading to a peace agreement and a new constitution. Beyond these rather superficial changes, some attempts may be noted where co-governance institutions eventually found recognition by the State, existing alongside the State while not being vested with powers beyond self-governance. Self-governance as a success story on its own could only develop, it is argued, if seen in its particular historical context in Europe, that of a desecuritization, and the vanishing fear minorities may "*collaborate with the enemy of the State*".[86]

[80] Posner et al. (2010).

[81] Mamdani (2012).

[82] Lindroth and Sinevaara-Niskanen (2022).

[83] Barth (2008).

[84] Ringelheim (2008).

[85] de Gaay Fortman (2011), p. 286.

[86] Kymlicka (2008), p. 24.

Illustrative may certainly be the recently established 'Parlamento Indígena do Brasil' or the comparatively more powerful Sámediggi (Sami parliaments) in Northern Europe, established in the 1990s as part of the State system with an "*ethnically defined electorate*".[87] In the case of the Sámi in Finland, for instance, the Sami parliament is considered a State authority as such while it does show clearly integrated into the State, as it operates under the administrative sector of the judiciary.[88] Certain doubts remain as to the genuine attribution of powers given that the Sámediggi do retain decision-making powers limited to internal affairs, yet not extending to responsibilities regarding third party interests such as land or forestry owners.[89] The issue of land issues may be emblematic here, revealing the State's reluctance as to transferring decision-making powers to the Sámediggi whenever third party or conflicting interests are at stake.[90] Another related systemic issue concerns the very positioning of the Sami Parliament given its role as firstly, a government agency and the fact that policies and other decisions taken by the Swedish National Assembly are simply implemented, and secondly, (sometimes contrary) commitments made among its own elected members, political programmes etc. which reflected the difficulties arising with questions of representation.[91] What is more, a few decisions clearly revealed the nature of such relationship, that is, the hierarchical relation between the State and the indigenous parliament with the Sámediggi acting as a purely "*administrative authority under the Swedish government*".[92] In that sense, becoming part of the integrationist and harmonising architecture of the State endows indigenous institutions with certain powers, without however placing its legislative powers on equal footing with the State, especially as far as issues of public interest are concerned.

Equality may however also be sought in relation to other actors such as multilateral institutions such as the UN[93] or through commitments made in the colonial age, so-called treaty settlements.[94] Interestingly, political agreements with States may prove detrimental where constitutional structures discourage indigenous jurisdictions and their representatives from approving certain UNDRIPS provisions.[95] Indeed, State sovereignty may ultimately prevent indigenous peoples from benefiting from the protective realm of international law. Indeed, settler colonialism commonly found further articulation through treaties,[96] one of its most known

[87] Lawrence and Mörkenstam (2016), p. 107.

[88] Samediggi/Saamelaiskäräjät (2022) The Sámi Parliament – The Representative Self-Government Body of the Sámi. Retrieved from https://www.samediggi.fi/task/?lang=en.

[89] Lawrence and Mörkenstam (2016).

[90] Ibid.

[91] Ibid.

[92] Ibid., p. 121.

[93] Charters and Stavenhagen (2012).

[94] Centre for International Governance Innovation (2020) and Te Aho (forthcoming).

[95] Gover (2015).

[96] See, for instance, Samson (2014).

principles being the *Terra Nullius* doctrine. Others have distinguished between treaty and colonial relationships, notably in the Canadian context where treaty relationship in which "*Aboriginal peoples and newcomer Canadians recognise each other as equal, coexisting and self-governing nations and govern their relations with each other by negotiations, based on procedures of reciprocity and consent, that lead to agreements that are then recorded in treaties or treaty-like accords of various kinds, to which both parties are subject*".[97] Colonial relationships would assume quite the opposite, that is, a denial of their status as equal, coexisting and self-governing nations; Indian Acts would administer such logics of domination.[98] Contrary to most treaty relations, the Chilean context, for instance, allows for a rather positive reading of old established agreements—while not being uncontested—that were made in the era of parliaments bringing together the Mapuche people and representatives of the Spanish Crown, one of the most known ones being the Quillín Parliament of 1647.[99] In indigenous contexts, equality orders are necessarily to be understood across time, their formal and informal engagements with a number of actors including colonial powers, the contemporary State, but also in the light of emerging actors such as NGOs[100] and corporate companies.

### 2.3.1 Equality Beyond Classical Liberal Constitutionalism: The Call for Pluralism

Returning to the classical differentiation made between *de jure* and *de facto* equality, we shall understand equality in the present context as an attempt to create level-playing-fields between State law on the one hand and alternative justice systems such as indigenous jurisdictions or minority justice frameworks on the other. These underlying conditions inevitably play into the operating and functioning of the State, eventually setting the stage for its eventual re-building, as powerfully demonstrated in Andean States.[101] This inevitably brings us to one of the most needed debates in the legal discipline and beyond, that of legal pluralism.[102] Just as other approaches discussed in the present work, legal pluralism is expected to respond to the question if it actually pretends to represent a single theory,[103] possibly even more so since its

[97] Tully (2008), p. 226.

[98] Ibid.

[99] Zavala Cepeda (2015). See also José Bengoa's work for that matter.

[100] See, for instance, Hirsch (2003).

[101] Yrigoyen Fajardo (2016).

[102] Pluralism may indeed refer to a variety of meanings throughout the present book, embracing, inter-alia legal, political, economic, cultural, linguistic or religious pluralism. A wide range of pluralisms has found constitutional recognition in the plurinational frameworks of the Bolivian and Ecuadorian States principally.

[103] Schiff Berman (2020a).

proponents largely show critical of traditional legal theory and its preparedness to open up for legal pluralistic forms of law. If simplified, it could be said these approaches challenge the Rawlsian idea of a single theory of justice.[104]

At large, pluralism may be understood in a multiplicity of ways. To start with, society itself is increasingly—and rightly—described as plural; the commonly used term '*plural societies*'[105] hence dominates debates on multiculturalism, common identities and difference(s). This piece rather engages with the institutionalised forms of pluralism, including the question of minority-majority that shines through the State's institutional design. Indeed, 'pluralism' has come to be understood as the opposite to what has been termed the sovereign 'nation-State',[106] even as one of its most prominent counter forces when recalling its inability to deal with diversity and political autonomy:[107] a historical line was followed when assuming such State constituted 'the requisite political form' and by basing itself on nationalism as the presumably most appropriate response to governing diversity.[108] In the current age, this, of course, no longer holds, however neither individual nor minority rights do succeed in "*mitigat(ing) the harms and inequalities entailed by the allocation of sovereignty to nation-states by the international legal and political system*".[109] Indeed, the global has commonly played a key role when shaping the local and vice versa in the way pluralism has become articulated.[110] The current contribution however, tries to examine the matter at an abstract level rather than contextualising the global or the local at deeper levels.

When discussing pluralism(s), the scholarly community has further demonstrated an active interest in interactions between different spheres, including so-called jurisdictional battles.[111] While this may be of interest as an illustration of norm conflict or legal hierarchies, we will be focussing our attention on the groups making these claims and, above all, the surrounding institutional logics and their mitigating (or not) effect on the communities' positions. In that sense, it has been observed what kinds of tools legal pluralism may provide for indigenous legal traditions and the communities, also when juxtaposing these with settler law.[112] The difficulties associated with introducing legal pluralism into the institutional landscape of dominant society may also visualise other systemic ills, it has been argued, such as "*authoritarianism, lack of autonomy, and lack of internal critique*"; this becomes apparent in the current Brazilian political scenario.[113] Legal pluralists would trace

[104] Ibid.

[105] See e.g. Foblets et al. (2018) and von Busekist (2018).

[106] Arato and Cohen (2018).

[107] Ibid.

[108] Ibid., p. 2.

[109] Ibid., p. 3. Macklem (2015).

[110] see Sally Engle Merry's work on the matter. Also: Goodale (2007) and Schiff Berman (2020b).

[111] Barrera (2012) and Benton (2020).

[112] Gover (2020).

[113] Chalmers (2020), p. 292.

the beginnings back to a (predominant) "*legal consciousness focused on the modern State*".[114] While this may reflect a sober view on State law and its predominance, legal pluralists have also drawn our attention to ethic objections, holding that "*the modern state reproduces the conditions for the excesses of modern capitalist economies and erases more emancipatory forms of ordering from the legal consciousness*".[115]

Indeed, answers may be found in socio-legal and socio-political as well as anthropological accounts of (State) law. While legal pluralism would certainly serve as a facilitating tool to enhance collective rights, State law needs to be read in the light of power relations, of the ruling power and those subjected to it, which becomes accentuated in the case of minorities. Questions of power and powerlessness become apparent in such situations of inequality,[116] where the law operates, where it is appropriated[117] and may be masking power or elitist undertakings, rather than being employed as an '*emancipatory tool for vulnerable people*'.[118] Power differentials may be found between parties in a legal conflict, requiring mitigating tools that are often inexistent.[119] Legal pluralism may be emblematic here as "*choices from among different legal systems have real consequences*" with the law accommodating different forms of power relations such as social, symbolic or economic ones.[120] This may however not only concern parties to a dispute, but also extend to those institutions mandated to deal with disputes with the objective of "*garner(ing) their authority*".[121] For legal pluralism to be effective, it inevitable needs to transcend the law and its institutions, and in that sense—eventually—fulfil transformative functions. What is more, practices and processes are understood as underlying the anthropological concept of legal pluralism, requiring us to examine the "*practices within each legal or quasi-legal regime, the processes by which they interact with and influence each other, and the relative power exercised by each regime*".[122] More complexities are added if we were to examine the historical background of the law in indigenous contexts where the settler State legal order would meet with indigenous legal systems, forming "*an often violent and always contested area of legal pluralism*"[123] to say the least. The predominating legal doctrine 'Terra Nullius' applied in the colonies[124] would clearly render a parallel understanding of territoriality, land use and the entire conception of land less valid.

---

114 Ibid., p. 301.

115 Ibid., p. 301. de Sousa Santos (2002).

116 Gaventa (1980).

117 Comaroff and Comaroff (2008).

118 Merry (2006).

119 von Benda-Beckmann and Turner (2020).

120 Ibid., p. 78.

121 Ibid., p. 78.

122 Merry (2020), p. 169.

123 Schiff Berman (2020c), p. 803.

124 See, for instance, Samson and Gigoux (2017) and Anaya (2004).

Legal theoretical accounts too have been dealing with legal pluralism as a proper object of inquiry. Critical voices have shown reluctant in accepting its genuine contributions to and recognition of legal pluralism. What has been termed as '*legal theory's pluralism problem*' could be subsumed under the following points of critique or claims: that "*law is necessarily state law*", that it would represent law or could be considered the "*best form of law*", and finally, that legal theory would "*neglect nonstate forms of law*".[125] When engaging more closely with legal theoretical work though, the first claim seems largely unfounded while the second claim shows to be less implicit in practice with legal theorists simply seeming to place a different focus (other than on pluralist approaches) in their work; the last claim focussing on the field's ignorance when considering nonstate law seems to be vanishing in the current age.[126] Instead, legal pluralism may be conceived as relational, it is argued elsewhere, as captured by the concept of '*legal interactionism*', referring to the multiplicity of relatively autonomous legal orders which may differ in the extent to which these are actually autonomous or intertwined.[127] Global legal developments in the field of indigenous rights may be illustrative of this, having absorbed indigenous demands as they were introduced by indigenous representatives throughout several decades, taking the form of working groups principally.[128] Another relevant conceptual framework is proposed by de Sousa Santos in an attempt to decolonise the State, notably by establishing a so-called '*inter-legal space*' or '*inter-legality*' while considering the different levels, interpretative views, dynamics and intersections emerging in these spaces.[129] According to the scholar, we shall not lose sight of the centrality of State law, as an important political variable and a result of processes of socialisation,[130] which in a way exert some form of invisibilising function. Similarly, what has been termed '*jurisprudence of hybridity*' significantly helped in making sense of continuing inequalities relating to indigenous law.[131] More precisely, such jurisprudence of hybridity is based on the threefold idea that for mixed legal spheres to arise, the mind would need to be decolonised, based on a more inclusive understanding of indigenous law; colonial legal authority would need to be destabilised; and legal orders to be transformed from being monist-pluralistic to a '*pluralist-pluralism*'.[132]

Let us engage with plurinational constitutionalism for a moment, being perhaps the most emblematic manifestation of constitutionalised pluralism of the current age. In Latin American frameworks, Yrigoyen Fajardo distinguished between different post-authoritarian constitutional eras, initiating with the period of '*multicultural*

[125] Mac Amhlaigh (2020), p. 267.

[126] Ibid.

[127] van der Burg (2020).

[128] Charters and Stavenhagen (2012).

[129] de Sousa Santos (1987) and Eichler (2022a).

[130] de Sousa Santos (1987).

[131] Nursoo (2018).

[132] Ibid.

*constitutionalism*' (1982–1988) and its emphasis on cultural diversity, multilingual and multicultural societal contexts and the recognition of cultural identity as well as related rights granted to indigenous peoples, followed by '*pluricultural constitutionalism*' (1989–2005) which demonstrably built on the previous cycle by embracing cultural diversity and multiculturalism—this time, however, by envisaging a redefinition, a rebuilding of the State.[133] First manifestations of legal pluralism came to the fore, rather explicitly, in that period, including the indigenous struggle for recognition of their proper legal orders, the embracement of indigenous law by the international legal framework, the growing of multicultural discourse and finally systemic State reforms on the matter.[134] While Yrigoyen Fajardo identifies a fourth cycle elsewhere, that of an eco-constitutionalism (2008–ongoing) with nature becoming a subject of rights,[135] we shall focus on '*plurinational constitutionalism*' (2006–2009) as the cycle demonstrating the greatest match with the idea of legal pluralism and relevant empirical foundations.

Embedded in Bolivian and Ecuadorian constitutionalism and international law (UNDRIPS at the time), we move away from the mere acknowledgement of multiculturalism and diversity; instead, self-determination is explicitly referred to, including a variety of consequences such the very '*plurinational State*' and its new division of powers and, expressly '*equal legal pluralism*' and '*equal dignity of peoples*'.[136] Elsewhere, it is maintained that plurinational States in their essence show open towards and accommodate self-governing entities and again, generally approve the idea of indigenous and Afro-descendent peoples' self-determination.[137] What is more, when defining the plurinational State, it is referred to '*equality among groups*' based on ethnic difference and their recognition as '*collective political actors*'; indigenous peoples and their institutions(!) were henceforth understood as constituting "*transversal dimensions of the whole state structure*".[138] Indeed, the plurinational State is generally understood as an accommodating framework, to actively include indigenous peoples' rights under its protective umbrella and to eventually "*redesign State institutions to guarantee those rights, going beyond the concept of multiculturalism*".[139]

[133] Gover (2020).

[134] Ibid.

[135] Yrigoyen Fajardo (2021).

[136] Yrigoyen Fajardo (2016), p. 167.

[137] Schilling-Vacaflor and Kuppe (2012) and de Sousa Santos (2010).

[138] Schilling-Vacaflor and Kuppe (2012), p. 365.

[139] von Bogdandy et al. (2017a), p. 18.

### 2.3.2 *Equality and Its Inadequate Dealing with Multiethnicity and Multiculturalism*

From a juridical point of view, 'generic' equality principles at least may be seen as an exceptionalism—at least in international human rights law—given the predominance of an anti-racist paradigm enshrined in the law that makes sure discrimination on ethnic grounds is (explicitly) addressed by the law. Nevertheless, different levels of protection easily become discernible, hence creating different scopes in dealing with difference, and ultimately equality. The EU Racial Equality Directive may be emblematic as it establishes that equality principles may not prevent those measures from being maintained or adopted that are meant to mitigate disadvantage based on ethnic background or race: such disadvantage has been interpreted as implying structural manifestations, also constituting societal and institutional problem.[140] However, the EU framework on the matter could be criticised based on its rather cautious approach on any resulting positive measures to be taken while the ECtHR and ICERD frameworks clearly advocate for a positive action approach addressing historical and current discrimination in the case of the European Court of Human Rights.[141] This latter instance has come to generally pronounce itself on positive measures in recent years,[142] being derived from its very founding instrument, the European Convention on Human Rights and Fundamental Freedoms that explicitly establishes obligations to '*secure*' specific rights.[143] What is more, an integrative and systematic role has been attributed to the Court when dealing with positive obligations.[144] International human rights law, by contrast, generally embraces a positive action approach; ICESCR, for instance, proscribes the taking of steps to achieve the full realisation of the rights stipulated therein, by all appropriate means. Constitutional frameworks may lag behind in that sense, with the French and German constitutions pretending to adhere to universalistic constitutional principles that fall short of addressing particularisms generally.[145]

Let us refine the question however, why would positive measures—as opposed to equality principles—prove particularly apt to respond to ethnic or cultural grounds rather than what ordinary equality law has to offer. Answers may be sought in institutional developments on the matter, such as the establishment of equality institutions in the EU that would adopt a '*judicialised equality approach*'.[146] In this context, it remains absolutely crucial to distinguish between equality as a de jure quality and equality in effect/de facto, with the latter predominating institutional

[140] Barskanmaz (2019).

[141] Ibid. See also *Horváth and Kiss vs Hungary*, European Court of Human Rights in 2013.

[142] Dickson (2010), Xenos (2011) and Mowbray (2004).

[143] Eichler (2022b).

[144] Ibid. Barth (2008).

[145] Vilain (2015).

[146] Krizsan et al. (2012), p. 210.

equality frameworks, the first being the Racial Equality and Employment Directives adopted in 2000. Despite progressive developments such as the '*procedural turn*'[147] including e.g. the reversal of the burden of proof, and a gradual "*cross-national trend to amalgamate equality institutions*",[148] a few critical remarks shall be made. A common institutional ill concerns the question of implementation or enforcement, in the case of racial discrimination, the Racial Equality Directive was complemented by Council Framework Decision 2008/913/JHA on combating certain forms and expressions of racism and xenophobia by means of criminal law. This also concerns judicial enforcement with few cases on new grounds such as racial discrimination being litigated by the European Court of Justice.[149] Generally, Member States have been showing a certain reluctance in complying with these norms, illustrative being lengthy transposition periods.[150] At a broader political level, it has been argued internal market principles would commonly enjoy priority wherever minority rights were at stake.[151] It may be concluded for now that the systemic nature of violations as they relate to ethnic background may require stronger levels of cross-institutional mainstreaming, more political leverage and domestic policy alignment given the persisting difficulties in implementing relevant EU policies.

The claim for multiculturalism opens yet a wider debate on the (missing) aptitude of equality paradigms in living up to the demands of multiculturalism and multiethnicity widely speaking. It could be argued that classical models of deliberative democracy are associated with the "*privatisation of issues of cultural difference*", instead, deliberative democracy is engaged with universalising "*equal rights and entitlements to all citizens regardless of their difference*".[152] Culture and identity are relegated to the private sphere, forming what Rawls called '*background culture*'[153] and perceiving the State as a neutral actor without supposedly "*privileging or favouring a particular culture*".[154] Indeed, many deliberative democracy theories show largely ignorant of culture, context and history in aiming for equality and justice; in that sense, only marginal attention (if at all) is paid to historical injustices and the demands of certain groups.[155] Similar arguments shine through Mouffe's radical democracy when critically engaging with the concept of citizenship, she identifies some inherent difficulties as it "*ignores the limits imposed on the extension of pluralism by the fact that some existing rights have been constituted on the very exclusion or subordination of the rights of other categories. Those identities must*

[147] Muir and de Witte (2017). See also: Belavusau and Henrard (2019).

[148] Muir and de Witte (2017), p. 142.

[149] Belavusau and Henrard (2018).

[150] Ibid.

[151] Kochenov (2018).

[152] Bashir (2012), p. 62.

[153] Rawls (1999b).

[154] Bashir (2012), p. 62.

[155] Ibid.

*first be deconstructed if several new rights are to be recognised*".[156] This would fundamentally apply to de jure forms of equality (Mouffe understands equality as an achievement): how would equality and positive discrimination find a place in the same legal provision, and more importantly, in the same framework such as constitutionalism, charters or treaties? To what extent do we need to deconstruct equality in the first place? Put differently, equality principles can only apply wherever relations of domination have been challenged to start with.[157] Proponents of positive discrimination approaches or collective rights would probably view this endeavour with suspicious eyes as equality remains a difference-ignorant conception with the inherent dangers of abuse while constituting a fundamental underappreciation of the complex multidimensional contexts surrounding vulnerable groups. Indeed, it could be argued, as maintained by Mouffe, that we need to understand the "*struggle against the multiple forms in which (the category "women") is constructed in subordination*".[158]

Other authors too have shown a certain reluctance in viewing the benefits of equality principles and relatedly, citizenship as inclusive categories. Indigenous self-determination probably shows at its finest how ordinary citizenship may be contested, and its integrationist agenda:[159] to put it bluntly, indigenous peoples may "*prefer their own way of life to the supposed benefits of citizenship. There are also indigenous peoples campaigning (...) to be granted the benefits of citizenship and to retain significant elements of their own way of life*".[160] Equality may very serve as a guiding rationale ruling on relations between entire groups as the concept of co-citizenship may illustrate. Multiculturalism is specifically addressed as offering the space for e.g. migrants to be recognised as "*co-citizens within a pluralism in which all identities are respected*".[161] While not being mentioned as such, said pluralist space and the very concept of citizenship presuppose a conception of equality that regulates relations between different groups of persons. Citizenship, however, necessarily creates '*representations of Otherness*' and hence clearly demonstrates exclusionary effects; these are largely attributable to the law and its categorisations, showing detrimental impacts such as the creation of '*identity boundaries*'.[162] On the bright side, the law operates as a virtuous countervailing force in other regards, such as the creation of dedicated rights holder groups that are granted special protection. In a way, equality relations between groups presuppose and build on the prior recognition by the law, requiring us indeed to understand equality as it is demanded in different phases of the process of recognition. Seen from a yet different angle, equality would be understood as a regulating principle

[156] Mouffe (1992a), p. 112.

[157] Ibid.

[158] Mouffe (1992b), p. 143.

[159] Muldoon (2012).

[160] Ibid., p. 130. Hindess (2004).

[161] Kastoryano (2018), p. 3.

[162] Ibid., p. 4.

amongst individuals, disclosing its classical orientation towards individual rights while it assumes different regulating functions amongst recognised groups, communities, holders of collective rights. In both scenarios, we need to be reminded of the issue of power permeating such relations—majority-minority conditions easily become absorbed by the equality discourse, inviting us yet again to engage more closely with context(s) and historical injustices.

### 2.3.3 Postcolonial Thought and Its Critique of Equality Paradigms

Inequality and neo-colonial discourse commonly go hand in hand, referring in this case to global power relations as it was maintained by Bertrand Badie: "*La forte inégalité de puissance (...) s'est révélée à la faveur d'une décolonisation manquée*" (The strong inequality of power has shown favourable to a failed decolonisation process).[163] Indeed, the decolonisation process can hardly be constrained to local realities or domestic politics, but requires global (re)thinking, and with it a broader conception of equality. The two—the global and the local—are often juxtaposed, making sense of social processes that develop across multiple boundaries.[164] Both global and local are certainly marked by a neo-liberal market rationale, permeating different spheres, creating the space for inequalities to emerge. These may be imagined at different levels, including—famously—socio-economic inequalities, access to vital resources, education and basic health services, but also decision-making spaces and the operation of institutions such as the State.

Unsurprisingly, respective transformations have initiated at the very epistemological level, as defended famously by de Sousa Santos in "*Descolonizar el saber, reinventar el poder*" (Decolonising knowledge, reinventing power)[165] or following Tuhiwai Smith "Decolonizing Methodologies"[166] approach to start with. Indigenous rights have been thought through and subjected to the colonisation critique for a long time,[167] demanding equality at yet a different level, with self-determination constituting the most vehemently demanded right with the view to eventually transform the relations maintained with the State. Indeed, we may feel compelled to revisit the initial projection of the present (hypo)thesis that understands equality as coexisting at different levels, in multiple orders.

Returning to the epistemological dimension of the debate, by far not being a minor concern, we get entangled with the question of whether we would need to classify current State relations as forming a postcolonial order, as reflecting a

[163] Badie (2018), p. 244.

[164] Goodale (2007).

[165] de Sousa Santos (2013).

[166] Smith (2012).

[167] See, for example, Irene Watson's or Val Napoleon's work.

neo-colonial reality, or as being situated in a continuing process of decolonisation. We may very well also think of a complete reversal of the colonial order[168] which has been voiced by indigenous peoples early on (consider the concept of *pachakuti* for that matter). While we may reach different answers on the matter, colonial heritage necessarily builds on a two-tier relationship or what Said called '*positional superiority*',[169] reflected in not only military strength, but also extended to imperial knowledge.[170] This dual-dimensional view on current State relations and the world order has been questioned, resembling the critique on the binary divide between Global North and Global South logics, the latter following the colonial rationale in particularly emblematic ways. Indeed, it has been argued elsewhere that the focus is placed wrongly, instead, attention is to be paid to legal globalisation dynamics generally speaking, unpacking the interrelatedness of the legal, economic, social and cultural drivers of globalisation.[171] Relatedly, the 'from above' and 'from below' distinction[172] may be subjected to severe criticism, given that the Global South converts to a passive agent, often suppressed by the Global North. A different position is maintained here, broadly embracing systemic considerations on the (re)-distribution of power that ultimately also underlie the present critical engagement with equality orders.

As a matter of fact, colonial heritage and its current manifestations prove emblematic of how indigenous peoples and (other) minorities remain dependent on and subjected to external rule, limited in their capacities as '*shapers and makers*'[173] on an equal level with the State. Epistemological conditions, it is argued, serve as a perpetuating, if not foundational factor in that regard. Let us explore some major points of epistemological critique from a postcolonial perspective in the following. It is often maintained that knowledge is constructed *on* the Other instead of together with the Other.[174] These processes of objectification, we could say, transcend the disciplines and the current dominant academic consensus[175] in the social sciences. Along these lines, it was critically remarked in the Aotearoa/New Zealand context: "*We have a history of people putting Maori under a microscope in the same way a scientist looks at an insect. The ones doing the looking are giving themselves the power to define*."[176] Indeed, we easily witness a spirit that seeks complete detachment from the social world, including persisting hierarchies of agents and decision-makers. It is in this light that de Sousa Santos

---

[168] Rivera Cusicanqui (2012).

[169] Said (1978).

[170] Smith (2012).

[171] Ballakrishnen and Dezalay (2021).

[172] Rajagopal (2003).

[173] Cornwall and Gaventa (2001).

[174] de Sousa Santos (2017).

[175] For further engagement with the concept, see relevant contributions produced by the philosophy of sciences such as Kuhn (1962).

[176] Smith (2012). Mita (1989), p. 30.

carefully observed that scientific knowledge did not prove very useful in spurring social struggles in its own terms after all, if these weren't related to the context they find themselves embedded in, the so-called '*ecology of knowledges*' which closely surround these struggles in order to ultimately reinforce them.[177]

Albeit relatedly, a final consideration worthy further exploration concerns firstly, the construction of the subject and secondly, subject-holdership according to State or official law. As maintained by a book written by indigenous scholars, "*naming and constructing who we are is essential to the colonial project and its long campaign to subjugate the 'natives' to colonial power*".[178] We may also think of current manifestations of stereotypisation in that regard, with hate crime but also mundane forms of racial discrimination contributing to these processes of exogenous subjectification, often institutionalised through the apparatus of the State, police detention and interventions in particular.[179] Similar observations have been made in relation to racial profiling by criminal justice personnel, impacting indigenous peoples in particular, and in terms of hate speech and incitement to hatred.[180] The second malaise relates to the aforediscussed question of legal pluralism: indigenous laws have been considered non-existent, hence reinforcing the colonial mindset and undignified notions such as 'backward natives'[181] or the 'civilisation' discourse. Indeed, State law has been understood as a domination process, with States imposing legal norms of their own imagination without seeking the consent of those they intend to subject (indigenous peoples) in a given geographical space.[182]

## 2.4 Forms of Equality and Individual Subject Holdership

We may indeed want to examine in more detail to what extent subject holdership becomes a relevant question when understood in the context of de facto equality, that is, the way minorities and indigenous peoples eventually gain a position as citizens or enter into similar categories of protection as part of the (constitutional) architecture of the State. Not only that, we shall understand such positions as channelling

[177] de Sousa Santos (2017). In the original language: "*...l'utilité de la connaissance scientifique pour les luttes sociales ne dépend pas tant de cette science elle-même que de leur adéquation par rapport au contexte dans lequel elles s'inscrivent, c'est-à-dire l'écologie des savoirs qui se tisse au fil des luttes pour les renforcer*", p. 146.

[178] Watson (2018b), p. 2.

[179] *Hickey vs. Australia*, UN Human Rights Committee in 1995.

[180] UN Committee on the Elimination of Racial Discrimination (2020) *General Comment N° 36: On Preventing and Combating Racial Profiling by Law Enforcement Officials.*

UN Committee on the Elimination of Racial Discrimination (2013) *General Comment N° 35: Combating Racist Hate Speech.*

[181] de Sousa Santos (2017).

[182] Newcomb (2018).

juridical constructs that ultimately ensure recognition at eye level and as a translation of legal pluralism into the institutional ambit of the State.

Some answers are probably to be found in a State's founding document, commonly establishing basic equality provisions and dedicated catalogues protecting group rights. The degree to which autonomies are being granted thereby determines the level of de facto equality such positions are endowed with. To be sure, we are not thinking of territorial or governmental autonomy to start with, instead, the focus is placed on the subject—individual minority member or collective entity—and the very position assumed by the rights holder vis-à-vis the State. This concerns, first and foremost, creating a level playing field with firstly, other rights holders, and secondly, autonomous powers as integrated into or co-existing with the State's very own institutional architecture.[183] If we were to start with the former, we shall recall basic equality and non-discrimination provisions, constituting predominant elements in contemporary constitutional law. It seems too difficult to refute the foundational rationale of human rights, as argued elsewhere, based on the "*twin ideas that human beings are born equal in dignity and rights, and that all human beings have to be treated with equal concern and respect*".[184] We may object for several reasons, starting with the unequal socio-economic conditions into which we are born,[185] different degrees of enjoying civil and political rights as in the context of totalitarian governance or the very underlying deficient (living) conditions, requiring mitigation beyond 'equal concern'. Secondly, by understanding subject-holdership in relation to the State, we necessarily think of collective rights, given that individual rights (holders) would hardly legitimately claim any eye level position with the State on their own regard. Demands for collectivised forms of sovereignty have been viewed suspiciously though if we consider indigenous long lasting struggle for lands and resources[186] on the one hand and the contentious nature of negotiations around recognising new States, as it becomes apparent at the UN.[187] Similar logics permeate the constitutional level where the State's (exclusive) sovereignty over land and resources remains undisputed whereas exceptions are granted in the case of ad hoc procedures, famously shown by prior consultation and consent processes.[188]

---

[183] For a detailed examination on different forms and scales of indigenous autonomies and decision-making instances in relation to the State, see the following report Expert Mechanism on the Rights of Indigenous Peoples (2010) *Progress Report on the Study on Indigenous Peoples and the Right to Participate in Decision-Making.*

[184] Clapham (2015), p. 143.

[185] Social Justice theories to be revisited in that regard.

[186] See e.g. Doyle (2015).

[187] For further insights on the matter, kindly check the Montevideo Convention on the Rights and Duties of States (1933), particularly art. 1 which defines the qualifications a State would need to live up to, namely "*a) a permanent population, b) a defined territory, c) government, d) capacity to enter into relations with the other States.*"

[188] Wright and Tomaselli (2019), Doyle (2015), Rodríguez-Garavito (2011), Fontana, and Grugel (2016) and Szablowski (2010).

Another relevant factor to consider concerns the very entitlements attached to said positions. While these may become visible from the outset, a rather complicated picture may be drawn where rights and responsibilities intersect—a common phenomenon being indigenous roles as guardians of the earth and holders of environmental rights,[189] giving rise to some sort of indigenous (intergenerational) stewardship.[190] It does not come as a surprise that international legal documents have been working with utilitarian minded diversity discourses, focussed on the contributions indigenous peoples and minorities may make to society.[191] In fact, utilitarian approaches have been heavily criticised in the field of human rights for a multiplicity of reasons. Classical Rawlsian theories of justice prove emblematic here portraying utilitarian arguments as pragmatic only, to be contrasted with schools of thought based on principles.[192] Others would even maintain that rights serve as safeguard when subjecting rights holders' interest to any utilitarian calculus, more specifically "*if a right-holder has a right to do something, V, then typically no non-right claims can override the right-holder's right to V*".[193]

Relatedly, relevant frameworks may demonstrate a clear orientation towards responsibilities, rather than rights only—in that sense, broadening the idea of subject-holdership. Indeed, responsibility approaches have become a common point of reference in contemporary human rights approaches, especially with the formalisation of rights in the African human and peoples' rights framework and its dedicated focus on communities and peoples.[194] These could be contrasted with the aforementioned utilitarianist approach on human rights which gives rise to a negative conception of rights, viewing "*rights as some sort of side-constraints on others' actions*"; such duties may be of different nature, including but not limited to juridical and ethical duties.[195] It could be argued that legal pluralism, at least in part, imposes responsibilities on the individual; it is reasoned that the individual "*is no longer responsible just for her private life, but is now responsible for the success and equity*

[189] See, for instance, MacPherson (2021).

[190] Bennett and Bavikatte (2015), Winter (2022) and Page (2017).

[191] See e.g. Framework Convention for the Protection of National Minorities (1995) "*Considering that the upheavals of European history have shown that the protection of national minorities is essential to stability, democratic security and peace in this continent (...) considering that the creation of a climate of tolerance and dialogue is necessary to enable cultural diversity to be a source and a factor, not of division, but of enrichment for each society*" (preambular paragraphs). See also Indigenous and Tribal Peoples Convention N° 169 (1989) "*Calling attention to the distinctive contributions of indigenous and tribal peoples to the cultural diversity and social and ecological harmony of humankind and to international co-operation and understanding*" (preambular paragraphs). See also Indigenous and Tribal Populations Convention N° 107 (1957), several preambular and operative paragraphs of the treaty.

[192] Mendus (2015).

[193] Liao (2015).

[194] Dersso (2006). See also relevant developments, starting with the Universal Declaration of Human Rights, art. 29(1) stating that "*Everyone has duties to the community in which alone the free and full development of his personality is possible*". See also: Baldwin and Morel (2009).

[195] Flikschuh (2015), p. 657. Kant (1797).

*of social institutions. Duties of guardianship, foresight and comity are thrust on her*".[196] Emblematic may be, again, indigenous practices and community procedures which may indeed envisage regulating not only organisational questions, but establish duties on the individual.[197]

### 2.4.1 Citizenship and Its Exclusionary Implications

As it becomes apparent from the above, citizenship could be regarded as an exclusive,[198] homogenising legal construct, rarely living up to the particularities and distinguished claims raised by minorities and indigenous peoples. While we could easily delve into related fundamental concerns of importance to migrants, refugees and other non-citizen groups in that context,[199] our focus shall remain on so-called 'recognised minority groups', those by and large benefiting from the regime, in principle. This does not, of course, diminish the significance of exploring the logics and institutions of exclusion as these affect non-citizens in a given domestic jurisdiction. As it is maintained elsewhere, "*citizenship is 'Janus-faced', simultaneously projecting the warm embrace of inclusion while excluding those who are outside the borders of belonging*".[200] Instead, the present piece strives to further disentangle such 'warm embrace of inclusion' inherent to citizenship as it is argued, by critically examining its potential in recognising difference.

Commonly, citizenship is regarded as a self-preserving legal construct, facilitating a homogenising vision ignorant of difference(s) in the name of (de jure) equality. Similar issues are debated globally, considering citizenship "*as a key force behind the preservation of the status quo where the poor are poor and the rich are rich (...) thus emerging as the key tool for the preservation of global inequality*".[201] Rather, we shall explore micro levels here, the very encounters of the State and its subjects, usually articulated through the legal concept of citizenship in constitutional law. It is narrated elsewhere that "*social and political movements have formed to redefine the*

---

[196] Chalmers (2007), p. 302.

[197] See, e.g., work developed by Kirsty Gover, Val Napoleon. Also check relevant cases such as *Sandra Lovelace vs. Canada*, UN Human Rights Committee in 1977; *Ivan Kitok vs. Sweden*, UN Human Rights Committee in 1985; Individual opinion of Olivier de Frouville in *Tiina-Sanila-Aikio vs. Finland*, UN Human Rights Committee in 2017; *Käkkäläjärvi vs. Finland*, UN Human Rights Committee in 2017.

[198] Indeed, reflecting a common complaint by political theorists on the question (of exclusive citizenship), see, for instance: Balot (2017), p. 839.

[199] With birthright citizenship probably constituting one of the most exclusionary and brutal forms, resembling property inheritance and hence giving rise to important re-distributional obligations attributable to those people actually benefitting from the inheritance of membership, check: Shachar (2009).

[200] Volpp (2017), p. 153. Bosniak (2008).

[201] Kochenov (2019) and Milanovic (2016).

*boundaries of citizenship by restricting membership to a given ethnonational group*",[202] reflecting the old idea of the 'Nation State' and other racist tendencies. Indeed, we shall recall, the law is rarely objectively constructed; it involves a wide range of players, and often dominant majorities[203] that steer the juridification process, ultimately determining who will be granted constitutionally embedded special rights. On a positive note, such movements may also act in favour of group rights, as famously shown by constitutional reform processes in the Andes that would reverse the colonial orientation of the law, re-build the entire State, steered towards so-called 'plurinational' identities and groups. At least its theoretical foundations convey a promising impression on the recognition of inclusive or plural-citizenship. Relatedly, another fundamental point of discussion concerned the explicit recognition and constitutional embedment of indigenous justice systems which was in fact driven by the most powerful social actor, the Movement for Socialism (MAS) in Bolivia.[204] We may, however, be mindful of the exceptional situation of plurinational constitutionalism (see Bolivian, Ecuadorian and Chilean cases), as an inclusive manifestation of citizenship if compared to other constitutional developments around the globe.

Despite the (somewhat superficial) multicultural umbrella of many contemporary State architectures, these have been described as difference-ignorant citizenship models,[205] often under the guise of the harmonising notion of equality. Conversely, difference may assume a defining role in the sense of building on binary opposites: State-based citizenship, is has been argued, is necessarily defined by difference; it is assumed for there to exist a form of 'other' which assumes a demarcating function, or to put it differently, citizenship builds on the distinctiveness of a particular domestic community.[206] In that sense, we may have to distinguish between the 'other' or the 'different' as a category that becomes concealed under the broad notion of citizenship on the one hand (e.g. indigenous peoples, minorities), and as a manifestation of difference that is excluded altogether from the domestic category of citizenship (e.g. migrants). The former—remaining the focus of our attention—have also been dubbed 'internal exclusions' elsewhere, referring to a long history of exclusion in terms of inter-alia equal participation in political decision-making, or co-authoring of the laws, and instead they were to be considered as "*subjects to be ruled paternalistically and coercively rather than as citizens*".[207] Similar arguments could be made in relation to colonial imperialism and its "*graded, racialised, and hierarchical citizenship practices which excluded the vast majority of imperial subjects from equal membership*".[208] Indeed, it is maintained elsewhere that

[202] Yashar (2012), p. 32.

[203] Kymlicka (2013).

[204] Schilling-Vacaflor (2010).

[205] Shachar (2001), Kymlicka (1995), Taylor (1994) and Benhabib (2002).

[206] Spiro (2020).

[207] Kymlicka and Donaldson (2017), p. 839.

[208] Sadiq (2017), p. 184.

subjectship was "*determined by racial ancestry and which carried differential access to rights*"[209] in the colonial era. Yet other accounts refer to a distinguished category of subject-citizenship in the colonial age whose main differentiators were based on race and class.[210] To be sure, in that age we would understand those imperial subjects referred to as pertaining to those 'others' that were not admitted in the first place, unable to access[211] citizenship to start with.

Let us return to the current dilemma inherent to the allegedly inclusive conception of citizenship for a moment. It is assumed among a notable circle of academics that internal exclusions would now have disappeared, attributable, for instance, to the achievement of an almost universal citizenship while building on the rationale refuted by the present (hypo)thesis, that is, for modern citizenship to be "*democratic and* egalitarian, *committed to recognising* equal *belonging, an* equal *right of all members to contribute to and benefit from social cooperation, and an* equal *right to influence the norms of shared society*".[212] Indeed, we easily become trapped in a conceptual paradox here, as clarified by Kymlicka and Donaldson, arguing that a

> 'difference-centred' conception of citizenship is not about flattening differences, and imposing a one-size-fits-all model of how to enact citizenship. Rather the aim is to be responsive to everyone's desire to control and shape their world in meaningful ways, and supporting them in the development of their competence and responsibility. (…) It does mean (…) implementing mechanisms that ensure that these perspectives and expressions actually shape society. In other words, it is about providing avenues for excluded individuals' concerns to get onto the political agenda, not about conscribing them into our pre-set agenda. When as a society, we ask: what matters to this person?.[213]

Indeed, citizenship may fail to meet minority needs on grounds of its generic, all-encompassing umbrella, its institutions, procedures and equal rights, it might however also be criticised for its very pretensions and assumptions that rely on its "*promise of universal inclusion*".[214] It is argued here, this may distract from its inability to critically engage with its underlying rationale, that of equality and its suitability in addressing difference and respective claims arising. Pretentious terminology such as the universality claims, even inclusive or internal universality concepts,[215] may pose methodological dilemmas, proving alien or ignorant at best to any more foundational critique: by building on binary divides such as citizens vs. non-citizens or sub-citizens,[216] we tend to forget to critically approach its surrounding legal framework, the catalogue of rights established therein, its

---

[209] Ng'weno and Obura Aloo (2019), p. 147. Lee (2011).

[210] *Op. cit.* Ng'weno and Obura Aloo (2019).

[211] On the importance of accessing rights in the first place, please see the following conference paper: Ganty (2022).

[212] Kymlicka and Donaldson (2017), p. 839.

[213] Ibid., p. 856.

[214] Bosniak (2017), p. 318.

[215] Ibid.

[216] Ibid.

individualistic orientation, prioritisation of certain categories or typologies of rights and the necessary space for new articulations and juridification processes.

## 2.5 The Missing Ingredient: (The) Social Justice Dimension(s)

Yet another constitutional malaise inherent to the equality rationale lies in its ignorance of social justice, or to put it differently, in allowing individuals and groups alike to access human rights equally, irrespective of their socio-economic situation. Rather than returning to the Rawlsian imaginary, hypothetical veil of ignorance,[217] we shall engage with socio-economic background as such. We easily uncover the myth when returning to the origins of European constitutionalism(s), the way civil and political rights have been prioritised ever since the embracement of the Déclaration des Droits de l'Homme et du Citoyen, in turn, giving rise to equality orders, meant to—in the first place—alienate themselves from medieval hierarchies, abuse of power and clientelism.[218] A paradigm shift would only occur in post-World War II European constitutionalism, based on an appreciation of social welfare as "*an integral part of the legal model of the constitution*"[219] which would be declared *Estado social de derecho*, *État social* or *sozialer Rechtsstaat*.[220] We could also understand the current constitutional deficiency in the light of a missing integrated approach on rights, instead, staying loyal to the old-established taxonomy of human rights, including distinct dividing lines between civil and political rights on the one hand and economic, social and cultural rights on the other hand.[221] Clearly, what empirically seems to represent common practice, in theoretical terms we easily sense contradictions with the globally proclaimed nature of human rights, conceiving the latter as interdependent, interrelated, indivisible and universal according to the *Vienna Declaration and Programme of Action at the World Conference on Human Rights* of 1993.

It remains unexplored, however, why we would consider social justice a decisive matter from the perspective of distinct or group-specific rights. In fact, economic conditions may easily be dismissed in that context, also when defining group status that may exclude any socio-economic grounds.[222] Reasons may lie in the way violations are classified and ultimately weighted in that context: violations relating to accessing employment, social services or public administration, it is argued, are mostly classified as infringements upon minorities' right to identity, rather than an

[217] Rawls (1999a).

[218] Eichler (2020). See, for instance, rationale broadly developed in Baron Montesquieu (1892).

[219] Uprimny (2002), p. 55.

[220] Uprimny (2011), p. 1593.

[221] Vasak (1977) and Tomuschat (2014).

[222] Jovanović (2012)

interference with minorities' socio-economic rights.[223] A few key dimensions are mentioned in that regard, drawing on comparative research on minority and indigenous rights, including "*hindrance in de facto access to education (for religious or linguistic reasons), access to employment (inflexible working schedules make it impossible for you to get a job because you are a devout believer), access to social services*".[224]

The minority-poverty nexus has been explored in different contexts, giving it different turns and complexity. Economic opportunities, or the neglect thereof, may be connected to the minority condition by means of Sen's renown capabilities approach,[225] ultimately guided by the principle of self-determination: formal education, for instance, would enhance economic opportunities by facilitating job access and income, but also vesting an individual with social and cultural freedom, hence allowing her/him/x to enjoy basic political rights.[226] Now, indigenous, tribal and minority education, it is maintained here, may ironically violate such right to education—in its worst form amounting to linguistic genocide—on grounds of the "*choice of the wrong medium of education*", in other words 'dominant-language-only education'.[227] In a different study on minority languages and the socio-economic context, the debate is taken to a meta level by advocating that such particular (e.g. linguistic or social) identity variables impact on a person's socio-economic position.[228] More precisely, these variables "*interlock with minoritization and hierarchization processes that structure society by means of class, gender, ethnicity, caste, religion, and language*".[229] In other words, linguistic, religious or ethnic background need to be understood in the light of those processes undermining them, taking the shape of asymmetries and ultimately allowing the minority condition to arise from such dynamics, with socio-economic positions being shaped by the former. Resultantly, legal responses are expected to develop a certain sensitivity, paying due regard to the multiplicity of variables in play, ultimately constituting the minority condition, while being responsive or pre-emptive in view of any socio-economic implications related to such identity condition.

Considerable cleavages may however be noted between hard law standards and daily politics on the matter. The Framework Convention for the Protection of National Minorities does seem to offer clear directions on social justice questions, calling upon States to adopt measures towards effective equality in the field of economic life, paying due consideration to the specific conditions of 'national minorities' in its article 4. One systemic ill may lie in the focus placed on recognition and related questions of self-definition: one of the most prominent claims being

[223] Henrard (2013).

[224] Ibid., p. 2.

[225] Sen (1984).

[226] Mohanty and Skutnabb-Kangas (2013).

[227] Ibid., p. 162.

[228] Phillipson (2013).

[229] Ibid., p. 190.

considered by constitutional frameworks in Europe, comparatively speaking, concerns minorities' very cultural, traditional or linguistic identities, or territorial status;[230] a more contextual, beyond-the-law analysis would however allow us to also appreciate the socio-economic environment such collective demands are to be situated in. In Europe, this becomes most visible in the case of the Roma minority and their exposure to practices of segregation, often creating "*deplorable and inhumane social and economic conditions*".[231] Indicators may be manifold, among others, (adequate) housing and employment conditions, infant mortality rates, illiteracy rates or access to water,[232] complementing other severe infringements in the education sector and language practice.

International law, by contrast, develops a rather cautious positioning on the granting of socio-economic rights, as we may gather from the somewhat contrasting framing of duties in the case of ICCPR and ICESCR respectively, with the latter permitting some discretion in the way the rights established therein are to be realised.[233] In the aftermath of the adoption of both covenants, however, it would soon become clear that further reaching responsibilities would similarly concern economic, social and cultural rights,[234] emblematic being for these obligations to be (cultural) adequate, affordable, accessible, (culturally) acceptable, adaptable and to live up to a certain quality.[235] More hope may be placed in the collective right to self-determination, enshrined in both covenants, establishing rather unambiguously peoples' right to determine not only political status but to pursue their 'economic, social and cultural development'. Economic development certainly merits some thought, considering the frequently exploited nature of the term, especially if viewed from the perspective of external stakeholders: notably, economic development is not uncommonly contrasted with the anti-growth discourse that permeates many indigenous cosmogenic systems, illustrative being mother earth ideologies.[236] Similar to the individual dimension, these collective expressions of socio-economic rights

[230] Ringelheim (2008).

[231] Baarth (2008), p. 168.

[232] Ibid.

[233] According to art. 2(1), ICESCR, States are to "*take steps, individually and through international assistance and co-operation, especially economic and technical, to the maximum of its available resources, with a view to achieving progressively the full realization of the rights recognised in the present Covenant by all appropriate means, including particularly the adoption of legislative measures.*"

[234] Maastricht Guidelines on Violations of Economic, Social and Cultural Rights (1997).

[235] UN Committee on Economic, Social and Cultural Rights (2000) *General Comment N° 14 The Right to the Highest Attainable Standard of Health.*

UN Committee on Economic, Social and Cultural Rights (1999) *General Comment N° 13 The Right to Education.*

UN Committee on Economic, Social and Cultural Rights (1999) *General Comment N° 12 The Right to Adequate Food.*

UN Committee on Economic, Social and Cultural Rights (1991) *General Comment N° 4 The Right to Adequate Housing.*

[236] Gudynas (2011), Escobar (2014) and Solón (2017).

violations require important elements of self-determination to be in place, if not even more so, giving rise to perspectives that commonly stand in clear contrast with societal majority opinions. And yet again, equality orders may work towards opposite directions, being little perceptible to socio-economic difference, let alone structural impediments.

## 2.6 Negative and Positive Duties as a Response to Equality's Limited Scope of Protection

Conceptualisations around the principle of equality are diverse or fluid, given that the reasons for the belief in equality are multiple, but also considering the process of critical engagement with equality, in other words, processes of refinement and improvement are under way, new versions come to the fore.[237] Respectively, duties too have come to assume a variety of formats and developed transformative potential to varying degrees. Classical human rights language distinguishing between the obligation to *respect*, *protect* and *fulfil* shall serve as an important yardstick in that regard. Such triadic typology of obligations has come to enjoy wide recognition both in IHRL, notably separating between, firstly, a right to respect which would require States not to interfere with the exercise of a given right, in other words, not to impede or place a bar limiting such enjoyment;[238] secondly, a right to protect, invoking important monitoring obligations on the conduct of third parties, leading to prevent individuals or groups from accessing their rights; and thirdly, a right to fulfil, implying further reaching obligations on the part of States, steps to be taken,[239] notably by rendering rights available, (physical and economic) accessible, affordable, adaptable while ensuring their quality.[240] Key to such triadic obligations framework, it is being considered, is the work developed by the treaty monitoring

[237] Raz (2008).

[238] Tomuschat (2014).

[239] Ibid.

[240] These criteria are further spelt out by the UN Committee on Economic, Social and Cultural Rights in relevant general comments including but limited to the right to food, to education, to health, to housing, to work: UN Committee on Economic, Social and Cultural Rights (1999) *General Comment N° 13 The Right to Education*; UN Committee on Economic, Social and Cultural Rights (2000) *General Comment N° 14. The Right to the Highest Attainable Standard of Health* (Article 12 of the International Covenant on Economic, Social and Cultural Rights); UN Committee on Economic, Social and Cultural Rights (1999) *General Comment N°12 The Right to Adequate Food* (art. 11); UN Committee on Economic, Social and Cultural Rights (2016) *General Comment N°23 on the Right to Just and Favourable Conditions of Work* (article 7 of the International Covenant on Economic, Social and Cultural Rights). See also: Maastricht Guidelines on Violations of Economic, Social and Cultural Rights (1997). See also: Clapham (2015).

bodies that demonstrably applied those obligations to the right to non-discrimination in particular.[241]

According to the OHCHR & Equal Rights Trust guide "Protecting Minority Rights: A Practical Guide to Developing Comprehensive Anti-Discrimination Legislation", the *obligation to respect* comprises two main elements:

> States undertake to refrain from engaging in discriminatory acts or adopting, implementing, or pursuing policies that are discriminatory in purpose or effect (. . .) [and] States undertake to 'amend, rescind or nullify any laws and regulations which have the effect of creating or perpetuating' discrimination[242]

It has been maintained elsewhere that respective measures to prevent discrimination when relating discrimination to the right to food came to include the obligation of 'accessing' food or resources for food principally,[243] reading like a further reaching obligation. Interestingly, the Committee on Economic, Social and Cultural Rights also engages with the equality principle as in equality of opportunity. Notably, the Committee maintains that "*equality of opportunity requires that hiring, promotion and termination not be discriminatory*".[244] Also at a broader level, it stipulates that

> just and favourable conditions of work [to be] exercised without discrimination of any kind. Specifically, they have an obligation to guarantee that women enjoy conditions of work not inferior to those of men and receive equal pay for equal value, which requires the immediate elimination of formal and substantive discrimination. States must also combat all forms of unequal treatment arising from precarious employment relationships.[245]

Curiously, the Committee's understanding of non-discrimination and equality reveals some awareness of the immediacy of adopting measures and it also discloses a conscious dealing with the matter inclusively, that is, approaching unequal treatment in any possible form this may take. The Committee on the Elimination of Discrimination against Women further adds to this, by holding that the negative State obligation not to discriminate shall be protected in "*law, policy and practice*".[246]

Secondly, we shall focus on the second main human rights obligation, that is, the State *duty to protect* as it relates to the equality principle. Such obligation primarily

---

[241] OHCHR & Equal Rights Trust (2023) *Protecting Minority Rights: A Practical Guide to Developing Comprehensive Anti-Discrimination Legislation.*

[242] Ibid., pp. 2–3.

[243] Committee on Economic, Social and Cultural Rights (1999) *General Comment N°12 The Right to Adequate Food* (art. 11).

[244] Committee on Economic, Social and Cultural Rights (2016) *General Comment N°23 on the Right to Just and Favourable Conditions of Work* (article 7 of the International Covenant on Economic, Social and Cultural Rights), para. 31.

[245] Ibid., para. 53.

[246] Committee on the Elimination of Discrimination against Women (2010) *General Recommendation N°28 on the Core Obligations of States Parties under Article 2 of the Convention on the Elimination of All Forms of Discrimination Against Women*, p. 4.

OHCHR & Equal Rights Trust (2023) *Protecting Minority Rights: A Practical Guide to Developing Comprehensive Anti-Discrimination Legislation*, p. 2.

concerns the third sector—while corporate actors are broadly upheld to comply with due diligence obligations (e.g. 'Ruggie Principles'),[247] the State is called upon to protect against any such actions. One obligation arising from this concerns the adoption of anti-discrimination legislation which is addressed by several treaty monitoring bodies.[248] More precisely, jurisprudence developed by both international human rights bodies and regional mechanisms seems to suggest that the obligation to protect requires anti-discrimination legislation adopted to be comprehensive.[249] Some attempts have been made to interpret non-discrimination and equality as far as they relate to the duty to protect, notably in the contexts of education and work. Relevant obligations highlighted in that regard concerned, among other indicators, the "*time frame and coverage of policy or programme for equal access to education at all levels (...) or for equal access to decent work*",[250] or respective times frames, coverage as well as programmes to "*provide protection from discriminatory practices interfering with access to food, health, social security and housing (...) or the elimination of forced labour and other abuse at work, including domestic work*".[251]

Thirdly, equality principles may gain a particular place in the context of the most far reaching obligation, that of *fulfilment* or guarantees. As the committee probably most active in the field of positive obligations, the Committee on Economic, Social and Cultural Rights pronounced itself on positive measures in relation to non-discrimination and equality, stating that "*in addition to refraining from discriminatory actions, States parties should take concrete, deliberate and targeted measures to ensure that discrimination (...) is eliminated*".[252] When examining treaty body jurisprudence generally, a few special measures stand out as they relate to non-discrimination and equality:

---

[247] Office of the High Commissioner for Human Rights (2011) *Guiding Principles on Business and Human Rights: Implementing the United Nations 'Protect, Respect and Remedy' Framework.* See also: Bilchitz and Deva (2013).

[248] The aforementioned report "Protecting Minority Rights" engages in detail with the obligation to adopt anti-discrimination legislation, broadly interpreting such obligation to protect, as follows "the law shall prohibit any discrimination and guarantee to all persons equal and effective protection against discrimination (...) [for the State to] take the necessary steps (...) to adopt such laws or other measures as may be necessary to give effect" to the rights established by the treaties. The report refers to arts. 26 and 2(2) ICCPR in stipulating such obligations while also referring to art. 2 (1) ICESCR, art. 2(1)(d) ICERD, art. 2(a) CEDAW and art. 4(1) CRPD.

[249] OHCHR & Equal Rights Trust (2023) *Protecting Minority Rights: A Practical Guide to Developing Comprehensive Anti-Discrimination Legislation.*

[250] Office of the High Commissioner for Human Rights (2012) *Human Rights Indicators: A Guide to Measurement and Implementation*, p. 100.

[251] Ibid., p. 100.

[252] OHCHR & Equal Rights Trust (2023) *Protecting Minority Rights: A Practical Guide to Developing Comprehensive Anti-Discrimination Legislation*, p. 3.

Committee on Economic, Social and Cultural Rights (2009) *General Comment N° 20 Non-Discrimination in Economic, Social and Cultural Rights* (Article 2, para. 2).

> the development of policies, plans and strategies; data collection and analysis; public reporting; public education, training and awareness-raising; and the establishment of institutions.[253]

As it becomes apparent, the duty to fulfil may not only concern State action in a strict sense, but shall include relevant incentivising measures oriented towards other key players including civil society entities. Institutional spaces stand at the forefront of these endeavours with education, public information and institution-building informing any conceptualisation of the duty to fulfil. Another observation worth mentioning concerns the close alignment of such duty with substantive equality. A list of indicators on the right to non-discrimination and equality developed by experts of the OHCHR allows for such derivation, including the following relevant special measures to be adopted:

> Time frame and coverage of policy to implement special and temporary measures to ensure or accelerate equality in the enjoyment of human rights (...) Proportion of targeted population groups accessing positive action or preferential treatment measures aiming to promote de facto equality (e.g. financial assistance, training)[254]

To be sure, the above wording suggests that equality is to be understood as an outcome or guarantee and as an objective to be complied with in actual practice; even more unequivocally, positive measures shall strive for de facto equality. Only rarely, as in the present case, the duty to fulfil is oriented as strongly towards equality as an outcome rather than the—undoubtedly quintessential—sheer enumeration of measures to be adopted by the State as a result. As it becomes apparent, such guarantees represent the most effective form of a human rights obligation, living up to the State's (international) commitments in implementing or enforcing the law.

Finally, it may be worth examining jurisprudence developed by the Committee on the Rights of Persons with Disabilities establishing what it terms '*inclusive equality*', a new equality paradigm introduced in a dedicated comment on equality and non-discrimination.[255] It similarly refers to the term '*equalization of opportunities*', the latter constituting a general principle of the treaty, to be considered a "*significant development from a formal model of equality to a substantive model of equality*".[256] Inclusive equality permeates the covenant, defined as a

> substantive model of equality (...) and [it] extends and elaborates on the content of equality in (a) a fair redistributive dimension to address socioeconomic disadvantages; (b) a recognition dimension to combat stigma, stereotyping, prejudice and violence and to recognise the dignity of human beings and their intersectionality; (c) a participative dimension to reaffirm

---

[253] OHCHR & Equal Rights Trust (2023) *Protecting Minority Rights: A Practical Guide to Developing Comprehensive Anti-Discrimination Legislation.* See in particular Committee on Economic, Social and Cultural Rights (2009) General Comment N° 20 *Non-Discrimination in Economic, Social and Cultural Rights* (Article 2, para. 2).

[254] Office of the High Commissioner for Human Rights (2012) *Human Rights Indicators: A Guide to Measurement and Implementation*, p. 100.

[255] Committee on the Rights of Persons with Disabilities (2018) *General Comment N°6 on Equality and Non-Discrimination*, para. 11.

[256] Ibid., para. 10.

> the social nature of people as members of social groups and the full recognition of humanity through inclusion in society; and (d) an accommodating dimension to make space for difference as a matter of human dignity.[257]

Interestingly, the Committee hereby combines not only different grounds of discrimination including its intersectional manifestations, it also addresses discrimination in its pre-mature stage, including various forms of exclusion, marginalisation, ultimately inequality. For the right to equality and non-discrimination to be effective, the Committee on the Rights of Persons with Disabilities requires States to adopt dedicated enforcement measures.[258] It also understands the principle of 'inclusive equality' as to give rise to specific measures to be adopted vis-à-vis persons with disabilities including people suffering intersectional discrimination.[259] As a pre-condition for measures to be adopted in such cases, the Committee calls upon States to

> (they must) collect and analyse appropriate data and research information in order to identify inequalities, discriminatory practices and patterns of disadvantage, and analyse the effectiveness of measures promotion equality (...) and for developing effective anti-discrimination and equality measures. (...) States should also conduct appropriate research on disability discrimination and equality rights.[260]

## 2.7 The Respect, Protect, Fulfil Framework Beyond IHRL

As it may become apparent from the above, IHRL could probably be considered as the most shaping legal framework as to the triadic human rights obligation to respect, protect and fulfil.[261] Nevertheless, domestic developments may reveal to what extent old-established equality paradigms continue shaping the wide range of human rights

---

[257] Ibid., para. 11.

[258] Ibid. While not exhaustive in kind, the Committee refers to specific enforcement measures to be adopted in that regard, including (not limited to): "*(a) measures to raise the awareness of all people about the rights of persons with disabilities under the Convention, the meaning of discrimination and the existing judicial remedies; (b) measures to ensure rights contained in the Convention are actionable in domestic courts and provide access to justice for all persons who have experienced discrimination; (c) protection from retaliation, such as adverse treatment or adverse consequences in reaction to a complaint or to proceedings aimed at enforcing compliance with equality provisions; (d) the legal right to bring a lawsuit to court and to pursue claims through associations, organisations or other legal entities that have a legitimate interest in the realisation of the right to equality; (e) specific rules relating to evidence and proof to ensure that stereotyped attitudes about the capacity of persons with disabilities do not result in victims of discrimination being inhibited in obtaining redress; (f) effective, proportionate and dissuasive sanctions for breach of the right to equality and adequate remedies; (g) sufficient and accessible provision of legal aid to ensure access to justice for the claimant in discrimination litigation.*" para. 31.

[259] Ibid.

[260] Ibid., paras. 34–35.

[261] See, illustratively, British Institute of International and Comparative Law (2018) *When National Law Conflicts with International Human Rights Standards: Recommendations for Business.*

obligations to be complied with in the current age, hence reflecting a modest stance on such commitments. A critical engagement with such obligations requires us to examine its underlying principles more closely: rather than merely giving rise to a duty 'not to do harm', the obligation to respect could be understood as entailing the 'responsibility not to dehumanise'.[262] In one way or another, constitutional debates have shown open towards such framework, illustrative being the South African case where constitutional experts and a technical committee would recommend the additions of the terms 'promote' and 'fulfill' to section 7 of the 1996 constitutional draft, referring to IHRL standards.[263] Indeed, the obligation to respect, protect and fulfil socio-economic rights needs to be respected by the South African State, forming part and parcel of the Bill of Rights under the South African constitution and to be interpreted by the courts to "*promote human dignity, equality and freedom*".[264] Similar expert recommendations were issued on the catalogue of fundamental rights in the Belgian constitution (Title II) calling for a human rights clause embedding the "*classic triad to respect, to fulfil and to protect*".[265] These specific obligations certainly find their roots in international law principally, as (a) main source(s) of reference but also as important frames of interpretation. What may be called the 'constitutionalization of human rights treaties' illustrates such top-down logics vividly.[266] The latter principally implies that human rights treaties would benefit from constitutional rank, but also more broadly, human rights treaties have become transposed into domestic law acquiring a special status, that way, "*guarantee[ing] their precedence vis-à-vis domestic statutes, and (it) prevent [ing] human rights treaties from subsequent statutory invalidation*".[267] In that sense, the duty to respect, protect and fulfil assumes an extra-recommendatory role, serving as an important guidance for spelling out human rights domestically, resembling the function exerted by regulations in the domestic legal order.

Also regionally, the triadic human rights obligation enjoys prominence. Typically, in the European Ius Commune, the duty to 'secure' human rights is called for: the aforediscussed *Belgian Linguistic case* dating back to the 1960s coined the term in relation to the right to education; positive discrimination was then further developed to protect the right to life in *Makaratzis vs. Greece* and the right to access information on origins and childhood in *Gaskin vs. the United Kingdom.*[268] At a

See also: United Nations (2022) The Foundation of International Human Rights Law. Retrieved from https://www.un.org/en/about-us/udhr/foundation-of-international-human-rights-law.

[262] Karp (2019).

[263] Panel of Constitutional Experts and Technical Committee (South Africa) (1996) *Memorandum: Section 7 The State Must Respect, Protect, Promote and Fulfil the Rights in this Bill of Rights.*

[264] Barrett (2016), p. 19.

[265] Velaers (2016), p. 277.

[266] Góngora-Mera (2017).

[267] Ibid., p. 238.

[268] Volou (2022). See also the following decisions: *Airey vs. Ireland*, European Court of Human Rights in 1979; *Marckx vs. Belgium*, European Court of Human Rights in 1979; *X and Y vs. The Netherlands*, European Court of Human Rights in 1985. See also Dröge (2003).

more structural level, the ECtHR is confronted with the ever present principle of deference or subsidiarity which delegates respective obligations to the State Parties as it is stated elsewhere, unequivocally, "*the task of ensuring respect for the rights enshrined in the Convention lies first and foremost with the authorities in the Contracting States rather than with the Court*".[269] Nevertheless, a few general observations may be made in relation to positive obligations under the ECtHR umbrella. Far from establishing any uniform positioning, jurisprudential developments generically require action for positive obligations to be complied with; instead, the Court upholds certain principles to be adhered to, namely for respective guarantees to be 'practical' and 'effective', having "*explicitly declined to develop any 'general theory' of positive obligations*".[270] In other words,

> positive obligations have thus been created as a consequence of applying the effective and dynamic interpretation of the ECHR to protect the rights of individuals. The foundation and the content of positive obligations in the Convention system – the so-called 'standard of effectiveness' – lies thus in the recognition that a purely negative approach to the protection of human rights cannot guarantee their effective protection.[271]

When concerning ourselves with the tripartite typology distinguishing between human rights respect, protection and fulfilment, it is argued that the Court has never "*explicitly endorsed the tripartite typology but remains loyal to the bipartite typology of positive and negative obligations*"[272]—in that sense, any such attempt to categorise duties accordingly would require a rather "*artificial interpretative exercise to reconstruct the Court's positive obligations case law*".[273] According to such reading of the case law, the tripartite duty paradigm does not always allow for an easy fit for competing categories or, alternatively, proves difficult to cope with a certain blurriness. In other words, such typology is being challenged on grounds of the inability of categories to do justice to the complexity of human rights infringements, also called 'category scepticism'.[274] Interestingly, the Court does refer to the tripartite obligation in relation to a non-derogable norm, without however exploring such duty in depth, notably by establishing the State's 'utmost responsibility' and relatedly, the "*obligation to respect, protect and fulfil the right of individuals not to be subjected to torture or to inhuman or degrading treatment or punishment*".[275] Instead, it could be argued that the duty to 'secure effective rights' takes its place, as such duty "*does not mean merely the absence of an interference but may require the State to take various forms of positive action*"[276] which seemingly takes shape in a

---

[269] Brems (2017), p. 22.

[270] Medda-Windischer (2016), p. 29. See, for instance, *Platform 'Ärzte für das Leben' vs. Austria*, European Court of Human Rights in 1988.

[271] Medda-Windischer (2016), p. 29. See also Xenos (2011).

[272] Lavrysen (2017), p. 12. See also Koch (2005).

[273] Lavrysen (2017), p. 12.

[274] Ibid., p. 13.

[275] *Premininy vs. Russia*, European Court of Human Rights in 2011, para. 85.

[276] Lavrysen (2017), p. 58.

constraining context, commonly limited to the enforcement of judgements and regarding the hearing of witnesses. Equivalent protection may also be granted by what has been termed "*protection in the absence of interference*",[277] being tantamount to the obligation to fulfil, notably, requiring State assistance to enable a human right to be exercised in the first place or to provide certain means proving facilitating in that regard.

As it is to be expected, the EU legal order has demonstrated a somewhat cautious attitude on the matter: it is argued that necessary measures to be adopted with the objective of fulfilling positive obligations could not be taken given the "*only limited competences to protect fundamental rights*".[278] From the outset, it needs to be stated that fundamental rights "*have not shaped its jurisprudence decisively, even if some recent decisions show a clearer fundamental rights-oriented profile*".[279] Reasons may be sought in the historical-institutional developments of the Union, without having been declared rights as such, these could be considered of the functionalist—rather than constitutionalist—path of the EU, in that sense, representing a fruitful side-effect of institution-building.[280] This does not stand in contradiction with certain principles created to foster fundamental rights, emblematic being the principle of 'effectiveness' guiding the adherence to and implementation of fundamental rights.[281]

Despite the lack of a systematic approach on the matter, a few observations can be made as to a possibly common position embraced by the EU's judicial institutions. In quite a few cases, positive measures do not directly follow from the specific provision that stipulates a given right, rather, the CJEU would formulate such duty in an individual case considering the individual circumstances.[282] Again, the principle of '*effective judicial protection*' is invoked in the case of positive obligations, requiring, for instance, remedies to be created or vesting specific powers to public authorities.[283] This becomes quintessential for basic equality principles to be meaningfully applied, if the principle was understood as aiming for substantive equality or equality of outcome, turning effective protection an important pre-condition. Also more transversally-speaking, attempts have been made to further define positive measures as these arise in the EU legal order, for instance, understanding that positive duties (other than negative obligations)

> (i) do not follow (directly) from provisions on fundamental rights and their structure, but need to be implied in individual cases; (ii) require states to take active measures which can

---

[277] Ibid., p. 79. See also Xenos (2011).

[278] Beijer (2017), p. 7.

[279] von Bogdandy (2012), p. 45.

[280] Ibid.

[281] Beijer (2017).

[282] Ibid. See also: *T. Port GmbH & Co. KG vs. Bundesanstalt für Landwirtschaft und Ernährung*, Court of Justice of the European Union in 1996.

[283] Ibid. See also: *The Queen vs. Secretary of State for Transport, ex parte: Factortame Ltd.*, Court of Justice of the European Union in 1990; *Unibet (London) Ltd and Unibet (International) vs. Justitiekanslern*, Court of Justice of the European Union in 2007.

> (only) relate to certain gaps in their policies; (iii) and have an 'alternative' structure, which means that they leave a choice as to the measures which need to be taken by states.[284]

Finally, the CJEU proposes two criteria that shall apply to positive obligations, namely for such obligations to be 'intrinsic' and 'supportive' which are further defined throughout its case-law:

> Intrinsic types of positive obligations require measures to be taken so that fundamental rights can actually be enjoyed by individuals. (. . .) Supportive positive obligations are necessary to secure that public authorities do in fact comply with the negative obligation to protect fundamental rights.[285]

Similarly, the Inter-American human rights system has been establishing a duty to 'respect' and 'ensure' rights as stipulated in its founding instrument, the American Convention on Human Rights. Attention shall be paid to the specific historical context giving rise to positive obligations: in the case of the Americas, specific obligations in that regard include the duty to prevent, investigate, punish and repair but also obligations to secure substantive equality.[286] While the latter may not have become part of the typical legal jargon, a '*culture of human rights*' is generally considered as an important precondition for achieving substantive equality; this may include stereotypes as reflected in policies contributing to the subordination of women as argued in *González et al. ("Cotton Field") vs. Mexico.*[287] Also more expressly, the Court has developed a firm positioning on such duty, "*recognis[ing] that the principle of non-discrimination requires more than mere formal equality*"[288] in its *Advisory Opinion on the Juridical Condition and Rights of Undocumented Migrants*. Instead, it calls upon States to

> take affirmative action to reverse or change discriminatory situations that exist in their societies to the detriment of a specific group of persons. This implies the special obligation to protect that the State must exercise with regard to acts and practices of third parties who, with its tolerance or acquiescence, create, maintain or promote discriminatory situations.[289]

Also elsewhere the Court pronounced itself on the obligation to grant preferential treatment, to take positive steps to revert the impacts caused by third parties, or relatedly, for States to promote the equality of conditions.[290] Indeed, positive obligations have become part of the regional order in the Americas, initiating with the *Velásquez-Rodríguez vs. Honduras* judgement.[291]

---

[284] Beijer (2017), p. 265.

[285] Ibid., p. 274.

[286] Lavrysen (2014).

[287] Ibid.

[288] Ibid., p. 111.

[289] Ibid. *Advisory Opinion on the Juridical Condition and Rights of Undocumented Migrants*, Inter-American Court of Human Rights in 2003, para. 104.

[290] Lavrysen (2014). See also: *Case of the "Mapiripán Massacre" vs. Colombia*, Inter-American Court of Human Rights in 2005; *Furlan and Family vs. Argentina*, Inter-American Court of Human Rights in 2012.

[291] Volou (2022).

Relatedly, the African human and peoples' rights system requires measures to be adopted according to its founding document, the African Charter on Human and Peoples' Rights: State Parties "*shall have the duty to promote and ensure (...) the respect of the rights [established therein]*" according to its art. 25. The duty to respect, protect and fulfil has gained prominence in the field of economic, social and cultural rights: in its article 1, the Pretoria Declaration on Economic, Social and Cultural Rights in Africa unequivocally refers to the duty to respect, protect, promote and fulfil the rights enshrined in the African Charter on Human and Peoples' Rights which include economic, social and cultural rights, hence further articulating the rights stipulated in the Charter. Positive obligations generally shine through the Charter in its art. 1 stipulating respective duties by maintaining that Member States "*shall undertake to adopt legislative or other measures to give effect to them*".[292] Relevant jurisprudential development further reinforce such perspective. In that sense, the Commission has been pronouncing itself not only in favour of the obligations codified in art. 1, but on the legal value of such duties:

> The Commission is mindful of the positive obligations incumbent on States Parties to the Charter in terms of Article 1 not only to 'recognise' the rights under the Charter but to go on to 'undertake to adopt legislative or other measures to give effect to them' [art. 1]. The obligation is peremptory, States 'shall undertake'.[293]

More specifically, the Commission has been referring to the triadic duty to respect, protect and fulfil in its case-law, more specifically pronouncing itself on such duties as they can be derived from IHRL:

> Internationally accepted ideas of the various obligations engendered by human rights indicate that all rights (...) generate at least four levels of duties for a State (...) namely the duty to respect, protect, promote, and fulfil these rights.[294] These obligations universally apply to all rights and entail a combination of negative and positive duties.[295]

---

[292] See also: Mba (2009).

[293] *Legal Resources Foundation vs. Zambia*, African Commission on Human and Peoples' Rights in 2001. See also: Mba (2009).

[294] The triadic obligation is further spelt out in the present judgement, defined as follows: "*At a primary level, the* ***obligation to respect*** *entails that the State should refrain from interfering in the enjoyment of all fundamental rights; it should respect right-holders, their freedoms, autonomy, resources, and liberty of their action. At a secondary level, the State is* ***obliged to protect*** *right-holders against other subjects by legislation and provision of effective remedies. This obligation requires the State to take measures to protect beneficiaries of the protected rights against political, economic and social interferences. Protection generally entails the creation and maintenance of an atmosphere or framework by an effective interplay of laws and regulations so that individuals will be able to freely realize their rights and freedoms. This is very much intertwined with the tertiary obligation of the State to promote the enjoyment of all human rights. The State should make sure that individuals are able to exercise their rights and freedoms, for example, by promoting tolerance, raising awareness, and even building infrastructures. The last layer of obligation requires the State to* ***fulfil*** *the rights and freedoms it freely undertook under the various human rights regimes. It is more of a positive expectation on the part of the State to move its machinery towards the actual realisation of the rights. This is also very much intertwined with the duty to promote mentioned in the preceding paragraph.*" (paras. 45–47).

[295] *The Social and Economic Rights Action Center and the Center for Economic and Social Rights vs. Nigeria*, African Commission on Human and Peoples' Rights in 2001; para. 44.

In relation to the positive duties, the Commission takes the chance of further spelling them out in a clarificatory manner, namely by stating that "*if a state neglects to ensure the rights in the African Charter, this can constitute a violation, even if the State or its agents are not the immediate cause of the violation*".[296] If we were to relate this to the principle of equality, we would expect such duties to apply to the Charter in its entirety and hence also require equality to be achieved in practice, rather than merely de jure.

## References

Anaya J (2004) Indigenous peoples in international law. Oxford University Press, Oxford

Arato A, Cohen JL (2018) Introduction: forms of pluralism and democratic constitutionalism. In: Arato A, Cohen JL, von Busekist A (eds) Forms of pluralism and democratic constitutionalism. Columbia University Press, New York

Aristotle (1984) Nichomachean ethics. In: Barnes J (ed) Complete works of Aristotle: the revised Oxford translation. Princeton University Press, Princeton

Arneson R (2013) Egalitarianism. The Stanford encyclopedia of philosophy. https://plato.stanford.edu/archives/sum2013/entries/egalitarianism/

Arneson R (2015) Equality of opportunity. The Stanford encyclopedia of philosophy. https://plato.stanford.edu/cgi-bin/encyclopedia/archinfo.cgi?entry=equal-opportunity

Baarth WK (2008) On cultural rights: the equality of nations and the minority legal tradition. BRILL, Leiden

Badie B (2018) Quand le Sud réinvente le monde: Essai sur la puissance de la faiblesse. La Découverte, Paris

Badie B, Vidal D (2017) Un Monde d'Inégalités. La Découverte, Paris

Baldwin C, Morel C (2009) Group rights. In: Evans MD, Murray R (eds) The African Charter on human and peoples' rights: the system in practice. Cambridge University Press, Cambridge

Ballakrishnen SS, Dezalay S (2021) Invisible institutionalisms: collective reflections on the shadows of legal globalisation. Hart Publishing, Oxford

Balot R (2017) Revisiting the classical ideal of citizenship. In: Shachar A, Bauböck R, Bloemraad I, Vink M (eds) The Oxford handbook of citizenship. Oxford University Press, Oxford

Baron Montesquieu CLS (1892) Esprit des Lois. Hachette Livre, Paris

Barrera A (2012) Turning legal pluralism into state-sanctioned law: assessing the implications of the new constitutions and laws in Bolivia and Ecuador. In: Schilling-Vacaflor A (ed) New constitutionalism in Latin America: promises and practices. Ashgate, Farnham

Barrett D (2016) The importance of equality law and human rights in addressing socio-economic inequality. In: Cuypers D, Vrielink J (eds) Equal is not enough. Intersentia, Antwerp

Barrios Suvelza F (2018) El Control Contramayoritario como Marco de Análisis de la Influencia del Nuevo Constitucionalismo Latinoamericano sobre la Democracia. Revista Española de Ciencia Política (47)

Barskanmaz C (2019) Recht und Rassismus: Das menschenrechtliche Verbot der Diskriminierung aufgrund der Rasse. Springer, Cham

Barth WK (2008) On cultural rights: the equality of nations and the minority legal tradition. Martinus Nijhoff Verlag, Leiden

[296] *Commission Nationale des Droits de l'Homme et des Libertés vs. Chad*, African Commission on Human and Peoples' Rights in 1995; para. 20.

Bashir B (2012) Accommodating historically oppressed social groups: deliberative democracy and the politics of reconciliation. In: Kymlicka W, Bashir B (eds) The politics of reconciliation in multicultural societies. Oxford University Press, Oxford
Beijer M (2017) The limits of fundamental rights protection by the EU: the scope for the development of positive obligations. Intersentia, Antwerp
Belavusau U, Henrard K (2018) EU anti-discrimination law beyond gender. Hart Publishing, Oxford
Belavusau U, Henrard K (2019) A bird's eye view on EU anti discrimination law: the impact of the 2000 equality directives. German Law J 20(5)
Benhabib S (2002) The claims of culture: equality and diversity in the global era. Princeton University Press, Princeton
Bennett T, Bavikatte KS (2015) Community stewardship: the foundation of biocultural rights. J Hum Rights Environ 6(1)
Benton L (2020) Empires and jurisdictional politics: legal pluralism and the search for global order. In: Schiff Berman P (ed) The Oxford handbook of global legal pluralism. Oxford University Press, Oxford
Besson S (2015) Human rights and constitutional law: patterns of mutual validation and legitimation. In: Cruft R, Liao SM, Renzo M (eds) Philosophical foundations of human rights. Oxford University Press, Oxford
Bilchitz D, Deva S (2013) Human rights obligations of business: beyond the corporate responsibility to respect? Cambridge University Press, Cambridge
Bosniak L (2008) The citizen and the alien: dilemmas of contemporary membership. Princeton University Press, Princeton
Bosniak L (2017) Status non-citizens. In: Shachar A, Bauböck R, Bloemraad I, Vink M (eds) The Oxford handbook of citizenship. Oxford University Press, Oxford
Brems E (2017) The 'logics' of procedural-type review by the European Court of Human Rights. In: Gerards J, Brems E (eds) Procedural review in European fundamental rights cases. Cambridge University Press, Cambridge
Breton R (1985) Les Institutions et les Réseaux d'Organisations des Communautés Ethnoculturelles. In: Fédération des Francophones hors Québec (eds) État de la Recherche sur les Communautés Francophones hors Québec. Fédération des Francophones hors Québec, Ottawa
Carbonneau J-R (2017) La Complétude Institutionnelle des Sorabes de Lusace depuis l'Unification des États Allemands. Politique et Sociétés 36(3)
Carbonneau J-R, Gruschke A, Jacobs F, Keller I (2017) Dimensionen kultureller Sicherheit: Einführung. In: Carbonneau J-R, Gruschke A, Jacobs F, Keller I, Wölke S (eds) Dimensionen kultureller Sicherheit bei ethnischen und sprachlichen Minderheiten. Zeitschrift für sorbische Sprache, Geschichte und Kultur | Časopis za rěč, stawizny a kulturu Łužiskich Serbow 64(2)
Centre for International Governance Innovation (2020) UNDRIP implementation: comparative approaches, indigenous voices from CANZUS, special report. Centre for International Governance Innovation, Waterloo
Chalmers D (2007) Constituent power and the pluralist ethic. In: Loughlin M, Walker N (eds) The paradox of constitutionalism. Oxford University Press, Oxford
Chalmers D (2020) Constituent power and pluralist ethic. In: Schiff Berman P (ed) The Oxford handbook of global legal pluralism. Oxford University Press, Oxford
Charters C, Stavenhagen R (2012) Making the declaration work: the United Nations Declaration on the Rights of Indigenous Peoples. International Work Group for Indigenous Affairs, Copenhagen
Clapham A (2015) Human rights: a very short introduction. Oxford University Press, Oxford
Comaroff J, Comaroff JL (2008) Law and disorder in the postcolony. Chicago University Press, Chicago
Corntassel J (2007) Partnership in action? Indigenous political mobilization and cooptation during the first UN indigenous decade (1995–2004). Hum Rights Q 29

Cornwall A, Gaventa J (2001) From user and chooser to makers and shapers: repositioning participation in social policy. IDS Working Paper 127
Cossette-Lefebvre H (2020) Direct and indirect discrimination: a defense of the disparate impact model. Public Aff Q 34(4)
Craig R (2007) Systemic discrimination in employment and the promotion of ethnic equality. Martinus Nijhoff Publishers, Leiden
Crowley J (2001) The political participation of ethnic minorities. Int Polit Sci Rev 22(1)
de Gaay Fortman B (2011) Minority rights: major misconception? Hum Rights Q 33
de Sousa Santos B (1987) Law: a map of misreading. Toward a postmodern conception of law. J Law Soc 14(3)
de Sousa Santos B (2002) Toward a new legal common sense. Cambridge University Press, Cambridge
de Sousa Santos B (2010) Refundación del Estado en América Latina: Perspectivas desde una epistemología del Sur. IILS, Lima
de Sousa Santos B (2013) Descolonizar el saber, reinventar el poder. LOM ediciones, Santiago de Chile
de Sousa Santos B (2017) Épistémologies du Sud et militantisme académique. Entretien avec Boaventura de Sousa Santos, réalisé par Baptiste Godrie. Sociologie et sociétés 49(1)
Dersso SA (2006) The jurisprudence of the African Commission on human and peoples' rights with respect to peoples' rights. Afr Hum Rights Law J 6
Dickson B (2010) Positive obligations and the European Court of Human Rights. North Ireland Leg Q 61(3)
Doyle O (2007) Direct discrimination, indirect discrimination and autonomy. Oxf J Leg Stud 27(3)
Doyle CM (2015) Indigenous peoples, title to territory, rights and resources: the transformative role of free prior and informed consent. Routledge, Abingdon
Dröge C (2003) Positive Verpflichtungen der Staaten in der Europäischen Menschenrechtskonvention. Beiträge zum ausländischen öffentlichen Recht und Völkerrecht 159
Dworkin R (1977) Taking rights seriously. Harvard University Press, Cambridge
Eichler J (2020) "Migrating recognition" or "constitutionalism reversed": relating Andean plurinational constitutionalism and European integration politics. Hum Rights Q 42(4)
Eichler J (2022a) Disentangling the vernacular in Bolivia and decolonising the law: epistemological-legal perspectives on the encounters between indigenous peoples and the state. Int J Min Group Rights
Eichler J (2022b) The transformative forces of international law? Questioning equality regimes from a multi-level perspective. Global Constitutionalism
Eichler J, Doyle C, Howard S (forthcoming) United Nations Declaration on the Rights of Indigenous Peoples: article-by-article commentary. Beck/Hart/Nomos, München/Baden-Baden/Oxford
Escobar A (2014) Sentipensar con la Tierra: Nuevas Lecturas sobre Desarrollo, Territorio y Diferencia. Ediciones UNAULA, Medellín
Flikschuh K (2015) Human rights in Kantian Mode: a sketch. In: Cruft R, Liao SM, Renzo M (eds) Philosophical foundations of human rights. Oxford University Press, Oxford
Foblets M-C, Graziadei, Dundes Renteln A (2018) Personal autonomy in plural societies: a principle and its paradoxes. Routledge, Abingdon
Fontana LB, Grugel J (2016) The politics of indigenous participation through "free, prior informed consent": reflections from the Bolivian Case. World Dev 77
Fraser N (1998) Social justice in the age of identity politics: redistribution, recognition, participation. Wissenschaftszentrum Berlin für Sozialforschung Discussion Papers FS 98-103
Ganty S (2022) A right to the effective access to rights: a pleonasm? ICON•S annual conference, Wrocław
Gaventa J (1980) Power and powerlessness: quiescence and rebellion in an Appalachian Valley. University of Illinois Press, Urbana

Góngora-Mera ME (2017) The block of constitutionality as the doctrinal pivot of a Ius Commune. In: von Bogdandy A, Ferrer MacGregor E, Morales Antoniazzi M, Piovesan F (eds) Transformative constitutionalism in Latin America: the emergence of a new Ius Commune. Oxford University Press, Oxford

Goodale M (2007) Introduction: locating rights, envisioning law between the global and the local. In: Goodale M, Engle Merry S (eds) The practice of human rights: tracking law between the global and the local. Cambridge University Press, Cambridge

Gosepath S (2021) Equality. The Stanford encyclopedia of philosophy. https://plato.stanford.edu/archives/sum2021/entries/equality/

Gover K (2015) Settler-state political theory, 'CANZUS' and the UN Declaration on the Rights of Indigenous Peoples. Eur J Int Law 26(2)

Gover K (2020) Legal pluralism and indigenous legal traditions. In: Schiff Berman P (ed) The Oxford handbook of global legal pluralism. Oxford University Press, Oxford

Gudynas E (2011) Buen Vivir: today's tomorrow. Development 54(4)

Henrard K (2008) Equality of individuals. Max Planck encyclopedias of international law. https://opil.ouplaw.com/view/10.1093/law:epil/9780199231690/law-9780199231690-e788?rskey=MyxtkC&result=1&prd=MPIL

Henrard K (2011) Boosting positive action: the asymmetrical approach towards non-discrimination and special minority rights. ZaöRV 71

Henrard K (2013) Introduction. In: Henrard K (ed) The interrelation between the right to identity of minorities and their socio-economic participation. Martinus Nijhoff Publishers, Leiden

Hindess B (2004) Citizenship for all. Citizensh Stud 8(3)

Hirsch SM (2003) The emergence of political organisations among the Guaraní Indians of Bolivia and Argentina: a comparative perspective. In: Detlef E, Muñoz E (eds) Contemporary indigenous movements in Latin America. Rowman & Littlefield Publishers, Lanham

Hobbes T (1588-1679) Leviathan. Oxford University Press, Oxford

Hohmann J, Weller M (2018) The UN Declaration on the Rights of Indigenous Peoples: a commentary. Oxford University Press, Oxford

Honneth A, Fraser N (2003) Redistribution or recognition? A political philosophical exchange. Verso, New York

Itçaina X (2017) Entre Incomplétude Institutionnelle et Mobilisation Sociale. Le Cas de la Langue Basque en France. Politique et Sociétés 36(3)

Jovanović M (2012) Collective rights: a legal theory. Cambridge University Press, Cambridge

Kant I (1797) The metaphysics of morals. Cambridge University Press, Cambridge

Karp DJ (2019) What is the responsibility to respect human rights? Reconsidering the 'respect, protect, and fulfill' framework. Int Theory 12(1)

Kasım C (2022) Building bridges between dismissal protection and non discrimination law: re-opening the debate on equality principles and social groups. In: Eichler J, Topidi K (eds) Minority recognition and the diversity deficit: comparative perspectives. Hart Publishing, Oxford

Kastoryano R (2018) Multiculturalism and interculturalism: redefining nationhood and solidarity. Comp Migr Stud 6(17)

Koch IE (2005) Dichotomies, trichotomies or waves of duties? Hum Rights Law Rev 81

Kochenov D (2015) The European Union's troublesome minority protection: a bird's-eye view. In: Boulden J, Kymlicka W (eds) International approaches to governing ethnic diversity. Oxford University Press, Oxford

Kochenov D (2018) When equality directives are not enough: taking issue with the missing minority rights policy in the EU. In: Belavusau U, Henrard K (eds) EU anti-discrimination law beyond gender. Hart Publishing, Oxford

Kochenov D (2019) Citizenship. MIT Press, Boston

Krizsan A, Skjeie H, Squires J (2012) European equality regimes: institutional change and political intersectionality. In: Krizsan A, Skjeie H, Squires J (eds) Institutionalising intersectionality: the changing nature of European regimes. Palgrave Macmillan, London

Kuhn TS (1962) The structure of scientific revolutions. University of Chicago Press, Chicago
Kymlicka W (1995) Multicultural citizenship: a liberal theory of minority rights. Oxford University Press, Oxford
Kymlicka W (2008) The internationalization of minority rights. Int J Constitutional Law 6(1)
Kymlicka W (2013) Multicultural odysseys: navigating the new international politics of diversity. Oxford University Press, Oxford
Kymlicka W, Donaldson S (2017) Inclusive citizenship beyond the capacity contract. In: Shachar A, Bauböck R, Bloemraad I, Vink M (eds) The Oxford handbook of citizenship. Oxford University Press, Oxford
Lavrysen L (2014) Positive obligations in the jurisprudence of the Inter American Court of Human Rights. Inter-American and European Human Rights Journal/Revista Interamericana y Europea de Derechos Humanos 7:1–2
Lavrysen L (2017) Human rights in a positive state: rethinking the relationship between positive and negative obligations under the European Convention on Human Rights. Intersentia, Antwerp
Lawrence R, Mörkenstam U (2016) Indigenous self-determination through a government agency? The impossible task of the Swedish Sámediggi. Int J Minority Group Rights 23
Lee C (2011) Jus soli and jus sanguinis in the colonies: the interwar politics of race, culture, and multiracial legal status in British Africa. Law Hist Rev 29
Letsas G (2015) Rescuing proportionality. In: Cruft R, Liao SM, Renzo M (eds) Philosophical foundations of human rights. Oxford University Press, Oxford
Liao SM (2015) Human rights as fundamental conditions for a good life. In: Cruft R, Liao SM, Renzo M (eds) Philosophical foundations of human rights. Oxford University Press, Oxford
Lindroth M, Sinevaara-Niskanen H (2022) The colonial politics of hope: critical junctures of indigenous-state relations. Routledge, Abingdon
Mac Amhlaigh C (2020) Does legal theory have a pluralism problem? In: Schiff Berman P (ed) The Oxford handbook of global legal pluralism. Oxford University Press, Oxford
Macklem P (2015) The sovereignty of human rights. Oxford University Press, Oxford
MacPherson E (2021) Paper presented at the Taller International: Armonía, con la Naturaleza en el Contexto del Marco Global de Biodiversidad Posterior al 2020. FILAC, Ministerio de Relaciones Exteriores de Bolivia, Ministerio de Medio Ambiente y Agua
Mamdani M (2012) Define and rule: native as political identity. Harvard University Press, Boston
Mba O (2009) Positive obligations under the African Charter on human and peoples' rights: the duty of the Nigerian Government to enact a freedom of Information Act. Commonwealth Law Bull 35(2)
Medda-Windischer R (2016) Housing rights and the inclusion of Roma and travellers: towards positive action measures from the rulings of the European Court of Human Rights? In: Cuypers D, Vrielink J (eds) Equal is not enough. Intersentia, Antwerp
Mendus S (2015) Care and human rights: a reply to Virginia held. In: Cruft R, Liao SM, Renzo M (eds) Philosophical foundations of human rights. Oxford University Press, Oxford
Merino R (2018) Reimagining the nation-state: indigenous peoples and the making of plurinationalism in Latin America. Leiden J Int Law 31(4)
Merry SE (2006) Anthropology and international law. Annu Rev Anthropol 35
Merry SE (2020) An anthropological perspective on legal pluralism. In: Schiff Berman P (ed) The Oxford handbook of global legal pluralism. Oxford University Press, Oxford
Milanovic B (2016) Global inequality. Belknap Press of Harvard University, Cambridge
Mita M (1989) Merata Mita On... New Zealand Listener
Mohanty A, Skutnabb-Kangas T (2013) MLE as an economic equaliser in India and Nepal: mother tongue based multilingual education fights poverty through capability development and identity support. In: Henrard K (ed) The interrelation between the right to identity of minorities and their socio-economic participation. Martinus Nijhoff Publishers, Leiden
Mouffe C (1992a) Democratic citizenship and the political community. In: Martin J (ed) Hegemony, radical democracy, and the political. Routledge, London

Mouffe C (1992b) Feminism, citizenship and radical democratic politics. In: Martin J (ed) Hegemony, radical democracy, and the political. Routledge, London
Mowbray AR (2004) The development of positive obligations under the European Convention on Human Rights by the European Court of Human Rights. Hart Publishing, Oxford
Muir E, de Witte B (2017) The procedural and institutional dimension of anti-discrimination law. In: Rossi LS, Casolari F (eds) The principles of equality in EU law. Springer International Publishing, Cham
Mukhayer H (forthcoming) Article 36. In: Eichler J, Doyle C, Howard S (eds) United Nations Declaration on the Rights of Indigenous Peoples: article-by-article commentary. Beck/Hart/Nomos, München/Baden-Baden/Oxford
Muldoon P (2012) 'The very basis of civility': on agonism, conquest, and reconciliation. In: Kymlicka W, Bashir B (eds) The politics of reconciliation in multicultural societies. Oxford University Press, Oxford
Newcomb S (2018) Domination in relation to indigenous ('dominated') peoples in international law. In: Watson I (ed) Indigenous peoples as subjects of international law. Routledge, Abingdon
Ng'weno B, Obura Aloo L (2019) Irony of citizenship: descent, national belonging, and constitutions in the postcolonial African State. Law Soc Rev 53(1)
Nursoo I (2018) Indigenous law, colonial injustice and the jurisprudence of hybridity. J Leg Pluralism Unofficial Law 50(1)
Page EA (2017) Intergenerational justice of what: welfare, resources or capabilities? Environ Polit 16(3)
Palermo F (2011) Territorial solutions for managing diversity and their changing role. In: European Commission for Democracy through Law (Venice Commission) (ed) The participation of minorities in public life. Council of Europe Publishing, Strasbourg
Phillipson R (2013) English as pandemic? In: Henrard K (ed) The interrelation between the right to identity of minorities and their socio-economic participation. Martinus Nijhoff Publishers, Leiden
Posner EA, Spier KE, Vermeule A (2010) Divide and conquer. J Leg Anal 2(2)
Postero N (2017) The indigenous state: race, politics, and performance in plurinational Bolivia. University of California Press, Oakland
Rajagopal B (2003) International law from below: development, social movements, and third world resistance. Cambridge University Press, Cambridge
Rawls J (1999a) A theory of justice: revised edition. Harvard University Press, Cambridge
Rawls J (1999b) The law of peoples. Harvard University Press, Boston
Raz J (2008) On the value of distributional equality. Legal research paper series N° 41
Ringelheim J (2008) Minority protection and constitutional recognition of difference: reflections on the diversity of European approaches. In: Verstichel A, Andre A, de Witte B, Lemmens P (eds) The Framework Convention for the Protection of National Minorities: a useful pan-European instrument? Intersentia, Cambridge
Rivera Cusicanqui S (2012) Violencias (re)encubiertas en Bolivia. Otramérica, Santander
Rodríguez-Garavito C (2011). Ethnicity.gov: global governance, indigenous peoples, and the right to prior consultation in social minefields. Indiana J Glob Leg Stud 18(1)
Rodríguez-Piñero Royo L (2010) Political participation systems applicable to indigenous peoples. In: Weller M, Nobbs K (eds) Political participation of minorities: a commentary on international standards and practice. Oxford University Press, Oxford
Rosanvallon P (1998) Le peuple introuvable. Histoire de la représentation démocratique en France. Gallimard, Paris
Sadiq K (2017) Postcolonial citizenship. In: Shachar A, Bauböck R, Bloemraad I, Vink M (eds) The Oxford handbook of citizenship. Oxford University Press, Oxford
Said E (1978) Orientalism. Vintage Books, New York
Samson C (2014) Dispossession and Canadian land claims: genocidal implications of the Innu nation land claim. In: Woolford A, Benvenuto J, Laban Hinton AL (eds) Colonial genocide in indigenous North America. Duke University Press, Durham

Samson C, Gigoux C (2017) Indigenous peoples and colonialism: global perspectives. Polity Press, Malden

Sauer B (2019) Das repräsentationalistische Paradox. Dekonstruktivistische und postkoloniale Kritik an den Verkürzungen der Repräsentationsdebatte und staatstheoretisch-feministische Erweiterungen. In: Voigt R (ed) Repräsentation: Eine Schlüsselkategorie der Demokratie. Nomos, Baden-Baden

Sawyer S (2004) Crude chronicles: indigenous politics, multinational oil, and neoliberalism in Ecuador. Duke University Press, Durham

Schiff Berman P (2020a) Developing and contesting a philosophical theory of global legal pluralism. In: Schiff Berman P (ed) The Oxford handbook of global legal pluralism. Oxford University Press, Oxford

Schiff Berman P (2020b) From local to global: introductory stories of global legal pluralism. In: Schiff Berman P (ed) The Oxford handbook of global legal pluralism. Oxford University Press, Oxford

Schiff Berman P (2020c) Global legal pluralism and indigenous communities. In: Schiff Berman P (ed) The Oxford handbook of global legal pluralism. Oxford University Press, Oxford

Schilling-Vacaflor A (2010) Recht als umkämpftes Terrain: Die neue Verfassung und indigene Völker in Bolivien. Nomos, Baden-Baden

Schilling-Vacaflor A, Eichler J (2017) The shady side of consultation and compensation: 'divide-and-rule' tactics in Bolivia's extraction sector. Dev Change 48(6)

Schilling-Vacaflor A, Kuppe R (2012) Plurinational constitutionalism: a new era of indigenous-state relations? In: Nolte D, Schilling-Vacaflor A (eds) New constitutionalism in Latin America: promises and practices. Ashgate Publishing, Farnham

Sen A (1984) Resources, values and development. Cambridge University Press, Cambridge

Sen A (1992) Inequality reexamined. Clarendon Press, Oxford

Shachar A (2001) Multicultural jurisdictions: cultural differences and women's rights. Cambridge University Press, Cambridge

Shachar A (2009) The birthright lottery: citizenship and global inequality. Harvard University Press, Cambridge

Smith LT (2012) Decolonizing methodologies. Zed Books, London

Solón P (2017) Alternativas Sistémicas: Vivir Bien, Decrecimiento, Comunes, Ecofeminismo, Derechos de la Madre Tierra y Desglobalización. Fundación Solón, Focus on the Global South and Attac France, La Paz

Spiro PJ (2020) Membership and global legal pluralism. In: Schiff Berman P (ed) The Oxford handbook of global legal pluralism. Oxford University Press, Oxford

Stavenhagen R (2002) Indigenous peoples and the state in Latin America: an ongoing debate. In: Sieder R (ed) Multiculturalism in Latin America: indigenous rights, diversity and democracy. Palgrave Macmillan, London

Stiglitz J (2016) Inequality and economic growth. In: Mazzucato M, Jacobs M (eds) Rethinking capitalism. Wiley-Blackwell in association with The Political Quarterly, Hoboken

Stojanović N (2013) Dialogue sur les quotas: Penser la représentation dans une démocratie multiculturelle. Presses de Sciences Po, Paris

Szablowski D (2010) Operationalizing free, prior, and informed consent in the extractive industry sector? Examining the challenges of a negotiated model of justice. Canadian Journal of Development Studies/Revue Canadienne d'études du développement 30:1–2

Taylor C (1992) Multiculturalism and the 'politics of recognition'. Princeton University Press, Princeton

Taylor C (1994) Multiculturalism. Princeton University Press, Princeton

Te Aho F (forthcoming) Article 37. In: Eichler J, Doyle C, Howard S (eds) United Nations Declaration on the Rights of Indigenous Peoples: article-by-article commentary. Beck/Hart/Nomos, München/Baden-Baden/Oxford

Thornberry P (2000) Self-determination and indigenous peoples: objections and responses. In: Aikio P, Scheinin M (eds) Operationalizing the right of indigenous peoples to self-determination. Institute for Human Rights, Åbo Akademi University, Turku
Tomuschat C (2014) Human rights: between idealism and realism. Oxford University Press, Oxford
Toniatti R (1996) Minorities and protected minorities: constitutional models compared. In: Bonazzi T, Dunne M (eds) Citizenship and rights in multicultural societies. Keele University Press, Keele
Tully J (2008) Public philosophy in a new key. Vol I: Democracy and civic freedom. Cambridge University Press, Cambridge
Uprimny R (2002) Constitución de 1991, Estado Social y Derechos Humanos: Promesas Incumplidas, Diagnósticos y Perspectivas. In: Moncayo VM et al (eds) El Debate a la Constitución. Universidad Nacional de Colombia, Bogotá
Uprimny R (2011) The recent transformations of constitutional law in Latin America: trends and challenges. Tex Law Rev 89
Van Cott DL (2005) From movements to parties in Latin America: the evolution of ethnic politics. Cambridge University Press, New York
van der Burg W (2020) Conceptual theories of law and the challenges of global legal pluralism: a legal interactionist approach. In: Schiff Berman P (ed) The Oxford handbook of global legal pluralism. Oxford University Press, Oxford
Vasak K (1977) A 30 year struggle: the sustained effort to give the force of law to the Universal Declaration of Human Rights. The UNESCO Courir 3
Velaers J (2016) Constitutional versus international protection of human rights: added value or redundancy? The Belgian Case, in the light of the advisory practice of the Venice Commission. Revue Interdisciplinaire d'Études Juridiques 2(77)
Verstichel A (2011) Special measures to promote minority representation in elected bodies: the experience of the OSCE High Commissioner on national minorities. In: European Commission for Democracy through Law (Venice Commission) (ed) The participation of minorities in public life. Council of Europe Publishing, Strasbourg
Vilain Y (2015) § 3 Verfassungsprinzipien. In: Marsch N, Vilain Y, Wendel M (eds) Französisches und Deutsches Verfassungsrecht: Ein Rechtsvergleich. Springer, Cham
Vizi B (2022) Participation in public life – the political background and central role of minority self-governments in Hungary. In: Eichler J, Topidi K (eds) Minority recognition and the diversity deficit: comparative perspectives. Hart Publishing, Oxford
Voigt R (2019) Dialektik der Repräsentation. Das Unsichtbare sichtbar machen. In: Voigt R (ed) Repräsentation: Eine Schlüsselkategorie der Demokratie. Nomos, Baden-Baden
Volou A (2022) When national laws and human rights standards are at odds. Verfassungsblog. https://verfassungsblog.de/at-odds/
Volpp L (2017) Feminist, sexual, and queer citizenship. In: Shachar A, Bauböck R, Bloemraad I, Vink M (eds) The Oxford handbook of citizenship. Oxford University Press, Oxford
von Benda-Beckmann K, Turner B (2020) Anthropological roots of global legal pluralism. In: Schiff Berman P (ed) The Oxford handbook of global legal pluralism. Oxford University Press, Oxford
von Bogdandy A (2012) Founding principles. In: von Bogdandy A, Bast J (eds) Principles of European constitutional law. Hart/CH Beck/Nomos, Oxford/München/Baden-Baden
von Bogdandy A, Ferrer Mac-Gregor E, Morales Antoniazzi M, Piovesan F, Soley X (2017a) Ius Constitutionale Commune en América Latina: a regional approach to transformative constitutionalism. In: von Bogdandy A, Ferrer MacGregor E, Morales Antoniazzi M, Piovesan F (eds) Transformative constitutionalism in Latin America: the emergence of a new Ius Commune. Oxford University Press, Oxford
von Bogdandy A, Ferrer MacGregor E, Morales Antoniazzi M, Piovesan F (2017b) Transformative constitutionalism in Latin America: the emergence of a new Ius Commune. Oxford University Press, Oxford

von Busekist A (2018) Conclusion: territorial pluralism and language communities. In: Arato A, Cohen JL, von Busekist A (eds) Forms of pluralism and democratic constitutionalism. Columbia University Press, New York

Watson I (2018a) Indigenous peoples as subjects of international law. Routledge, Abingdon

Watson I (2018b) Introduction. In: Watson I (ed) Indigenous peoples as subjects of international law. Routledge, Abingdon

Weller M, Nobbs K (2010) Political participation of minorities: a commentary on international standards and practice. Oxford University Press, Oxford

Winter CJ (2022) Subjects of intergenerational justice: indigenous philosophy, the environment and relationships. Routledge, Abingdon

Wright C, Tomaselli A (2019) The prior consultation of indigenous peoples in Latin America: inside the implementation gap. Routledge, Abingdon

Xenos D (2011) The positive obligations of the State under the European Convention of Human Rights. Routledge, Abingdon

Yashar DJ (2012) Contesting citizenship in Latin America: the rise of indigenous movements and the postliberal challenge. Cambridge University Press, Cambridge

Young RJC (2020) Postcolonialism: a very short introduction. Oxford University Press, Oxford

Yrigoyen Fajardo R (2016) The panorama of pluralist constitutionalism: from multiculturalism to decolonisation. In: Rodríguez-Garavito C (ed) Law and society in Latin America: a new map. Routledge, Abingdon

Yrigoyen Fajardo R (2021) Hacia la Descolonización del Derecho y la Justicia desde el Pluralismo Jurídico Igualitario y los Derechos de los Pueblos Indígenas. Conferencias introductorias para el evento intercontinental sobre Colonialismo, Descolonización y Neocolonialismo desde la Justicia y el Bien Común. Comité Panamericano de Juezas y Jueces por los Derechos Sociales y la Doctrina Franciscana y Pontificia Academia de las Ciencias Sociales

Zavala Cepeda JM (2015) Los Parlamentos Hispano-Mapuches, 1593-1803: Textos Fundamentales. Ediciones Universidad Católica de Temuco, Temuco

# Chapter 3
# Equality Principles and Institutionalism: Judicial Spill-Overs and Dialogues

## 3.1 A Regional Example of Equality Institutionalism: The EU and Its Anti-Discrimination Framework

EU law follows what could be termed a classical approach to equality law, conceptually, by thinking of equality and anti-discrimination law as inter-related when dealing with the individual dimension (rather that inter-State relations);[1] in other words, the Court has been considering the two as constituting one single principle, ruling out any different treatment of similar situations and the same treatment for different situations if not objectively justified.[2] The principle of equality in particular has been enjoying long-lasting recognition as a '*general principle of law*' in domestic constitutional law, but also as a '*basic principle of Community law*'[3]. In practice, there has been a growing academic consensus on the importance of the 2000 Equality Directives, described as "*marking the birth of EU anti-discrimination law as a field of its own right*"[4] while early steps were taken as early as 1964 in the *Mangold* judgement dealing with age-related grounds, indicative also being Directive 79/7 on Gender Equality in Social Security endorsed in 1979. Indeed, the Racial Equality and Employment Directives adopted in 2000 brought fresh air into EU anti-discrimination law and also minority rights,[5] protecting race and ethnicity, as well as religion, sexual orientation, age and disability respectively.

With the adoption of the Charter of Fundamental Rights of the European Union and its integration into the quasi-constitutional Lisbon Treaty in 2007, more grounds

---

[1] Rossi and Casolari (2017).

[2] Ibid. See also *Europe Chemi-Con GmbH vs. Council and Commission*, Court of Justice of the European Union in 2005.

[3] Bureau of the Convention (2010) *Explanations Relating to the Charter of Fundamental Rights of the European Union*. Chapter III Equality. Article 20 Equality before the law.

[4] Belavusau and Henrard (2019), p. 615.

[5] See, for instance, Busstra (2010).



J. Eichler, *An Interdisciplinary Journey from Non-Discrimination to Collective Rights*, https://doi.org/10.1007/978-3-031-54618-1_3

would find formal recognition: an entire chapter would be devoted to 'equality' (Title III), protecting not only gender (art. 23), the elderly (art. 25), and persons with disabilities (art. 26), but also the rights of the child (art. 24), and cultural, religious and linguistic diversity (art. 22) as distinct grounds. Importantly, it would spell out multiple grounds of discrimination, hitherto enjoying recognition under EU primary law, by stating

> any discrimination based on any ground such as sex, race, colour, ethnic or social origin, genetic features, language, religion or belief, political or any other opinion, membership of a national minority, property, birth, disability, age or sexual orientation (art. 21)

The same provision would also rule out discrimination on grounds of nationality in its art. 21(2). In practice, the two different sets of grounds may very well intersect; language-related discrimination was found as a derivative ground of 'nationality'.[6] To be sure, said (non-exhaustive) grounds are to be respected in relation to discriminatory practice engaged in by EU bodies and institutions as well as such discriminatory State practice falling under the implementation of Union law, in that sense adding to the Treaty on the Functioning of the European Union, protecting discrimination on (the exhaustive) grounds of "*sex, racial or ethnic origin, religion or belief, disability, age or sexual orientation*" (art. 19).[7]

Nevertheless and despite all efforts involved, EU non-discrimination law can hardly be perceived as a single response to the multiplicity of grounds concerned: in that sense, the safeguarding system has been described as '*a chorus with several different voices*'[8], alluding to the fragmented nature of EU discrimination law. Such multiplicities of grounds come with yet another related challenge, that of underlying inequality structures, as well as complex questions of identities and respective social relations.[9] Another related complexity may lay with the grounds the law actually addresses: while wide in scope, gender discrimination has become a prominent "*ground of status discrimination in EU law [accompanied by] extensive policy development*"[10] which has led to the frequent invoking of the present non-discrimination provision to gender equality cases in addition to art. 23 on equality between women and men.[11]

As EU non-discrimination law has become gradually embedded in the legal order, we can also speak of institutional developments, by way of implementing EU substantive rules, both procedurally and institutionally-speaking.[12] The role of the victims and her/his/x possibilities in accessing justice have been considered of

---

[6] Kilpatrick (2014). *Italy vs. Commission, Advocate-General Kokott's Opinion*, Court of Justice of the European Union in 2012.

[7] Bureau of the Convention (2010) *Explanations Relating to the Charter of Fundamental Rights*. Title III. Article 21 Non-Discrimination.

[8] Zaccaroni (2017).

[9] Xinidis (2019) and Baer (2017).

[10] Kilpatrick (2014), p. 582.

[11] *Test-Achats vs. Conseil des ministres*, Court of Justice of the European Union in 2011.

[12] Muir and de Witte (2017).

particular value in that regard.[13] Indeed, we could think of it as a '*procedural turn in EU Anti-Discrimination Law*',[14] materialising with the adoption of the Equality Directives in 2000, but also relying on previous directives on the prohibition of sex discrimination in employment,[15] self-employment[16] and social security[17], as well as a burden of proof directive[18]. Essentially, this would give rise to more advanced procedural rules which carry the following implications, namely judicial and/or administrative procedures for the enforcement of obligations available to all persons considering themselves wronged (in terms of equal treatment); a partial shift of the burden of proof relating to sex equality contexts; protection against victimisation in the form of retaliation impacting on the person filing a complaint; and regulating sanctions, penalties, compensation and reparation for the victims.[19]

Institutional transformations similarly mirror this rethinking of non-discrimination materialising in the law, which has been termed a gradual "*cross-national trend to amalgamate equality institutions*"[20], showing how pluralisation has been taken up at domestic levels, culminating in State policies in different European jurisdictions on a multiplicity of inequality grounds.[21] Indeed, we may think of such tendencies as a move towards an '*integrated approach to multiple inequalities*'[22], most likely to the advantage of multiple, intersecting inequalities,[23] doing justice to their social complexity and inherent disadvantages[24]. Indeed, it has been argued elsewhere that such "*integration of equality laws, bodies and policies*" allowed for a more effective dealing with multiple and intersecting forms of discrimination.[25]

Another novelty accompanying these developments concerns institutional transformation itself, in the sense that equality bodies would become more independent, disassociating them from governments, their dedicated priorities or other forms of politization.[26] Institutional approaches have been assuming a variety of forms and

---

[13] Ibid.

[14] Ibid., p. 135.

[15] Directive 75/117 on the approximation of the laws of the Member States relating to the application of the principle of equal pay for men and women. See also Directive 76/207.

[16] Directive 86/613 on the application of the principle of equal treatment between men and women engaged in an activity, including agriculture, in a self-employed capacity, and on the protection of self-employed women during pregnancy and motherhood.

[17] Directive 79/7 on the progressive implementation of the principle of equal treatment for men and women in matters of social security. See also Directive 86/378.

[18] Directive 97/80 on the burden of proof in cases of discrimination based on sex.

[19] Muir and de Witte (2017).

[20] Ibid., p. 142.

[21] Krizsan et al. (2014).

[22] Krizsan et al. (2012), p. 1.

[23] Eichler (2022).

[24] Xinidis (2019) and Fredman (2005).

[25] Kantola and Nousiainen (2009), p. 460.

[26] Choudhury (2006).

formats, such as through extending the mandate (Austria, Estonia, Liechtenstein, Lithuania, Malta, Norway, Slovenia, Sweden) or abolishing a previous gender-based anti-discrimination body to be replaced by a new integrated mechanism (Denmark, France, Ireland, the Netherlands, United Kingdom) or for entirely new institutions to be created in the context of EU accession (Bulgaria, Czech Republic, Hungary, Latvia, Romania, Slovakia) and beyond (Germany).[27] Consequently, stakeholders have argued, such institutional amalgamation may have led to a reprioritisation of gender as a distinct ground of protection, failing to, for instance, increase numbers of experts working in these institutions or the overall budget.[28] External factors such as the 2008 financial crisis have been impacting on the institutions' budgets and institutional frameworks, also to the detriment of their very way of operating.[29] As a response to the continuing challenges many Equality Bodies have been facing, a Commission Recommendation on Standards for Equality Bodies was adopted in 2018. One of the recurring arguments raised among scholarship in the field concerns the appropriateness of design and resources—as, it is argued, Equality Bodies "can be *crucial institutions to effectively 'respond' to discrimination*"[30] under the former conditions.

Interestingly, these forms of institutionalisation could also be read as a way to adopt an integrated approach, as a response to legal sources (the 2000 Directives) that use different standards for each ground of discrimination.[31] In that sense, it is hoped to harmonise differing treatment of protected grounds, preventing low standards to become established in relation to specific grounds. Finding institutional answers may also lay in the opportunities laying in ways of operating beyond the sheer enforcement of legislation with soft power gaining in prominence, enabling equality bodies to make recommendations, conveying good practice through different channels such as the very duty bearers and research.[32] Again, resource-related concerns may arise leading to a prioritisation of institutional duties with enforcement overriding soft law activities.[33]

More contextual insights may be needed to get a sense of the overall institutional context surrounding Equality Bodies in the European Union (also see last sub-chapter). Especially the initial economically grounded rationale of the European integration process deserves mentioning, impacting on the very first anti-discrimination developments.[34] But also current contexts may be indicative of the approach embraced initially, emblematic being the CJEU's approach on the matter which remains far from genuinely "*combating (of) societal oppression and*

[27] Ammer et al. (2010).

[28] Ibid.

[29] Benedi Lahuerta (2021).

[30] Ibid., p. 391.

[31] Ammer et al. (2010) and Holzleithner (2005).

[32] Kádár (2018).

[33] Ibid.

[34] Kantola and Nousiainen (2009).

*marginalisation*"[35], focussing on the market-driven mobility of goods, services and people instead. It is maintained that processes of Europeanization have been relegated to soft law indeed, and explicitly favour integrated Equality Bodies to address multiple discrimination as an efficient solution.[36] Some thought has been devoted to the distinct situation(s), old and new EU Member States have been facing; Eastern European States have been demonstrating a particular eagerness to effectively collaborate with the civil society sector.[37] Another particularity, as has been reported, lies in the level of cooperation between the different equality strands (or grounds) or agencies working on equalities.[38] At EU level, by contrast, critical voices have pointed to institutional failures in addressing inequalities by means of an intersectional approach, instead these were juxtaposed, not attributing equal weight to the different grounds.[39] Similarly, the EU's neglective attitude towards structural approaches to inequality has been viewed critically in that regard.[40] Also intra-/inter-institutionally, the dealing with multiple discrimination has been viewed sceptically, as not all inequalities were considered which were supposedly addressed by other specialised mechanisms such as the European Institute for Gender Equality which, in turn, requires procedures to coordinate among the EU's equality mechanisms to ensure intersecting grounds are paid due consideration in the policy process.[41] According to very critical voices, anti-discrimination at EU level has been viewed as a symbolic tool for a Union in search of legitimacy.[42] At the ending, we shall not forget about the nature of anti-discrimination law itself, based—first and foremost—on EU directives that are subject to the discretionary (interpretative) powers of the Member States, hence allowing for a wide room for manoeuvre in the domestic realm of non-discrimination law.

## 3.2 International Law, Legal Hierarchies and Judicial Dialogue

Ever since the *Kadi* and *Al Barakaat* decisions before the European Court of Justice,[43] questions of legal hierarchies touching upon fundamental rights questions can no longer escape scholarly attention. The cases at hand may certainly raise interesting debates on the legitimacy and validity of exceptions to human rights,

---

[35] Ibid., p. 463.

[36] Ibid. Squires (2009).

[37] Koldinská (2009).

[38] Ibid.

[39] Lombardo and Verloo (2009).

[40] Ibid.

[41] Lombardo and Verloo (2009).

[42] Kantola and Nousiainen (2009).

[43] See e.g. de Búrca (2012). See also more generally De Witte (2012).

namely limits on individual freedoms in the context of anti-terrorist measures and the security discourse.[44] What shows more important for the purpose of the present analysis concerns its implications for the authority of interpretative powers and their interrelation, in other words, possible conflicts of competence amongst (quasi)-judicial institutions or the simple manifestation of legal hierarchies. Critical voices may refer to a form of appropriation of human rights by international mechanisms such as the UN Security Council; at the ending, the ECtHR takes the liberty to exercise its judicial review functions by testing a community act implementing a Security Council resolution against its commensurability with human rights.[45] Again, we may be inclined to compare mandates and their human rights competence, we shall also, however, be reminded of the importance attributable to political development and regional integration,[46] turning the ECtHR and its supranational institutionality into a considerable institutional promoter of fundamental rights.

A different scenario presents itself with the Charter of Fundamental Rights of the European Union which seems to reverse the positioning of the ECtHR according to which it would refrain from reviewing EU legislation on grounds of the equivalent protection of human rights that is granted.[47] With the Charter having gained the same legal value as the Treaties, the EU human rights system has become more independent and more Charter-based, hence independent from the ECHR. In that sense, the effectiveness of fundamental rights does no longer depend on the so-called '*general principles*' approach that had hitherto been defended, but acquired its own order with the Charter, considered as the "*result of a pan-European political consensus that sought to make fundamental rights more visible to the citizens of the Union*"[48]. Such positioning—in relation to the value of the ECHR first and foremost—has gradually become common place,[49] especially after the adoption of Advisory Opinion 2/13[50] on the accession of the EU to the ECHR which was

[44] *Yassin Abdullah Kadi and Al Barakaat International Foundation vs. Council of the European Union*, Court of Justice of the European Union in 2008.

[45] See also Eichler (2022).

[46] Bantekas and Oette (2020).

[47] *Bosphorus Hava Yollari Turizm ve Ticaret AS vs. Ireland*, European Court of Human Rights in 2005.

[48] Lenaerts and Gutiérrez-Fons (2014), p. 1560.

[49] Krommendijk (2018).

[50] The Court ruled that the agreement on the accession of the EU to the ECHR was incompatible with art.6(2) TEU or Protocol n°8 relating to art.6(2) of the TEU on the accession of the Union to the ECHR on the following grounds: "*it is liable adversely to affect the specific characteristics and the autonomy of EU law in so far as it does not ensure coordination between Article 53 of the ECHR and Article 53 of the Charter, does not avert the risk that the principle of Member States' mutual trust under EU law may be undermined, and makes no provision in respect of the relationship between the mechanism established by Protocol No 16 and the preliminary ruling procedure provided for in Article 267 TFEU; it is liable to affect Article 344 TFEU in so far as it does not preclude the possibility of disputes between Member States or between Member States and the EU concerning the application of the ECHR within the scope ratione materiae of EU law being brought before the ECtHR; it does not lay down arrangements for the operation of the co-respondent*

considered incompatible by the CJEU. Especially institutionally-speaking, however—and as far as the European Ius Commune is concerned—it becomes clear that ECHR and EU do not operate in isolation, instead they engage in a cross-fertilising process.[51] Since the adoption of Advisory Opinion 2/13 the CJEU would adopt a reconciliatory position by developing an approach on the matter (reconciling the principle of mutual trust with fundamental rights) that showed fully in line with the ECtHR reasoning.[52] Similar conclusions may be reached on the three different systems operating side-by-side—the ECtHR, the CJEU and domestic constitutional courts—which have been described as a '*common constitutional space*'[53] in which these three instances maintain a constructive dialogue.[54]

Similar terminology has been used across legal frameworks in the field of human rights more specifically which have become formalised under the umbrella of a '*human rights jus commune*'[55] developed by means of cross-jurisdictional dialogue. Three scenarios may best capture cross-jurisdictional dialogue in relation to human rights, namely by means of a "*comparative law analysis as a means of identifying an emerging consensus*", often shared by Member State courts; it may also refer to "*domestic courts referring to the interpretation of a specialised monitoring body established under a human rights instrument for the application of that instrument*", hence seeking an advisory opinion or preliminary ruling on a matter; and "*international courts referring to the interpretation of the specialised monitoring body established under a human rights instrument for the application of that instrument itself*", again referring to dedicate competence on a given matter.[56]

Taken to a broader level, these processes of human rights interpretation shared among domestic and international human rights institutions have been subsumed under the umbrella term '*judicial dialogue*'[57]. Indeed, rather than presenting itself as an atmosphere of mere dual or co-existence, or, as reflecting a "*static juxtaposition of human rights regimes and of their conflicting authority claims*"[58], it could be argued, these become part of a dynamic and mutual process of positivization and legitimation. Nevertheless, a few notes need to be made as to the persisting, almost natural,

---

*mechanism and the procedure for the prior involvement of the Court of Justice that enable the specific characteristics of the EU and EU law to be preserved; and it fails to have regard to the specific characteristics of EU law with regard to the judicial review of acts, actions or omissions on the part of the EU in CFSP matters in that it entrusts the judicial review of some of those acts, actions or omissions exclusively to a non-EU body*" (para. 258).

[51] Lenaerts and Gutiérrez-Fons (2014).

[52] Krommendijk (2018). *Pál Aranyosi and Robert Căldăraru v Generalstaatsanwaltschaft Bremen*, Court of Justice of the European Union in 2016. *C. K. and Others v Republika Slovenija*, Court of Justice of the European Union in 2017.

[53] Groussot (2006).

[54] Lenaerts and Gutiérrez-Fons (2014).

[55] De Schutter (2018), p. 7.

[56] Ibid., pp. 10–16.

[57] Krisch (2010).

[58] Besson (2015), p. 280.

hierarchies in relation to interpretative powers—commonly known as subsidiary powers or *marge d'appréciation* exercised by domestic courts principally. This may refer to a given Court culture, it may however also reflect a consensus reached among several judicial systems, a '*joint interpretative endeavour*'[59] leading to a transnational interpretation which may eventually find consolidation in international human rights law. On a final note and as a general rule of thumb, we may want to recall that interpretations need to meet minimum standards irrespective of the judicial entity ruling on the matter; these standards ('saving clauses') couldn't possibly become less protective, in that sense, following a levelling-up rather than a levelling-down approach[60]—this applies to domestic and international instances alike.

### 3.2.1 Interactions, Legal Hierarchies and Their Impacts on (the) Equality Principle(s)

The equality principle may hardly be understood in isolation, that is, decontextualised, alienated from the constitutional or other foundational framework giving rise to such principle to start with. Accordingly, it has been argued that its realisation would depend on the conception of the State; such conception would, in turn, manifest a given legal or State philosophy.[61] As a consequence, the specific form of equality ultimately embraced is qualified by the legal or political philosophy shaping a particular State framework.[62] A certain controversy arises from this, given the variety in substance the equality principle potentially accommodates, as well as it would result from conflicts of ideological or cosmovisionist nature.[63] Indeed, considerable importance is attributed to the political ideology—commonly democratic—chosen at the time constitutions are first adopted, ranging from minimalistic approaches on equality, including formal equality, to positive discriminatory visions on equality, including the adoption of measures.

Some thought shall be spent on the positionality of individuals in the political community, giving rise to equality as a form of regulating principle, both vertically and horizontally. As famously stated by Arendt "*...we are not born equal; we become equal as members of a group on the strength of our decision to guarantee ourselves mutually equal rights*"[64]—or put differently, "*through mutual human rights, individuals become actors of their own equality and members of their*

[59] Ibid., p. 292.

[60] Ibid.

[61] Alexy (2018) and Scholler (1969).

[62] Alexy (2018) and Dreier (1976).

[63] Alexy (2018).

[64] Arendt (1951), pp. 147–182.

*political community*"[65]. These words convey a transformative vision, allowing individuals to gain equal rights in community with others—undoubtedly representing a considerable achievement in its own terms—while reflecting the idea of some form of social contract in essence, that is, a reciprocal relationship of duties and rights, freedoms and obligations of non-interference. In a next step, being of importance here, the position of members in a political community is to be further disentangled and, as a consequence, rights to be differentiated, notably between those applicable to all, and those being specific to specific groups of people. In a way, it may be claimed that the very universality,[66] the generality,[67] and general applicability of (unspecific) human rights under the umbrella of the often cited notion '*belong to all human beings by virtue of their humanity*' shall not be restricted to a specific genre or category of rights, but should, instead, also become invokable by specific groups. Very commonly, the articulation of cultural, ethnic, religious or linguistic minority rights depends on the specific legal framework which predetermines what extent and what shape these rights may take, far from any approximation to a universal or general applicability. In that sense, these specific rights do not only merit importance as to the particular vulnerability minorities face compared to groups confronting such situation, horizontally speaking, but they equally deserve a detailed examination as to the rights-duties relationship, in other words, the State-individual nexus, vertically speaking.

As suggested here, vertical relations may vary with minority rights enjoying recognition to different degrees which has led to differing positions among States, their judicial institutions and international mechanisms pronouncing themselves on equality principles. At the most general level, equality enjoys wide recognition without any immediate diverging interpretation discernible; it is considered a foundational value in accordance with EU primary law (art. 2, TEU). Similar arguments may be made for the sphere of international law: both treaty law (UN Charter, arts. 55 & 56; Universal Declaration on Human Rights, arts. 2 & 7; ICCPR; ICESCR) and State practice prove indicative of the recognition of equality globally;[68] racial discrimination has been declared customary international law.[69]

Our attention shall, however, rest on a more nuanced understanding of the equality principle as it is has been interpreted differently across different international and regional frameworks. A common point of departure certainly lies with its conception as a general principle of law.[70] Equality has been declared a general

---

[65] Besson (2015), p. 283.

[66] Donnelly (2003).

[67] Jovanović (2022).

[68] Shaw (2008).

[69] *Ethiopia vs. South Africa*, International Court of Justice in 1966; *Liberia vs. South Africa*, International Court of Justice in 1966 ('*South West Africa cases*') Dissenting Opinion of Judge Tanaka.

[70] General principles of (international) law were first defined by the Rome Statute, more specifically its art. 38(1)(c) stipulating "*The Court, whose function is to decide in accordance with international*

principle of EU law,[71] it enjoys general applicability in the EU legal framework, and manifests itself, specifically, in the anti-discrimination directives.[72] It thereby resembles an interpretation issued by the UN Human Rights Committee in its General Comment N° 18 on Non-Discrimination, which maintains "*non-discrimination, together with equality before the law and equal protection of the law without any discrimination constitute a basic and general principle relating to the protection of human rights*".[73] Importantly, the same Committee permits derogations[74] from obligations established by the same instrument such as in the case of public emergency; however, respective measures are not to involve discrimination while it also explicitly rules out advocacy of "*national, racial or religious hatred*" constituting incitement to discrimination.[75] Somewhat relatedly, the Committee refers to its art. 26 that provides safeguards complementing those of art. 2, highlighting that the former does not specify any limitations, and in that sense, it not only "*prohibits discrimination in law or in fact in any field regulated and protected by public authorities*", but also clarifies non-discrimination "*is not limited to those rights which are provided for in the Covenant*".[76] As early as 1935, the Permanent Court of International Justice (PCIJ) pronounced itself on the de jure and de facto quality of the equality principle to be protected by stating that "*equality in law precludes discrimination of any kind; whereas equality in fact may involve the necessity of different treatment in order to attain a result which establishes an equilibrium between different situations*"[77].

The Human Rights Committee further defines the equality principle by stipulating that the "*enjoyment of rights and freedoms on an equal footing, however, does not mean identical treatment in every instance*"[78]; it further specifies this, by stating that "*not every differentiation of treatment will constitute discrimination, if the criteria for such differentiation are reasonable and objective and if the aim is to achieve a purpose which is legitimate under the Covenant*"[79]. Relatedly, the Committee unequivocally establishes that the "*principle of equality sometimes requires States parties to take affirmative action in order to diminish or eliminate conditions which cause or help to perpetuate discrimination prohibited by the Covenant (...) As long as such action is needed to correct discrimination in fact, it is a case of legitimate*

*law such disputes as are submitted to it, shall apply (...) the general principles of law recognised by civilised nations.*"

[71] Wouters and Ovádek (2021).

[72] Benoît-Rohmer (2017).

[73] UN Human Rights Committee (1989) *General Comment N° 18 on Non-Discrimination*; para. 1.

[74] See e.g. Cassese (2012).

[75] UN Human Rights Committee (1989) *General Comment N° 18 on Non-Discrimination*; para. 2.

[76] Ibid., para. 12.

[77] *Advisory Opinion 'Minority Schools in Albania'*; Permanent Court of International Justice in 1935; p. 19. Shaw (2008).

[78] UN Human Rights Committee (1989) *General Comment N° 18 on Non-Discrimination*; para. 8.

[79] Ibid., para. 13.

*differentiation under the Covenant*"[80]. International law and European law establish similar thresholds in that regard with the ICJ considering differentiation acceptable as long as such treatment is just or reasonable[81] and the ECtHR[82] and IACtHR[83] holding that differentiation would need to be reasonably and objectively justified. In other words, comparable situations are not to be treated differently, and different situations not to be treated similarly unless objectively justified.[84] Restrictions may however be manifold including States exercising their discretionary powers as to those grounds prohibited under ICCPR, or as to the inapplicability of the treaty in relation to private discrimination or any direct third party effect.[85]

### 3.2.2 *Equality and Its Manifestations in Judicial Dialogue Across Judicial Systems*

A few common approaches may be explored here as far as the principle of equality is being interpreted by different judicial instances across international law, regional ius commune or constitutional levels. Given the generality of equality provisions, interpretative authorities have demonstrably examined the principle in-depth, including its conceptual roots and implications.

---

[80] Ibid., para. 10.

[81] *Liberia vs. South Africa*, International Court of Justice in 1966 ('*South West Africa cases*') Dissenting Opinion of Judge Tanaka. Shaw (2008).

[82] '*In the case "relating to certain aspects of the laws on the use of languages in education in Belgium" vs. Belgium*; European Court of Human Rights in 1968 (*'Belgian Linguistics' case*). The Court notably stated "*following the principles extracted from the legal practice of a large number of States (. . .) a difference in treatment is only discriminatory when it has no objective and reasonable justification*" (p. 34). Shaw (2008).

[83] *Advisory Opinion 'Proposed Amendments to the Naturalization Provisions of the Constitution of Costa Rica'*; Inter-American Court of Human Rights in 1984. The Court unequivocally held that "*Precisely because equality and non-discrimination are inherent in the idea of the oneness in dignity and worth of all human beings, it follows that not all differences in legal treatment are discriminatory as such, for not all differences in treatment are in themselves offensive to human dignity. (. . .) There may well exist certain factual inequalities that might legitimately give rise to inequalities in legal treatment that not violate principles of justice. They may in face be instrumental in achieving justice or in protecting those who find themselves in a weak legal position. (. . .) Accordingly, no discrimination exists if the difference in treatment has a legitimate purpose and if it does not lead to situations which are contrary to justice, to reason or to the nature of things. It follows that there would be no discrimination in differences in treatment of individuals by a State when the classifications selected are based on substantial factual differences and there exists a reasonable relationship of proportionality between these differences and the aims of the legal rule under review*" (paras. 56–57). Shaw (2008).

[84] Benoît-Rohmer (2017) and Brillat (2015). *Akzo Nobel Chemicals Ltd and Akcros Chemicals Ltd vs. European Commission*; Court of Justice of the European Union in 2010.

[85] Tomuschat (2019). For a debate on the principles of equality and non-discrimination as stipulated in ICCPR, see the following work: Ramcharan (2015).

A curious starting point lies with the criterion of 'intent' concerning the reason underlying discriminatory treatment which is, by and large, ruled out in International Human Rights Law.[86] Emblematic may be relevant hard law developments, including ICERD and CEDAW treaty texts according to which discrimination is understood as carrying the purpose or effect of limiting the exercise of human rights and freedoms (ICERD, art. 1(1); CEDAW, art. 1).[87] Jurisprudential developments similarly reflect such understanding across the international treaty monitoring system, illustrative being the Human Rights Committee's conception of discrimination which unequivocally disapproves '*discriminatory intention'*, for it not to constitute a "*necessary element of discrimination*"[88]. In the aforediscussed General Comment on Non-Discrimination, the Committee explicitly refers to the purpose or effect of not recognising any rights and freedoms to be enjoyed on an equal footing by all persons.[89] On the shadowy side, the Committee seems to have adopted a conservative stand on some occasions as relating to the effect or result, that is, assuming a clear positioning on substantive equality. It notably held that "*differences in result of the uniform application of laws do not per se constitute prohibited discrimination*"[90]. Following the line established by CEDAW and ICERD, the ECtHR maintains that art. 14 on the prohibition of non-discrimination is to include the effects of detrimental measures.[91]

Another illustrative point shall be made about one of the most contentious human rights questions, that of positive action to be taken by States, striving to transform societal structures and restructuring institutions.[92] We shall address the specific thresholds established in that context. The IACtHR clearly defended a position that would oblige the State to "*take affirmative action to reverse or change discriminatory situations that exist in their societies to the detriment of a specific group of persons*"[93]. Likewise, the ECtHR maintained that failing to mediate inequalities with the help of different treatment would be considered a violation of the right to be protected against non-discrimination.[94] A similar rationale is mirrored in the ICERD framework which regards preferences that take the form of special measures as not constituting discrimination,[95] which albeit takes a more modest approach on the

[86] Moeckli (2015).

[87] Ibid.

[88] Ibid., p. 62. *Simunek et al. vs. The Czech Republic*; UN Human Rights Committee in 1995. *Adam vs. The Czech Republic*; UN Human Rights Committee in 1996.

[89] UN Human Rights Committee (1989) *General Comment N° 18 on Non-Discrimination*; para. 6.

[90] *Vos vs. The Netherlands,* UN Human Rights Committee in 1989; p. 232. See also: *P.P.C. vs. The Netherlands*, UN Human Rights Committee in 1988. For a detailed discussion, see: Bayefsky (2015).

[91] Moeckli (2015). *Belgian Linguistics Case*, European Court of Human Rights in 1968.

[92] Moeckli (2015).

[93] *Advisory Opinion OC-18/03 'Juridical Condition and Rights of Undocumented Migrants'*, Inter-American Court of Human Rights in 2003, p. 99. Moeckli (2015).

[94] *Stec and Others vs. UK*, European Court of Human Rights in 2006. Moeckli (2015).

[95] Lerner (2015) and Bayefsky (2015).

matter, not assuming the form of positive obligations language shining through the above discussed regional interpretations of positive action.

Specific attention shall be paid here to the protection of specific groups resulting from affirmative action measures. In fact, respective measures were defined early on as a way to mediate unequal positions, affecting specific groups as maintained by the Special Rapporteur of the Sub-Commission on the Promotion and Protection of Human Rights in 2001, "*measures (. . .) aimed specifically at correcting the position of members of a target group in one or more aspects of their social life, in order to obtain effective equality*"[96]. Due consideration to be paid to specific groups may enter through the backdoor as shown by the Human Rights Committee's jurisprudence on the matter: accordingly, special measures are granted if they meet a general justification test, in other words, specific aims are to be set which, in turn, need to be pursued proportionately.[97] In that sense, preferential treatment is to be granted to such groups, thereby fulfilling a specific objective which may, however, not be indefinite in time.[98] Similar obligations have been established under other treaty monitoring bodies such as CEDAW, CESCR and CERD.[99] Distinct criteria were developed respectively, for special measures to be

> undertaken with certain limited purposes, namely to secure advancement in order to ensure equal enjoyment of human rights and fundamental freedoms, or the acceleration of de facto equality, temporary, cease when certain set objectives are achieved, namely, equality of opportunity and treatment, and not result in the maintenance of unequal or separate standards of rights[100].

In that sense, great resemblance is to be noted when comparing these developments with the interpretations issued by the Human Rights Committee.

Emphasis shall, however, be equally placed on the nature of obligations arising therewith; the Committee explicitly "*requires*" States to adopt special measures as discussed in its General Comment on Non-Discrimination.[101] More specifically, the Committee held that the prevention of discrimination "*requires not only measures of protection but also affirmative action designed to ensure the positive enjoyment of rights*"[102]. Also neighbouring regimes such as women's rights protection under CEDAW have been submitted to similar reasoning, emblematic being the right to equal remuneration for work of equal value, requiring, among other steps to be

---

[96]Ibid. Special Rapporteur of the Sub-Commission on the Promotion and Protection of Human Rights (2001) *Progress Report on the Concept and Practice of Affirmative Action*; para. 7.

[97]Moeckli (2015). *Stalla Costa vs. Uruguay*, UN Human Rights Committee in 1987. *Jacobs vs. Belgium*, UN Human Rights Committee in 2004. See also: Henkin (1981).

[98]Moeckli (2015).

[99]Bayefsky (2015) and Moeckli (2015).

[100]Bayefsky (2015), p. 97.

[101]UN Human Rights Committee (1989) *General Comment N° 18 on Non-Discrimination*; para. 10.

[102]UN Human Rights Committee (1981) *General Comment No. 4: Article 3 (Equal Right of Men and Women to the Enjoyment of All Civil and Political Rights)*; para. 2. Bayefsky (2015).

taken, implementation machineries to be put in place. The ECtHR also clearly adopted a positive positioning on the matter, explicitly addressing positive State obligations in relation to a variety of rights.[103] More precisely, the Court would discuss these comparing them with the less disputed negative obligations a State needs to comply with: notably, it would state "*there may be positive obligations*"[104], or even more strongly, "*fulfilment of a duty (...) on occasion necessitates some positive action*"[105]. In terms of the level of protection and legal value of positive obligations, there seems to be agreement across international and regional mechanisms, with positive duties having clearly gained recognition by relevant authorities of interpretation.

## 3.3 Equality Institutions and Their Shaping Potential: Towards a New Engagement with Equality?

In the following, we shall approach equality institutionalism principally through the eyes of the EU *Ius Commune* given the prominence attributed to equality ever since the adoption of the 2000 Directives, the Racial Equality and Employment Equality Directives, and the level of institutionalisation, which in turn provides us with a rich empirical landscape to explore such principle. Sheer numbers of existing institutions may be indicative of such tendency, with notably 27 Member States having established equality bodies that assume respective responsibilities on the grounds protected by the Directives, namely racial discrimination or ethnic origin and gender,[106] which would expand to include sex and citizenship-based discrimination for mobile workers.[107] We may similarly recall that grounds have been treated differently, institutionally speaking as some bodies would assume a multi-ground equality design while others would deal with one specific ground only, yet others would opt for integrated equality bodies and a separate one dedicated to a single ground.[108] A final distinction to be drawn concerns the very mandates and overall purpose guiding the work of the bodies, principally operating to "*generate findings on discrimination (tribunal-type bodies)*"[109] or to "*provide legal advice and support to victims of discrimination (promotional-type bodies)*"[110], both constituting

[103] *Marckx vs. Belgium*, European Court of Human Rights in 1978. *Airey vs. Ireland*, European Court of Human Rights in 1979.

[104] *Marckx vs. Belgium*, European Court of Human Rights in 1978; para. 31. *X & Y vs. The Netherlands*, European Court of Human Rights in 1985; para. 23.

[105] *Airey vs. Ireland*, European Court of Human Rights in 1979; para. 25.

[106] Ammer et al. (2010).

[107] Benedi Lahuerta (2021).

[108] Ammer et al. (2010). See also: Muir and de Witte (2017).

[109] Ammer et al. (2010), p. 63.

[110] Ibid., p. 63.

relevant points of departure to explore further how equality has been embraced as a principle and right.

Indeed, some conclusions have been drawn elsewhere portraying Equality Bodies as '*fundamental enforcement tools*'[111] to effectively combat discrimination if well designed and resourced. Complementing their role in enforcing equality legislation, Equality Bodies have similarly been described as '*soft powers*' aiming for achieving equality in society at large.[112] Hope has also been placed in a relevant pan-EU instrument, the 2018 EU Recommendation on Standards for Equality Bodies,[113] which has however been criticised on grounds of its uncompelling language and soft-law nature.[114] Similar criticism has been directed towards the Equality Bodies in the EU in the light of a particular socio-political climate threatening to "*undermine their independence, effectiveness, and even their existence*"[115]. In the following, we shall hence examine to what extent the principle of equality has come to enjoy recognition, a further spelling out of obligations, and relatedly, assumed a stronger position in a context of enhanced levels of institutionalisation.

### 3.3.1 Making Sense of Equality Institutionalism: Between Human Rights Conservatism and Responsive Governance

A positive reading of EU equality law and its particular institutionalised form suggests that the rise of integrated Equality Bodies dealing with multiple grounds has shown better equipped to work on intersecting manifestations of equality, the wide range of grounds and their social complexity.[116] Cautious voices may however draw our attention to the politicisation of the issue, given that most bodies, at least in some way, operate under the umbrella of or are associated with governmental entities: accordingly, institutional transformations have been undergone, disassociating these specialised mechanisms from governments, and respectively, from specific agendas or programmes.[117] Reasons for such cautious attitude may be

[111] Benedi Lahuerta (2021), p. 407.

[112] Kádár (2018).

[113] Principally, the Recommendation strives to set out measures that are to "*improve the equality bodies' independence and effectiveness, in particular as regards their capacity to ensure that individuals and groups that are discriminated against can fully enjoy their rights*" (chapter 1 (1)). The Recommendation further spells out functions to be covered by the equality bodies' mandates including "*providing independent assistance to victims (...) carry out independent surveys regularly (...) publish independent reports regularly and present them to the public institutions concerned (...) promote equality and diversity*" (Chapter 1.1.2. (1)–(12)).

[114] Benedi Lahuerta (2021).

[115] Kádár (2018), p. 11.

[116] Krizsan et al. (2012).

[117] Choudhury (2006).

found in the very directives giving rise to their institutional formalisation as the Racial Equality Directive states: "*…these bodies may form part of agencies charged at national level with the defence of human rights or the safeguard of individual rights*" (art. 13), hence building strong connections with National Human Rights Institutions which, evidently, fall short of complying with independence criteria as much as NGOs would. The 2018 Recommendations give us a sense of the importance of independent operating of Equality Bodies by way of mainstreaming, inter-alia, independent assistance to victims, independent surveying and independent reporting throughout their institutional machinery (Chapter 1.1.2. (1)–(9)).

Generally, Equality Bodies have found themselves exposed to critical examination of many sorts, identifying a few transversal challenges including "*a reduction of resources, restructuring, threats to independence, lack of expertise*"[118] among others. All these challenges seem indeed to reflect exogenous failures attributable to executive or legislative forces that show unresponsive to on-the-ground realities, also deeply ingrained in institutional matters rather than embracing a specifically directed critique on, for instance, some discriminatory grounds left outside the body's scope, lacking enforcement or other institution-endemic factors. A study assessing domestic Equality Bodies in 27 EU Member States and three EFTA States identifies five key areas that are yet to be developed further throughout the States examined, namely "*improving the situation of individuals who experience discrimination (such as by levelling down discriminatory structures); enabling change in policies, procedures and practices of organisations; improving quality of policy and legislation; improving stakeholder action; improving public attitudes*"[119]. Very visibly, the role of Equality Bodies expands that of a classical judicial institution, turning it a key actor vested with powers in the public space, to trigger change both in governmental policies and other relevant actors in the field, including societal transformation. In that sense, we may not only understand Equality Bodies as instances of implementation in a strict sense, but possibly also as standard-enhancing, if not standard-setting mechanisms—hence bearing considerable two-way potential in the struggle for non-discrimination.

A different picture may be drawn if we consider Equality Bodies' direct involvement in judicial proceedings. With the proceduralisation of Equality Law, organisations have become enabled to represent groups facing inequality in their absence or on their behalf.[120] This may also enable equality bodies to assume the position of a plaintiff organisation,[121] thereby clearly contributing to progressive standards through litigation. On a different note, we may recall that some equality institutions had existed prior to the adoption of the directives, such as in the case of the United Kingdom and the Netherlands which, as it may be argued, triggered respective

[118] Belavusau and Henrard (2019).

[119] Ammer et al. (2010), p. 178.

[120] Belavusau and Henrard (2019).

[121] *Centrum voor gelijkheid van kansen en voor racismebestrijding vs. Firma Feryn NV*, Court of Justice of the European Union in 2008. See also: Henrard (2009).

institutional transformations at EU level.[122] Similar observations may be made in the case of the ombudsman tradition in Scandinavian States or its strong influence in Southern Europe.[123] In these cases, it is reported, equality bodies assumed an active role in mobilising domestic courts to ultimately enforce the rights of those being discriminated.[124] Other influential developments include institutional transformations leading to Equality Bodies merging into National Human Rights Institutions,[125] which, in the worst case, may imply additional dependencies and exposure to political pressures, that way, threatening judicial independence and the potential to engage in proceedings or other forms of assuming a victims-oriented approach. Despite institution-specific advantages such as the availability of personnel and financial resources, Equality Bodies may find themselves exposed to higher levels of dependencies while also jeopardising their autonomies when dealing with individual victims, victims groups, or determining agendas.

## References

Alexy R (2018) Theorie der Grundrechte. Suhrkamp Taschenbuch Verlag, Frankfurt a.M.

Ammer M, Crowley N, Liegl B, Holzleithner E, Wladasch K, Yesilkagit K (2010) Study on equality bodies set up under Directives 2000/43/EC, 2004/113/EC and 2006/54/EC. Human European Consultancy and Ludwig Boltzmann Institut für Menschenrechte, Utrecht/Vienna

Arendt H (1951) The origins of totalitarianism. Penguin Books, London

Baer S (2017) Speaking law: towards a nuanced analysis of "cases". German Law J 18

Bantekas I, Oette L (2020) International human rights law and practice. Cambridge University Press, Cambridge

Bayefsky AF (2015) The principle of equality or non-discrimination in international law

Belavusau U, Henrard K (2019) A bird's eye view on EU anti discrimination law: the impact of the 2000 equality directives. German Law J 20(5)

Benedi Lahuerta S (2021) Equality bodies: advancing towards more responsive designs? Int J Law Context 17

Benoît-Rohmer F (2017) Lessons from the recent case law of the EU Court of Justice on the principle of non-discrimination. In: Rossi LS, Casolari F (eds) The principles of equality in EU law. Springer International Publishing, Cham

Besson S (2015) Human rights and constitutional law: patterns of mutual validation and legitimation. In: Cruft R, Liao SM, Renzo M (eds) Philosophical foundations of human rights. Oxford University Press, Oxford

Brillat M (2015) Le Principe de Non-Discrimination à l'Épreuve des droits européens. Institut Universitaire Varenne, Paris

Busstra M (2010) The implications of the racial equality directive for minority protection within the European Union. Eleven International Publishing, The Hague

Cassese A (2012) Realizing Utopia: the future of international law. Oxford University Press, Oxford

[122] Belavusau and Henrard (2019).

[123] de Witte (2011).

[124] Muir and de Witte (2017).

[125] Ibid.

Choudhury T (2006) The Commission for equality and human rights: designing the big tent. Maastricht J Eur Comp Law 311(13)
de Búrca G (2012) The ECJ and the international legal order: a re-evaluation. In: de Búrca G (ed) The worlds of European constitutionalism. Cambridge University Press, Cambridge
De Schutter O (2018) The formation of a common law of human rights. In: Bribosia E, Rorive I (eds) Human rights tectonics: global dynamics of integration and fragmentation. Intersentia, Antwerp
De Witte B (2011) National equality institutions and the domestication of EU non-discrimination law. Maastricht J Eur Comp Law 18(1–2)
De Witte B (2012) The European Union as an international legal experiment. In: de Búrca G (ed) The worlds of European constitutionalism. Cambridge University Press, Cambridge
Donnelly J (2003) Universal human rights in theory and practice. Cornell University Press, Ithaca
Dreier R (1976) Zur Problematik und Situation der Verfassungsinterpretation. In: Dreier R, Schwegmann FG (eds) Probleme der Verfassungsinterpretation: Dokumentation einer Kontroverse. Nomos, Baden-Baden
Eichler J (2022) The transformative forces of international law? Questioning equality regimes from a multi-level perspective. Global Constitutionalism
Fredman S (2005) Double trouble: multiple discrimination and EU law. Eur Anti-Discrimination Law Rev 13(2)
Groussot X (2006) General principles of community law. European Law Publishing, Groningen
Henkin L (1981) The international bill of rights: the covenant on civil and political rights. Columbia University Press, New York
Henrard K (2009) The first substantive ECJ Judgement on the racial equality directive. NYU Jean Monnet Working Paper Series 1
Holzleithner E (2005) Mainstreaming equality: dis/entangling grounds of discrimination. Transnatl Law Contemp Probl 14(3)
Jovanović M (2022) Making social groups visible to and in law – essentialisation and law's generality. In: Eichler J, Topidi K (eds) Minority recognition and the diversity deficit: comparative perspectives. Hart Publishing, Oxford
Kádár T (2018) Equality bodies: a European phenomenon. Int J Discrimination Law 18(2–3)
Kantola J, Nousiainen K (2009) Institutionalizing intersectionality in Europe. Int Femin J Polit 11(4)
Kilpatrick C (2014) Article 21: non-discrimination. In: Peers S, Hervey TK, Kenner J, Ward A (eds) The EU Charter of Fundamental Rights: a commentary. Hart Publishing, Oxford
Koldinská K (2009) Institutionalizing intersectionality. Int Femin J Polit 11(4)
Krisch N (2010) The open architecture of European Human Rights Law. In: Krisch N (ed) Beyond constitutionalism: the pluralist structure of postnational law. Oxford University Press, Oxford
Krizsan A, Skjeie H, Squires J (2012) Institutionalising intersectionality: the changing nature of European regimes. Palgrave Macmillan, London
Krizsan A, Skjeie H, Squires J (2014) The changing nature of European equality regimes: explaining convergence and variation. J Int Comp Soc Policy 53(30)
Krommendijk J (2018) Opinion 2/13 as a game changer in the dialogue between the European courts? In: Bribosia E, Rorive I (eds) Human rights tectonics: global dynamics of integration and fragmentation. Intersentia, Antwerp
Lenaerts K, Gutiérrez-Fons JA (2014) The place of the charter in the EU constitutional edifice. In: Peers S, Hervey T, Kenner J, Ward A (eds) The EU Charter of Fundamental Rights: a commentary. C. H. Beck/Hart/Nomos, Munich/Oxford/Baden-Baden
Lerner N (2015) The U.N. Convention on the elimination of all forms of racial discrimination. BRILL, Leiden
Lombardo E, Verloo M (2009) Institutionalizing intersectionality in the European Union? Int Femin J Polit 11(4)
Moeckli D (2015) Equality and non-discrimination. In: Farrior S (ed) Equality and non-discrimination under international law. Ashgate Publishing Limited, Farnham

Muir E, de Witte B (2017) The procedural and institutional dimension of anti-discrimination law. In: Rossi LS, Casolari F (eds) The principles of equality in EU law. Springer International Publishing, Cham
Ramcharan BG (2015) Equality and non-discrimination. In: Henkin L (ed) The international bill of rights: the covenant on civil and political rights. Columbia University Press, New York
Rossi LS, Casolari F (2017) Preface. In: Rossi LS, Casolari F (eds) The principle of equality in EU law. Springer International Publishing, Cham
Scholler H (1969) Die Interpretation des Gleichheitssatzes als Willkürverbot oder als Gebot der Chancengleichheit. Duncker-Humblot, Berlin
Shaw MN (2008) International law, 6th edn. Cambridge University Press, Cambridge
Squires J (2009) Intersecting inequalities: Britain's equality review. Int J Femin Polit 11(4)
Tomuschat C (2019) Equality and non-discrimination under the International Covenant on Civil and Political Rights. In: von Münch I (ed) Staatsrecht – Völkerrecht – Europarecht. De Gruyter, Berlin
Wouters J, Ovádek M (2021) The European Union and human rights: analysis, cases, and materials. Oxford University Press, Oxford
Xinidis R (2019) Multiple discrimination in EU anti-discrimination law: towards redressing complex inequality? In: Belavusau U, Henrard K (eds) EU anti-discrimination law beyond gender. Hart Publishing, Oxford
Zaccaroni G (2017) Differentiating equality? The different advancements in the protected grounds in the case law of the European Court of Justice. In: Rossi LS, Casolari F (eds) The principle of equality in EU law. Springer International Publishing, Cham

# Part II
# Redefining Recognition

Collectivisation processes, it could be argued, may prove inefficient where these are not paralleled by respective socio-political transformations. It is in this context that we shall think about the question of recognition, the politics of difference to be considered vital where collective rights are to be juridified. Indeed, much depends on, inter-alia, the political couleur of those governing, on the governance order in place as determined by constitutional law, or the political spirit of the time including societal tendencies showing more or, alternatively, less eager to respond to difference and minority situations. Multiculturalism and other State theories cannot be reduced to the law but require profound transformations including at institutional level (the daily institutional realities and mindsets), affecting the mundane operating of the State but also daily politics. Indeed, recognising difference cannot remain delegated to the political periphery, but instead needs to find due consideration in any policy decision, in other words, to be mainstreamed throughout any legislative endeavour, resembling the largely accepted gender-based approach. A particular focus shall hence be placed on right wing populism, parties and formations, proving particularly inimical to difference broadly speaking and minorities to considerable extent.

In a way, the present debate follows up on the equality discourse and its codification in the law, its institutionalisation, its socialisation, which is commonly utilised by the political right to promote a harmonising, assimilating understanding of the State. The right wing however also essentially participates actively in the construction of exclusive, imaginary categories such as the 'nation', the 'people' or, as a corollary, categories it shows inimical to, notably through processes of othering. It hence appears easy enough to conclude that any form of collectivisation or the recognition of minority rights, including LGBTIQ+ rights, are ruled out, categorically, from the start. Instead, the opposite is the case, processes of othering, of alienating and delegitimating, or blaming practices in crisis contexts, dominate the political discourse, often perpetuated through the media. Rather than witnessing an on-going discrimination and exclusion of particular groups in society, and often long-lasting histories of subalternity, minorities are commonly invoked, whenever felt appropriate, to be placed in the context of contemporary dilemmas societies are facing. Rather than what may be assumed when thinking about equality, namely for right wing parties and movements to reject the equality discourse due to its potential to grant rights to those it strives to exclude, quite the opposite has been observed: right wing discourse has been attempting to normalise and streamline its views and underlying logics with the help of equality's rationale, and its homogenising function. This might not only further complexify ideological critique on the matter, but diversify strategies used by the political right in its positioning towards group identities and respective rights to be recognised. Discourses and directions become much less tangible, in a way escape the analytical reach of many scholarly endeavours, it could be argued. Indeed, the equality discourse has been employed by movements and parties of different political couleur, albeit serving very different agendas and purposes.

It is against this background that recognition politics or, alternatively, the politics of difference need to be seen, as a response to growing right wing trends, notably in Europe, with the need to be further spelt out rather than being left 'somewhere out there', as a lose conceptual project without teeth (see Chap. 5 for such spelling out). In a way, this represents a new articulation with the multicultural realities of today's societies and respective needs that arise in that context, rather than turning an indifferent (at best!) eye to these questions as it is commonly being practiced by right wing formations. In that sense, equality has clearly become outdated as an appropriate, responsive paradigm dating back to eighteenth century Europe where equal rights and citizenship had to be considered as important preconditions given the recent experience with totalitarian, elitist rule and lacking democratic safeguards, let alone fundamental rights. Others may argue it is in people's mindsets that transformations must be spurred or even initiated, raising awareness of difference and respective correlations with vulnerability or marginalised, unequal positions in relation to society at large, as an ever more important field requiring institutional and societal attention.

Ongoing difficulties to do so may exactly lie in the somewhat opposite direction this ought to take (as opposed to views entrenched in the equality logics or even exclusionary practice), evidently remaining unconsidered or unthought, possibly deemed as too ambitious yet quintessential given the persisting threats to society's minorities. In other words, the existing judicial framework dating back to eighteenth century Europe does not show an easy fit with multicultural and plural realities and might require a rethinking that goes beyond or even initiates beyond the law, especially given the systemic nature of the matter. Possibly owing to the ever present threats attributable to right wing ideologies and formations, the politics of difference remain an ever present and necessary demand, an incarnation of resistance. But before turning to collective and group rights, it is argued here, we need to first think of difference as a more global objective to be considered throughout any policy goal or any form of State measure with the objective of also transforming societal perspectives. Election results throughout Europe need to be taken seriously, being indicative of a growing acceptance of (extreme) right wing politics. Indeed, this might require a dedicated effort to work on reconceptualising difference to turn to the salience of the question, to make first steps towards (judicial) recognition, and also for society to become aware of stereotyping trends and overall normalising attitudes, in a way equipping society to distinguish and to identify patterns or accepted conduct that ought to be questioned to say the least. The politics of difference and politics of recognition possibly represents the most known step into that direction.

What recognition strives to visualise, amongst a variety of other factors, concerns one of the weakest points of the law, that of a thorough, contextual background analysis that shows typical of and is urgently needed as far as minority groups are concerned, or those facing minority situations such as indigenous peoples. The rather to-the-point, ad-hoc nature of legal codes and jurisprudence may prove inhibiting in that regard, often overlooking histories of past injustices, their contemporary effects including intergenerational suffering, the systematic nature of many violations and those impacts on minorities that lay below the threshold of qualifying as a violation such as, famously, stereotypisation and other degrading conduct such as 'othering' impacting on people's/peoples' psychological integrity in a systematic manner and its long term effects. Indeed, recognition demands a conscious alienation from a purely isolated view that, instead, takes societal context into account, including, fundamentally, group-specific violations that may not easily come to the surface when studying an individual case. The situation of indigenous peoples may exemplify such scenario at its finest, given the long history of genocide, forced removal from lands, neo-colonial practices that impose specific visions in one way or another on indigenous communities including specific education, language or religious practices. Large-scale targeting practices including the persecution of leaders and imposed barriers in relation to questions of representation further add to the collective burden indigenous peoples are sharing in the contemporary world. Rather clearly then, violations cannot be separated from and need to be understood in the collective context in which they occur. Rather than serving as a tool of evidence-gathering that could assist in the legal process or the like, it is argued here that recognition of difference is to be considered as an effective measure in its own terms, starting where the slightest manifestation of subjugation or forms of exclusion become apparent in practice, and also by considering the dealing with difference holistically and as a long-term endeavour, requiring respective transformations in people's mindsets, in institutions, and ultimately also in the law.

Admittedly, a complex scenario presents itself with minority situations, often introducing a multiplicity of overlapping claims that may not easily be discerned and identified from the outset. At times, these may not be mirrored in the law itself and in those cases require an active court to make use of its wide interpretative powers. Another related phenomenon concerns the fragmentation of jurisprudence developed that—given the only sporadic mentioning of minority rights in legal codes—hardly does justice to the multiplicity of claims, their interrelatedness and again, the needs arising with minority situations. Indeed, intersectional violations have only been addressed by (quasi)legal institutions in recent years despite progressive developments in academia reaching back to the twentieth century. Now, a successful politics of difference takes a different direction, namely by fully appreciating the nuanced, multivariate nature of identities, also sometimes referred to as identity politics. Indeed, claims may be complex where individual rights do not immediately seem to coincide with his/her/x responsibilities towards the group, where individual and collective rights seem to clash. Identity debates may indeed open up the space for ideas on the construction or deconstruction of these through the law but also in the very interaction of minority groups with society at large, initiating with questions on self-identification but also encompassing their positioning towards other minority groups or communities belonging to the same minority group at large. Interestingly, theoretical debates on recognition hardly ever engage too closely with very specific groups, rather with minority situations at large or the multiplicity of parallel claims to be considered. Much emphasis is placed on majority-minority relations, histories of dispossession or the general 'configuration' and organisation of society, institutions, or the dealing with colonial past.

This is not for us to become completely isolated from legal contexts: in fact, common categories such as citizenship, minority or indigenous rights necessarily require a profound judicial understanding to be in place, to appreciate its various implications, to grasp the sheer meaning of specific rights and to develop an awareness of relevant jurisprudence, to name a few qualities needed here. What however escapes such strictly legal understanding of rights concerns the premises on which the State is built, on which equality relies and entire catalogues of rights are based on. Recognition politics, it is advanced here, critically approach such underlying rationale, allowing us to examine how political realities demonstrably impact on such understanding, what kind of policies would be needed to reform the law in the long run, or how to disentangle such underlying common sense that is played out to the detriment of groups in minority situations.

We are indeed confronted with a complex scenario of unwilling stakeholders, commonly rooted in right wing ideologies; a State whose structures are yet to be overhauled by alienating itself from the status-quo and its basic guiding principles such as sovereignty and an absolute conception of its integrity; and a society that shows unwilling to great extents to give up on majority positions, hidden under the veil of democratic principles and the rule of law. Recognition hence assumes the role of a panacea, considering such persisting societal ill and respective insensibility towards minority situations but also institution-wide, as a systemic problem deeply rooted in the State's very architecture; recognition of difference however also confronts epistemological truth and entire ontologies on which theories are built, starting with conceptual preconditions that remain unquestioned, entering our daily vocabulary and working definitions. In that sense, we are facing a nuanced interplay of normative expectations, that is, a complete reform of the State and majority-minority relations, and on the other side, empirical realities entrenched in a human rights conservatism that only sporadically allows for difference to be recognised to the degree necessary for minority situations to be genuinely mediated in practice.

# Chapter 4
# Equality Paradigms and Contemporary Politics of Recognition

## 4.1 Introducing Recognition Politics and the Politics of Differentiation

The question of recognising and accommodating cultural diversity has been declared as one of the most '*pressing questions*' of the twenty-first century, as famously defended by James Tully.[1] He thereby refers to different minority groups including language minority groups, indigenous peoples or recently migrated groups. In view of the current piece's major orientation towards collective rights (in an abstract manner), his thesis proves highly interesting: Tully notably examines to what extent the cultural and political demands raised by these groups may coincide and, at the same time, lead to an amalgamation of '*intercultural demands*' as these concern the public sphere and institutions.[2] Others, notably Ayelet Shachar, has termed such manifestation of recognition a '*legal accommodation of difference*' which ought to transform the commonly-embraced understanding of citizenship to not merely problematise the citizenship-cultural accommodation nexus, but to allow for self-governance in accordance with a group's customs.[3] Relatedly, Will Kymlicka's conceptualisation on the matter, that is '*group-differentiated citizenship*', approaches similar manifestations of differentiation, drawing on polyethnic rights—reflecting those claims raised by immigrant groups and religious minorities—and self-government rights as they are advocated by indigenous peoples and 'national minorities', mirroring the different demands of the groups in question.[4] Somewhat relatedly, the so-called politics of recognition have come to reflect different 'strands'

[1]Tully (2012).

[2]Ibid., p. 2.

[3]Shachar (2001), p. 17.

[4]Kymlicka (1995), p. 44.



J. Eichler, *An Interdisciplinary Journey from Non-Discrimination to Collective Rights*, https://doi.org/10.1007/978-3-031-54618-1_4

in contemporary politics as it is demanded by inter-alia minority or subaltern groups, feminist thought or the politics of multiculturalism at large.[5]

Some thought may also be spent on the fragmentation of claims, with identity politics or the politics of recognition often being portrayed as separate from questions of redistribution or claims for social equality.[6] Not uncommonly, questions of recognition prove intrinsically tied to political participation, representation or (self-) governance matters, being historically separated from social rights if we were to follow classical human rights taxonomies.[7] Inevitably, struggles for recognition have commonly come to absorb the demands raised by social movements, as important channels for social justice agendas or translators of collective socio-economic claims. Yet another considerable ground is laid by the socio-psychological damage suffered being attributable to the misrecognition of groups where "*a confining or demeaning or contemptible picture of themselves [is] mirrored back to them (...) by the people or society*".[8] Another societal malaise may lay in what Taylor identifies as ignorance of difference which he traces back to Rousseau's Discourse on Inequality, the latter advocating for a society where "*all can share equally in the light of public attention [in which] he sees the source of health*".[9] By and large, he appears critical of the "*claim[s] made (...) on behalf of 'difference-[ignorant]' liberalism [in] that it can offer a neutral ground on which people of all cultures can meet and coexist*".[10] Much may be derived from the origins of classical liberal thought and its premisses, built on a culturally homogenous State: both John Stuart Mill and the contemporary John Rawls draw on a misconception according to which a unifying public opinion could impossibly be formed in "*a country made up of different nationalities*".[11] The realities of even minorities' internal diversity and the complexities of group formation clearly escaped the proclaimed objective of forming a single, valid public opinion—also ignorant of any politically powerful opposition to identity politics, constituting a majority until today. Indeed, the normative (the *ought to question* relating to equality paradigms or differentiated treatment) and the empirical (*on the ground realities* of inequalities) enter a contested field of negotiation here, with the often contrasting portrayals of societal (in)equality and the diverging views on difference and recognition thereof.

Despite the value laying with differentiated treatment as such, specific emphasis shall be placed on group-specific differentiation here, requiring a more systemic, also systematic approach that promises to adequately deal with group-related vulnerabilities. A major contribution lies with Kymlicka's '*group-differentiated*

[5] Taylor (1992), p. 25.

[6] Fraser (1998).

[7] See e.g. Tomuschat (2014).

[8] Taylor (1992), p. 25.

[9] Ibid., p. 35.

[10] Ibid., p. 62.

[11] Freeman (1995), p. 26. Mill (1910) and Rawls (1999).

*rights*',[12] resembling the notion of collective rights, while more specifically tailored to group identities and respective demands arising from such group category. To be sure, it is referred to rights "*reflect[ing] a collectivist or communitarian outlook*", vested with considerable 'powers' to protect the group from "*internal dissent, e.g. the decision of individual members not to follow traditional practices or customs (...) and the impact of external decisions, e.g. the economic or political decisions of the larger societies*".[13] Importantly, however, Kymlicka maintains—by way of avoiding any false dichotomies—collective rights may be accorded to and exercised by individual members of such group.[14] The focus here certainly remains on external impacts, which in turn, require specific safeguards to be put in place. A common weakness shining through such differentiation paradigm however lies in the definition of groups included by the protection scheme: Kymlicka adopts a positivistic stance by referring to language rights as a classical manifestation of group-specific rights which are reserved to 'national minorities' as opposed to immigrant groups. Indeed, we are witnessing a largely exclusive approach inherent to current recognition politics, differentiating between so-called old and new minorities.[15] In that sense, the current debate remains aspirational, building on the empirical foundations in the field of indigenous rights and (mostly 'national') minorities without neglecting their potential of transfer, that is, establishing similar standards for hitherto un-recognised minority groups.

## 4.2 Juridified Ways of Dealing with Difference: Assimilating and Integrationist Agendas and Effects

Examining 'difference' necessarily requires us to understand the concept from the perspective of and as interpreted in coexisting orders. Almost evidently, domestic constitutionalism has proven conservative towards both protected categories of rights including 'national minorities' and in extending its safeguarding umbrella to include non-citizens, migrated persons in particular. An influential role has been attributed, instead, to international developments as it may become apparent from a historical reading of 'national minority' protection in Europe.[16] With the commencement of the post-cold war period, the status and treatment of those minorities was absorbed by multilateral endeavours, declared as "*matters of legitimate international concern*",[17] also against the background of the recent experience with violent ethnic

[12] Kymlicka (1995).

[13] Ibid., p. 35.

[14] Ibid.

[15] See e.g. Kochenov (2015), Henrard (2011), Medda-Windischer (2009), Eide (2004) and Medda-Windischer et al. (2020).

[16] Kymlicka (2013).

[17] Ibid., p. 173.

conflicts. Reasons may be manifold, not least to mention political aspirations, notably, an opening towards and eventually integration into institutional structures of Europe. The adequate dealing with 'national minorities' was considered a test of political maturity accordingly,[18] one way of "*measuring a country's moral progress*".[19] A similar positioning was assumed in the context of official accession criteria for joining the European Community; amongst the criteria qualifying for membership, the Presidency of the European Council included the "*achieve[ment of] human rights and respect for and protection of minorities*" which were adopted during its 1993 Copenhagen meeting.[20] A similar wording shines through the EU's 'constitutional order' finding formalisation with the Treaty of Lisbon in 2009: according to art. 2 of the Treaty on European Union, the Union is founded on specific values including, importantly, the rights of persons belonging to minorities, hence representing a foundational matter to be referred to and to be implemented.

In a way, the dealing with difference is subjected to yet a different instance, with its own understanding of group rights. This is the case for the Council of Europe with its large number of members—and home(s) to minorities—considerable definitional influences are to be traced back to its normative framework, notably the Framework Convention for the Protection of National Minorities. It should be noted from the outset, however, that its protective realm principally affects individual rights.[21] Insights on the assimilative nature of difference-based treatment (here: minority rights) and its prevention may be drawn from the Convention itself: in its Explanatory Report on art. 5(2), the Ad Hoc Committee for the Protection of National Minorities specifies that members of such minorities are to be protected from assimilation against their will which is, however, not to prohibit voluntary assimilation (para. 45). Paradoxically, in discussing the same provision, the Ad Hoc Committee explicitly allows States to take "*measures in pursuance of their general integration policy*" while it refers to the importance of social cohesion and cultural diversity which shall enrich society (para. 46). Similar observations have been made in relation to indigenous peoples where the term '*assimilation policies*' is commonly invoked, in the colonial context and beyond; in fact, in the US context, historical patterns point to policy shifts taking place every 20 years promoting assimilative practices vis-à-vis indigenous peoples in one way or another.[22]

Some thought shall be spent on the positioning on difference as it emerges from the interaction of co-existing judicial systems. Indeed, domestic constitutionalism may find itself not only exposed to jurisprudence developed in the regional Ius Commune, it may also have to comply with decisions made by, for instance, the European Court of Justice. Emerging concepts finding formalisation, and ultimately institutionalisation, include that of '*European homogeneity*' or even more widely

---

[18] Ibid.

[19] Ibid., p. 174. Burgess (1999).

[20] Presidency of the European Council (1993) Conclusions of the Presidency, para. 7(A)(iii).

[21] Kugelmann (2007).

[22] Corntassel and Witmer (2008).

embraced, the notion of the '*European democratic deficit*'.[23] An interesting turn is taken however through the '*marge d'appréciation*'[24] doctrine as well as, relatedly, references to the '*common constitutional traditions of the Member States*'[25] which we shall explore as they relate to difference. Interestingly, a middle ground is found as far as the principle of equality and non-discrimination is concerned:

> the Directive does not itself lay down the principle of equal treatment in the field of employment and occupation which derives from various international instruments and from the constitutional traditions common to the Member States, but has the sole purpose of laying down, in that field, a general framework for combating discrimination on various grounds[26]

In relation to the related principle of non-discrimination, the CJEU develops a clear stance, not only as far as its understanding of non-discrimination is concerned, but also in terms of the question of legal hierarchies in that regard:

> ...it [is] for the national court, hearing a dispute involving the principle of non-discrimination on grounds of age (...), to provide (...) the legal protection which individuals derive from European Union law and to ensure the full effectiveness of that law, disapplying if need be any provision of national legislation contrary to that principle[27]

Rather unequivocally, the Court refrains from deriving the non-discrimination principle from the common constitutional traditions of the Member States. What is more, the Court assumed a positive stance on the direct applicability of the general principle of non-discrimination on the basis of age which, in turn, widened the scope of EU law, hence reflecting what has been deemed '*interpretive activism*'.[28] As a consequence, critical voices have been referring to the Court as acting as the legislature rather than as the judicial power.[29]

Relevant insights may also be drawn from the margin of appreciation doctrine as it has been practiced by the European Court of Human Rights. This materialises to a particularly visible extent as far as minority rights are concerned, constituting a politically sensitive matter indeed: in that sense, the margin of appreciation doctrine as applied by the ECtHR has been deemed problematic or inappropriate in the

---

[23] Mangiameli (2013).

[24] See e.g. Greer (2000), Kratochvíl (2011), Akerø-Stueland (2021), Arai-Takahashi (2013), Brauch (2005), Arai-Takahashi (2013) and Agha (2017).

[25] See e.g. Cassese (2021).

[26] Ibid., p. 598. The author quotes the Römer decision here (C-147/08), Court of Justice of the European Union in 2011. *Cresco Investigation GmbH vs. Markus Achatzi*; Court of Justice of the European Union in 2017; *Mangold vs. Helm*, Court of Justice of the European Union in 2005; see also *Kücükdeveci vs. Swedex GmbH & Co. KG*, Court of Justice of the European Union in 2010; *Jürgen Römer gegen Freie und Hansestadt Hamburg*, Court of Justice of the European Union in 2011.

[27] *Kücükdeveci vs. Swedex GmbH & Co. KG*, Court of Justice of the European Union in 2010.

[28] Fichera and Pollicino (2019).

[29] Herzog and Gerken (2008).

minority rights context.[30] Reasons may be manifold, including its deferential use in decisions delegated to domestic instances which resulted in an insufficient protection of minority rights.[31] Some would go as far as arguing that the doctrine would not only distort the objectives established by the international system, but to also entirely neglect the obligation to protect the '*democratically challenged minorities*';[32] hence clearly understanding minority matters as a systemic ill of democratic principles which continue enjoying recognition as founding rationales of a convincing majority of today's State orders. The necessity of retaining considerable powers at domestic level in the form of judicial scrutiny shines through decisions that are based on, for instance, '*weighty reasons*' or '*derogation cases*' such as declarations of emergency,[33] as they relate to minorities. At the end of the day, much depends on the interpretative scope exercised by domestic courts, as adherents to majority-led domestic laws or as promoters of minority rights as established in international and regional legal systems. We may however be reminded of the politically contentious contexts shaping international negotiation processes, only rarely do minority rights find expression in the law in their purest form. Difference, it could be easily argued, remains a much disputed concern across different orders and levels, subject to majority-oriented orders and principles, the invisibilising veil of equality law or its isolated, contextualised appearance in the case law demonstrating ignorant of larger, systemic implications.

## 4.3 Obstacles to a Successful Pursuit of Recognition Politics: Political Couleur Under Focus

So far, the debate around recognition politics has been devolving around constitutional matters principally, constituting a valuable venue to explore for systemic transformations of majority-minority relations, for specialised rights to be established, allowing for participation in the functioning and daily operating of the State, or relatedly, specific procedures to be put in place to facilitate access to State institutions and basic governance functions. Challenges may be manifold, commencing, indeed, with the underlying principles of the State's architecture, that is, equality principles, non-discrimination paradigms or human rights '*non-specificism*' that shows ignorant of the specific needs and demands raised by minority groups.

Our attention shall, however, be directed to the daily realities of recognition politics as these find further application and operationalisation against the background of the changing panorama of governance processes, political alliances and the dangers for minority situations as they are posed by the political right or the right

[30] Benvenisti (1999) and Gross and Ní Aoláin (2001).

[31] Born et al. (2020).

[32] Ibid., p. 88. See also: Benvenisti (1999).

[33] Letsas (2006) and Gerards (2017).

wing pushing moderate parties away from identity politics.[34] Indeed, the related term '*identity politics*' merits our attention for a moment, as a concept capturing the wider context and political realities minority groups are exposed to while also addressing their very own struggle. Accordingly, the term has been defined as to encompass

> a wide range of political activity and theorizing founded in the shared experiences of injustice of members of certain social groups. Rather than organizing solely around belief systems, programmatic manifestos, or party affiliation, identity political formations typically aim to secure the political freedom of a specific constituency marginalised within its larger context. Members of that constituency assert or reclaim ways of understanding their distinctiveness that challenge dominant characterisations, with the goal of greater self-determination.[35]

And yet, identity politics in the current age—other than famously suggested by Fraser[36]—has been attributed negative connotations, having been associated with inter-alia social conflicts and confrontations as induced by the politicisation of ethnic and specifically indigenous identity.[37] It may easily be countered however, collective identity struggles and the response thereto by governments carry an inherently and necessary political element.

In other words, the "political project" proves key in not only "*reconcil[ing] antagonism and competition rooted in cultural and identity differences*" but also in "*provid[ing] legitimacy to the institutionalised framework of coexistence*".[38] Such political project seems little ambitious though, with coexistence being largely silent on distribution of power questions or representation matters. In fact, such political project—whenever successful—would result in the loss of cultural differences as illustratively narrated in the following:

> ... the importance of identity politics will gradually be suppressed by the emphasis of equality, even if the political project does not expressly target the 'cultural genocide' of the given communities.[39]

These developments seem to resonate, albeit in a reversed sense, with the early beginnings of the term 'identity politics' in the 1970s which was supposed to "*reshape movements that had until then prioritised the monotony of sameness over the strategic value of difference*".[40] Political projects have however also been described as bearing considerable potential in the case where "*divided States (to) bec[a]me genuine political communities, or in the form of polycentric political communities*".[41] As alluded to earlier, the homogenising potential remains a real

---

[34] See, for instance, Catalano Weeks and Allen (2022).

[35] Heyes (2020).

[36] Fraser (1998).

[37] Mähler and Pierskalla (2015).

[38] Salat (2021), p. 45. Schnapper (1994).

[39] Salat (2021), p. 46.

[40] Garza (2019), p. 1.

[41] Salat (2021), p. 46. For a detailed account on these arrangements, see Kukathas (2014). Also see Márquez (2011).

danger to ethnic or cultural minority groups, providing only small scale prospects to genuinely engage with the dominant political community.

### *4.3.1 Instrumentalising of Equality Paradigms: Right-Wing Party Formation and (Other) Ideologies*

In a way and in the light of the above, the struggle around identity politics has been portrayed as a false one, as directing us to make false choices.[42] Rather than understanding collective identity groups and their dedicated needs as given, representatives of the political conservative have been engaging in quite the opposite, that is, by deconstructing or invisibilising difference: conservative movements, it has been argued, have opted for

> neutrality [as] strategic to maintain white, heterosexual, male, cisgendered power, at the expense of everyone who does not occupy those social positions (. . .) they have identified that inequality resulting from race and gender, and other social indicators that have economic implications, is best left undiscussed.[43]

Rather often, it has been observed elsewhere, far right political discourse shows critical of any endeavours directed towards substantive equality as far as "*historically marginalised groups*" are concerned "*suggesting that these ideologies and associated policies take away valuable resources from native working class populations*", reflecting, indeed, a popular argument of the political right.[44] What is more, it has been observed that mainstream political parties have demonstrably shown responsive to the right wing conception of equality and its application on the ground, resulting in changes of their position on migration and multiculturalism.[45]

With the increasing popularity of right wing formations in Europe throughout the past decade, a few observations may be made as they relate to or actively invoke the equality discourse. Gender equality may be illustrative here, representing one of the most studied equality paradigms in that regard: in Central Europe, Hungary and Poland more precisely, illiberal transformation has been positioning itself in "*opposition to the liberal gender equality paradigm*",[46] or as becoming apparent in the discourse of the radical right, "*ranging from 'ethnosexism' against immigrants, to 'anti-genderism'*".[47] In fact, gender-based equality may serve as a noteworthy illustration of the right wing orientation towards difference, systemically thought, as it has also been witnessed among scholars active in the field:

---

[42] Garza (2019).

[43] Ibid., para. 37.

[44] Catalano Weeks and Allen (2022), p. 1. See also: Sakki and Pettersson (2016).

[45] Catalano Weeks and Allen (2022).

[46] Gwiazda (2021), p. 682. See also Grzebalska and Pető (2018).

[47] Dietze and Roth (2020), p. blurb.

> ...an important dimension of right-wing populism research, for us, is the observation that populism is not only concerned with gender as an issue itself but also with gender as a meta-language for negotiating different conditions of inequality and power in the context of current struggles over hegemony, and over resources forged by neoliberalism.[48]

Another notable nuance or differentiation is needed when taking gender equality as an example: capitalist market logics have been conducting to what has been termed '*neoliberal equality*', benefiting educated women, also described as one of the facilitating conditions of '*femonationalism*' which has been contrasted to intersectional forms[49] of feminism. These would, importantly, base themselves in the

> structural and inseparable entanglements of different axes of oppression and inequalities such as race, class, and gender – which practice a variety of forms of resistance against White mainstream feminisms, who often side with right-wingers in their anti-immigration stance. Intersectional feminists provide platforms against right-wing populism in the U.S., in Latin America, and Europe[50]

Indeed, intersectionality proponents in particular have been demonstrating quite powerfully how the debate on difference needs to be widened, deepened, and understood in its complexity, also with the objective of exposing inequalities and the wider collective struggle against right wing politics.

Observations may however also be made as they relate to equality discourses on other forms of difference as the former become instrumentalised by right wing formations. When examining data from a range of European States (Austria, Great Britain, The Netherlands, France, Germany, Hungary) and the US on the difference between right wing and left wing populism[51] in the dealing with Islamophobia and Antisemitism and other minority situations, it is referred to recurring features. These relate to explicit and indirect linguistic forms of exclusion used by right wing populist parties, emblematic being manifestations of '*othering*':

> all right-wing populist parties instrumentalise some kind of ethnic/religious/linguistic/political minority as a scapegoat for most if not all current woes and subsequently construe the respective group as dangerous and a threat 'to us', to 'our' nation; this phenomenon manifests itself as a 'politics of fear'; and all right-wing populist parties seem to endorse what can be recognised as the 'arrogance of ignorance'[52]

Further distinguishing features that may prove salient in view of the rightist endorsement of the equality paradigm include the embracement of an '*anti-pluralist*' stance or the "*appeal to a quasi-homogenous ethos as salient for such movements*", or relatedly "*serving the interests of an imagined homogenous people inside (...) a State*".[53]

---

[48] Ibid., p. 8.

[49] See, for instance, Atrey (2022).

[50] Dietze and Roth (2020), p. 10. See also: Roth (2020).

[51] See also: Dieckhoff et al. (2019).

[52] Wodak and Nugara (2017), p. 166. See also: Wodak (2015).

[53] Wodak and Nugara (2017), p. 166.

Other strategies originating from and attributable to the political right wing or conservative circles concern a certain (conscious) ignorance of persisting inequalities. The commonly used arguments associated with abstract liberalism concern, indeed, a critical engagement with critical race theory[54] and an ignorant attitude towards inequality-conscious language:

> Demonizing CRT and limiting the language associated with racial inequality severely takes away from the language, concepts, and words one can use to talk about race and history in a critical way. This illustrates how 'abstract liberalism' is tied to whites rejecting the idea that they have structural advantages over people of colour and marginalised groups (. . .) it [racial progress] misses the ways that racial inequality has been restructured through viewpoints, such as the ones, above that dismiss the presence of white supremacy today. This viewpoint sees racism as an attitude or ideology versus a structure that is sustained socially, politically, economically, and emotionally.[55]

Indeed, inequalities demonstrably persist at a structural level, facilitated by the difference-ignorant veil of equality, its mundane manifestations, and its usage by majorities interested in maintaining the status quo. Albeit relatedly, we could think of the equality discourse as a disguising strategy, showing ignorant of any root causes and contexts that prove foundational for minority positions in society:

> . . . that the narrative of (. . .) liberalism, as a political discourse of progress and equality, is a form of discourse control because it validates whites' position in society as earned and deserved rather than a product of these structural and material mechanisms of race thinking.[56]

Giving yet a different turn to the equality debate, equality may very well serve as a conscious strategy with deterring potential vis-à-vis unrecognised or minority positions, vesting the ruling majority with considerable legitimacy while absolving those in power from any duties towards both persisting minority positions, and any attempts to engage in transformative action.

---

[54] Critical Race Theory could be defined as follows "*intellectual and social movement and loosely organized framework of legal analysis based on the premise that race is not a natural, biologically grounded feature of physically distinct subgroups of human beings but a socially constructed (culturally invented) category that is used to oppress and exploit people of colour. Critical race theorists hold that racism is inherent in the law and legal institutions of the United States insofar as they function to create and maintain social, economic, and political inequalities between whites and nonwhites, especially African Americans. Critical race theorists are generally dedicated to applying their understanding of the institutional or structural nature of racism to the concrete (if distant) goal of eliminating all race-based and other unjust hierarchies.*" (see entry 'critical race theory: social sciences' in Encyclopaedia Britannica).

[55] Allen (2022), p. 98. See also: Harris (1993).

[56] Ibid., p. 98.

### 4.3.2 *Institutional Approval of the Diversity Deficit: How Equality Materialises in the Functioning and Daily Operating of the State*

Equality principles have certainly found their way into the institutional architecture of the State through specialised institutionalism, that is, dedicated equality bodies that have come to form part of the State's Ombudsman's Office or 'National Human Rights Institutes' or, alternatively, as independent mechanism operating on single or multiple equality grounds.[57] These developments have fallen on fruitful ground in European institutional landscapes, acting in sheer compliance with the EU Equality Directives[58] and, as a consequence, having resulted in institutional reform processes, the amalgamation of discriminatory grounds, or the establishment of entire new institutions.

As a cornerstone of a wide range of constitutional frameworks, equality has also occupied a more transversal position, permeating the State's daily functioning and operating on the ground. While generally benefiting from an approving attitude in the State's architecture, the principle of equality has sometimes been viewed as standing in opposition to federalism but also self-rule as autonomies come with different rules for each unit and the citizens of a State.[59] Accordingly, it has been hypothesised the nature of the State system very much qualifies equality approaches while demonstrating a certain proneness or otherwise negating attitude towards such principle:

> ...there is an important but largely unexplored theoretical and conceptual difference in the understanding of the principle of equality in federal and decentralised States which grant autonomy to regions and, on the other hand, unitary States which provide for homogenous rules applied uniformly throughout the country. Furthermore, there are challenges with regard to the protection of minorities on the federal level and the protection of minorities within minorities in autonomous regions.[60]

As it becomes very visible here, the principle of equality operates at different levels under the State's umbrella, revealing different degrees of institutionalisation of the autonomy question which may or may not include, even formalise, minorities' demands for collective self-determination. Leaving regional autonomies aside though, equality and its operationalisation assume an important space in such very arrangements, either decentralised or unitary States, carrying considerable implications for collective identities and ultimately rights to find further articulation (or not).

---

[57] Muir and de Witte (2017) and Belavusau and Henrard (2019).

[58] The 2000 Racial Equality Directive stipulates in its art.13 in that regard: "*Member States shall designate a body or bodies for the promotion of equal treatment of all persons without discrimination on the grounds of racial or ethnic origin. These bodies may form part of agencies charged at national level with the defence of human rights or the safeguard of individuals' rights.*"

[59] Belser and Zünd (2021).

[60] Ibid., p. 2.

As history shows, most States have been building on centralised top-down designs with the contemporary State "*structured around the idea of a shared homogeneous national identity (...) orchestrated top-down and enforced by assimilation policies*".[61] Similar arguments could be raised about the idea of equality principles introduced in such contexts; it could be argued that revolutionary movements at the time—emblematic being eighteenth/nineteenth century Europe—were primarily concerned with balance of power questions and putting an end to social status questions such as those separating the king, aristocracy and the common people while allowing for citizen participation.[62] Citizenship as a catch-all concept would be maintained until the current age, vesting the former with ever new rights, deemed a sheer necessity in the context of new technological or societal developments. Equality could hence be regarded as an important safeguard against the sovereign or any other external power threatening the existence of the individual and respective rights. Internal differences thereby easily escape the protective realm of the law, steered towards the individual whilst hostile towards any differentiated approach or group-specific rights. It may not come as a surprise that minorities in such position have considered statehood as an attractive solution to pursue which would allow these groups to benefit from other forms of equality, namely international guarantees of equality between States.[63]

Let us return to 'internal equality' for a moment, understood as those equality paradigms operating under the State's institutional umbrella. A concept that merits further consideration in that regard concerns so-called '*constitutional asymmetry*',[64] relating to power-sharing arrangements between the majority and minority group(s), mostly in federal contexts. In relation to the principle of equality, constitutional asymmetry strongly correlates with the former, albeit without clearly showing if and to what extent this would result in de facto equality from the perspective of minority groups. Instead, the principle of equality (in its de facto manifestation) takes several turns, revealing a complex attitude towards minority recognition as it was to be expected:

> ... constitutional asymmetry affects the principle of equality and can be seen – and often is seen – as a threat to the legitimacy and stability of a State. (...) Constitutional asymmetry (...) can have numerous and complex implications for the principle for equality. It can serve the principle of equality by allowing all nations, not just the majority group, to determine their fate autonomously and to have an equal say in the making of shared rule. Constitutional asymmetry can then help in implementing the principle of equality by equalising existing power relations and give all the nations a fair chance for effective self-governance and participation. At the same time, constitutional asymmetry can harm the principle of equality. Such is the case when it allows communities and regions, which enjoy a high level of bargaining power thanks to economic or political power, natural resources, military strength or support by neighbouring or kin nations, to negotiate rights and privileges other

[61] Belser (2021), p. 415.

[62] See, for instance, Montesquieu's work: Baron Montesquieu (1892).

[63] Belser (2021). See also: Kelsen (1944).

[64] Sahadžić (2021), p. 37.

> communities and regions do not have and cannot bargain for. Constitutional asymmetry then does not (only) compensate existing (cultural) inequalities on the ground, but has the potential to exacerbate (political, economic, and social) inequalities.[65]

Rather clearly then, a de facto perspective on equality is assumed, attributing important co-governance functions as well the capacity to exercise internal self-determination to minority groups. Interestingly, (de facto) equality is thereby pictured as a premise, possibly as standing hierarchically above '*constitutional asymmetry*'; it is to be operationalised through re-distributive processes with constitutional asymmetry playing a key part. What is more, equality is interpreted as serving the objective of establishing important self-governance functions and wider participatory rights for all minority groups, hence expanding upon the common practice of reserving rights for 'national minorities' only. Quite clearly then, equality is understood as giving rise to further reaching obligations, resembling those articulated as positive measures. Conversely, constitutional asymmetries are placed into the contentious context of differences materialising across minority contexts, that is, inequalities persisting among different minority groups. This proves particularly salient for unrecognised minority groups and those not benefiting from territorial or political autonomy arrangements. Again, the debate returns to probably the most sensitive political issue in minority matters, that of sovereignty and external self-determination which is often labelled as a secessionist endeavour, hence perceived as a threat to the State's integrity and basic sovereignty matters.

When concerning ourselves with the daily realities in which equality finds operationalisation, we necessarily need to engage more closely with the political structure of the State(s) examined, hence carrying implications for questions of implementation. Theory and practice differ, for instance, in the case of unitary States which guarantee equality to their citizens and redistribute resources without living up to these guarantees in practice.[66] Related dangers are attributable to centralist governments manifesting themselves in ethnic, linguistic and cultural discrimination—governments that are being perceived as guarantors of equality by their populations but in reality seem to favour a small partisan group.[67] A special focus of attention shall hence be placed on multicultural State designs here, promising considerable potential for discovering de facto equality at work. The constitutional reform process in Ethiopia, for instance, reveals how patterns of dominance exerted by one group vis-à-vis all other groups came to an end with the embracement of "*constitutional equality for all peoples, nations, and nationalities*".[68] Interestingly, Ethiopian constitutional practice has been prioritising collective rights over the individual's right to equal treatment which would, in turn, discriminate against members affiliated with non-dominant groups, materialising in the area of self-

---

[65] Belser (2021), p. 418. See also: Sahadžić (2021).

[66] Belser (2021).

[67] Steytler (2021).

[68] Belser (2021), p. 421. For further debates on the matter, see: Tesfaye Fessha (2021).

governance arrangements.[69] Constitutional practices have not proven effective in "*prevent[ing] minorities within minorities from suffering from the autonomy of the other people's right to self-determination*":[70] as a result, effective constitutional enforcement processes have been demanded to be put in place.[71] Equality between groups is similarly discussed, emblematically, in the case of multinational Bosnia and Herzegovina; one major shortcoming of the introduced equality of the three groups (Croats, Serbs, Bosniaks) included discriminatory effects this would have for other groups and their members.[72]

Interestingly, broader conclusions are drawn as to the proneness to equality principles as it varies across political systems: whereas unitary States are portrayed as prioritising unity over diversity, multinational federal systems are generally considered as compromise and consensus-seeking rather than following any majoritarian political reasoning.[73] Indeed, the principle of equality in its de jure manifestation may disguise difference, having become an important part to play in the daily operating of the unitary State. Responses may instead be sought among multinational federal designs as presented above, seeking de facto equality between different groups, resembling the idea of proper statehood. At the same time, considerable challenges become apparent in the process, including the situation where un-recognised minorities may not benefit from such arrangements or individual members—so-called minorities within minorities—may similarly be left out. We may hence preliminarily conclude that institutional approval of and structural arrangements around de facto equality do indeed represent a major premise for minority rights to be upheld in practice, yet miss to address the complexity inherent to and the breadth of collective rights that would need to be considered in that regard.

### *4.3.3 The Two-Way Construction of a Non-Discrimination Gap: Public Discourse and its Exploitative Use by the Right Wing*

Domestic politics in contemporary Europe may certainly be considered emblematic for what could be regarded as a right turn[74] and respective organisational

---

[69] Tesfaye Fessha (2021). See also scholarly debates on membership rights, customs and traditions, including rights and responsibilities attributed to the individual, such as: Gover (2011).

[70] Belser (2021), pp. 421–422.

[71] Ibid.

[72] Vanjek (2021).

[73] Ibid.

[74] Observer Editorial (2022) The Observer View on the Dangerous Rise of the Far Right in Europe. *The Guardian*. Retrieved from https://www.theguardian.com/commentisfree/2022/sep/18/observer-view-dangerous-rise-of-far-right-europe. Wodak et al. (2013).

developments,[75] by absorbing the societal disapproval of any difference-based paradigm by means of electoral vote—a form of human rights regression as far as difference is concerned. For good reasons, such developments have been captured by Wodak in the following: "*A spectre is haunting Europe, the spectre of radical right-wing populism*", alluding to what has been described as exponential increases in presence and influence of right-wing populist parties in Europe.[76] Relatedly, such developments have been described as a "*sudden upsurge of right-wing populism*" whose "*rise and success is certainly not a recent or momentary phenomenon*".[77] The origins are multiple, one of its main predecessors certainly being the fall of the Iron Curtain and respective socio-political transformations including migration movements which would "*provide right-wing political parties with opportunities of using anti-immigration and xenophobic rhetoric immediately after 1989*".[78] In fact, in the last two decades we have not only been witnessing right wing parties finding sufficient popular support to gain parliamentary seats as in the case of AfD in Germany, Vox in Spain, Partij voor de Vrijheid in the Netherlands or Rassemblement National in France, but also to find acceptance as coalition partners as in the recent cases of Northern League in Italy or as a de facto governing party in the case of the Sweden Democrats in Sweden. Relatedly, centre-right parties with tendencies to radicalise have become governing parties in some cases such as PiS in Poland and Fidesz in Hungary. Rather visibly, these political developments have been accompanied and actually driven by an anti-immigration spirit, a rejection of European multilateralism,[79] hostility towards progressive gender rights,[80] Islamophobic positioning,[81] Antisemitism, discrimination of Roma and other minorities, but also showing hostile towards any politics of difference generally.

The electoral victories as pictured above certainly speak for themselves in terms of the societal construction of a non-discrimination gap, a difference-ignorant positioning shared among considerable members of society. What is more, it could be argued that right wing ideology has more easily spread across society as data from Western Europe suggests: notably, the populist radical right has been "*remarkably successful setting the agenda of the public discourse*" from 2006 onwards.[82] Reasons for such success have been attributed to the public media principally, which have been described as decisive for electoral success, by attracting attention and setting agendas on the media, by provocation and scandalisation notably.[83] In other words, Wodak repeatedly argues this could be subsumed under the term '*right-wing*

[75] Ellinas (2020).

[76] Cossarini (2015), p. 951.

[77] Wodak, and Krzyżanowski (2017), p. 471.

[78] Ibid., p. 473.

[79] See, for instance, Beauzamy (2013).

[80] See, for instance, Caielli (2022).

[81] See, for instance, Kallis (2013) or also: Betz (2021).

[82] Karstens (2019), p. 46.

[83] Randeria and Wodak (2021). See also: Wodak (2015).

*populist perpetuum mobile*', referring to provocation and scandalisation, but also the launching of conspiracy theories and victimisation.[84] In a way, the media could be attributed a powerful intermediary role here, channelling right wing politics into the mundane spaces of society and public opinion. This form of mediatisation has demonstrably allowed populist agendas to spread more widely and for these to become 'normalised' both in European politics and the general public.[85] More specifically, alternative web spaces have been serving to "*spread exclusionary or outright discriminatory populist ideologies and imaginaries*".[86] Similar arguments may be made in relation to the steadily increasing pluralisation of online media allowing us to understand how "*political actors avoid both overt and implicit barriers to popularising extreme positions*".[87] Indeed, hate speech and related criminal content only gradually finds its way into legislation.[88]

If we were indeed to return to the object of the debate, that is, the positioning towards difference and equality, we may be attentive to right wing attempts in reconstructing history, a return to ethnonationalism, blood and soil ideology.[89] Building on previous narratives, we are witnessing a form of scapegoating, of accusing minorities, mostly Muslims, Muslim migrants, but also Roma and Jews in contemporary Europe.[90] A related strategy includes what has been termed a '*colonisation of liberal frames*' while attacking political correctness which becomes apparent where gender is misappropriated by the political right to, for instance, ascribe specific gender roles to religious minorities.[91] If we were now to delve deeper into the rationale constructed by the right wing in Europe as far as difference is concerned, we are firstly witnessing a form of difference-ignorant positioning building on homogeneity.[92] Another common rationale lies with the appeal to 'the people', the so-called '*argumentum ad populum*' in an overtly generalising way, hence proving ignorant of the complexity of society.[93] Paradoxically and tragically, such homogenising image is combined with processes of '*othering*'. This shines through, for instance, the security discourse demonising migration and a general "*rhetoric against the enemy, the ethically, culturally and religiously foreign*".[94] As it becomes apparent here, far from criticising the foundations of positive discrimination, right wing proponents in Europe seek an entirely different starting point,

[84] E.g. Wodak (2015).

[85] Wodak and Krzyżanowski (2017). See also: Wodak (2015).

[86] Wodak and Krzyżanowski (2017), p. 475.

[87] Littler and Feldman (2017), p. 510.

[88] See, for instance, Caielli (2022).

[89] Randeria and Wodak (2021).

[90] Ibid.

[91] Ibid.

[92] Ibid.

[93] Cossarini (2015).

[94] Ibid., p. 952.

commencing with the equality framework established in the late eighteenth century Europe.

Some attention may indeed be devoted to the functionality and impacts of discourses employed by right wing movements. It has been observed elsewhere that radical or even racist discourse has not only found its way into the public sphere, but has undergone normalisation by means of wider processes of "*strategically orchestrated discursive shifts*", by introducing extreme positions into the wider right-wing populist agenda, that way becoming normalised.[95] This may concern the discourses around 'the people', a constructed conception operating to exclude groups.[96] Indeed, a discursive perspective on exclusionary populism gives more insights on the matter: exclusionary populism, it is brought forward, refers to a "*fantasmatic transcendental signified (the nation, race, etc.)*".[97] In that sense, any groups not complying with such characteristics are left out of the process which may carry serious complications as to accessing rights or questions of inclusion generally. In other words, "*discursive units in extreme right discourse often function as naturalised, original (mythical) points of reference, as Derridean 'transcendental signifies' attempting to fix signification once and for all*".[98] As it easily becomes apparent here, plural society hardly finds a place under fixed, unitary terms while its fluidness across time is hardly taken account of. As we can easily imagine, minority positions can hardly expected to find due consideration, explicit recognition, under such frames, instead, processes of othering are explicitly envisaged by the right wing.

## References

Agha P (2017) Human rights between law and politics: the margin of appreciation in post-national contexts. Hart Publishing, Oxford

Akerø-Stueland KV (2021) The European Court of Human Rights, the margin of appreciation and European consensus: strengthening or diluting minority rights. LSE Law Review Blog. https://blog.lselawreview.com/2021/03/european-court-of-human-rights-the-margin-of-appreciation

Allen ER (2022) Inequality and liberal ideology: a critical discourse analysis of conservative white opposition to critical race theory in the United States. Transcience 13(1)

Arai-Takahashi Y (2013) The margin of appreciation doctrine: a theoretical analysis of Strasbourg's variable geometry. In: Føllesdal A, Peters B, Ulfstein G (eds) Constituting Europe: the European Court of Human Rights in a national, European and global context. Cambridge University Press, Cambridge

Atrey S (2022) Feminist constitutionalism: mapping a discourse in contestation. Int J Constitutional Law

Baron Montesquieu CLS (1892) Esprit des Lois. Hachette Livre, Paris

[95] Krzyżanowski (2020), p. 503.

[96] Rydgren (2017).

[97] Stavrakakis (2017), p. 530.

[98] Ibid., p. 530.

Beauzamy B (2013) Explaining the rise of the front national to electoral prominence: multi-faceted or contradictory models? In: Wodak R, Khosravi Nik M, Mral B (eds) Right-wing populism in Europe: politics and discourse. Hart Publishing, London
Belavusau U, Henrard K (2019) A bird's eye view on EU anti discrimination law: the impact of the 2000 equality directives. German Law J 20(5)
Belser EM (2021) Concluding remarks. In: Belser EM, Zünd L (eds) The principle of equality in diverse states: reconciling autonomy with equal rights and opportunities. Brill, Leiden
Belser EM, Zünd L (2021) Introduction. In: Belser EM, Zünd L (eds) The principle of equality in diverse states: reconciling autonomy with equal rights and opportunities. Brill, Leiden
Benvenisti E (1999) Margin of appreciation, consensus and universal standards. N Y U J Int Law Polit 31(843)
Betz H-G (2021) Mosques, Minarets, Burqas and Other Essential Threats: the Populist Right's Campaign against Islam in Western Europe. In: Wodak R, KhosraviNik M, Mral B (eds) Right-Wing Populism in Europe: Politics and Discourse. Hart Publishing, London
Born G, Morris D, Forrest S (2020) "A margin of appreciation": appreciating its irrelevance in international law. Harv Int Law J 61(1)
Brauch JA (2005) The margin of appreciation and the jurisprudence of the European Court of Human Rights: threat to the rule of law. Columbia J Eur Law (11)
Burgess A (1999) Critical reflections on the return of national minority rights to east/west European affairs. In: Cordell K (ed) Ethnicity and democratisation in the new Europe. Routledge, London
Caielli M (2022) Freedom of expression revisited: limiting free speech to stop silencing women and vulnerable minorities. In: Eichler J, Topidi K (eds) Minority recognition and the diversity deficit: comparative perspectives. Hart Publishing, Oxford
Cassese S (2021) Ruling from below: common constitutional traditions and their role. NYU Environ Law J 29
Catalano Weeks A, Allen P (2022) Backlash against "identity politics": far right success and mainstream party attention to identity groups. Politics, Groups, and Identities
Corntassel J, Witmer RC (2008) Forced federalism: contemporary challenges to indigenous nationhood. University of Oklahoma Press, Norman
Cossarini P (2015) Book review on right-wing populism in Europe: politics and discourse. Democratization 22(5)
Dieckhoff A, Jaffrelot C, Massicard E (2019) L'Enjeu Mondial. Populismes au Pouvoir. Presses de Sciences Po, Paris
Dietze G, Roth J (2020) Right-wing populism and gender: a preliminary cartography of an emergent field of research. In: Dietze G, Roth J (eds) Right-wing populism and gender: European perspectives and beyond. Transcript Verlag, Bielefeld
Eide A (2004) The rights of "old" versus "new" minorities. Eur Yearb Min Issues 2(3)
Ellinas AA (2020) Organising against democracy: the local organisational development of far right parties in Greece and Europe. Cambridge University Press, Cambridge
Fichera M, Pollicino O (2019) The dialectics between constitutional identity and common constitutional traditions: which language for cooperative constitutionalism in Europe? German Law J 20(8)
Fraser N (1998) Social justice in the age of identity politics: redistribution, recognition, participation. Wissenschaftszentrum Berlin für Sozialforschung Discussion Papers FS:98–103
Freeman M (1995) Are there collective human rights? Polit Stud XLIII
Garza A (2019) Identity politics: friend or foe? Othering & Belonging Institute, University of California. https://belonging.berkeley.edu/identity-politics-friend-or-foe
Gerards J (2017) The margin of appreciation doctrine, the very weighty reasons test and grounds of discrimination. In: Balboni M (ed) The European Convention on Human Rights and the principle of non-discrimination. Editoriale scientifica, Napoli
Gover K (2011) Tribal constitutionalism—states, tribes and the governance of membership. Oxford University Press, Oxford

Greer S (2000) The margin of appreciation: interpretation and discretion under the European Convention on Human Rights. Council of Europe Publishing, Human Rights files N°17
Gross O, Ní Aoláin F (2001) From discretion to scrutiny: revisiting the application of the margin of appreciation doctrine in the context of Article 15 of the European Convention on Human Rights. Hum Rights Q 23(625)
Grzebalska W, Pető A (2018) The gendered modus operandi of the illiberal transformation in Hungary and Poland. Women's Stud Int Forum 68
Gwiazda A (2021) Analysing the "what" and "when" of women's substantive representation: the role of right-wing populist party ideology. East Eur Polit 37(4)
Harris C (1993) Whiteness as property. Harv Law Rev 8
Henrard K (2011) Boosting positive action: the asymmetrical approach towards non-discrimination and special minority rights. ZaöRV 71
Herzog R, Gerken L (2008) Stop the European Court of Justice. EU Observer. https://euobserver.com/opinion/26714
Heyes C (2020) Identity politics. The Stanford encyclopedia of philosophy. https://plato.stanford.edu/entries/identity-politics/
Kallis A (2013) Breaking taboos and 'mainstreaming the extreme': the debates on restricting Islamic symbols in contemporary Europe. In: Wodak R, Khosravi Nik M, Mral B (eds) Right-wing populism in Europe: politics and discourse. Hart Publishing, London
Karstens F (2019) How public discourse affects attitudes towards freedom of movement and Schengen. Eur Union Polit 21(1)
Kelsen H (1944) The principle of sovereign equality of states as a basis for international organization. Yale Law J 53(2)
Kochenov D (2015) The European Union's troublesome minority protection: a bird's-eye view. In: Boulden J, Kymlicka W (eds) International approaches to governing ethnic diversity. Oxford University Press, Oxford
Kratochvíl J (2011) The inflation of the margin of appreciation by the European Court of Human Rights. Netherlands Q Hum Rights 29(3)
Krzyżanowski M (2020) Discursive shifts and the normalisation of racism: imaginaries of immigration, moral panics and the discourse of contemporary right-wing populism. Soc Semiot 30(4)
Kugelmann D (2007) The protection of minorities and indigenous peoples respecting cultural diversity. Max Planck Yearbook of United Nations Law, p 11
Kukathas C (2014) A definition of the state. Univ Queensland Law J 33(2)
Kymlicka W (1995) Multicultural citizenship: a liberal theory of minority rights. Oxford University Press, Oxford
Kymlicka W (2013) Multicultural odysseys: navigating the new international politics of diversity. Oxford University Press, Oxford
Letsas G (2006) Two concepts of the margin of appreciation. Oxf J Leg Stud 26(4)
Littler M, Feldman M (2017) Social media and the cordon sanitaire: populist politics, the online space, and a relationship that just isn't there. J Lang Polit 16(4)
Mähler A, Pierskalla JH (2015) Indigenous identity, natural resources, and contentious politics in Bolivia: a disaggregated conflict analysis, 2000-2011. Comp Pol Stud 48(3)
Mangiameli S (2013) The European Union and the identity of member states. L'Europe en Formation 3(369)
Márquez X (2011) Models of political community: the nation-state and other stories. In: Filibi I, Cornago N, Frosini JO (eds) Democracy with(out) nation? Old and new foundations for political communities in a changing world. Universidad del País Vasco, Bilbao
Medda-Windischer R (2009) Old and new minorities: reconciling diversity and cohesion; a human rights model for minority integration. Nomos, Baden-Baden
Medda-Windischer R, Boulter C, Malloy TH (2020) Extending Protection to Migrant Populations in Europe: Old and New Minorities. Routledge, London
Mill JS (1910) Considerations on representative government. Dent, London

Muir E, de Witte B (2017) The Procedural and Institutional Dimension of Anti-Discrimination Law. Rossi, Lucia Serena, and Casolari, Federico (eds.) The Principles of Equality in EU Law. Cham, Springer International Publishing
Randeria S, Wodak R (2021) Language and public discourse in the success of right-wing political movements. Podcast 'Democracy in Question'. https://softauthoritarianisms.uni-bremen.de/podcast/s3e2-language-and-public-discourse-in-the-success-of-right-wing-political-movements/
Rawls J (1999) The law of peoples. Harvard University Press, Boston
Roth J (2020) Intersectionality strikes back: right-wing patterns of en-gendering and feminist contestations in the Americas. In: Dietze G, Roth J (eds) Right-wing populism and gender: European perspectives and beyond. Transcript Verlag, Bielefeld
Rydgren J (2017) Radical right-wing parties in Europe: what's populism got to do with it? J Lang Polit 16(4)
Sahadžić M (2021) Constitutional asymmetry and equality in multinational systems with Federal arrangements. In: Belser EM, Zünd L (eds) The principle of equality in diverse states: reconciling autonomy with equal rights and opportunities. Brill, Leiden
Sakki I, Pettersson K (2016) Discursive constructions of otherness in populist radical right political blogs. Eur J Soc Psychol 46(2)
Salat L (2021) Political community and normative pluralism. In: Malloy TH, Salat L (eds) Non-territorial autonomy and decentralization: ethno-cultural diversity governance. Routledge, Abingdon
Schnapper D (1994) La Communauté des Citoyens. Sur l'Idée Moderne de Nation. Éditions Gallimard, Paris
Shachar A (2001) Multicultural jurisdictions: cultural differences and women's rights. Cambridge University Press, Cambridge
Stavrakakis Y (2017) Discourse theory in populism research: three challenges and a dilemma. J Lang Polit 16(4)
Steytler N (2021) Equality and advantage in emerging federations and the dilemma of non-renewable resources: the cases of the Solomon Islands and Trinidad and Tobago. In: Belser EM, Zünd L (eds) The principle of equality in diverse states: reconciling autonomy with equal rights and opportunities. Brill, Leiden
Taylor C (1992) Multiculturalism and the 'politics of recognition'. Princeton University Press, Princeton
Tesfaye Fessha Y (2021) In the name of diversity: the disenfranchisement of citizens in an African Federation. In: Belser EM, Zünd L (eds) The principle of equality in diverse states: reconciling autonomy with equal rights and opportunities. Brill, Leiden
Tomuschat C (2014) Human rights: between idealism and realism. Oxford University Press, Oxford
Tully J (2012) Strange multiplicity: constitutionalism in an age of diversity. Cambridge University Press, Cambridge
Vanjek D (2021) Federal equality in multinational Bosnia and Herzegovina. In: Belser EM, Zünd L (eds) The principle of equality in diverse states: reconciling autonomy with equal rights and opportunities. Brill, Leiden
Wodak R (2015) The politics of fear. What ring-wing populist discourses mean. Sage Publications, London
Wodak R, Krzyżanowski M (2017) Right-wing populism in Europe & USA: contesting politics & discourse beyond 'Orbanism' and 'Trumpism'. J Lang Polit 16(4)
Wodak R, Nugara S (2017) Right-wing populist parties endorse what can be recognised as the "arrogance of ignorance". Les Languages Du Politique, Mots, p 115
Wodak R, Khosravi Nik M, Mral B (2013) Right-wing populism in Europe: politics and discourse. Hart Publishing, London

# Chapter 5
# Principles of Recognition: Or How to Move Forward?

The present piece certainly adds to predominant political theoretical thought on what has generally been termed as '*politics of difference*', or alternatively, '*politics of recognition*' against the premise of a multicultural outlook of society and its institutional mirror. Its distinguished contribution however does not lie with a re-conceptualisation of difference, the majority-minority nexus or how these would be reflected in current institutional realities. Instead, political theoretical thought is supposed to undergo processes of translation that consider alternative legal models as valuable venues to respond to the lasting inequalities which, as it is argued here, find their beginnings, are being perpetuated or reinforced through the equality principle. In a sense, Kymlickan and beyond thinking is being spelt out further, living up to the collective claims minorities may be making beyond their somewhat isolated frameworks of rights. Different strategies and principles are presented here as a way to not only juridify difference-based thinking but to think in technical terms—an attempt to uncover the merit lying in alternative theoretical models that could potentially add to or eventually replace equality as an accepted, one-size-fits all approach permeating current constitutional thinking, European legal orders and beyond.

More precisely, four different theoretical attempts are made that shall find further articulation in the following, in other words, the following constituent elements shall serve as a theoretical basis for a potential reconceptualization, and in view of a paradigm that clearly departs from the persisting ad-hocism that finds political approval in constitutional, but also regional ius commune and international legal realities. This shall include a form of '*principlization*', a legal technical channel permitting pluralisms to be streamlined and formally codified throughout the multiplicity of legal orders. A second attempt is made with the '*proceduralisation*' of collective rights that may take the form of special(ised) participatory rights, allowing minorities' most vehement requests for autonomy and self-determination to be channelled into the protective realm of the law. Indeed, the importance of procedural law in establishing standing rights, as ways to ultimately vindicate rights, is an often neglected dimension throughout the debates on self-determination. Thirdly,

 
J. Eichler, *An Interdisciplinary Journey from Non-Discrimination to Collective Rights*, https://doi.org/10.1007/978-3-031-54618-1_5

difference-based thinking in legal terms shall be operationalised through '*speciali-sation*', within constitutional and other foundational orders, complementing rather than replacing those rights applicable to all by the very nature of their quality as human beings. Some progress has been achieved in the field of group-specific rights which find dedicated mentioning in international human rights law, often confronted with a certain unease at domestic levels. Finally, juridifying difference requires some structural rethinking, demanding a form of '*pluralisation*' of the legal conceptual space that, in its current state, clearly demonstrates a certain proneness towards the equality paradigm, its corollary, the non-discrimination principle, and their influential harmonising powers throughout (the) justice orders. We may understand such pluralisation both systematically, including the ambitious objective of questioning the majority-driven status quo beneficial to the equality principle, and also as far as internal differences are concerned, that is, by way of amplifying the conceptual scope of collective rights in their own regard.

## 5.1 Principlisation

Now, '*principlisation*' processes shall serve as a useful technical legal tool which would (potentially) allow pluralisms to be acknowledged and recognised, then formalised and codified, and eventually streamlined into the law, across the multiplicity of legal orders that is. At a very general level, human rights may be emblematic of such undertaking which becomes clearly visible in the EU legal order: ever since the *Stauder vs. City of Ulm* decision dating back to the late 1960s, fundamental rights are to be considered General Principles of EU law.[1] Another source of inspiration giving rise to these Principles lies with the constitutional traditions of the Member States as well as international human rights treaties, as established in *Nold vs. Commission* in 1974.[2] A similar status has been reserved for the European Convention on Human Rights and Fundamental Freedoms and recently, the EU Charta of Fundamental Rights.[3] As it easily becomes apparent here, the sources of these principles are multiple, to be traced back to domestic constitutional, regional and international orders.

As it may easily be assumed, the principle of equality has been gaining a key position both in domestic constitutionalism and the European Ius Commune.[4] Related developments would follow as far as non-discrimination is concerned in

[1]Eichler (2021).
for a comprehensive overview, see: Amalfitano (2018).

[2]Craig and de Búrca (2015).

[3]Bogdandy Armin von (2012).

[4]Muir and de Witte (2017).

EU law,[5] which has however proven limited in the field of minority rights.[6] Relevant questions in that regard also concern the scope of applicability of said principle; some accounts distinguish—in its application of the equality principle—between federal and decentralised States on the one hand and unitary States on the other.[7] It seems that the particular manifestation of '*principlization*' that is envisaged here creates a space of co-existence, not opting for one while excluding the other, but as reflecting a parallel existence of equality and positive discrimination:

> All States subscribe to the principle of equality, view equal rights and opportunities for all as a fundamental aspect of justice, and have committed to guaranteeing equal rights and freedoms to all without discrimination. At the same time, all States deal with diversity and most have adopted special regimes or autonomy arrangements for some regions or groups, such as islands, unpopulated territories, capitals, metropolitan areas, national minorities or indigenous groups.[8]

Interestingly, these last mentioned 'special regimes' or 'autonomy arrangements' appear to be treated in isolation from equality and respective principlization processes, again, understanding equality primarily in its de facto sense which, rather evidently, is to be distinguished from the much further reaching obligations attributable to group rights and collectivisation.

### 5.1.1 *General Principles and Principlisation*

The debate on principles of law as a welcome venue for recognition politics could be mirrored in the case of collective rights, constituting a promising method for introducing collective rights into dominant orders. Especially when making use of unwritten sources of law, general principles are considered key to protect human rights; what is more, these acquire an autonomous meaning and are to be understood as mandatory.[9] Again, EU law merits mentioning here, given the fact that the EU Charter of Fundamental Rights does not have direct application, hence creating certain dependencies on general principles.[10] Indeed, the general principles could at times be considered as the only source to protect fundamental rights in which cases resorting to the principles would be regarded as compulsory and would vest these with an autonomous meaning, indeed in relation to the Charter or other written

---

[5]Belavusau and Henrard (2018).

[6]Kochenov (2018).

[7]Belser and Zünd (2021).

[8]Ibid.; p. 2.

[9]Amalfitano (2018).

[10]As explained by Chiara Amalfitano, "*three different instances can be detected in which the general principle operates in a complementary and alternative way with respect to the Charter, namely: (i) when the latter is not (yet) applicable ratione temporis; (ii) when some of its provisions cannot be applied ratione personae; or (iii) when some of its provisions might not apply to certain Member States*" (p. 148).

sources of law.[11] Its origins may also be traced back to the general principles[12] of law established in art.38(1)(c) of the Statute of the International Court of Justice as they are to be applied by the Court. It may be noted here however that general principles as they find consideration in or are being established by domestic law (*foro domestico*) demonstrate an equivalent relevance to international courts or tribunals.[13] More precisely, general principles as they shine through existing case law are understood as being "*derived from commonly accepted domestic rules*".[14] To put this differently, the Court has been focussing itself on the degree of convergence on a specific issue among the different domestic judicial orders.[15] Seen from a more meta perspective, general principles have been portrayed as rather diverse given their nature and functioning.[16] Indeed, scholarly opinions on the matter differ to a great extent while some common trends may be observed in the field of human rights: these have demonstrably shown influential on the meta understanding of general principles with some having been "*accepted and recognised as binding, even peremptory, by the international community of States as a whole*".[17] In that sense, the present channel, that of '*principlisation*', presents a very effective method to introduce new developments and eventually codify these.

Let us explore in the following to what extent equality has entered the realm of general principles, hence disclosing potential to find broader acceptance through processes of '*principlisation*'. Again, the EU legal order may be illustrative here with equal treatment to be considered a general principle of EU law.[18] To be sure, general principles are to be considered a standard of review of EU measures; any measures adopted breaching the general principles are to be regarded as void.[19] From the outset, it must be stated EU law distinguishes between different categories of principles which come with different levels of enforceability, including guiding principles, existing principles, basic principles, uniform principles, fundamental principles, general principles and general principles; to be sure, the equality principle as also enshrined in the EU Charter of Fundamental Rights and it is to be regarded as

[11] Ibid.

[12] General Principles (of international law) include, inter-alia, "*the principle of good faith, the obligation to make reparation for international wrongs, the principle of res judicata, the principle of estoppel, the principle of jus novit curia, equality of the parties to a dispute, the rights of the defence, and respect for fundamental rights*" (p. 196) O'Boyle and Lafferty (2013).
see also: Dallier et al. (2009).

[13] Gaja (2020).

[14] O'Boyle and Lafferty (2013), p. 196.

[15] Ellis and Watson (2012).

[16] Ibid.

[17] Ibid.; p. 196.
see also Cassese (2012b).

[18] Belavusau and Henrard (2019).
see also: Prechal (2010).

[19] Ellis and Watson (2012).

an enforceable principle of Community law.[20] Relevant scholarly writings present the principle as one following the Aristotelian understanding of equal treatment which suggests that equal matters to be treated equally and different matters to be dealt with differently, qualified by the extent of the difference—representing a somewhat unambitious approach on the question.[21] If we were to follow this line of argumentation, it could be stated that differential treatment may not always be justified where equality demands equal treatment, however, it may also imply differential treatment where a person's special characteristics are to be considered.[22] As a matter of principle, the former approach will not be dealt with here, not only with the focus placed on indigenous and minority rights and their special characteristics, but also owing to the rationale that such violations may hardly ever be separated from the person and the general, long-term, and systemic situation of vulnerability he/she/x is in. Related tribute has been paid to equality and non-discrimination as principles: the Inter-American Court of Human Rights considers these principles to have gained *jus cogens* status and to confer erga omnes obligations binding upon all States.[23]

If we were to draw connections between collective rights and the debate on general principles, we are easily confronted with a conservative attitude on the part of law-makers. This concerns, above all, collective rights in their entirety to be granted some higher rank, and as a consequence, special protection being established. Noteworthy is certainly indigenous peoples' right to prior consultation which was declared a general principle of international law in the *Sarayaku vs. Ecuador* decision.[24] It is expected for such interpretation to be referred to by other relevant (international) mechanisms given the Court's prominent role in protecting indigenous rights,[25] and in that sense take a decisive role in standard-setting generally. Quite remarkably, such right has come with far-reaching consequences for indigenous land and resource rights, including the multiple impacts of (external) measures on indigenous livelihoods, integrity, health, food and water but also identity and religious practice. While this dates back to the early 1990s, it was maintained back then that collective rights such as those held by indigenous peoples

---

[20] von Bogdandy (2010).

[21] Belavusau and Henrard (2019).

[22] see e.g. Henrard (2007).

[23] O'Boyle and Lafferty (2013).

Inter-American Court of Human Rights (2003) Advisory Opinion on the Juridical Condition and Rights of Undocumented Migrants.

[24] See also: Brunner and Quintana (2012).

In view of the Court's interpretation that understands the obligation to consult as a general principle of international law, this implies such obligation applies irrespective of a State's ratification of relevant treaties, by holding that "*there is currently a clearly recognised right to consultation*" to be derived from the Court's and Commission's understanding of indigenous peoples' property rights which is to be situated in international instruments and the case-law of, for instance, constitutional courts (Brunner and Quintana 2012).

[25] Ibid.

would need to be considered in historical-legal terms rather than general human rights principles[26]—which, back then, were distinguished based on their exclusive focus on the individual, more than today. Indeed, it has been maintained elsewhere that the doctrinal debate on general principles has been focussing on the protection of the rights of the individual.[27] Some value certainly lies with the *lex specialis* nature of general principles, and in that sense complement other sources or even become immersed into written codes, gaining yet additional legal value.[28] Another collective right meriting attention here concerns the right to self-determination often discussed in indigenous contexts. As Cassese argues, by deeming self-determination a general principle, the latter should indeed be considered as part of the body of peremptory norms,[29] discussed earlier, hence assuming a particularly powerful and enforceable norm in international law and beyond. Somewhat resembling the debate on prior consultation, collective self-determination stands out due to its multidimensionality, its umbrella functions, essentially, with its meaning varying from political or territorial demands including State secession, but also extending to self-determined forms of cultural or economic development including, famously, alternatives to developments, or linguistic and educational manifestations. For that reason, States have proven unwilling to grant self-determination to indigenous peoples in its fullest sense, fearing possible conflicts with a State's integrity. Conversely, collective self-determination has become a particularly noteworthy right, given its underlying rationale that strives to decolonise ontological and epistemological common sense as it is defended in the Global North. In that sense, self-determination as a collective right demonstrates most convincingly the extent to which '*principlisation*' may serve as an effective procedural venue for collective rights to enter legal vocabulary, eventually entire State orders, and possibly the world of practice.

### *5.1.2 Peremptory Norms and Principlisation*

The processes of principlization discussed here may or may not build on or include peremptory norms such as the aforediscussed collective right to self-determination—it is yet to be discussed to what extent *jus cogens* norms in particular may fulfil the purpose of complementing the picture where written sources demonstrate bias towards equality. Our attention shall indeed be placed on hierarchies in the law: not uncommonly, domestic constitutionalism—and hence constitutionalisation processes[30]—constitute an important source of relevant principles, initiating as

[26] Sanders (1991).

[27] Groussot and Lindholm (2022).

[28] Shao (2021).

[29] Saul (2011).

[30] Klabbers et al. (2009).
Klabbers (2004).
De Wet and Vidmar (2012).

early as 1215 with the *Magna Carta* in the United Kingdom, to which '*habeas corpus*' is largely attributed.[31] Similar observations may be made in relation to the *Declaration des Droits de l'Homme et du Citoyen* proclaimed in 1789, finding resonance in the 1791 French Constitution and the 1776 *Declaration of Independence*, being mirrored in the *US American Bill of Rights* ratified in 1791. A noteworthy role is also assumed by the *Universal Declaration of Human Rights* and its influence on constitutionalism around the world; for good reasons the International Court of Justice referred to the provisions of the Declaration as "*relevant principles to be taken into account in its judgements*".[32] Despite their considerable impact, said codes need to be seen in the spirit of the time, that is, by curtailing totalitarian power or arbitrary rule, hence presenting a homogenising picture of a State's population and respective rights to be exercised. A certain diversity-proneness or pluralistic orientation requires *principlization* processes to be initiated beyond those classically envisaged by traditional human rights codes.

Peremptory (*jus cogens*) norms certainly represent an important point of departure for group-specific rights to enter into negotiation with the predominant legal order,[33] eventually to become part of the latter. This may concern the prohibition of racial discrimination, genocide, but even more so peoples' right to self-determination.[34] In fact, a fixed set of principles has been identified by Cassese including violations of a distinct collective nature, it could be argued, including the ban on genocide, forcible denial of self-determination, the acquisition of territory by force, or slavery.[35] Again—and the principle cannot be referred to enough—it has come to enjoy wide acceptance, being understood as a jus cogens rule falling under the definition of an international crime:

> *. . .a serious breach of an international obligation of essential importance for safeguarding the right of self-determination of peoples, such as that prohibiting the establishment or maintenance by force of colonial domination* (art.19(b), Draft Articles on State Responsibility)

In many ways, self-determination could be regarded as a principle vested with important umbrella functions, for channelling indigenous or minority demands into predominant orders. *Jus cogens* principles exemplify at its finest how recognition processes may become operationalised without the need for collective rights to fit into the constraining frame of legal codes—and, even more powerfully, for *jus*

---

[31] O'Boyle and Lafferty (2013).

[32] Ibid.; p. 220.

[33] For gaining a first overview, see the following works:
Lagerwall (2017).
Frowein (2013).
Tomuschat and Thouvenin (2006).

[34] *Legal Consequences of the Construction of a Wall in the Occupied Palestinian Territory (Advisory Opinion)*, International Court of Justice in 2004; *East Timor (Portugal vs. Australie)*, International Court of Justice in 1995.

[35] Cassese (2012a).

*cogens* obligations to depend on a possible higher status ascribed to other norms, with the former being inherently '*intransgressible*', or '*non-derogable'*.[36] Yet another opportunity for collective rights may be given by the very nature of *jus cogens*: in contrast to other legal sources, jus cogens is viewed as introducing values into the law; a form of moralisation of (international) law is taking place.[37] This may indeed enable collective norms such as self-determination to challenge legal positivism that demonstrably perpetuates the law's adherence to individual rights in its daily operating.

Alongside the collective right to self-determination we may think of the prohibition of genocide as a key jus cogens obligation in the collective sense.[38] Indeed, we may derive genocide from the individual right to physical and psychological integrity which is extended to a group, often persecuted on ethnic or cultural grounds. In these cases, violations are targeted against a specific group in particular, often with the outright intention to eliminate its members, hence resulting in mass atrocities, turning these crimes into probably the most cruel manifestations of a human rights violations. Indigenous contexts are to be considered particularly emblematic here, with intergenerational harm having become a common point of reference, permeating and accompanying many related violations. It may not come as a surprise then that genocide was placed before other international crimes such as crimes against humanity, war crimes or the crime of aggression in the Rome Statute of the International Criminal Court, and would include physical, biological and cultural forms of genocide according to the Convention on the Prevention and Punishment of the Crime of Genocide.[39] The question of definitional scope is particularly pertinent here as it has been maintained that the legal significance and the conceptual reach of genocide have been subjected to a minimalizing analysis in a way that has been contributing to the genocide of indigenous peoples.[40] Some progress may be reported here though: while first definitional attempts limited themselves to understanding genocide in its physical dimension whereas current accounts also regard physical and mental harm which has been broadened in the context of indigenous rights with Clavero referring to "*the perpetration of genocide by destroying or harming a group's cultural heritage*".[41] Challenges similarly arise in relation to the scope of application of the Genocide Convention which was not supposed to apply to the colonies; while indigenous peoples would remain protected by virtue of living within the State's borders, it is upon the State to decide if such peoples would

[36] Tomuschat (2006).

[37] Tavernier (2006).

[38] Cassese (2012a).

see also: *Armed Activities on the Territory of the Congo (Congo vs. Rwanda)*, International Court of Justice in 2006; *Application of the Convention on Genocide (Bosnia and Herzegovina vs. Serbia and Montenegro)*, International Court of Justice in 2007.

[39] see also: Eichler and Bacca (2020).

[40] Ibid.; see also: Schabas (2005).

[41] Clavero (2009), p. 2.

be considered as belonging to a specific territory.[42] Again, we are confronted with definitional questions to start with, relying on criteria seemingly established by the State, hence infringing upon indigenous self-identification and ultimately self-determination. Wherever such question is relegated to indigenous peoples themselves, the ban on genocide with its multidimensional impacts to be considered does constitute a considerable safeguard as a jus cogens norm, hence turning the latter into an impactful principle accommodating other human rights at stake.

A final debate worthy further thought concerns slavery, constituting a key inspiration for indigenous rights to have found their way into the ILO framework, emblematic being the early Recruiting of Indigenous Workers Convention N°50 (1936).[43] In any case, slavery assumes a strong group character, targeting specific groups which are subjected to inhumane conditions, including while not limited to undignified working conditions. Oftentimes and especially in contemporary contexts, slavery or slavery-like conditions take the form of a specific racialised conduct. In the case of indigenous peoples, we can easily relate slavery-like conditions to the colonial context, patterns of subjugation, modern forms of debt-bondage or other inter-group dynamics revealing master-peon relations.[44] The violations described prove particularly impactful on affected groups, causing intergenerational trauma including a collective sense of inferiority and subconsciousness that hardly vanishes with a few years or a judicial process in favour of the victims. As it becomes apparent in this context, protection against slavery allows for a multiplicity of safeguards to be put in place, in the short and long term, that may become invokable and find recognition through processes of *principlisation*. Especially the slavery context gives rise to a number of interrelated *jus cogens* violations at individual and group level, being interwoven with human dignity. The absolute prohibition thereof hence operates as a safeguard against multiple collective rights violations which may concern indigenous peoples or (other) ethnic minorities. Wherever hard law on the matter is yet to be put in place, *principlisation* may serve as a useful tool to introduce respective safeguard sporadically, albeit not less powerfully, given the significance of *jus cogens* norms.

---

[42] Eichler and Bacca (2020).

see also: United Nations Permanent Forum on Indigenous Issues (2011) Study on International Criminal Law and the Judicial Defense of Indigenous Peoples' Rights.

[43] Two of ILO's eleven fundamental instruments may be relevant here, including the Abolition of Forced Labour Convention N°105 (1957) and the Discrimination (Employment and Occupation) Convention N°111 (1958), but also other relevant conventions such as the Violence and Harassment Convention N°190 (2019); the Recruiting of Indigenous Workers Convention N°50 (1936); the Contracts of Employment (Indigenous Workers) Convention N°86 (1947); the Abolition of Penal Sanctions (Indigenous Workers) Convention N°104 (1955).

[44] see e.g. Inter-American Commission on Human Rights (2009) *Captive Communities: Situation of the Guaraní Indigenous People and Contemporary Forms of Slavery in the Bolivian Chaco.*

### 5.1.3 Founding Principles and Other Systemic Routes as a Way to Principlise

Principles may however also take a more systemic route, namely by laying the grounds for a legal order. Indeed, so-called '*founding principles*'[45] may be emblematic given their shaping potential vis-à-vis entire legal orders: in fact, it has been maintained in the EU context that the constitutional character of EU primary law would find its clearest articulation in the founding principles.[46] The EU context indeed represents an interesting thought experiment here with its founding principles that are "*rooted in the tradition of European constitutionalism, but at the same time should do justice to the specifics of the Union and thus concretise the sui generis character of the Union*".[47] Such amalgamation of sources represents a common phenomenon, resembling our earlier debate on general principles[48] and their roots traceable to both domestic and international law. This particularity becomes relevant if we engaged more closely with the sources of inspiration of legal principles—a key consideration in view of the redefinition of recognition: by their very nature, these principles may show open enough for accommodating grassroots demands including alternative justice models such as customary law, hence providing fruitful ground for indigenous law or minority customary practice to find general acceptance through processes of '*principlization*'. Principles in particular may prove sufficiently broad in scope in order for the rich blend of indigenous customary law, organic community laws, other codes but also entire paradigms such as Good Living (*Buen Vivir/Vivir Bien*) to be translated into the State-centric realm of the predominant legal order. Especially the inherent diversity of indigenous laws requires enough room for development which, in principle, is provided by legal principles, proving more open and flexible by their very nature than rigid, detailed codes. In theory, processes of *principlization* establish an important bottom-up-directed space of articulation, allowing not only complex legal systems to eventually be recognised, but for rights holder groups to take an active part in the construction or reform of the predominant legal and institutional framework.

Understanding the founding principles of a given order as bearing transformative potential may however prove to be an illusion. As advanced earlier, equality principles enjoy wide recognition, not least owing to their embedment in the constitutional order and hence being vested with higher status. In that sense, any principlising endeavour will necessarily come with certain systemic challenges, that is, resistance on the part of majority approved principles and rights. What is more, equality-prone principles are enshrined in early human rights documents. Illustrative

[45]These have been discussed more extensively in the context of the regional *ius commune*: Yihdego (2011).
von Bogdandy (2012).

[46]von Bogdandy (2012).

[47]Ibid.; p. 12.

[48]O'Boyle and Lafferty (2013).

may be the case of Declaration of Independence of 1776 whose founding principles were interpreted by Lincoln as promoting "*liberty and ultimate emancipation*".[49] Interestingly, he was reproached for magic tricks as he would "*make people think that he's the one fighting for the Declaration and the Founder's Constitution, when in fact he's against them*".[50] In turn, Lincoln's public campaign against slavery was presented as a "*massive fraud on the public*", namely by "*transforming the nation's Founding document from one that was irrelevant to slavery, compatible with slavery, and even affirmed the right of 'insiders' to enslave 'outsiders', into one that proclaimed universal human freedom – as if the words 'all men are created equal' and 'are endowed by their Creator' with the rights to 'Life, Liberty and the pursuit of Happiness' actually meant that all human beings had a right to be free*".[51] Far from establishing any collective rights, these founding principles did remind politicians in times of slavery and other cruel human rights violations to return to these basic safeguards that explicitly and necessarily had to be applied to ethnic minorities.

If we return to the legal theoretical debate on the meaning of principles, our attention necessarily rests on its abstract conception rather than its concrete terms for principles to be applied.[52] By their very nature then, (funding) principles lend themselves particularly well for accommodating entire alternative justice ideas or any other basic justice paradigms to find recognition in the predominant order. Another purpose commonly ascribed to legal principles concerns their systematising potential vis-à-vis legal norms.[53] In that sense, principles may actually serve to not only introducing new justice ideas but to provide for necessary methodological potential in mainstreaming these and vesting these with articulating powers to find alignment in preexisting orders. Indeed, the positioning in existing orders is key to appreciate the meaning of founding principles and, at the same time, their potential in channelling alternative justice orders into State law. Such potential becomes particularly visible in a decision delivered by the Supreme Court of Canada which refers to the constitution as "*embrac[ing] the entire global system of rules and principles which govern the exercise of constitutional authority... It is necessary to make a more profound investigation of the underlying principles animating the whole of the Constitution.... Those principles must inform our overall appreciation of the constitutional rights and obligations*".[54] Importantly, founding principles are attributed a holistic value, serving as a general orientation and thereby also assuming relevant shaping powers, possibly ideological orientation, guiding entire constitutional frameworks. And, as it becomes apparent here, these principles are also to

---

[49] Bessette (2023), p. 287.

[50] Ibid.; p. 287.

[51] Ibid.; p. 288.

[52] Wolfrum (2010).

[53] Ibid.

[54] Ibid.; para.12.

*Reference re Secession of Quebec*, Supreme Court of Canada in 1998.

orient constitutional rights and their interpretation. The exact phrasing of equality provisions thereby necessarily assumes a wider significance, being detrimental to the particularities of the law.

It is important to understand constitutionalism in a wide sense, not being limited to the domestic realm but in the way it establishes a general, overarching, foundational and hierarchically superior while constituent order. To put this differently, we may understand these as 'underlying principles' of a given legal code or other principles such as self-determination that may give rise to specific obligations not necessarily enshrined in the law.[55] This will, of course, raise questions as to the applicability of such principles, especially wherever these are not spelt out in treaties and would base themselves on bilaterally or multilaterally agreed norms. Similar to the case of *jus cogens* norms however, founding principles may, by contrast, establish obligations with an *erga omnes* effect, that is, to be applicable towards everybody. The very constitutional or foundational nature of the norms in question would in fact suggest this. Indeed, the nature and functionality of principles may differ to great extents, which may allude to their embedment into a specific norm or, more overarchingly, in the sense that these would be "*inherent or underlying a particular legal system*".[56] For the purpose of the present work, *principlisation* shall not be limited to one or the other, instead, it is referred to the transformative effect of principles, as to its potential in altering majority-minority relations. Examples are manifold with principles finding their way into specific non-discrimination and equality provisions, or as they may define the political ideological nature of an entire constitutional order. Principlisation shall open the door for any form of shift with the prospect of introducing collective rights (at best), either taking the rather technical route of provisions, or/and by altering the overall orientation of predominant ((quasi)constitutional) orders.

It may indeed be worthwhile to revisit the debate on founding principles in the EU legal order, as a particularly illustrative case of constitutionalism beyond the domestic realm. Ever since the Lisbon Treaty was adopted, we may speak of a quasi-constitutional framework, which inevitably includes a set of founding principles to orient the entire order. Elsewhere is has been argued that the constitutional character ascribed to EU treaty law becomes particularly apparent in the founding principles.[57] To put this differently, the doctrine of principles is to be considered not only a passive witness of the process of constitutionalism, but instead to be regarded as part of such process.[58] Somewhat relatedly, the European unification process at large is being oriented by a couple of guiding principles, that is, '*reconciliation*', '*effective solidarity*', '*subsidiarity*', and '*supra-nationality*'.[59] If interpreted literally, supranationality, for instance, may bear considerable potential in alienating itself from

[55] Wolfrum (2010).

[56] Ibid.; p. 20.

[57] von Bogdandy (2010).

[58] Ibid.

[59] Krijtenburg (2018).

domestic sovereignty questions, potentially being more prone towards minority matters. Subsidiarity too may not only allow for powers to be delegated to regional administrative levels, it may also permit regional minorities to exercise autonomy.[60] Even more visibly, the founding principles find expression in EU primary law, art.2 (the homogeneity clause) in particular, including human dignity, freedom, democracy, equality, the rule of law, human rights and the rights of persons belonging to minorities. Again, given the focus of the present work, we shall focus on equality which, interestingly, assumes two distinct meanings, firstly, as a principle that prescribes equal treatment of European citizens in a formal and substantive sense as a constitutional right, and secondly, as an organising principle of the EU, regulating relations between sovereign Member States, attributable to federal theory but also international law doctrine.[61] Particularly noteworthy may be the minority rights doctrine here though. From the outset, it needs to be stated that recognition of minority rights as such is to be found in the EU's accession criteria; EU anti-discrimination law such as the 2000 Anti-Racism Directive establishes a broader measure of protection such as—while far-reachingly—positive discrimination which is not to be considered as breaching the principle of equal treatment.[62] A 'structural principle' having become recognised in the field of minority rights concerns the respect towards the ethnic, cultural, linguistic and religious identity of members belonging to a minority group as well as "*creat[ing] appropriate conditions enabling them to express, preserve and develop this identity*".[63] Indeed, identity-related group rights might provide for ample of space for other rights to become articulated, broadly fitting with proper customs and procedures for which identity serves as an umbrella, and also with the overall purpose of *principlisation*.

## 5.2 Proceduralisation

Yet a different important channel established by the law lies in proceduralization processes. Operating as so-called '*umbrella rights*', procedural rights have commonly facilitated the exercise of substantive rights, emblematic being decision-making rights or those permitting to access justice. The case of free, prior and informed consultation and consent has often been referred to in such context,[64] allowing indigenous peoples to invoke, inter-alia, basic subsistence rights, cultural

[60] see, for instance, Calvès (2010).

[61] Mangiameli (2013).

[62] Ibid.

[63] Ibid.; p. 134.

[64] Wright and Tomaselli (2019).
Doyle (2015).
Rodríguez-Garavito (2011).
Fontana and Grugel (2016).
Szablowski (2010).

rights or health-related rights. Similarly, the right to a healthy environment has come to be understood in procedural terms, establishing the right to accessing justice, to information and participation.[65] While procedural rights represent a rather common form of invoking rights, actually constituting human rights on their own regard, these prove quite critical seen from the perspective of indigenous peoples and minorities. For good reasons, it is commonly referred to indigenous proper customs, laws, procedures and practices that are to be paid due regard to when establishing or implementing procedural rights. These certainly represent a form of hybrid format where State law co-exists with vernacular—as in indigenous or minority practices—laws and justice orders.

Indigenous and other procedural rights might however also be granted where these concern procedural rights as they are attributable to or emanate from collective justice orders which may include proper decision-making processes, mandate-holdership or other questions of representation or language issues to be considered throughout justice processes. *Proceduralisation* thereby represents a unique tool to translate these collective expressions, even rights, into the predominant legal framework and also to establish respective channels for (collective) substantive rights to become effective ultimately. It is indeed the procedural, whilst powerful, dimension that is commonly not paid enough attention to with the exception of dedicated procedural rights such as those to access justice or due process rights. Ultimately, when examining the underlying rationale of procedural rights, we are commonly confronted with unequal power relations that these might actually ignore when taken in the most formal sense:[66] in other words, the right to information, for instance, is to consider language-related aspects, expert knowledge and related inequalities which are to be addressed when granting procedural rights.

### 5.2.1 Proceduralisation and its Derivative Functions

The derivative, facilitating nature attributable to procedural rights has been described elsewhere, maintaining that

> procedural rights (. . .) are normatively defensible only by reference to a complete elaboration of the substantive rights at stake when such procedural rights are invoked.[67]

We easily identify a corollary, conditional character of procedural rights here which, however, in no way diminishes the inherent power of these rights in terms of human rights protection. The significance of procedural rights in relation to substantive rights has attracted attention under the review procedures of the European Court of

---

[65] see, for instance, Aguilera Bravo (2023).

See also: Regional Agreement on Access to Information, Public Participation and Access to Justice in Environmental Matters in Latin America and the Caribbean (Escazú Agreement).

[66] See, for instance, Rodríguez-Garavito (2011).

[67] Alexander (1998), p. 19.

Human Rights,[68] also known as 'procedural turn' which relates to two distinct manifestations:

> ...the first is the procedural rights approach whereby explicit procedural requirements are increasingly interpreted into different Convention provisions. Thus, they become part of the protective scope of the right in question alongside issues relating to the substance of the relevant right. (...) The second form of the procedural turn, however, is that which can be referred to as procedural review stricto sensu. Here, the focus is not on if and how procedural elements are made explicit as part of the protective scope of Convention rights, but on their significance among the balance of reasons when the Court pronounces on the substantive merits and assesses the proportionality or reasonableness of a measure.[69]

We shall concern ourselves with the former manifestation that discloses a certain rapprochement between both categories of rights, for procedural rights to be introduced into the substantive rights context and, importantly, assuming essential safeguarding functions. At an even broader (as in meta) level, proceduralization has been classified as follows:

> In its broadest sense, and from a systemic perspective, the proceduralisation of law refers to the establishment of procedures designed to enhance the quality of the legal system. In the narrower sense, and form a more contentious perspective, the proceduralisation of a right refers to the establishment of procedural mechanisms to improve the enforcement of that right. It has a narrower scope and aims at enabling the realisation of a right. From this second meaning, proceduralisation denotes a process intended to reinforce the protection of a substantive right guaranteed in international human rights law.[70]

As it becomes apparent from the above, procedural rights may very well be understood as an ordinary manifestation of a well-functioning rule of law order and basic judicial guarantees, but also provide technical detail in terms of the extent to which a right becomes accessible, enforceable.

It may also be asked to what extent procedural rights could be considered as assuming an independent status or not, or, alternatively, could be understood as substantive rights:[71] in any case, certain dependencies may be found, or, reaching further, procedural rights may be derived from substantive rights. Their specific role has thereby been defined as "*securing our substantive rights and thus minimizing the risks thereto*",[72] in a way operating as an additional safeguard. Also elsewhere it is being maintained that substantive rights are rendered effective by virtue of procedural rights.[73] Others may argue basic human rights including due process guarantees "*do not derive from antecedent moral procedural rights*" as "*absent special circumstances, there are no preinstitutional procedural rights, not even a right*

[68] See also generally: Panagoulias (2011).

[69] Mjöll Arnardóttir (2017), p. 14.
See also: Brems (2013).

[70] Amani Cirimwami (2020), p. 3.
See also: Dubout (2007).

[71] Alexander (1998).

[72] Ibid.; p. 19.

[73] Uzelac and van Rhee (2017).

*against being punished without first being found guilty by a fair and reliable process*" as it is argued States build on a different rationale for their citizens not to be (over)punished or the like.[74] Others have viewed this perspective critically, arguing in favour of "*a class of general, moral, judicial, procedural rights*" as these would (co-)constitute a considerable part of the rule of law and make sense of the specific form punitive institutions take.[75] Similarly, it has been held that "*easily accessible, fair, short and effective judicial procedures*" are key to the rule of law without which rights cannot be enforced.[76] Along similar lines, by following Waldron, it is alluded to the quasi-independent nature of procedural rights, hence far from establishing any derivative relation vis-à-vis substantive rights by stating that "*when we disagree about each others' moral rights and duties, and we must decide what those rights and duties are, we have no choice but to recognise that each of us has a right to participate in the decision*".[77] An interesting case to be studied further concerns the granting of participatory rights in the derivative sense, indeed often becoming apparent where procedural rights are at stake.[78] As a general remark, we may refer to the value of procedural rights against the background of democratic backsliding; procedural rights thereby provide for "*concrete protection for ordinary people*".[79] Relatedly, it has been observed that a couple of contemporary developments are not favourable to procedural rights, including the economic crisis and a gradually increasing level of emergency cases; in the former case, austerity would lead to resource constraints affecting judicial resources, in the latter case, armed conflicts would result in a shift in the hierarchy of values with human rights being subordinated to other political agendas.[80]

Again, arguments as to the overall effectiveness of human rights may be raised, which may also concern rights spelt out in a collective sense, as it happened to be the case before the IACtHR which interpreted participatory rights widely, giving rise to the right to prior consultation and consent. Indeed, progressive developments in the field of indigenous rights have been assuming a strong procedural dimension under the IACtHR, mingling land and territorial rights with participatory rights and their procedural particularities which became most pronounced in the jurisprudence of the Inter-American Court and Commission. The right to prior consultation and consent would be considered emblematic in that regard,[81] with its multivariate implications

---

[74] Health Wellman (2014), p. 306.

[75] Adams (2019), p. 3.

[76] Barkhuysen and van Emmerik (2023), p. 282.

[77] Alexander (1998), p. 41.

[78] Altwicker (2011).

See the following decisions in particular: *National Union of Belgian Police*, European Court of Human Rights in 1975; *Relating to certain aspects of the laws on the use of languages in education in Belgium*, European Court of Human Rights in 1968.

[79] See also: Uzelac and van Rhee (2017), p. 4.

[80] Ibid.

[81] See, for instance, James Anaya's work on the matter, for consultation and consent to be understood as procedural rights in the first place.

for the exercise of other rights such as cultural identity, health, environmental rights, or basic subsistence rights. It may be argued that procedural rights in the participatory sense could be regarded as a particularly essential safeguard as they relate to collective rights, since they provenly extend classical participatory rights to do justice to communal decision-making structures, mandate-holdership or party formation.

### 5.2.2 Proceduralization as a Channel for Recognition (of Novel Rights)

*Proceduralization* has indeed come to be understood as unleashing considerable supplementing potential, vesting the court with powers that ultimately "*secure minimum safeguards in complex or highly contested situations where it would otherwise hesitate to engage too actively*".[82] Similar arguments may be raised in relation to substantive collective rights and their dependencies on respective venues; procedural rights may constitute the only viable channel for group-specific rights to find realisation, and hence guarantee indigenous and minority standards, even from a minimalistic standpoint. Also elsewhere, *proceduralization* is denoted as a process that amplifies (substantive) obligations, it is stated that

> the proceduralization of substantive rights, as an offshoot of judicial activism, seeks to ensure the concretisation of rights by both widening the scope of obligations and strengthening the requirement for their protection (. . .) Proceduralization is an interpretative tool arising from judicial activism. It makes human rights protection more effective and reinforces procedural values.[83]

Other than *principlization* processes, *proceduralization* clearly builds on regulatory detail, in other words, specific legal parameters and a further spelling out of obligations.[84] What is more, *proceduralization* has been subject to interpretative exercise, with new challenges arising in that regard, resembling the emergence of entire new legal rules.[85] In that sense, the broad scope could prove sufficiently flexible for accommodating those rights hitherto unrecognised. A further widening of obligations could very well imply a (further) strengthening of collective rights, both in terms of standing—the collective wielding of rights—and substantially, as in land or language rights.

Particular insights may be gained from the field of procedural environmental rights, as an emerging field of international law with its multivariate implications from a procedural point of view. First attempts of bringing together human rights and

---

[82] Mjöll Arnardóttir (2017), p. 14.
See also: Brems and Lavrysen (2013).

[83] Amani Cirimwami (2020), pp. 1, 14.

[84] Ollino (2022).

[85] Ibid.

environmental protection were made in the early 1970s, notably the right to a safe and healthy environment; amongst those rights that would qualify the enjoyment of effective environmental protection, procedural rights stand out, notably those to "*access environmental information, public participation in decision making, and access to justice and remedies in the event of environmental harm*".[86] This was also confirmed institutionally, in Principle X of the Rio Declaration on Environment and Development of 1992, taking an evident procedural turn, which declared environmental issues to be addressed with the participation of affected citizens at respective levels.[87] Another noteworthy development not to be missed concerns the adoption of the *Convention on Access to Information, Public Participation in Decision Making, and Access to Justice in Environmental Matters (Aarhus Convention*) with its emphasis on duties towards the people(s) and NGOs, also to be considered "*a driving force for environmental democracy in Europe and at the forefront of developing the legal framework in this respect worldwide*".[88] Participation may be further spelt out by taking the form of consultation and free, prior and informed consent (FPIC) which is more specifically regulated in the field of indigenous rights where the principle enjoys particular legal recognition. A final noteworthy attempt to codify procedural environmental rights was made with the Paris Agreement on Climate Change.

Now, procedural environmental rights are not only seen as methods to foster participatory democracy but also as "*effective instrument of monitoring compliance with – and enforcement of – environmental law*".[89] More functionalities need to be presented in that context, with Principle X principally representing an "*international benchmark against which the compatibility of national standards could be compared and as a forecast of the creation of new procedural rights which could be granted to individuals through international law and exercised at the national and possibly international level*".[90] Indeed, the principle contributes to standard-setting in the field of procedural environmental rights, also by way of codifying ground-setting procedural rules. Some critical voices lament that human rights hardly find expression in the field; in fact, procedural environmental rights could be seen as a way to strengthen the human rights-based approach in the field of environmental rights.[91] This may become manifest by relating on the one hand the "*importance of public access to environmental information*" and on the other "*the recognition of a*

[86] Anton and Shelton (2012), p. 356.
See also: Kiss (1976).

[87] Anton and Shelton (2012).
On public participation in environmental matters see also *Aarhus Convention (Convention on Access to Information, Public Participation in Decision Making, and Access to Justice in Environmental Matters, Aarhus).*

[88] Jendrośka (2017), p. xviii.

[89] Ibid.; p. xvii.

[90] Ibid.; p. xvii.
See also: Sands and Peel (2018).

[91] Misonne (2017).

*subjective right to such access to information*", thereby for environmental rights to assume a human rights dimension.[92] When turning to the more theoretical level of the present debate, it is stated that procedural dimensions have been facilitating the recognition or affirmation of substantive rights, and have been not only triggering but also enabled the public to follow-up of environmental matters.[93] The right in question, that is, the right of access to information has also been conceived as a condition for the enjoyment of other procedural rights, notably public participation and accessing justice.[94] If we now turn to the right to access justice indeed, standing rights have proven to be most contentious with determining who could actually seek judicial review, often curtailed by a constrained view limiting itself to those directed affected.[95] Indeed, a particularly strict application of standing may prove constraining in terms of accessing justice, especially as far as public interest litigation is concerned.[96] In that sense, standing should not be employed to avoid or sidetrack from uncomfortable global question which may be of concern to everybody in this world.[97] And as a corollary, a wide range of relevant substantive environmental human rights claims could be translated into the justice order, eventually.

### *5.2.3 Procedural (Re-)Inventions in Regional Human Rights Orders*

Another procedural development worth mentioning concerns the '*procedural turn*'[98] in EU law as it relates to anti-discrimination law: as discussed earlier, the turn relates to the reversal of the burden of proof in favour of the victim and an amalgamation of equality bodies in several EU States,[99] hence facilitating the dealing with intersectional forms of discrimination. At the same time, such institutionalisation has manifestly led to a general approval of specific discrimination grounds which, in a second step, could result in a reinvention of the recognition paradigm towards a firmer commitment to positive discrimination. Also classically speaking, the Lisbon Treaty framework has been contributing to enhanced legal protection in the field of procedural rights; this includes the new human rights order

---

[92] Ibid.; p. 478.

[93] Ibid.

[94] Ibid.

[95] Varvaštian (2017).

[96] Ibid.

[97] Ibid.

[98] Muir and de Witte (2017).
See also: Belavusau and Henrard (2019).

[99] Muir and de Witte (2017).

established with the EU Charter of Fundamental Rights[100] which explicitly foresees the establishment of effective remedies and right to a fair trial, guarantees for criminal proceedings, basic procedural requirements such as impartial, fair and timely treatment, but also the right to be heard generally (arts.41, 47, 48). The Lisbon framework would only systematically codify these basic procedural guarantees, much had been developed in the CJEU's jurisprudence, for instance, through processes of *principlisation*.[101]

In the Council of Europe order, *proceduralization* has similarly taken a technical route, dealing with classical procedural guarantees such as due process rights, possibly given the necessity of dealing with procedural rights if we were to understand human rights protection as a holistic exercise. In a creative attempt, the ECtHR would derive the right to access to a court despite any lacking legal basis, notably art.6's silence on the matter: in the *Golder* decision, the Court notably referred to fair, public and expeditious proceedings which lacked any meaningfulness if respective judicial proceedings did not exist.[102] It continued, the right to access to a court needed to be effective, requiring respective steps to be taken[103]—these would necessarily assume a procedural dimension. Respective safeguards are, almost evidently, not limited to the basic right to accessing a court, but similarly embrace accessing an independent and impartial court or tribunal, a fair and public hearing within reasonable time, special procedural requirements in the context of criminal charges, or effective legal protection including effective remedy.[104]

Further observations may be made on pan-African jurisprudence, notably through proceduralization the African Court on Human and Peoples' Rights has been enabled to refer back to substantive rights,[105] again in the sense of providing further strength to these latter rights. Its proper approach on procedural rights is traceable throughout the African Charter, and secondly, due to its consideration of domestic proceedings in its decisions.[106] References to collective rights or peoples' rights—constituting key categories of its normative framework—have hitherto remained absent from the proceduralization debate, without however categorically denying the existence of procedural norms as relevant to group-specific rights.

A final view shall be shed on relevant developments in the Inter-American human rights system. Just as argued in different contexts presented earlier, the Inter-American order expects procedures to be clear and transparent, also in view of the individual petitions, as part of judicial protections as stipulated in art.25 of the American Convention on Human Rights, and to eventually serve the final objective,

[100] Barkhuysen and van Emmerik (2023).

[101] Ibid.

[102] Ibid.

[103] Ibid.

[104] Ibid.

[105] Amani Cirimwami (2020).

[106] Ibid.

that of protecting and guaranteeing human rights.[107] Indeed, Inter-American bodies refer to ordinary procedural guarantees established also elsewhere, including legal certainty which is translated to a trustworthy environment and due process conditions.[108] Similar to legal theoretical considerations made elsewhere, basic process guarantees are to be considered an instance of conflict resolution which, in a balanced way, guarantees procedural rights to the parties, and as a consequence, confidence in and compliance with their decisions.[109] The interwovenness of these basic guarantees becomes apparent in the case of the right to a fair trial[110] and the right to judicial protection which have been analysed in conjunction by the Court.[111] An important obligations arising in that regard also concerns the right to remedy: notably in Fernandez Ortega and Others vs. Mexico, the Court would establish the State obligation to put in place "*effective remedies and guarantees of due process before the competent authorities and (...) to ensure due application of these remedies and guarantees*".[112] Overall, it is established for remedies to exist in domestic law, for these to be applied effectively, and for remedies to be appropriate and effective in view of the violation in question.[113] Especially the condition for remedies to be appropriate merits further discussion as far as collective rights concerns, as large-scale crimes in particular require comprehensive remedying measures to live up to the particular vulnerability context victims are facing.

## 5.3 Specialisation

Ever since the adoption of the *Universal Declaration of Human Rights* in 1948 and the virtually universal approval of the *International Bill of Rights*, but also considering recent categorisations such as human rights taxonomies,[114] we are confronted with a largely homogenising human rights landscape. Classical human rights codes, almost inevitably, build on the equality principle which may be emblematic of the

---

[107] Escobar-Gil (2011).

[108] Acosta-López and Amaya-Villarreal (2008).

[109] Ibid.

[110] See, for instance, *Chaparro Álvarez and Lapo Íñiguez vs. Ecuador*, Inter-American Court of Human Rights in 2007. It establishes the following main constituent elements, namely the right to presumption of innocence; granting the accused adequate time and means to prepare his defense; right of the accused to be assisted by legal counsel of his own choosing and right to be assisted by counsel provided by the State; reasonable time of the criminal proceedings; right to information about consular assistance.

[111] Cavallaro et al. (2019).

[112] Ibid.; p. 458.

[113] Ibid.

[114] See, in particular, debate on human rights generations as discussed in the following works:
Vasak (1977).
Tomuschat (2014).

harmonising forces of human rights. As a consequence, it is hardly differentiated between rights holder groups with the exception of the somewhat modest non-discrimination principle and its dedicated grounds. Group differentiation would however require yet a different threshold to be met for proper legal categories to emerge beyond the somewhat unambitious objectives of non-discrimination. Reasons may be manifold, not least owing to a specific ideological focus, placing emphasis on balance of power questions reaching back to the immediate post-French Revolution era or even the time of the *Magna Carta Libertatum* in the early thirteenth century when the first human rights codes came into being.

In other words, the law's generality may be critically approached based on its universalistic claims made in the field of human rights for instance,[115] which may, at the ending also diminish the value of these in practice, and as a consequence, be questioned as a legal construct as to their effective role, for instance.[116] The question of legal hierarchies may be asked as a consequence, or that concerning the legal value of relevant documents. Firstly, to what extent would general human rights treaties building on the generic premises of equality principles prevail over those treaties that advocate for human rights specialisation such as in group rights. At the ending, this may turn out to be a purely technical question, depending on a State's ratification status, but it may also not be seen as a conflict of rights situation, in a way ignoring those provisions that establish generic equality rights. In a way, group rights approaches may very well be favoured under the *lex specialis derogat legi generalis* approach,[117] being more specific than general equality law. Again, these may not be perceived as conflicting in the first place. Secondly, another difficulty may arise with the guiding nature of even non-binding documents such as the *Universal Declaration of Human Rights*, hence relating to the legal value of the law. This is often the case for collective rights instruments, such as the UN Declaration on the Rights of Indigenous Peoples or the UN Declaration on the Rights of Persons Belonging to National or Ethnic, Religious and Linguistic Minorities. Relevant commentary refers to these soft law developments as requiring "*particular attention (. . .) to be paid to it*",[118] while "*reflect[ing] a political intention to act in a certain way*".[119] Specialisation hence proves to create valuable opportunities for group-specific rights to be spelt out further which almost inevitably comes with certain limitations, such as rights spelt out in an individual fashion only or for only specific rights to be included with more contentious matters to be left outside the judicial realm of protection.

[115] Jovanović (2022).

[116] See, for instance, Rajagopal (2003); Kennedy (2005).

[117] See, for instance, Shaw (2008).

[118] Ibid.; p. 117.
See also: Boyle and Chinkin (2007).
Gómez Isa (2016).

[119] Shaw (2008), p. 118.

### 5.3.1 Specialisation as a Response to Equality's Failures

More work may be needed in terms of the popular conceptions of anti-discrimination law: anti-discrimination law is commonly viewed as tantamount to creating special rights.[120] Such view clearly overlooks the intrinsic connection between equality and non-discrimination, at the same time as it underappreciates the pertinence of creating conditions for special rights to be put in place, beyond the somewhat sporadic, exceptional application of non-discrimination law. Relatedly, critical voices point to the blurriness of the concept, highlighting the lack of consensus which concerns both equality in its substance and how it would be operationalised after all.[121] In other words, despite its importance as an end and as a key component of social justice, equality needs to be viewed as a means through which to achieve social justice.[122] It is hence its functionality, operationalizability that necessarily deserves a space in the debate on recognition of difference, again, operating as an end (in terms of 'outcome') with a mediating potential, and as a means to eventually achieve social justice in the broader picture.

What is more, equality as a paradigm may be dismissed altogether, even as a frame of reference, as it may distract from the true needs of those systematically left out. Without any doubt, special rights would potentially allow groups to finally access rights that are exercised by others,[123] commonly the majority, in other words, minority groups would come to enjoy rights equally. Otherwise, it has been argued, this would potentially bypass their material needs which would require a proper strategy to be pursued.[124] Equality law may also be ruled out or lose in validity since it could create unnecessary, possibly irrelevant divides as it has been observed in relation to gender rights:

> Not all questions which concern feminists are of necessity questions of equality or discrimination. Not all such questions and issues need to nor should they be met with a factionalism which divides the class of human beings up into male and female[125]

This may exactly be the point of human rights specialization, that of providing a more specific, informed response to the victims, also in view of the complexity of violations and situations caused therewith, including the important question of intersectionalities.[126] Another point of criticism revolves around the broader patterns of discrimination that are easily dismissed when making equality the sole objective of (re)mediatory treatment:

---

[120] Rubin (1998).

[121] Baker (2020).

[122] Ibid.

[123] Ibid.

[124] Krieger and Cooney (1983).

[125] Baker (2020), p. 64.

[126] See, for instance, Atrey (2019).

> . . .that we need to keep ourselves oriented from a point of view of social justice; we need to take into consideration just what it is we want to be equals in[127]

Indeed, considerations of whatever equality pretends to mediate necessarily sidesteps the self-determined nature group claims ought to reflect and be sensitive towards. So too, any form of directionality as it is demanded by the quote gets absorbed by the generality inherent to and promoted by the equality principle.

Rather visibly, equality becomes part of a wider strategy to uphold the status-quo in the law, it could be argued, dispossessing diasporic voices from important shaping powers while showing ignorant towards the multifaceted demands naturally arising from the grassroots. It thereby develops harmonising, integrating, but also oversimplifying potential. Such undertaking may very well be attributable to a form of disciplinary bias; indeed, the equality paradigm exerts decisive influence on our view and what we see, building on specific legal theories, resembling Kuhn's idea of paradigm(s).[128] Indeed, we easily observe tendencies, if not a consensus, that largely approves equality as a valid foundation to build on, as the current and predominant legal paradigm of constitutional law but also traceable in influential international legal codes. Special rights hence assume the important task of '*rebalanc[ing] the scales*',[129] with the potential of firmly establishing a social justice paradigm with a clear, transversal commitment to difference and recognition thereof by the law and its multijurisdictional channels.

Answers may also be sought in the debates on human rights universalism and particularism, with the former demonstrating stronger adherence to equality principles and classical human rights language and the latter proving more prone towards local manifestations and questions of pluralism. In that sense, human rights particularism brings ample of opportunities for classical human rights to be spelt out further, to be more attentive towards local needs, and for translating local demands including justice constructs into classical law. We may however want to distinguish between the law's universality and its specific contents; universality is often proclaimed in the case of human rights,[130] and shall not be subjected to debate here, given that the main idea of human rights is understood as universal—for rights to be attributed to rights holders, for duties to be held by States and third parties, or for rights to be effective, enforceable. Instead, the human rights landscape is widened and deepened, illustrative being recent charters and codes such as the African Charter on Human and Peoples' Rights with its emphasis on peoples' rights, including environmental rights or the collective right to economic, social and cultural development, or duties towards family society or community.

Oftentimes, '*cultural relativism*' is invoked to further illustrate the need for (further) adaptation of human rights[131] as they are spelt out in widely recognised

---

[127] Baker (2020), p. 65.

[128] Krieger (2000).

[129] Green (2000), p. 68.

[130] Tomuschat (2014).

[131] see, for instance, Donnelly (1989).

treaties and declarations, starting with the *Universal Declaration on Human Rights*. When placing cultural relativism in the broader theoretical context of human rights, the following could be said by way of further defining it, namely for "*the philosophy of cultural relativism [to] further assert that outsiders are not competent to solve problems that are internal to another culture. This allegation is often raised in support of the argument that a particular interpretation of human rights (...) may be alien to a particular culture. Such a culture (...) should not be judged by standards derived from external sources*".[132] Interestingly, such critique builds not only on conceptual matters such as neutral depoliticised categories, but for them to be placed into drafting and negotiation processes, to consider questions of sovereignty, jurisdiction and competence, entire justice systems, playing into this. The distinction between human rights' universalism and cultural relativism also opens the debate on group rights raised earlier, it could be confidently argued that "*the standard liberal argument for human rights is based upon individualism and universalism, while the argument for cultural relativism typically assigns moral status to some collective entity such as 'culture' or 'community'*".[133] Also elsewhere bridges are built between these supposedly conflicting schools of thought, that is, the universalist claim vs. the relativist divide in human rights debates,[134] with the former position reflecting a form of liberal view embraced in many human rights codes and treaties with their emphasis on individual rights, transcending any forms of boundaries.[135] We may juxtapose this with a pluralist critique that is emerging in the human rights literature, ultimately permitting group rights to find fruitful territory.

Human rights '*specialisation*' could be considered a necessary response to contemporary human rights developments, also given that in the light of, for instance, religious or cultural differences "*no truly common denominator could be found*".[136] This may not come as a surprise not least owing to the multiplicity of human rights having become codified across different legal orders. In the very drafting process leading to international treaties we may witness what is called reservations and declarations made by the States to ensure some provisions do not find application in their jurisdictions.[137] Not uncommonly, these cases reflect objections to specific gender standards or represent issues considered contentious by some governments. As we enter the world of group-specific rights, we may indeed be confronted with a wide range of coexisting categories that each require to be examined in their own regard. Differences may be considerable, whether we concern ourselves with 'national' minorities, indigenous peoples or migrant groups, each

---

[132] Freeman (1994), pp. 494–495.

[133] Ibid.; p. 495.

[134] e.g. Monshipouri (2019).

[135] for instance Farren (2009).

[136] Tomuschat (2014), p. 47.

[137] See, for instance, Hill (2016). Neumayer (2007).

demanding a proper form of specialisation, hence expanding—and arguably further regulating—the human rights landscape.

### 5.3.2 *Group Differentiation and Collectivisation as Processes of Specialisation*

In that sense, group-specific, let alone collective rights hardly find an appropriate legal frame that could do justice to the specific demands and needs arising in group contexts. In other words, group-differentiated rights[138] or collective rights[139] as these apply to groups in minority situations remain far from being generally accepted or, resultantly, formally juridified. Specialization processes would indeed refer to those rights established for specific groups, hence demonstrating a clear collective orientation. So-called person-specific rights[140] undoubtedly laid the foundations for a largely individualised human rights framework, both internationally and domestically, which was to experience a paradigmatic shift—extending its protective scope to include women's rights, the rights of the child, persons with disabilities or elderly persons. Special rights find dedicated mentioning in the literature as the following scholarly dictionary entry shows:

> Special rights are rights that pertain to a limited group of agents or have a specified range of application. That is, special rights are limited to a restricted set of rights holders or have content that is restricted to certain rights holders. So, with respect to legal rights – that is, rights pertaining to citizens within a given legal system – certain specified groups or individuals have certain rights that others do not.[141]

Rather clearly then, special rights are tailored to the specific situation a group of people shares. Also elsewhere it is unequivocally maintained that special rights could be understood by "*certain special facts*" that are not applicable to the rest of the world.[142] Interestingly, other scholarly attempts are made to relate special rights to its binary opposite, equality that is: notably, it is differentiated between equality of treatment (as in formal equality) and equality of effect with special rights achieving such equality of effect.[143] In other words, "*special rights are created in order to guarantee the possibility of exercising an equal right*".[144] This latter understanding manifestly differs from the definition presented above in that the focus seemingly remains on the same rights (as applicable to all) which are exercised by a specific

[138] For a detailed engagement with the concept, see Kymlicka (1995).

[139] See, for instance, Jovanović (2022).

[140] See Rodríguez-Piñero Royo's work for a more elaborated terminological debate on the matter.

[141] Boersema (2011), p. 1032.

[142] Engle (1998).

[143] Krieger (2000).

[144] Green (2000), p. 68.

group in a distinct manner while, on the contrary, special rights appear as derivative or further specified rights in relation to rights exercised by all.

More scholarly attempts have been made as far as the constituent components of special rights are concerned, understanding the doctrine of special rights as a paradigm—and as different from liberalism—that I) considers differences as they emerge in the actual world paying due regard to the surrounding circumstances, that II) distances itself from the need to live up to a form of "*universal conformity to an implied ideal*" and for such standards to qualify the way rights can be accessed, and that III) assumes a pragmatic stance by firstly examining what is being achieved by equality of effect, and secondly, establishing rights responding to such objective.[145] The approach taken here actively addresses the gaps ordinary equality principles are producing, that of a sheer acknowledgement of difference, that of a claim for exclusivity understanding itself as the sole standard to adhere to, and its lacking flexibility which would require rights to be responsive to actual needs. In a way, we are witnessing a form of dissociation from what we would expect the law to do, that is, curing injustices, finding tailored responses to violations, showing enough flexibility to adjust to new realities and demands arising. A paradigmatic shift towards the recognition of difference as it materialises in the form of collective rights seems like an inevitable corollary. For good reasons, it has been maintained that the "*conception of individuals and their rights is sometimes a misguided way of addressing justice*".[146] Again, conceptualising rights according to individual rather than group needs may stand in the way of fighting injustices comprehensively, ultimately truly non-discriminatorily.

Let us approach human rights specialisation, that is special rights, from yet another angle: classical theoretical accounts such as those defended, classically, by Waldron referring back to H. L. A. Hart who understands special rights—as opposed to general rights—as defining a specific relationship between two persons, a 'special transaction' or, alternatively, a 'special relationship' established between the two which, in turn, gives rise to specific rights and respective obligations in that very context.[147] A few objections may be raised in view of the present theoretical endeavour. Firstly, we necessarily understand rights holders and duty bearers more broadly, usually by juxtaposing State and individual, representing what we classically understand as a public law perspective, reaching back to social contract theory. Secondly, what is at stake here and what essentially differs from other legal constructs concerns the special position that is assumed by the rights holders, being particularly vulnerable, minoritized or unequal vis-à-vis non-rights-holders, that is majority society. This is not to say that the particular relationship between a minority group and the ruling majority wouldn't add an important rationale here, that of contextualising a violation, demonstrating its systemic nature. Minority positions may however be rather complex, with vulnerability not always becoming manifest

---

[145] Ibid.; p. 69.

[146] Wolgast (2020), p. 27.

[147] Waldron (1990).

where a legal relationship is established between two persons or entities. What lies at the heart of recognition concerns in fact the active dealing with difference, being attributable to a specific group, also by way of appreciating the collective, systematic, long-term, comprehensive and holistic nature of the violation incurred. What results from the above are special or group-specific rights. Elsewhere special rights are referred to as distinct and robust—distinct in the way they are conceptually justifiable, and to be treated differently as a result while it is to be asked to what extent such rights would be considered sufficiently distinct to justify the construction of a proper right and independent reference to it.[148] Secondly, special rights are portrayed as robust in the sense that it establishes a certain degree of protection; it is refrained from presenting robustness as absolute or even necessary.[149] In the case of group-specific rights, we do indeed build on a common rationale, that of positive discrimination, commonly built on a shared background of inequality, minoritisation and related disadvantage, however effective human rights protection is not necessarily provided with group rights often relegated to soft law.

Yet another way of understanding special rights is through discourse analysis with special rights constituting a concept meriting further semantic exploration, most prominently in terms of its societal acceptance. What is being portrayed as being posited in diametrically opposite sides of such ‘spectrum of acceptance’ concerns firstly, a constitutional mobilisation that considers special rights as resources for social change which is to be contrasted with a widely spread resentment over the achievements made by historically powerless parts of the population.[150] Interesting from the perspective of the rights talk, special rights are considered as unfair by advocates of this latter approach, standing in contradiction with individual merit and equality of opportunity, but also perceiving these groups as threats or scapegoating them.[151] More far reaching transformations may be noted at the socio-political level though, as the legal mobilisation would assist in rebuilding the social order that would eventually show more proneness towards egalitarian reform.[152] Also elsewhere, much merit is seen in studying movements and counter-movements mobilising (or not) for special rights; this, it is argued, also promises to further analyse the constitutive role of rights, that way adopting an inclusive approach of the law, tracing respective discourses as they are utilised by said movements and counter-movements.[153] Insightful may be the ‘*no special rights*’ slogan which was eventually supported by a majority of the Oregon electorate to vote in favour of anti-LGBTIQ+ bills, but which will most likely also be embraced by conservative judges in the future, scholars are afraid.[154] Indeed, LGBTIQ+ rights allow for a

[148] Kendrick (2017).

[149] Ibid.

[150] Dudas (2005).

[151] Ibid.

[152] Ibid.

[153] Adam and Cooper (2017).

[154] Schultz (2021).

comprehensive view on possible counter arguments to the debate given their contentious nature in many parts of the world till the current day and age. In that sense, not only have '*preferential treatment*' or affirmative action or quotas been perceived as negative while identical treatment has been suggested as an immediate result of equal rights, this also concerns the term '*special rights*' itself which is being viewed as tantamount to "*negative and inappropriate action generally*".[155] Also elsewhere special rights have been regarded as a negative development, portraying the movement behind it as a "*threat to efforts to achieve equality*" bearing two essential dangers, that of attracting wide-spread popular support, and as it could shape popular ideas of the nature of anti-discrimination law generally.[156] Somewhat relatedly, special rights may be employed by opponents with the dedicated aim of misguiding the public about the substance of antidiscrimination laws, with special rights considered as a preference leading to discrimination against those not benefiting from such preference.[157] Ironically, those supposed to be protected by such laws often feel they are protected less than equal treatment.[158] Similarly, it has been observed that members of the protected group suffer a "*continued disadvantaged position*" leading the author to speak of "*a vitality of the special rights objection [which] actually demonstrates the continued need for such laws*".[159] Critical theory, it is argued, has allowed us to return to the basic meaning of relevant concepts such as rights, equality or discrimination, and their very embedment into struggles.[160] We may hence be reminded of the pertinence of movements, and civil society generally in spurring these struggles for the recognition of special rights, including their socialisation and general acceptance.

## 5.4 Pluralisation

Processes of pluralisation may take the first steps in the preambular part of a constitutional framework, allowing for indigenous justice, educational, political, religious, economic or language systems to take a shaping role on the State's general architecture and very operating. In the Bolivian and Ecuadorian constitutional orders this would allow for a wide range of pluralisms to gain in symbolic (and beyond) recognition. Pluralisation is understood as a technique, principally, to widen the legal framework concerned to include rights hitherto left out, commonly collective or other group-specific rights. Certainly, the notion could be declared tantamount to 'system change' or an extensive constitutional reform or re-building of the State as it

---

155 Engle (1998), p. 1302.

156 Rubin (2019), p. 565.

157 Ibid.

158 Ibid.

159 Ibid.; p. 567.

160 Engle (1998).

strives to open up the legal scenery to other entire legal systems and paradigms. In other words, pluralising efforts are being formalised through the law, commonly by means of codification processes that prove sufficiently prone towards new legal amalgams, principles, entire justice systems and for these to eventually become embedded in the predominant legal order. Related concepts meriting further exploration in that regard concern '*legal culture*', '*legal consciousness*' and '*legal mobilisation*'.[161]

Let us first make some definitional attempts for the purpose of the present work. In an often-cited article Merry maintains "*given a sufficiently broad definition of the term legal system, virtually every society is legally plural, whether or not it has a colonial past. Legal pluralism is a central theme in the reconceptualization of the law/society relation*".[162] Elsewhere, she however explicitly refers to the colonial context in that regard, stating that "*they (scholars) recognised that the introduction of European colonial law created a plurality of legal orders but overlooked, to a large extent, the complexity of previous legal orders*".[163] Similarly Merry describes elsewhere "*during colonialism, the colonial power typically added a new layer of law and justice conceptions over existing ones*".[164] Another attempt is made by way of bringing together different strands of legal pluralism, materialising in the "*dynamic interaction of legal orders has, thus, a role to play in the globalization of the legal mind of [domestic] elites (Arthurs); in the confrontation of different communitarian legal cultures (Cotterrell); in the evolution of the dominant legal doctrine upon contact with a colonised culture (Melançon); in the contradictions and ruptures created within the official legal ideology by the autonomous aspirations of individuals and groups (Fecteau); and in the narrative practices of local communities (Blomley), of primary groups (Merry) and of subjects (Kleinhans and Macdonald)"*.[165] As it becomes apparent from the above, legal pluralism may find articulation in between forms of colonised or non-dominant laws, but also, most essentially, relative to the predominant legal order. Somewhat relatedly, two distinct forms of what has been termed 'plurality of pluralities' have been identified, referring both to the relative nature of legal pluralism and to an internal manifestations of pluralism, notably "*the plurality of law can refer to the inherent plurality of the singular system of state law, or it can refer to the existence of a plurality of legal systems*".[166] Both defining elements merit further thought as far as, for instance, indigenous justice frameworks are concerned, as autonomous, stand-alone orders and as they gain their place in the State's very architecture. Another central idea certainly lies with the State as a main reference and persisting authority in view of the predominant legal framework in place; accordingly legal pluralism has been framed

[161] Merry (2012).

[162] Merry (1988), p. 869.

[163] Ibid.; p. 869.

[164] Merry (2012), p. 67.

[165] Belley (1997), p. 9.

[166] Davies (2017), p. 239.

and oriented around it, defined as "*a model of statehood [that] also referenced the diversity of its constitutive people in terms of normativity*".[167]

Another thought meriting further elaboration concerns the notion of unofficial or hitherto unrecognised law, for indigenous law or vernacular norms to enter official legal vocabulary. This inevitably carries considerable implications as to the external side of the recognition process, often conveying the view that parallel legal systems would not qualify as such. The field was notably shaped by the discipline of anthropology early on, starting with non-State societies which counted with legal orders which also proved useful in the struggle against ethnocentrism.[168] Along these lines, the discipline exerted a noticeable impact on the eventual recognition of indigenous law, and the very definitional issues underlying these questions, which becomes apparent in the following "*with the admitted difficulty of pinning down precisely what 'law' is, anthropologists took for granted that it need to be attached to the state, and they were taught to see 'law' in terms of cultural systems of social order*"[169] with a dedicated focus placed on indigenous institutions. Others have attributed the difficulties associated with such dualism to what is termed 'the myth of centralism' elsewhere which is, in turn, ascribed to "*orthodox, mainstream or dominant theories of law*" with jurisprudence continues to focus on State law or the predominant legal order.[170]

From the early conceptual beginnings of legal pluralism, two distinct disciplinary directions may be discernible, firstly, what is commonly called '*a doctrinal legal pluralism*', and secondly, a '*social-scientific pluralism*', with the former, seeking to "*pluralise legal forms by beginning within the frame of official law*", and the latter "*social scientific conception has come to drive the legal pluralism agenda*".[171] This may concern the recognition of autonomous orders operating independently of State law. Relatedly, the concept of '*social fact legal pluralism*' has come to the fore, including a few defining features such as being a social fact and representing normative pluralism at the same time; as a manifestation of State legal pluralism, legal polycentricity and the coexistence of a plurality of orders; as being traceable in any multicultural society; as persistent across time in its institutionalised normative manifestation; as sources of advice, norms and fora; as giving rise to conflict and competition; as focussing on questions oriented on institutionalised normative orders and being empirically founded.[172] A related concept concerns '*empirical legal pluralism*' which was defined as "*a social state of affairs in which the behaviour of an actor is subject to different and possibly conflicting behavioral expectations (e.g., when the rules that obtain among the participants in a particular economic*

[167] Benda-Beckmann and Turner (2018), p. 256.

[168] Tamanaha (1993).
See principally Malinowski (1985).

[169] Tamanaha (1993), pp. 203–204.

[170] Fabra-Zamora (2022), p. 158.

[171] Kleinhans and Macdonald (1997), p. 30.

[172] Twining (2012).

*activity differ from those of state law)*" which is discussed by comparing the former concept with juridical legal pluralism and its focus on the formal legal order and its approach on diversity.[173]

Another noteworthy consideration concerns the situating of the very concept of legal pluralism amidst the multiplicity—and with it, layers—of (the) law(s). In fact, what is required to start with is a historical consideration and a dedicated positioning of the concept in the field of legal anthropology. A growing transnationalisation of the law initiated such period of multi-layeredness, giving due consideration to new actors, but also studying these questions critically, that is, terming these '*processes of hegemonic globalisation*' and in that sense triggering responses including the "*rejection or appropriation of transnationalised legal models*"[174] by a wide variety of actors including local people showing a negative positioning vis-à-vis neo-liberal globalisation. Likewise, critical voices have referred to the often-debated divide between universal human rights as enshrined in international codes and local manifestations, describing the related "*expansion of human rights (...) a new form of imperialism*".[175] In an albeit more neutral way, Merry describes these

> multiple legal orders [as] arrayed side by side in various geographical locations as well as up and down in local, state, national, regional, and global systems. These orders are not autonomous, but in constant interaction: the power of each is constrained by the power of the others. As considerable research on legal pluralism indicates, in both its side-to-side and up-and-down manifestations, the nature of these orders and their relationships are locally and historically variable. This multiplicity is not new, but the relative importance of each legal order and the nature of the interactions among them is constantly changing.[176]

Very apparently, these orders are viewed as fluid, bearing certain opportunities for non-predominant law to be recognised but also lacking stability for alternative legal justice orders to enjoy the necessary stability. From a conceptual view, global legal pluralism[177] too is considered a "*helpful description of law in the world*", making three main claims, namely for "*law [to] include both state law and non-state law, [for] there [to be] a plurality of laws, [for] laws [to] overlap and interact in certain ways*".[178] Throughout many scholarly contributions on legal pluralism, the question of multiple legal spheres remains undiscussed; instead, the focus is clearly placed on the different forms legal pluralism may take, that is, coexisting legal orders, dynamics between such orders, or forms of appropriation to name a few key elements.[179]

'*Pluralisation*' may assume two distinct meanings here, as discussed in the following sub-chapters, firstly, in the way new pluralisms, that is, system-

[173] Griffiths (2015), p. 757.

[174] Benda-Beckmann and Benda-Beckmann (2006), p. 3.

[175] Merry (1997), p. 249.

[176] Ibid., p. 250.
de Sousa Santos (1987).

[177] see also: Twining (2009).

[178] Michaels (2020), p. 629.

[179] Benda-Beckmann and Benda-Beckmann (2006).

transforming principles are being introduced, secondly, in the way the human rights landscape is widened to include group-specific rights not formerly envisaged by the law. In the former sense it is indeed alluded to a re-invention of the State and its institutions by way of introducing pluralising thinking. This may include new institutions and procedures that allow for specific groups to gain voice under the umbrella of the State, it means extending the State's operating to do justice to the particularities of dedicated groups, through ad-hoc procedures but also in an all-encompassing way. In practical terms, this would include dedicated values and principles assuming a guiding function throughout the entire framework concerned. In the latter sense, it is referred to the strictly technical exercise of introducing new rights into the predominant legal order. Commonly this gives rise to collective rights under the State's umbrella or for other progressive tendencies to become formalised in the constitutional order or other legal frameworks. This may include specific provisions only or it may give rise to entire catalogues of rights that are embraced by the State legal system.

### *5.4.1 Introducing System-Transforming Principles as a Manifestation of Pluralism*

Let us begin with the former, the way pluralism(s) as a legal construct per se may be embraced by the predominant legal order. As a matter of example, indigenous legal traditions have been seen as a

> much-needed corrective to the totalising tendency of settler law and could usefully assist to curb its preoccupation with absoluteness and universality, but only if Indigenous legal traditions are given their due in the practice and study of law in settler societies.[180]

Quite visibly, legal pluralism[181] adds a considerable counterweight in view of the predominant State legal order, ultimately inherited from the colonial age.[182] For understandable reasons, the relationship between '*Settler State legal systems*' and the '*legal systems of indigenous communities*' has been described as an "*often violent and always contested area of legal pluralism*", turning the "*core claims of legal pluralism (...) at least at times unresolvable through dialogue, inclusion, accommodation, and tolerance*", or to put it even more bluntly, these mirror a broader matter deeply ingrained in the legal sphere, that of "*multiple legal systems that on a fundamental level cannot be resolved into a unified system*".[183] Questions of recognition are similarly approached on both sides; both State and indigenous

[180] Gover (2020), p. 847.

[181] Consider, for instance, Sally Engle Merry's definition of legal pluralism referring to a "*situation in which two or more legal systems co-exist in the same social field*".
cited in: Napoleon (2019).

[182] See, for instance, Clavero (2010).

[183] Schiff Berman (2020), p. 803.

communities are viewed as not recognising each other's legitimacy, however, they are placed in a situation of needing to interact and find compromises, even if provisionally.[184] This might remind us of Sousa Santos' theoretical imaginations of an inter-legal space, providing important entry points for indigenous law to be further articulated at eye level with the predominant system.[185] In the real world, such co-spaces of justice hardly become reality, at least in the sense of vesting indigenous law with equal powers. Would we then consider (legal) pluralism as an effective venue for a difference-oriented form of recognition?

The way pluralisms are ultimately recognised in the predominant order varies to remarkable extents, ranging indeed from specific rights to a systemic overhaul of the constitutional order. In fact, existing approaches differ considerably between strong forms and weak forms such as in the former case continued colonialism, or in the latter situation integration into the State's architecture.[186] In the progressive sense, an entire "*reformulation of the relationship between State law and indigenous law*" is commonly embraced, including the creation of a new "*space (made) for the very categories, definitions, and epistemologies of the indigenous legal order*",[187] including adequate leverage for principles to actually gain legal teeth. Legal pluralist theories differ in the way such leverage is pursued further, with many rejecting the "*myth and ideology of legal centralism*", the latter being understood as "*imposing a reductive normative system on the pluralistic social fields contained in post-colonial societies*".[188] As Anaya concisely points out in relation to the interplay between the two systems:

> Within the architecture of domestic State legal orders, doctrines derived from colonial-era practice continue to rear their heads and impede the reversal of the status quo that has been left by the colonizing process. Of course there are advances and there are spaces within the domestic legal order for recognition of Indigenous law, but these impediments remain.[189]

A much recurred to debate in that regard concerns what could be regarded as an ostensible manifestation of pluralism, or empty promise, also dubbed '*pluralism of empire*' which "*acknowledges the plurality of human experience even as it insists on a universal conception of human agency and requires the recognition of a unifying authority*", reflecting indeed a narrow conception of agency.[190] Indeed, the depth and width of respective powers to be attributed to parallel orders remains largely undefined, also in existing scholarship with legal pluralism largely understood as "*a*

---

[184] Newman (2020).

[185] de Sousa Santos (1987).

[186] McKerracher (2022).
See also: Schiff Berman (2020).

[187] Schiff Berman (2020).
See also Tuhiwai Smith (2012), p. 804.
Also relevant in that regard: Watson (2018).

[188] Thornhill et al. (2018), p. 441.

[189] Anaya (2007), p. 4.

[190] Pratt (2013), p. 25.

*broad empirical and comparative concept that calls attention to the* possibility *that more than one legal system could be relevant for social interaction*".[191] As it might easily become perceptible when engaging in empirical observation, it cannot be grounded in any "*standardised relationship between the State and non-State system*".[192] Such call for multiplicities, both in substance and in methods, allows for considerable spaces of articulation for indigenous rights to be truly recognised; on the downside, however, respective legal guarantees are missing, hence establishing certain dependencies on the goodwill of States in sharing the legal space.

It seems clear enough from the above that for processes of *principlisation* to be effective, these need to truly provide the space for alternative justice systems and other pluralisms, entering into negotiation with the predominant order. It remains unexplored though what kind of principles would serve for triggering or spurring constitutional or, more broadly, systemic transformation. A certain threshold needs to be met in that regard, namely for principles to be overarching enough to accommodate a multiplicity of claims, rather than showing limited to singular rights to become embedded (see following section). To begin with, we shall concern ourselves with self-determination as an important umbrella right,[193] proving quintessential not only in the political sense, but also being facilitating in relation to cultural practices, religious or spiritual customs or educational rights. Indeed, self-determination has at times been portrayed as a procedural right, allowing for substantive rights to find realisation. Somewhat relatedly, the concept of autonomies[194] stands out as an umbrella right that assumes considerable political functions which gets shape in the form of self-governance, but also, famously, territorial autonomies. The right to development has similarly evolved into a dedicated umbrella right, providing fruitful soil for broader conceptual reflection as shown in the following extract which understands the right to development as

> a composite right to a process of development; it is not just an 'umbrella' right, or the sum of a set of rights. The integrity of these rights implies that if any one of them is violated, the whole composite right to development is also violated. The independent expert describes this in terms of a 'vector' of human rights composed of various elements that represent various economic, social and cultural rights as well as the civil and political rights. The realization of the right to development requires an improvement of this vector, such that there is improvement of some, or at least one, of those rights without violating any other[195]

Another important threshold is established here, with particular violations affecting the exercise of what is termed an umbrella right, in its entirety. The extract also demonstrates rather vividly how the wide panoply of human rights constitutes the

---

[191] Benda-Beckmann and Turner (2020).
cited in: Napoleon (2019).

[192] Napoleon (2019), p. 5.

[193] See, for instance, Aikio and Scheinin (2001).
Barelli (2011).

[194] see, for instance, Hirsch (1999).

[195] Marks (2004), p. 149.

umbrella right in question. A somewhat related noteworthy aspect concerns the integrity of rights that finds accommodation here, allowing for umbrella rights to do justice to the interrelatedness of claims by means of *principlisation*. Indeed, *principlisation* processes allow for a wide range of interrelated claims to eventually find recognition, clearly exerting channelling functions that show promising in view of a systemic transformation of constitutional orders and beyond.

### *5.4.2 Pluralising Human Rights*

Pluralisation may also concern wider juridifying processes with the objective of widening the human rights landscape to include dedicated rights, collective rights in particular. Despite the merits lying with the drafting of entire catalogues or chapters filled with difference-based provisions, and for the sake of establishing holistic human rights safeguards, we may be mindful of the way these eventually prove system-transforming (or not) or able to provoke genuine change in indigenous peoples' lives.

Most emblematic in that regard may be the collective right to self-determination[196] and autonomies invoked either as rights on their own or as a powerful umbrella claims. This also concerns respective derivative rights that are ultimately attributable to indigenous long-lasting struggles for collective self-determination, such as prior consultation and consent,[197] as well as, relatedly, land and resource rights.[198] Both dimensions intrinsic to the right to self-determination, that is, its internal and external manifestations,[199] show particularly far-reaching, with internal self-determination placing emphasis on indigenous proper institutionality, self-governance and related procedures, and external self-determination referring to questions of representation vis-à-vis external actors. Despite its important political value in the sense of strengthening indigenous governance structures and other organisational forms, self-determination is similarly applied to other matters.

[196] see, for instance, Marimán (2017).
See also: Aikio and Scheinin (2001).
Barelli (2011).
Xanthaki (2007).
Shrinkhal (2021).

[197] Wright and Tomaselli (2019).
Doyle (2015).
Rodríguez-Garavito (2011).
Fontana, and Grugel (2016).
Szablowski (2010).

[198] See, for instance, Monteiro de Matos (2020).
See also: Gilbert (2006).

[199] See, for instance, Hannum (2023).

Another highly contentious question in fact lies with economic growth,[200] exerting considerable pressures on local indigenous communities, pursuing a specific idea of development. In that sense, indigenous alternative development models[201] have not only become part of international discourses on degrowth and sustainable development, but do constitute, at the same time, an important collective claim.

Self-determination and development in particular have also assumed complementary functions, so-called umbrella functions, by guaranteeing other rights specific to indigenous ways of life. These have proven key not only for guaranteeing a holistic, contextual approach of the law, but also building connections between different rights of existential value for indigenous peoples, including physical and cultural survival,[202] and in that sense, adopting a pluralising approach. The virtually non-exhaustive nature and wide panoply of rights attributable to indigenous peoples in particular becomes apparent where attempts are made in actually defining these rights. Mirroring much of the foregoing, these rights have been understood as including, inter-alia, the "*rights to the land, rights to subsistence resources and activities, the right to self-determination and self-government, and the right to practice one's own culture and customs including language and religion*".[203] As an important addition to those standards existing in general terms, that is, those applicable to all, we may want to refer to indigenous customs and procedures[204] which operate as rights on their own terms and transversally, as a crucial component to consider when enforcing other rights, that way indigenising relevant rights.

Yet a different right that shall merit consideration on its own regard concerns the collective right to development which is to be understood beyond a purely economic meaning, often accommodating indigenous proper visions on development such as *Buen Vivir/Vivir Bien*,[205] based on a degrowth approach which stands in opposition to the common economic form of development. Collective forms of development do indeed extend the horizon of the human rights framework, being a concept commonly reserved for dedicated policies rather than entering human rights vocabulary. In indigenous contexts in particular, the concept has been stretched to include indigenous proper ways of live, cosmovisions, spiritualities which prove quintessential for maintaining and developing collective identities. It may further serve as an overarching principle that shall guide the exercise of other rights, that is, for commonly applicable human rights to be read in a specific light. The right to education, for instance, is not to be limited to public or private education in line

---

[200] For further insights on the matter, please check the 'resource curse' debate, for instance, in Ross (2015).

[201] See, for instance, Farah and Vasapollo (2011).

[202] See, for instance, *Case of the Kichwa Indigenous People of Sarayaku vs. Ecuador*, Inter-American Court of Human Rights in 2012.

[203] Hanson (2009), para.1.

[204] See, for instance, Van Cott (2000).

[205] Gudynas (2011).
Escobar (2014).
Sol6n (2017).

with a State's specific educational policies, but shall be adopted to indigenous languages, proper ways of transmitting knowledge, being considerate of entire knowledge systems. Relatedly, maintaining cultural identities necessarily includes a linguistic component where indigenous peoples continue practicing their proper language: contrary to what may be commonly expected, language rights reach beyond those linguistic practices that are upheld in the communities, but also concern the State's administrative proceedings including recognition of indigenous languages throughout the State's daily operating.

A proper glance shall similarly be shed on indigenous proper customs and procedures, clearly extending the classical human rights landscape. Indeed, a proper examination shall concern what we may call a procedural dimension of indigenous rights, articulating further the extent to which indigenous peoples participate in the State's operating but also as concerning their internal decision-making instances. Respecting indigenous customs and procedures however reaches far beyond participatory rights; instead it shall be understood as an overarching principle and right informing how human rights—both general applicable and specific rights—are to be interpreted. These are grounded in indigenous ancestral traditions informing any collective endeavour, especially in the context of encounters with the State and its institutions: it may concern the particularities of consensual decision-making[206] or specific mandate holdership which informs the internal working of indigenous assemblies, and as a corollary, is to be respected when taking share in the State's operating, such as electoral vote. Another famous illustration lies with legal pluralism and the need for State law to open up in terms of the personal, territorial and material indigenous jurisdictions operating here.[207] We may take this further, understanding a transversal approach on the matter as a way to decolonise classical human rights categories, that is, for indigenous customs and procedures to be considered, and in that sense to inform the application or localisation of human rights. Indeed, these developments need to be viewed in the colonial context in which indigenous proper laws and institutions started being subjected to classical contract law and colonial institutions, which in a way triggered institutional developments in the communities as far as questions of external representation were concerned.[208] Maintaining and developing indigenous proper procedures and customs hence demonstrate more than a manifestation of legal pluralism, but represents an ever-present claim for rights to be reconciled with indigenous identities and collective rights.

Also more broadly, indigenous specific rights have come to be classified as a proper category following human rights terminology, namely being subsumed under a so-called '*taxonomy of aboriginal rights*'.[209] Basing itself in jurisprudential

[206] See, for instance, Villoro (2000).

[207] See, for instance, Barrera (2012).

[208] See, for instance, Hirsch (2003).

[209] Slattery (2007).

analysis, it is broadly distinguished between indigenous specific and generic rights in the following:

> Specific rights are rights whose nature and scope are defined by factors pertaining to a particular Aboriginal group. As such, they vary in character from group to group. (. . .) By contrast, generic rights are rights of a uniform character whose basic contours are established by the common law of Aboriginal rights. All Aboriginal groups holding a certain generic right have basically the same kind of right. The essential nature of the right does not vary according to factors peculiar to the group.[210]

Indeed, indigenous rights themselves may have to undergo processes of standardisation to, for instance, enter the sphere of predominant legal orders; both categories clearly represent pluralisation in their own way, adding to classical State law. As the case of indigenous law clearly demonstrates, pluralisation may be operating at different levels, ultimately owing to a form of '*diversity within diversity*', hence complexifying the legal landscape of difference-based law. Rather than considering pluralisation as a fixed conglomerate of specific rights then, it may be regarded as a suitable method to absorb the diverse space of co-existence, of internal pluralism, characterising indigenous law(s) in relation to the predominant legal order.

## References


Acosta-López JI, Amaya-Villarreal AF (2008) Aporte para la Garantía del Equilibrio Procesal en el Sistema Interamericano de Protección de Derechos Humanos: La Acumulación de Etapas y las Garantías Procesales. Revista Colombiana de Derecho Internacional 11

Adam EM, Cooper BL (2017) Equal rights vs. special rights: rights discourses, framing, and lesbian and gay antidiscrimination policy in Washington state. Law Soc Inq 42(3)

Adams NP (2019) Grounding procedural rights. Legal Theory 25

Aguilera Bravo MG (2023) Environmental human rights in Latin America and the Caribbean: a regional contribution to sustainable development. Brill, Leiden

Aikio P, Scheinin M (2001) Operationalizing the right of indigenous peoples to self-determination. Institute for Human Rights, Åbo Akademi University, Turku/Åbo

Alexander L (1998) Are procedural rights derivative substantive rights? Law Philos 17

Altwicker T (2011) Menschenrechtlicher Gleichheitsschutz. Springer, Heidelberg

Amalfitano C (2018) General principles of EU law and the protection of fundamental rights. Edward Elgar Publishing, Cheltenham

Amani Cirimwami E (2020) Fashioning rights in the African court on human and peoples' rights: understanding the proceduralisation of substantive rights. Afr Human Rights Yearb 4

Anaya J (2007) Indigenous law and its contribution to global pluralism. Ind Law J 6(1)

Anton DK, Shelton DL (2012) Environmental protection and human rights. Cambridge University Press, Cambridge

Atrey S (2019) Intersectional discrimination. Oxford University Press, Oxford

Baker GS (2020) Is equality enough? Hypatia J Fem Philos 2(1)

Barelli M (2011) Shaping indigenous self-determination: promising or unsatisfactory solutions? Int Commun Law Rev 13(4)


[210] Ibid.; p. 114.

Barkhuysen T, van Emmerik M (2023) Procedural rights. In: Gerards J (ed) Fundamental rights: the European and international dimension. Cambridge University Press, Cambridge

Barrera A (2012) Turning legal pluralism into state-sanctioned law: assessing the implications of the new constitutions and laws in Bolivia and Ecuador. In: Schilling-Vacaflor A (ed) New constitutionalism in Latin America: promises and practices. Ashgate, Farnham

Belavusau U, Henrard K (2018) EU anti-discrimination law beyond gender. Hart Publishing, Oxford

Belavusau U, Henrard K (2019) A Bird's eye view on EU anti discrimination law: the impact of the 2000 equality directives. Germ Law J 20(5)

Belley J-G (1997) Le Droit comme terra incognita: Conquérir et construire le pluralisme juridique. Canadian J Law Soc / La Revue Canadienne Droit et Société 12(2)

Belser EM, Zünd L (2021) Introduction. In: Belser EM, Zünd L (eds) The principle of equality in diverse states: reconciling autonomy with equal rights and opportunities. Brill, Leiden

Benda-Beckmann F, Benda-Beckmann K (2006) The dynamics of change and continuity in plural legal orders. J Leg Plur:53–54

Bessette JM (2023) Staying true to the founding principles: a review article. Polit Sci Q 138(2)

Boersema D (2011) Special rights. In: Chatterjee DK (ed) Enyclopedia of Global Justice. Retrieved from https://link.springer.com/referenceworkentry/10.1007/978-1-4020-9160-5_391

Boyle A, Chinkin C (2007) The making of international law. Oxford University Press, Oxford

Brems E (2013) Procedural protection—an examination of procedural safeguards read into substantive convention rights. In: Brems E, Gerards J (eds) Shaping rights in the ECHR—the role of the European court of human rights in determining the scope of human rights. Cambridge University Press, Cambridge

Brems E, Lavrysen L (2013) Procedural justice in human rights adjudication: the European court of human rights. Hum Rights Q 35(176)

Brunner L, Quintana K (2012) The duty to consult in the inter-American System: legal standards after Sarayaku. Insights 16(35)

Calvès G (2010) La discrimination positive. Presses Universitaires de France, Paris

Cassese A (2012a) For an enhanced role of jus cogens. In: Cassese A (ed) Realizing utopia: the future of international law. Oxford University Press, Oxford

Cassese A (2012b) Realizing utopia: the future of international law. Oxford University Press, Oxford

Cavallaro JL, Vargas C, Sandoval C, Duhaime B (2019) Doctrine, practice, and advocacy in the inter-American human rights system. Oxford University Press, Oxford

Clavero B (2009) Genocide and indigenous peoples in international law. Paper presented at the Indigenous Peoples' Rights Lecture Series, Columbia University

Clavero B (2010) Original Latin American constitutionalism. Zeitschrift des Max-Planck-Instituts für europäische Rechtsgeschichte 16

Craig PP, de Búrca G (2015) Human rights in the EU. In: Craig PP, de Búrca G (eds) EU law: text, cases, and materials. Oxford University Press, Oxford

Dallier P, Forteau M, Pellet A (2009) Droit international public. Librairie Générale de droit et de jurisprudence, Paris

Davies M (2017) Plural pluralities of law. In: Roughan N, Halpin A (eds) In pursuit of pluralist jurisprudence. Cambridge University Press, Cambridge

Monteiro de Matos M (2020) Indigenous land rights in the inter-American system: substantive and procedural law. Leiden & Boston, Brill Nijhoff

de Sousa Santos B (1987) Law: a map of misreading: towards a postmodern conception of law. J Law Soc 14(279)

De Wet E, Vidmar J (2012) The hierarchy of international law. In The place of human rights. Oxford University Press, Oxford

Donnelly J (1989) Universal human rights in theory and practice. Cornell University Press, Ithaca

Doyle CM (2015) Indigenous peoples, title to territory, rights and resources: the transformative role of free prior and informed consent. Routledge, Abingdon

Dubout E (2007) La Procéduralisation des Obligations relatives aux Droits Fondamentaux Substantiels par la Cour Européenne des Droits de l'Homme. Revue Trimestrielle des Droits de l'Homme 69(397)
Dudas JR (2005) In the name of equal rights: "special" rights and the politics of resentment in post-civil rights America. Law Soc Rev 39(4)
Eichler J (2021) Die Rechte indigener Völker im Menschenrechtssystem: Normen, Institutionen und gesellschaftliche Auswirkungen. Nomos, Baden-Baden
Eichler J, Bacca PI (2020) Contemporary forms of cultural genocide in the natural resource sector: indigenous peoples' perspectives from Bolivia and Colombia. Canadian J Dev Stud/Revue Canadienne d'études du développement 42(4)
Ellis E, Watson P (2012) EU anti-discrimination law. Oxford University Press, Oxford
Engle K (1998) What's so special about special rights? Denver Law Rev 75(4)
Escobar A (2014) Sentipensar con la Tierra: Nuevas Lecturas sobre Desarrollo, Territorio y Diferencia. Ediciones UNAULA, Medellín
Escobar-Gil R (2011) Controversias Procesales en el Sistema Interamericano de Derechos Humanos. Revista Colombiana de Derecho Internacional 19
Fabra-Zamora JL (2022) The conceptual problems arising from legal pluralism. Canadian J Law Soc / Revue Canadienne Droit et Société 37(1)
Farah H, Vasapollo L (2011) Vivir Bien: ¿Paradigma no capitalista? CIDES-UMSA, La Paz
Farren S (2009) Human rights in the South Pacific: challenges and changes. Routledge, Cavendish
Fontana LB, Grugel J (2016) The politics of indigenous participation through "free, prior informed consent": reflections from the Bolivian case. World Dev 77
Freeman M (1994) The philosophical foundations of human rights. Hum Rights Q 16
Frowein J (2013) Ius Cogens. Max Planck Encyclopedia of Public International Law. Retrieved from https://opil.ouplaw.com/display/10.1093/law:epil/9780199231690/law-9780199231690-e1437?rskey=2XVPxO&result=1&prd=EPIL
Gaja G (2020) General principles of law. Max Planck Encyclopedia of Public International Law. Retrieved from https://opil.ouplaw.com/display/10.1093/law:epil/9780199231690/law-9780199231690-e1410
Gilbert J (2006) Indigenous peoples' land rights under international law. From victims to actors. Transnational Publishers, Ashley Park
Gómez Isa F (2016) The role of soft law in the progressive development of indigenous peoples' rights. In: Lagoutte S, Gammeltoft-Hansen T, Cerone J (eds) Tracing the roles of soft law in human rights. Oxford University Press, Oxford
Gover K (2020) Legal pluralism and indigenous legal traditions. In: Schiff Berman P (ed) The Oxford handbook of global legal pluralism. Oxford University Press, Oxford
Green P (2000) The logic of special rights. Hypatia J Fem Philosophy 2(1)
Griffiths J (2015) Legal Pluralism. International Encyclopedia of the Social & Behavioral Sciences, p 13
Groussot X, Lindholm J (2022) General principles: taking rights seriously and waving the rule-of-law stick in the European Union. In: Ziegler K, Neuvonen PJ, Moreno-Lax V (eds) Research handbook on general principles in EU law. Edward Elgar, Cheltenham
Gudynas E (2011) Buen Vivir: today's tomorrow. Development 54(4)
Hannum H (2023) Legal aspects of self-determination. Encyclopedia Princetoniensis. Retrieved from https://pesd.princeton.edu/node/511#:~:text=Internal%20self%2Ddetermination%20is%20the,of%20their%20own%20independent%20state
Hanson E (2009) Aboriginal rights. The University of British Columbia, First Nations & Indigenous Studies. Retrieved from https://indigenousfoundations.arts.ubc.ca/aboriginal_rights/
Health Wellman C (2014) Procedural rights. Legal Theory 20
Henrard K (2007) Equal rights versus special rights: minority protection and the prohibition of discrimination. Office for Official Publication of the European Communities, Luxembourg
Hill DW (2016) Avoiding obligation: reservations to human rights treaties. J Confl Resolut 60(6)

Hirsch SM (1999) The Capitanía of the Izozo: the struggle for political autonomy among the Guaraní Indians of Eastern Bolivia. In: Miller ES (ed) Peoples of the Gran Chaco. Greenwood Publishing Group, Westport
Hirsch SM (2003) The emergence of political organisations among the Guaraní Indians of Bolivia and Argentina: a comparative perspective. In: Detlef E, Muñoz E (eds) Contemporary indigenous movements in Latin America. Rowman & Littlefield Publishers, Lanham
Jendrośka J (2017) Introduction: procedural environmental rights in theory and practice. In: Jendrośka J, Bar M (eds) Procedural environmental rights: principle X in theory and practice. Cambridge University Press, Cambridge
Jovanović M (2022) Making social groups visible to and in law –essentialisation and law's generality. In: Eichler J, Topidi K (eds) Minority recognition and the diversity deficit: comparative perspectives. Hart Publishing, Oxford
Kendrick L (2017) Free speech as a special right. Philos Public Aff 45(2)
Kennedy D (2005) The dark side of virtue: reassessing international humanitarianism. Am J Int Law 99
Kiss A-C (1976) Peut-on définir le droit de l'homme à l'environment? Revue Juridique de l'Environment 15
Klabbers J (2004) Constitutionalism Lite. Int Organ Law Rev 1
Klabbers J, Peters A, Ulfstein G (2009) The constitutionalization of international law. Oxford University Press, Oxford
Kleinhans M-M, Macdonald RA (1997) What is a critical legal pluralism. Canadian J Law Soc/La Revue Canadienne Droit et Société 12(2)
Kochenov D (2018) When equality directives are not enough: taking issue with the missing minority rights policy in the EU. In: Belavusau U, Henrard K (eds) EU anti-discrimination law beyond gender. Hart, Oxford
Krieger LJ (2000) Through a glass darkly: paradigms of equality and the search for a woman's jurisprudence. Hypatia J Fem Philos 2(1)
Krieger LJ, Cooney PN (1983) The Miller-Wohl controversy: equal treatment, positive action, and the meaning of women's equality. Golden Gate Univ Law Rev 13(3)
Krijtenburg M (2018) Europe, dare to be yourself! Founding principles as guidelines for EU today and tomorrow: Schuman's frame of reference. Online J Model New Europe 28(2)
Kymlicka W (1995) Multicultural citizenship: a liberal theory of minority rights. Oxford University Press, Oxford
Lagerwall A (2017) Jus Cogens. Oxford Bibliographies. Retrieved from https://www.oxfordbibliographies.com/display/document/obo-9780199796953/obo-9780199796953-0124.xml
Malinowski B (1985) Crime and custom in savage society. Routledge, Abingdon
Mangiameli S (2013) Article 2 [the homogeneity clause]. In: Blanke HJ, Mangiameli S (eds) The treaty on European Union (TEU). Springer, Berlin & Heidelberg
Marimán JA (2017) Autodeterminación: Ideas Políticas Mapuche en el Albor del Siglo XXI. LOM Ediciones, Santiago de Chile
Marks S (2004) The human right to development: between rhetoric and reality. Harv Human Rights J 17
McKerracher K (2022) Relational legal pluralism and indigenous legal orders in Canada. Glob Const 12(1)
Merry SE (1988) Legal pluralism. Law Soc Rev 22(5)
Merry SE (1997) Global human rights and local social movements in a legally plural world. Canadian J Law Soc/La Revue Canadienne Droit et Société 12(2)
Merry SE (2012) Legal pluralism and legal culture: mapping the terrain. In: Tamanaha BZ, Sage C, Woolcock M (eds) Legal pluralism and development: scholars and practitioners in dialogue. Cambridge University Press, Cambridge
Michaels R (2020) Global legal pluralism and conflict of Laws. In: Schiff Berman P (ed) The Oxford handbook of global legal pluralism. Oxford, Oxford University Press

Misonne D (2017) Access to information, the hidden human rights touch of the Paris agreement? In: Jendrośka J, Bar M (eds) Procedural environmental rights: principle X in theory and practice. Cambridge University Press, Cambridge
Mjöll Arnardóttir O (2017) The "procedural turn" under the European convention on human rights and presumptions of convention compliance. Int J Const Law 15(1)
Monshipouri M (2019) Reza Afshari and cultural relativism. Hum Rights Q 41
Muir E, de Witte B (2017) The procedural and institutional dimension of anti-discrimination law. In: Rossi LS, Casolari F (eds) The principles of equality in EU law. Springer International Publishing, Cham
Napoleon V (2019) Ngā ture o ngā iwi taketake—Indigenous Law. Māori Law Review (November)
Neumayer E (2007) Qualified ratification: explaining reservations to international human rights treaties. J Leg Stud 36(2)
Newman D (2020) Indigenous rights and intrastate Multijuridicalism. In: Schiff Berman P (ed) The Oxford handbook of global legal pluralism. Oxford University Press, Oxford
O'Boyle M, Lafferty M (2013) General principles and constitutions as sources of human rights law. In: Shelton D (ed) The Oxford handbook of international human rights law. Oxford, Oxford University Press
Ollino A (2022) Due diligence obligations in international law. Cambridge University Press, Cambridge
Panagoulias KI (2011) La Procéduralisation des Droits Substantiels Garantis par la Convention Européenne des Droits de l'Homme. Limal, Anthemis
Pratt SL (2013) Indigenous agencies and the pluralism of empire. Philos Top 41(2)
Prechal S (2010) Competence creep and general principles of law. Rev Eur Adm Law 3(20)
Rajagopal B (2003) International law from below: development, social movements, and third world resistance. Cambridge, Cambridge University Press
Rodríguez-Garavito C (2011). Ethnicity.gov: global governance, indigenous peoples, and the right to prior consultation in social minefields. Indiana J Glob Leg Stud 18 (1)
Ross ML (2015) What have we learned about the resource curse? Ann Rev Polit Sci 18
Rubin PJ (1998) Equal rights, special rights, and the nature of antidiscrimination law. Mich Law Rev 97(2)
Rubin PJ (2019) Equal rights, special rights, and the nature of antidiscrimination law. Mich Law Rev 97(2)
Sanders D (1991) Collective rights. Hum Rights Q 13(3)
Sands P, Peel J (2018) Principles of international environmental law. Manchester, Manchester University Press
Saul M (2011) The normative status of self-determination in international law: a formula for uncertainty in the scope and content of the right? Hum Rights Law Rev 11(4)
Schabas W (2005) Cultural genocide and the protection of the rights of existence of aboriginal and indigenous groups. In: Castellino J, Walsh N (eds) International law and indigenous peoples. Martinus Nijhoff Publishers, Leiden & Boston
Schiff Berman P (2020) Global legal pluralism and indigenous communities. In: Berman S, Paul (eds) The Oxford handbook of global legal pluralism. Oxford University Press, Oxford
Schultz W (2021) The rise and fall of "no special rights". Or Hist Q 122(1)
Shao X (2021) What we talk about when we talk about general principles of law. Chinese J Int Law 20
Shaw MN (2008) International law, 6th edn. Cambridge University Press, Cambridge
Shrinkhal R (2021) "Indigenous sovereignty" and right to self-determination in international law: a critical appraisal. AlterNative 17(1)
Slattery B (2007) A taxonomy of aboriginal rights. In: Foster H, Raven H, Webber J (eds) Let right be done: aboriginal title, the Calder case, and the future of indigenous rights. UBC Press, Vancouver and Toronto
Smith LT (2012) Decolonizing methodologies. Zed Books, London

Solón P (2017) Alternativas Sistémicas: Vivir Bien, *Decrecimiento, Comunes, Ecofeminismo, Derechos de la Madre Tierra y Desglobalización*. La Paz, Fundación Solón, Focus on the Global South and Attac France

Szablowski D (2010) Operationalizing free, prior, and informed consent in the extractive industry sector? Examining the challenges of a negotiated model of justice. Canadian J Dev Stud/Revue Canadienne d'études du développement 30(1–2)

Tamanaha BZ (1993) The folly of the 'social scientific' concept of legal pluralism. J Law Soc 20(2)

Tavernier P (2006) L'Identification des Règles Fondamentales, un Problème Résolu ? In: Tomuschat C, Thouvenin J-M (eds) The fundamental rules of the international legal order: jus cogens and obligations Erga omnes. Leiden, Matinus Nijhoff

Thornhill C, Calabria C, Céspedes R, Dagbanja D, O'Loughlin E (2018) Legal pluralism? Indigenous rights as legal constructs. Univ Toronto Law J 68(3)

Tomuschat C (2006) Reconceptualizing the debate on Jus Cogens and obligations Erga Omnes—concluding observations. In: Tomuschat C, Thouvenin J-M (eds) The fundamental rules of the international legal order: jus cogens and obligations Erga omnes. Leiden, Matinus Nijhoff

Tomuschat C (2014) Human rights: between idealism and realism. Oxford, Oxford University Press

Tomuschat C, Thouvenin J-M (2006) The fundamental rules of the international legal order: jus cogens and obligations Erga omnes. Leiden, Matinus Nijhoff

Benda-Beckmann, Keebet von, & Turner, Bertram. 2018. Legal pluralism, social theory, and the state. J Leg Plur Unoff Law 50 (3)

Twining W (2009) Normative and legal pluralism: a global perspective. Duke J Comp Int Law 20

Twining W (2012) Legal pluralism. In: Tamanaha BZ, Sage C, Woolcock M (eds) Legal pluralism and development: scholars and practitioners in dialogue. Cambridge University Press, Cambridge

Uzelac A, van Rhee CH(R) (2017) Revisiting procedural human rights. Fundamentals of civil procedure and the changing face of civil justice. Cambridge University Press, Cambridge

Van Cott DL (2000) A political analysis of legal pluralism in Bolivia and Colombia. J Lat Am Stud 32

Varvaštian S (2017) Access to justice in climate change litigation from a transnational perspective: private party standing in recent climate cases. In: Jendrośka J, Bar M (eds) Procedural environmental rights: principle X in theory and practice. Cambridge, Cambridge University Press

Vasak K (1977) A 30 year struggle: the sustained effort to give the force of law to the universal declaration of human rights. The UNESCO Courir 3

Villoro L (2000) On consensual democracy: concerning Kwasi Wiredu's ideas. Forum Intercult Philos 2

von Bogdandy A (2010) Founding principles of EU law: a theoretical and doctrinal sketch. Revus 12

von Bogdandy A 2012. Founding principles. In: von Bogdandy A, Bast J (eds) Principles of European constitutional law (Oxford, München, Baden-Baden, Hart, CH Beck, Nomos)

Waldron J (1990) The right to private property. Oxford, Oxford University Press

Watson I (2018) Indigenous peoples as subjects of international law. Abingdon, Routledge

Wolfrum R (2010) General international law (principles, rules, and standards. Max Planck Encyclopedias of International Law

Wolgast E (2020) Wrong rights. Hypatia J Fem Philos 2(1)

Wright C, Tomaselli A (2019) The prior consultation of indigenous peoples in Latin America: inside the implementation gap. Routledge, Abingdon

Xanthaki A (2007) Indigenous rights and United Nations standards: self determination, culture and land. Cambridge University Press, Cambridge

Yihdego Z (2011) The African union: founding principles, frameworks and prospects. Eur Law J Rev Eur Law Cont 17(5)

# Part III
# Towards Collectivisation

We shall not remain confined to the somewhat unambitious objective of confronting systemic inequalities through classical non-discrimination and equality paradigms, that is, read through the lenses of formal or de jure equality. Collective vulnerabilities, it is argued, remain largely unaddressed or little mitigated by measures that are designed without taking context, scale, intensity and the very group nature into account. Grounds may be manifold, at times cumulative, hence rendering de jure equality ever more ineffective. What is more, the persistence of equality language in the daily discourse but also policies, on the institutional side and society alike, pretends societal relations to be equal and for differences to be irrelevant or constructed whether these may be biological or society-induced, attributable to family or educational background. The present piece engages with minority situations in particular and relatedly, indigenous peoples, showing immensely affected by the universalising pretensions of equality.

A particular accent is hence to be placed on equality's universalism and respective inadequacy in addressing the specifics of groups, their situations, their claims. This may concern equality as a basic paradigm and principle, some may extend the critique to human rights at large, entire frameworks being silent on group matters. In that sense, the present endeavour seeks to approach the question of distinct rights from a variety of perspectives, with a major emphasis being placed on collective rights, and resulting considerations, as to scale, its processes (of collectivisation) or rights holder groups as well as rights categories this could be relevant to. A debate meriting attention in its own terms concerns, relatedly, subject-holdership. Indeed, entire paradigms, legal frameworks, need to be rethought, de-individualised to permit collective rights to be introduced both procedurally and substantively. This would require a form of systemic transformation to be realised as alluded to earlier taking two main ways, as it is theorised here.

To start with, we shall concern ourselves with the very subject-category at stake. We will distance ourselves from the individual-driven legal language for a moment, permitting collective rights-holdership to be appreciated as a legal category in its own terms. Rather than pretending to present a holistic picture, by way of systematising findings across a large set of quantitative data, it is attempted to gain deeper insights into a couple of emblematic categories of rights-holdership in the collective sense. It is indeed the very context in which violations are committed that allow us to gain deeper insights into patterns of vulnerability, histories of injustices and other indicators hinting at the group nature of the violation incurred. Collective rights holdership as an alternative paradigm brings certain novelties that are being explored in the following. While we may understand procedural detail as a mere formal requirement for rights to be turned effective, it also allows us to deal with issues of representation, collective decision-making and mandate holding structures, touching upon crucial questions such as collective self-determination and autonomies that also shine through indigenous proper procedures and practices to be respected when substantive rights are being exercised. With the particular situation intrinsic to indigenous or minorities' ways of lives and their exposure to external pressures, we may argue existing rights may not be enough but require these to be spelt out and adapted to particular collective contexts. The particularities inherent to legal orders necessarily play into these debates, with 'national minority' rights, for instance, to assume very different meanings across coexisting legal orders. We may, of course, witness different needs, priorities, or interests depending on the local context or given the sheer diversity characterising rights holder groups. Nevertheless, a certain proneness to adhering to certain rules and principles governed by State sovereignty, necessarily shape the law drafting process, and ultimately juridifying processes leading to the recognition of collective subjects of rights. Reasons may be manifold, among others, the broader consequences of colonialisation, as well as the influence of majority thinking in the building of the State and daily functioning.

In a second moment, we shall concern ourselves with the very processes and scales 'collectivisation' may take, that is, juridifying processes around collective rights. This may take, to start with, the form of proper orders, *sui generis* orders, dedicated to collective rights. As argued earlier, we may indeed want to view not only individual rights in a critical light but understand these as transversal rationales permeating entire orders. In that sense, collective rights are not merely to be perceived as sporadic occurrences in a given legal order, resembling non-discrimination or equality principles, relegated to isolated provisions. Instead, we are to imagine a form of systemic transformation, a certain opening of legal orders allowing to rethink existing principles, provisions, duties and the like. What lays at the core of such thinking probably concerns the approach assumed, viewing collective rights as an order on its own, finding articulation in the form of dedicated rights catalogues but also throughout a legal code as a transversalising, also decolonising, endeavour. As the opposite side of the spectrum we can think of a fragmented legal landscape which may become difficult to be enforced where claims reach beyond the conceptual space defined by a given provision. Another scale of collectivisation we may identify here concerns what we may term 'constitutionalisation', to be thought of in a broad sense, rather than being limited to domestic constitutionalism. Classically, collective rights may indeed find entrance into the law through domestic constitutionalism as far as core principles are concerned but also regarding relevant collective rights. As a matter of fact however, collective rights primarily find articulation in international frameworks, including indigenous and minority rights regimes, also peasants' and environmental rights, or as some may say, solidarity rights. Taken to a more general level, collectivisation could be considered as a process, giving due weight to collective rights, for these to considerably gain in authority throughout a given order alongside the practicalities of juridifying collective rights, and hence allowing these to be recognised in a given order. In case of conflict, these may furthermore carry implications for their weight throughout the order, enjoying higher legal rank. Otherwise we may speak of principles with a low legal value, finding only isolated expression in many cases. More scales may be identified when it comes to actually embedding collective rights in existing legal orders, and making related efforts to mainstream these. Indeed, without any stronger embedment such as the recognition of collective rights in constitutional orders, these may fall short of developing legal teeth. Mainstreaming may indeed improve the visibility and therewith enhance the legitimacy of collective rights throughout legal orders and may take place at different levels, following diverse formats. This may take the form of regulations or other comparable legal instrument that specify obligations. It may similarly include protocols or neighbouring orders—as it becomes visible in the case of environmental rights, for instance—that extend or deepen specific norms of orders. In the case of indigenous peoples' rights this may be illustrated by the case of environmental rights more specifically which enjoy protection under the biodiversity convention and other socio-environmental standards. Similar to gender approaches, mainstreaming in the case of collective rights could be considered an institutional approach, that is, to be considered throughout relevant or competent institutions as a criterion to consider in relation to any policy measure. In that sense, we can think of these processes as both vertical and horizontal, transcending any institutional realm. On the opposite side, we may witness a form localism, describing the isolated, punctual nature collective rights may assume which is not uncommonly the case. On a final note, we may refer to standardisation processes. Similar to mainstreaming, these standardisation processes are to concern themselves with mainstreaming, however, not confined to the institutional sense. Instead, standardisation processes comprehend broader legal processes, juridification in other words. They also resemble constitutionalisation in the sense that specific rights undergo processes of codification, standard-setting. Standardisation is understood here also as a form to attribute a certain value to some norms in particular, those that find entrance into the standard-setting processes which suggests a certain priority to be granted to such norms—this may allude to human rights categories, norms enjoying less or more popularity respectively. This becomes particularly emblematic where, for instance, indigenous land rights or the right to collective self-determination or autonomy are referred to. The opposite, ad-hocism, refers to the isolated attempts of turning rights in the form of rules into legal obligations, generally those rights not becoming recognised as enforceable rights across a multiplicity of orders.

An often reoccurring theme running through the scholarly human rights landscape concerns the articulation of collective rights in the broader human rights debate with some considering collective rights part or a sub-category of the larger human rights scenery while others do not. The former would defend a view that demonstrates an inclusive approach on human rights with collective rights constituting a classificatory part of such scenery; the latter considers individual rights (the predominant part of a framework) and collective rights as to be placed on the opposite end of an imaginary spectrum respectively. It would, of course, also depend on one's view on the human rights landscape as being particularly value-loaded or not; in the way a given framework actually shows a certain proneness or openness towards collective rights; and the extent to which this could be concluded when considering the human rights landscape at large. A related question concerns the origins but also the ideological nature of both classifications, individual and collective rights, with individual rights commonly attributed to a largely classical approach originating in the Global North including an individualistic idea of property and other 'codified presumptions'. Collective rights and indigenous rights in particular find their origins in social movements, often originating in the Global South, clearly challenging these presumptions. Land and territorial rights in particular have spurred the struggle for recognising these as collective rights with a creative Inter-American Court of Human Rights. The collective rights discourse and its juridified manifestation have however not remained uncontested: its limits have become apparent in the way in which domestic minorities, so-called 'national minorities' including ethnic, cultural, linguistic or religious groups have become subsumed under the same movement or category, but also as these might disguise internal differences.

Indeed a relevant theoretical debate concerns the distinction between group and individual, or collective and individual rights, yet others would subsume such distinction under the term 'minorities within minorities'. Some refer to such differentiation as intersectionalities, cumulating different grounds of discrimination. Indeed, the focus of the present work is clearly not placed on the operating of the equality principle within groups, or otherwise identifying any such thing as 'cultural' practices threatening individual rights which often happens under the pretext of living up to a specific version of human rights, again, being attributable to legal paradigms originating in the Global North. While in some cases this might be very well justified, emblematic being serious human rights violations, autonomous justice orders very well protect the rights of the individual, giving it a proper accent, a distinct human rights language depending on the local context. In practice, critical voices refer to these questions as distracting or even undermining the value of collective rights, shifting the focus away from these which should be placed at the centre of our attention. Others have worked on the question of reconcilability between the two, placing emphasis on accommodating approaches or by distinguishing between external and internal dimensions respectively. The present work does explore intersectionalities as a proper (sub)question of inquiry, however, equality is largely understood as a matter to be approached from the perspective of groups including its implications on relations with the majority, its institutions, neo-colonial manifestations, or other systemic asymmetries—collectivisation processes being the most powerful response thereto.

# Chapter 6
# Exploring Counterbalancing Paradigms: Positive Discrimination and Collectivisation

## 6.1 From Equality's Universalism to Particularism and Distinct Rights

The commonly portrayed binary conceptualisation of equality-based paradigms and the contrasting particularism inherent to distinct or person-specific rights may very well represent one of the most impactful judicial malaises of current constitutional thinking. Let us explore the concept of particularism in the law for a moment. Reaching back to Aristotelian thought reflected in his Nicomachean Ethics, Jovanović describes two opposite poles, that of universalism and particularism: the former would essentially be captured by the idea of '*universal moral rights*' falling under Aristotle's '*natural justice*' concept, or, in other words, relate to "*pre-existing inherent rights of human beings*".[1] The *Universal Declaration of Human Rights*, it is argued, positivises or codifies these rights.[2] Indeed, universal rights—with equality certainly included—have largely entered the legal common sense in international law, but also as '*universal rights*' permeate constitutional frameworks. In practice, particularisms have come to be associated with specific groups, demands and frameworks in place. Famously, minority regimes have been attributed such status, commonly finding expression alongside or in direct opposition to individual rights laying at the heart of the idea of citizenship,[3] at least in Europe. This reaches back to Enlightenment universalism built on an '*undifferentiated human nature*'.[4] Also in relation to women's rights, universalising claims have undergone severe criticism. Quite openly universality has been described as a "*disavowal of the particular and a refusal of specificity*".[5] In relation to particularism, as feminist critics argue,

[1] Jovanović (2012), p. 177.

[2] Ibid.

[3] Wihtol de Wenden (2022).

[4] Mouffe (1988), p. 95.

[5] Ibid., p. 94.

 
J. Eichler, *An Interdisciplinary Journey from Non-Discrimination to Collective Rights*, https://doi.org/10.1007/978-3-031-54618-1_6

universal ideals have come to operate as mechanisms of exclusion.[6] To put it more bluntly, and again relating back to the universalising category of individualism, it is argued that "*we are all taught that the 'individual' is a universal category that applies to anyone or everyone, but this is not the case. 'The individual' is a man*."[7]

At the same time, we shall not exclude the possibility for particularistic claims to be universalised. This line of reasoning may help us in alienating ourselves from the idea of '*exceptionalism*' prominent among, for instance, so-called '*African (US) American exceptionalism*' which treats the situation of Black people in the US as completely distinct from the experiences of Afro-descendants in other States.[8] In fact, it has been commonly acknowledged for particularistic claims to enter even global frameworks, including the governance of multiethnicity.[9]

Quite clearly then, universalism may exert contrasting effects on the articulation of particularisms in the law. May the same argument be made in relation to equality principles? Equality has been accepted as an unquestioned legal principle for some time now, often considered as a 'fate' or as 'natural', defended by the Hegelian and Herderian schools of thought that would accept inequality as "*an inevitable consequence of the natural distribution of talents and traits*".[10] Particularism would also find expression in a distorted way, proving favourable to "*systems and rules (...) such as slavery, apartheid, colonialism and national socialism*".[11] In the present work, particularism is to be understood in relation to distinct or special rights only, or put differently, as an example of positive discrimination and its protective umbrella. Similarly, some advocates of the diversity paradigm have been placing emphasis on the importance of "*equalising opportunities across groups*" and relatedly, to "*make the provision of important services more equitable across societal groups*".[12] To be sure, such inter-group inequalities are considered a worthwhile idea to be followed; the present work however considers the multiplicity of groups solely in relation to the (ruling) majority.

Some answers in appreciating the relation between equality and distinct rights may be found in the idea of differential treatment. Theoretical considerations on the matter are manifold and widespread among legal and political theorists. Some have been tracing differential treatment back to Aristotle's justice theories demanding "*equals be treated equally and unequals be treated unequally*", following a basic justice rationale that may require people to be treated unequally in the name of equality.[13] Some accounts may very well understand differential treatment as a form of discriminatory treatment based on distinct grounds alongside such treatment that

[6] Ibid.

[7] Larmore (1990), p. 341.

[8] Davis (2021).

[9] Boulden and Kymlicka (2015).

[10] Solanke (2017), p. 40.

[11] Ibid., p. 40.

[12] Hull (2018), p. 414.

[13] Halldenius (2018), p. 109.

would discriminate in a positive way.[14] Actually, both forms may share similar logical foundations, following the definition established by Lippert-Rasmussen:

> X discriminates against (in favour of) Y in dimension W if: (i) X treats Y differently from Z (or from how X would treat Z, were X to treat Z in some way) in dimension W; (ii) the differential treatment is (or is believed by X to be) disadvantageous (advantageous) to Y; and (iii) the differential treatment is suitably explained by Y's and Z's being (or believed by X to be) (members of) different, social salient groups.[15]

We may hence be attentive to the nature of treatment itself and more particularly to the requirement of group membership as decisive in qualifying treatment differential in the sense of positive discrimination. In practice, any lines of differentiation may appear rather blurry in such taxonomy: for groups to be marginalised in the first place, a certain systemic treatment may figure as a precondition such as colonial contexts or racialised patterns inherent to social conduct. Conversely, it may argued, individuals and groups are born into such situation of (systemic) marginalisation, turning any differentiation between treatment and group rather redundant in practice.

On a final note, we may want to delve deeper into the conceptual particularities and implications related to so-called '*distinct rights*'. A wide array of relevant concepts comes to mind when considering rights that escape the supposedly inclusive, all-embracing umbrella of equality principles. They may find expression under the conceptual framework of the related protective categories of '*distinct rights*', '*particular rights*', '*specific rights*', '*person-specific rights*', and also coincide with the aforementioned categories '*collective rights*', '*group rights*' or '*minority rights*'. Other responses may be sought in positive discrimination or affirmative action frameworks (see Chap. 3). While valuable and instrumental in their own regard, and what remains a foremost concern here, relates to the significance of distinct rights in relation to the dominant equality paradigm.

Such inter-conceptual dialogue becomes absorbed by differential treatment, as discussed above, or it may also be considered under reasonable accommodation approaches, or, yet following a different venue, it may undergo codification processes resulting in dedicated sections or chapters in a State's constitution. Reasonable accommodation indeed constitutes an interesting angle from which to look at the '*distinct rights-equality nexus*', being defined as a consideration of "*whether reasonable steps have been taken to accommodate the rights of those being excluded*".[16] Not uncommonly, the principle is being applied in the context of disability rights,[17] but may extend to any excluded group distinct rights are designed for. Reasonable accommodation similarly enjoys recognition as a principle in the context of religion, employment and education:[18] while we may generically associate the term with the dominant, often State-centric legal framework for it to

---

[14] Lippert-Rasmussen (2018).

[15] Lippert-Rasmussen (2006), p. 168.

[16] Clapham (2015), p. 145.

[17] De Schutter (2005).

[18] See e.g. Alidadi (2018).

accommodate diversity, substantial accommodation is increasingly moved forward by newcomers or minorities, taking the shape of coping mechanisms.[19] At a more general level, it may be argued that reasonable accommodation could be considered a '*symmetrical right*', referring to it being applied to all, "*irrespective of (minority/ majority) religion or (non)belief, although in the current context it would be more relevant for minorities*".[20] Indeed, reasonable accommodation necessarily assumes a minority dimension when being confronted and contrasted with the all-embracing equality principle. Others have pronounced themselves on rather specific objectives, most prominently that of securing equal opportunities, notably by "*evening out barriers to full participation due to the interaction amongst personal characteristics and the way the society is structured*".[21] Similarly it was argued elsewhere that reasonable accommodation ought to "*allow everyone to participate fully in society on an equal footing as far as possible*".[22] When discussing concrete responsibilities and respective tasks to be fulfilled, it is generally distinguished between '*duties of reasonable accommodation*' consisting of, principally, duties of differential treatment oriented towards substantive equality, and '*accommodation measures*', serving as essential means to prevent or remedy indirect discrimination.[23]

Going one step further, Shachar proposes a related concept, that of '*transformative accommodation*', as it engages directly with the foundations of unequal treatment such as authority while enabling groups to access spaces of joint governance, notably she argues

> transformation accommodation (. . .) aims to establish an ongoing dialogue between different sources of authority as a means of eventually improving the situation of traditionally vulnerable group members without removing them from their nomoi groups.[24]

Very clearly, the present theoretical amalgam views integrationist approaches critically, placing—instead—dedicated emphasis on a group's integrity and its possibilities to negotiate at eye level with the State.

## 6.2 From Equality and Non-Discrimination to Particularism in the Regional Ius Commune

We may, almost naturally, think of regional orders as derivatives or simply as regional manifestations of international law if we consider its inter-governmental way of operating, or the persisting prevalence of State sovereignty. The opposite

---

[19] Alidadi (2017).

[20] Foblets (2017), p. IX.

[21] Belavusau and Henrard (2019), p. 28.

[22] Foblets and Bosset (2010), p. 37.

[23] Belavusau and Henrard (2019).

[24] Shachar (2001), p. 118.

may be true, however, if we were to shed light on its binding effects—consider supremacy and binding effect in the EU order[25]—or questions of institutionality, with supranational institutions having developed forms of sovereignty in key decision-making areas. In fact, the EU has been described as a proper order or, alternatively, an '*ill-defined sui generis legal construct*',[26] situated clearly beyond the international organisational context. This inevitably carries consequences on our analysis of equality and non-discrimination frameworks. The somewhat generic non-discrimination standards in the existing human rights treaty system[27] hardly resemble the degree of precision, of regulatory detail which has come to characterise regional discrimination orders. Not only that, we may speak of proper safeguarding standards, protecting dedicated groups, including 'national minorities' in Europe,[28] indigenous peoples and Afro-descendants in the Americas,[29] and peoples in Africa.[30] Reasons may lie in the very construction of orders, the juridification of rights. Given the scarcity of relevant legislation, especially in the early beginnings, regional systems have come to be subjected to and dependent on a wide *marge d'appréciation* exercised by the competent domestic courts in place. Under the EU's scope of protection, this may have arguably led to a redelegation of powers to the Member States, guided by their—somewhat paradoxically—'*constitutional traditions common to the Member States*',[31] enshrined in its very treaty documents, or following the often promoted '*unity in diversity*'. Emblematic may be the field of religion and similar sensitive matters which the CJEU feels, are to be addressed domestically,[32] also being indicative of political barriers permeating judicial institutions until today. A somewhat different understanding of its own powers has been conveyed by the Inter-American human rights system, proving particularly experimentally-minded when drawing on scarce legal sources, and, in turn, becoming a frontrunner in the field of human rights and collective rights in particular.[33] Let us problematise modus operandi and institutional approaches in turn, trying to reach deeper levels of understanding by examining each system in its own regard.

[25] See, for instance, *Costa vs. E.N.E.L.*, Court of Justice of the European Union in 1964; *Mangold vs. Helm*, Court of Justice of the European Union in 2005, see also *Kücükdeveci vs. Swedex GmbH & Co. KG*, Court of Justice of the European Union in 2010.

[26] De Witte (2012), p. 20.

[27] See, for instance, ICCPR, art. 2(1); ICESCR, art. 2(2); ICERD, art. 1(1) & 1(4).

[28] See, for instance, Verstichel et al. (2008) and Hofmann (2015).

[29] See, for instance, Cavallaro et al. (2019).

[30] Dersso (2006). See also: Baldwin and Morel (2009).

[31] von Bogdandy (2012).

[32] Chakim (2019).

[33] Cavallaro et al. (2019) and Rodríguez-Piñero Royo (2006).

### 6.2.1 Recognised and Unrecognised Minorities Under the Umbrella of the Council of Europe

Minorities under the protective umbrella of the Council of Europe follow clear forms of categorisation, falling short of providing safeguards for any imaginable or even common minority group such as migrating groups or individuals. The Council's main legal instrument (and monitoring framework) concerns 'national minorities', without attempting to further define these. Instead, respective guarantees are reserved to "*every person belonging to a national minority*" and entitling such person the "*freedom to choose to be treated or not to be treated as such*",[34] alluding to the important element of self-identification in that regard, as established by art. 3 (1) of the Framework Convention for the Protection of National Minorities and its Explanatory Report. The fact that a definition has failed to enter the convention's vocabulary has been criticised, principally due to its failing in bringing any clarity.[35] On the bright side, the treaty has remained more adaptable, open towards any possible changing circumstances throughout times and contexts.[36] Experts on the topic also draw our attention to the subjective criterion, that is, for individuals to freely decide on their membership status which may be understood too as an important safeguard against "*externally imposed ethnic markers or constructed social categories*",[37] allowing for exclusive categories. Indeed, it has been argued that "*categorising social realities based on perceptions and (often related) constructions may well serve a troubling nationalist discourse which inspired most of the post-1989 ethnic conflicts*"[38] which was, in turn, responded to by the Framework Convention. It may not seem far-fetched to assume that categorisations such as the current ones have served the State to harmonise policies, assimilate difference, and to bolster its integrative powers, legitimised by the idea of State sovereignty. Not only the instrument itself is in itself indicative of such cautious approach on the part of States; instead, a diversity of perspectives also becomes apparent in the declarations made by State Parties and questions of implementation that may prove more favourable to some groups than others,[39] yet again, revealing the dilemma of exclusiveness of the present concept.

The preambular paragraphs of the instrument provide further indication on those groups protected by its framework, by addressing ethnic, cultural, linguistic and religious identity which coincides with the criteria established by international law, the UN Declaration on the Rights of Persons Belonging to National or Ethnic, Religious and Linguistic Minorities. These, however, represent one of the rare

[34] Council of Europe (1995) *Explanatory Report to the Framework Convention for the Protection of National Minorities*, para. 34.

[35] Hofmann (2004).

[36] Marsal and Palermo (2018).

[37] Ibid., p. 93.

[38] Ibid., p. 93.

[39] De Witte (2008).

occasions on which the preamble closely engages with definitional or identity criteria, delving, otherwise, into the common utilitarian discourse on the protection of 'national minorities' as introducing an "*essential element of stability and democratic security*"[40] which is similarly to be found in the early instruments protecting indigenous rights, ILO Convention N° 107, to some minor extent N° 169.[41]

As the matter becomes decisive for indigenous peoples as far as definitional purposes are concerned, so too are minority groups granted important powers in defining membership though, in other words, subjective and objective criteria are introduced here. Very fundamentally though, objective criteria are not established to define groups externally, following early State practice initiating with the Martínez Cobo report,[42] but refer to a group's right to define membership[43] according to criteria established by the same group. Indeed, indigenous peoples had been struggling with criteria-setting, both domestically and globally, as it became apparent with the assimilationist ILO Convention 107.[44] As famously described by James Anaya, indigenous peoples are to be understood as "*groups that are descended from the original or long-time inhabitants of lands now dominated by others*",[45] other characteristics may be derived from the UN Declaration on the Rights of Indigenous Peoples.[46] The Declaration indeed puts an end to the struggle around objective criteria as defined by external actors, limiting definitional powers to the communities concerned.[47]

In the case of minority safeguards, more hope may be placed in interpretative standards and soft law that may very well counterbalance the constraining frame of the Convention: notably, the Advisory Committee has been ascribed a "*moral role beyond that of monitoring the provisions of the FCNM [Framework Convention on National Minorities]*",[48] essentially attributable to the Thematic Commentaries as part of the soft law developments on the matter. Emblematic may be the classification of the Roma, one of Europe's unwelcome minorities, as to be recognised under the framework.[49] It may indeed be argued that the personal scope has been extended

---

[40] Phillips (2018), p. 81.

[41] Swepston (2015) and Rodríguez-Piñero (2010).

[42] Martínez Cobo (1982). See also the following piece (chapters) discussing the historical origins of indigenous peoples' movements globally: Charters and Stavenhagen (2012).

[43] This may inevitably lead to conflicts with other human rights where the group's defining criteria encroach upon, for instance, women's rights and the defining of individual responsibilities: see e.g. *Sandra Lovelace vs. Canada*, UN Human Rights Committee in 1977; *Ivan Kitok vs. Sweden*, UN Human Rights Committee in 1985; Individual opinion of Olivier de Frouville in *Tiina-Sanila-Aikio vs. Finland*, UN Human Rights Committee in 2017; *Käkkäläjärvi vs. Finland*, UN Human Rights Committee in 2017.

[44] See e.g. Swepston (2015).

[45] Anaya (2004), p. vii.

[46] See preambular paragraphs in particular.

[47] Gover (forthcoming) and Imai and Gunn (2018).

[48] Caruso et al. (2013), p. 4.

[49] Ibid.

under the active lead of the Advisory Committee to be applicable to not only '*autochthonous minorities*', reflecting the initial understanding of several States when becoming State Parties to the Convention.[50] And yet, more precise indicators as to definitional detail or constituent criteria remain largely absent from, especially hard law developments.

By way of strengthening the above framework on 'national minorities', the Council of Europe introduced yet another legal tool, protecting minority languages specifically, notably, the European Charter for Regional or Minority Languages that entered into force in 1998. Similar to the Framework Convention, the Charter provides a rough definitional idea, limiting the application of the Charter to "*nationals of that State who form a group numerically smaller than the rest of the State's population*" in its article 1(a)(i). Indeed, the Charter is meant to promote a rather closed, if not xenophobic, view on rights holder groups as the Explanatory Report unequivocally states:

> The purpose of the charter is not to resolve the problems arising out of recent immigration phenomena, resulting in the existence of groups speaking a foreign language in the country of immigration or sometimes in the country of origin in case of return. In particular, the charter is not concerned with the phenomenon of non-European groups who have immigrated recently into Europe and acquired the nationality of a European State. The expressions 'historical regional or minority languages of Europe' and languages 'traditionally used' in the State show clearly that the charter covers only historical languages, that is to say languages which have been spoken over a long period in the State in question.[51]

Interpretative accounts differ as to possible constituent characteristics and the extent to which limits as stipulated in the Explanatory Report are to be defined in such a way as to exclude vulnerable minority groups.

A common criterion referred to concerns the existence of a historical community, including a certain level of institutionality, a shared geographical space, and language on the one hand, and the fact that such minority group would form only a small percentage of the State's overall population.[52] While presented as a rather accepted, commonly consented pan-European instrument, on the ground realities may reveal certain difficulties for languages to co-exist in a given jurisdiction, not always bearing peace-building potential: in that sense, the Belgian and Georgian cases may be emblematic of language-related conflicts which led to the refusal of signing the instrument, also disclosing difficulties in relation to basic questions of State sovereignty and territorial integrity,[53] questions that are vehemently defended by other States. Other politically sensitive cases bringing institutional integrity to the forefront of the debate concern Canadian Quebec, Catalonia in Spain,[54] or the

---

[50] Marko (2013).

[51] Council of Europe (1992) *Explanatory Report to the European Charter for Regional or Minority Languages*, para. 31.

[52] Byrd (2015) and Kymlicka (1995).

[53] Lebsanft and Wingender (2012). See also the following work for a critical engagement with these far-reaching terms: Boysen (2011).

[54] See, for instance, Jean-Rémi Carbonneau's work on these minority contexts.

Kurdish minority in Turkey,[55] especially the latter constituting a particularly urgent issue in terms of minority rights as recently shown by Erdogan's positive vote on Sweden and Finland joining the NATO in exchange for a shady memorandum on anti-terrorist measures and similar security jargon worded to the detriment of Kurdish minority members in Turkey and said States. Returning to the European institutional umbrella, it may be noted here that minority protection has come to be included in the political criteria for accession (Copenhagen Criteria) which has been phrased as '*a product for export*',[56] clearly ignorant towards the challenges this poses especially for un-recognised minorities.

Critical voices may however also be raised in relation to those left out altogether from the protective realm of regional safeguards. As a matter of fact, minority orders and the frameworks establishing indigenous peoples' rights remain reserved to dedicated groups, enjoying recognition under these special orders of human rights protection. Accordingly, an emerging group of scholars has drawn distinguishing lines between so-called '*long settled historical groups*' and '*new minorities, formed by recent immigration*'.[57] Also elsewhere is has been maintained that "*new minorities stemming from immigration in Europe*" would suffer from a particular form of discrimination beyond what is commonly known as direct and indirect discrimination in the law:[58] more precisely, scholarship has subsumed these "*beyond classical discrimination forms*" under the labels of '*institutional racism*' and '*structural discrimination*', with the former referring to a societal malaise that is "*based on generalised prejudices and thus the stigmatisation of groups and their members [as] a consequence of the ethnic stratification of societies*".[59] Indeed, new minorities deserve—while largely ignored by legal standards, political recognition or societal acceptance—a proper space of articulation, for distinct right to be recognised and formalised through legal standards, institutionalised throughout the State's machinery, and ultimately appropriated by society.

### 6.2.2 Indigenous Peoples and People(S) of African Descent in the Inter-American Human Rights Framework

The Inter-American Human Rights System could certainly be considered a frontrunner in safeguarding indigenous rights, and Afro-descendent rights to an albeit lesser extent, if considered from a comparative or cross-regional perspective.[60] Indeed, European human rights protection seems to predominantly focus on

---

[55] Lebsanft and Wingender (2012).

[56] Palermo (2013), p. 126. See also: De Witte (2000).

[57] Kochenov (2015), p. 81. Henrard (2011). See also: Baumgart (2020).

[58] Marko (2013), p. 99. Medda-Windischer (2009). See also: Medda-Windischer (2017).

[59] Marko (2013), p. 100.

[60] Sieder (2016).

'national' minorities with only sporadic consideration of North European indigenous groups while African institutions struggle with conceptual questions, yet they do reserve safeguarding measures for 'peoples' that may or may not include indigenous groups. Conceptual complexity may arise in a different sense in the Inter-American system which establishes dedicated protection measures for indigenous peoples, tribal peoples[61] and African descendant groups.[62]

While the Inter-American Human Rights System seems to sufficiently regard indigenous rights, its relation to equality remains worthy to be studied, especially as to its systemic nature. In one of the latest thematic (very interpretive) reports, the Commission refers to "*historical unequal relations between ethno-cultural groups during colonization*"[63] but also structural inequalities broadly conceptualised. While we would not want to deny the magnitude of what the Commission calls '*additional content*' or "*special and specific measures aimed at protecting, favouring and improving the exercise of human rights by indigenous and tribal peoples and their members*"[64] here, both Court and Commission depart from the premise that these groups "*enjoy all human rights in equality with other persons*".[65] Indeed, equality is commonly located in the context of an inclusive understanding of rights, that is, any rights stipulated in a given instrument or human rights order; such approach shines

[61] The Commission's understanding of 'tribal peoples' broadly follows the concept as stipulated in ILO C169 in its article 1(a) which "*regards them as peoples that are not indigenous or native to the region they inhabit but that like indigenous peoples share certain conditions that distinguish them from other sections of the national community*" (see Inter-American Commission on Human Rights (2019) *Situation of Human Rights of the Indigenous and Tribal Peoples of the Pan-Amazon Region*, para. 7). The Commission clarifies in that context that tribal peoples are to enjoy the same rights as those granted to indigenous peoples. Unfortunately the Commission also reverts back to objective criteria in addition to subjective elements elsewhere. Notably, it defines objective criteria as follows "*social, cultural and economic conditions [that] distinguish them from other sections of the national community (...) as well as being regulated wholly or partially by their own customs or traditions or by special laws or regulations*". The respective subjective element is "*related to the respective community's awareness of its distinct and group identity that makes its members assume themselves as members of a collectivity*". Inter-American Commission on Human Rights (2016) *Indigenous Peoples, Afro-Descendent Communities and Natural Resources: Human Rights Protection in the Context of Extraction, Exploitation, and Development Activities*, paras. 28–32.

[62] See especially the two recent reports on the matter: Inter-American Commission on Human Rights (2021) *Right to Self-Determination of Indigenous and Tribal Peoples*; Inter-American Commission on Human Rights (2021) *Economic, Social, Cultural and Environmental Rights of Persons of African Descent.*

[63] Inter-American Commission on Human Rights. 2021. *Right to Self-Determination of Indigenous and Tribal Peoples,* para. 8.

[64] Inter-American Commission on Human Rights (2009) *Indigenous and Tribal Peoples' over their Ancestral Lands and Natural Resources: Norms and Jurisprudence of the Inter-American Human Rights System*, para. 49. Inter-American Commission on Human Rights (2009) *Democracy and Human Rights in Venezuela*; *Maya Indigenous Communities of the Toledo District (Belize)*, Inter-American Commission on Human Rights in 2004.

[65] Inter-American Commission on Human Rights (2009) *Indigenous and Tribal Peoples' over their Ancestral Lands and Natural Resources*, p. 17; Inter-American Commission on Human Rights (2009) *Democracy and Human Rights in Venezuela.*

through the current regional context, it is also embraced by the UN Declaration on the Rights of Indigenous Peoples.[66] Internationally, two important thresholds are being established, namely for the rights stipulated therein to "*constitute minimum standards*" (art. 43) and, albeit relatedly, to establish limits, that is, interpretations of the Declaration—concerning co-existing, possibly conflicting rights—that could "*diminish or extinguish the rights indigenous peoples have now or may acquire in the future*" (art. 45).

In the case of Inter-American jurisprudence, the equality principle and positive measures are intrinsically related, which may be derived from the fact that equality principles are invoked, almost under the caveat that a particular treatment is granted. Whereas dedicated provisions stipulated by the American Convention on Human Rights (articles 1.1 and 24) establish the State duty to create conditions of equality in the exercise of the rights stipulated therein, the Court unequivocally maintains in two of its landmark decisions

> however, it is necessary to emphasise that to effectively ensure those rights, when they interpret and apply their domestic legislation, the States must take into account the specific characteristics that differentiate the members of the indigenous peoples from the general population and that constitute their cultural identity.[67]

Another particularity deserves further attention in that regard. Equality as embraced by the American Convention is to be conceived as a form of substantive equality which becomes apparent in the contentious context of land rights which the Commission courageously approaches as follows, being at the same time, emblematic of its general understanding of equality:

> ...the rights to equality before the law, equality of treatment and non-discrimination mean that States must establish the legal mechanisms which are necessary to clarify and protect indigenous and tribal peoples' right to communal property, in the same way that property rights in general are protected in the domestic legal system. States violate the rights to equality before the law, equal protection of the law and non-discrimination when they fail to grant indigenous peoples 'the protections necessary to exercise their right to property fully and equally with other members of the population'.[68]

Again, equality appears to explicitly invoke positive measures, in other words, for equality not to be separated from positive obligations which prove particularly central where indigenous proper organisational systems, justice orders or cosmovisions may conflict with the State-centric view as it has found

---

[66] Article 1 clearly conveys this understanding, "indigenous peoples have the right to the full enjoyment (...) of all human rights and fundamental freedoms as recognised in the Charter of the United Nations, the Universal Declaration of Human Rights and international human rights law." Yañez (forthcoming).

[67] *Yakye Axa Indigenous Community vs. Paraguay*, Inter-American Court of Human Rights in 2005, para. 51. *Sawhoyamaxa Indigenous Community vs. Paraguay*, Inter-American Court of Human Rights in 2006, para. 59.

[68] Inter-American Commission on Human Rights (2009) *Indigenous and Tribal Peoples' over their Ancestral Lands and Natural Resources*, para. 61. Inter-American Commission on Human Rights (2004) *Maya Indigenous Communities of the Toledo District (Belize)*, para. 171.

accommodation in the dominant legal order. In the case at hand, the Inter-American Court, importantly, refers to indigenous collective property systems within which the right to territorial property needs to be contextualised,[69] and ultimately ought to find articulation.

Given the scarcity of indigenous rights in the legally binding documents of the Inter-American Court of Human Rights, the Court and the Commission have shown creative in constructing a rationale for these rights to exist in the first place and for indigenous peoples' rights to find further articulation. In that sense, the Commission defends a position also rooted in international law, maintaining that special treatment shall not be considered discriminatory compared to society at large, again, referring to the principle according to which unequal treatment in unequal situations shall not classify as discrimination.[70] Elsewhere, the Court takes its first steps in developing indigenous rights as a legal concept, indigenous collective rights in particular, by relating specific property rights, collective rights and communal tradition, which, in their combination give rise to a new human rights regime, it could be argued:

> Given the characteristics of the instant case, some specifications are required on the concept of property in indigenous communities. Among indigenous peoples there is a communitarian tradition regarding a communal form of collective property of the land, in the sense that ownership of the land is not centred on an individual but rather on the group and its community. Indigenous groups, by the fact of their very existence, have the right to live freely in their own territory; the close ties of indigenous people with the land must be recognised and understood as the fundamental basis of their cultures, their spiritual life, their integrity, and their economic survival (for indigenous communities, relations to the land are not merely a matter of possession, and production but a material and spiritual element which they must fully enjoy, even to preserve their cultural legacy and transmit it to future generations).[71]

As it becomes clear, indigenous collectivity is derived from the idea that property is organised differently from the perspective of the dominant legal system, also being mirrored in indigenous cultural traditions and in organisational expressions of indigenous collectivity.

Yet another nuance to the understanding of equality is introduced: the Commission endorses the right to equality before the law, equality of treatment and non-discrimination which carry implications with them, notably, for States to "*establish the legal mechanisms which are necessary to clarify and protect indigenous and tribal peoples' rights to communal property in the same way that property rights in general are protected in the domestic legal system*".[72] The same could be

[69] Inter-American Commission on Human Rights (2009) *Indigenous and Tribal Peoples' over their Ancestral Lands and Natural Resources.*

[70] Ibid. *Saramaka People vs. Suriname*, Inter-American Court of Human Rights in 2007.

[71] *Mayagna (Sumo) Awas Tingni vs. Nicaragua*, Inter-American Court of Human Rights in 2001, para. 149.

[72] Inter-American Commission on Human Rights (2009) *Indigenous and Tribal Peoples' over their Ancestral Lands and Natural Resources*, para. 61. *Maya Indigenous Communities of the Toledo District (Belize)*, Inter-American Commission on Human Rights in 2004.

said about inter-subject relations, with different subjects falling under the safeguarding umbrella of domestic frameworks but also the regional *Ius Commune*; the Commission calls upon the States to guarantee indigenous peoples "*equality of treatment vis-à-vis non-indigenous peoples*".[73]

Also more transversally, the Commission establishes dedicated principles including relations amongst them: accordingly, equality and non-discrimination are to be regarded as '*guiding principles of human rights*' and as '*intrinsically correlated to each other*' whereas the principle of equality on its own is to be considered not only '*inherent to human nature*' but also not to be "*divorced from the essential dignity of the person and, therefore, it is incompatible with this precept that one human group is regarded as superior to and worthy of privileges over other groups*".[74] The Commission takes the chance to pronounce itself on the matter more transversally,[75] notably, in the Compendium 'Equality and Non-Discrimination: Inter-American Standards', which the Commission actively employs for definitional concerns. More precisely, the Commission understands the principle of equality as being derivative of a person's dignity and human nature and again, refers to superiority or privileged treatment of a group that is ruled out.[76] Conversely, groups deemed inferior are not to be discriminated against.[77] Similarly, the Commission draws larger conclusions for the concept of discrimination which is to be derived from international law, more precisely the International Convention on the Elimination of All Forms of Racial Discrimination and the Convention on the Elimination of Discrimination Against Women conceptualising discrimination as follows:

> any distinction, exclusion, restriction or preference based on any reason such as race, color, sex, language, religion, political or any other kind of opinion, national or social origin, economic status, birth, or any other social condition which has the purpose or effect of nullifying or impairing the recognition, enjoyment or exercise, on an equal footing, of

---

[73] Inter-American Commission on Human Rights (2009) *Indigenous and Tribal Peoples' over their Ancestral Lands and Natural Resources*, para. 90. *Mary and Carrie Dann vs. United States*, Inter-American Commission on Human Rights in 2002.

[74] Inter-American Commission on Human Rights (2021) *Economic, Social, Cultural and Environmental Rights of Persons of African Descent: Inter-American Standards to Prevent, Combat and Eradicate Structural Racial Discrimination*, para. 26.

[75] Also the following jurisprudential developments: *María Eugenia Morales de Sierra vs. Guatemala*, Inter-American Commission on Human Rights in 2001; *Rafael Ferrer-Mazorra* et al. *vs. United States of America*, Inter-American Commission on Human Rights in 2001; *Maya Indigenous Community of the Toledo District vs. Belize*, Inter-American Commission on Human Rights in 2004; *J.S.C.H. y M.G.S. vs. Mexico*, Inter-American Commission on Human Rights in 2015; *Miguel Ángel Millar Silva* et al. *(Radio Estrella del Mar Melinka) vs. Chile*, Inter-American Commission on Human Rights in 2016; *Marino López* et al. *vs. Colombia*, Inter-American Commission on Human Rights in 2011; *Ángel Alberto Duque vs. Colombia*, Inter-American Commission on Human Rights in 2014; *Rocío San Miguel Sosa* et al. *vs. Venezuela*, Inter-American Commission on Human Rights in 2015.

[76] Inter-American Commission on Human Rights (2019) *Compendium on Equality and Non-Discrimination. Inter-American Standards.*

[77] Inter-American Commission on Human Rights (2021) *Economic, Social, Cultural and Environmental Rights of Persons of African Descent.*

> human rights and fundamental freedoms in the political, economic, social, cultural or any other field of public life[78]

Relatedly, the Commission establishes dedicated '*protection against arbitrary differentiated treatment*' and the '*obligation of creating real equality conditions for groups that have been historically excluded and who have a higher risk of being discriminated*',[79] the latter giving rise to debates on dedicated groups which we shall explore in the following.

When it comes to rights holdership, the Commission at least approaches the question of who could fall under its protective umbrella by ruling that any forms of discrimination that "*disproportionately impact people who are exposed to situations of vulnerability*"[80] are to be eliminated. Somewhat relatedly, the Commission places a special focus on "*persons, communities, and groups who have been historically subject to discrimination and exclusion*";[81] elsewhere it addresses "*groups in a situation of vulnerability*" and "*groups in a situation of historical discrimination*".[82] To be sure, the American Convention does not refer to specific groups in that regard such as '*indigenous peoples in isolation*' while the Commission does clearly defend the position that equality before the law is to be considered "*potentially relevant for indigenous peoples living in voluntary isolation and initial contact*".[83] Tribal people find slightly clearer mentioning: the Commission clarifies these would not be (as) closely related to their livelihoods (as indigenous peoples), however, tribal people "*share certain conditions that distinguish them from other sections of the national community*" (also C169, art. 1(a))[84] and are to enjoy the same rights as those granted to indigenous peoples. A final group noteworthy mentioning concerns persons of African descent whose situation remains rather 'invisible' while it is referred to their collective suffering; the Commission maintains persons of African descent in the Americas "*have traditionally suffered and continue to suffer exclusion, racism, and racial discrimination*".[85] Problems initiate with the dilemma of accessing rights in the first place; the Commission laments there not to be systematic and reliable information on Afro descendants' living conditions and self-

---

[78] Inter-American Commission on Human Rights (2019) *Compendium on Equality and Non-Discrimination. Inter-American Standards*, para. 5.

[79] Ibid., para. 7.

[80] Ibid., para. 26. Inter-American Commission on Human Rights (2019) *Compendium on Equality and Non-Discrimination. Inter-American Standards.*

[81] Ibid., para. 9. Inter-American Commission on Human Rights (2017) *Strategic Plan 2017–2021.*

[82] Inter-American Commission on Human Rights (2019) *Compendium on Equality and Non-Discrimination. Inter-American Standards*, p. 11.

[83] Inter-American Commission on Human Rights (2013) *Indigenous Peoples in Voluntary Isolation and Initial Contact in the Americas*, para. 32.

[84] Inter-American Commission on Human Rights (2019) *Situation of Human Rights of the Indigenous and Tribal Peoples of the Pan-Amazon Region*, para. 7.

[85] Inter-American Commission on Human Rights (2011) *The Situation of People of African Descent in the Americas*, p. 1.

identification.[86] The situation is further aggravated by the fact that censuses and similar surveys have only recently included self-recognition criteria beyond merely considering the existence of ancestors as it was common practice in OAS States.[87] We shall then return to broader conceptualisations, such as vulnerability and in any case group rights approaches following the substantive equality rationale which has become a common frame of reference for equality principles to be further articulated according to Court and Commission.

### 6.2.3 *The African Human and Peoples' Rights System on Peoples' Rights*

The almost universally embraced doctrine of peoples and their distinct rights has not been paralleled beyond the African continent and its diverse landscape of institutionalisms while particular achievements may be noted in recent decisions issued by the African Commission and the African Court of Human and Peoples' Rights, the *Endorois vs. Kenya*, *Ogoni vs. Nigeria* and *Ogiek vs. Kenya* cases in particular. Resembling the debates on possible demarcation lines drawn between indigenous peoples and peasants in other world regions,[88] the question of indigeneity remains a highly disputed topic in African contexts,[89] often raising questions on overlapping identities with other groups, or possible shades of grey. Indeed, it has been maintained elsewhere that the differences between groups such as minorities, indigenous peoples and peoples lacks clarity in the African human and peoples' rights system:[90] what is more, a definition of 'peoples' was deliberately excluded from the Charter; emblematic also being the inapplicability of ILO C°169 and Kenya's abstention during the UNDRIPS vote in the UN General Assembly.

Despite such scarcity in definitional developments, the Banjul Charter (*African Charter on Human and Peoples' Rights*) itself provides several points of departure that engage rather explicitly with peoples and their rights.[91] Firstly, this may include peoples having been subjected to forms of colonisation or external rule (art. 19), turning any decolonising endeavours into an ever more prevalent issue as far as political independence is concerned, but also global economic dependencies (art. 20

---

[86]Ibid. Consider the Venezuelan, Peruvian, and Costa Rican cases on the matter (State reporting).

[87]Inter-American Commission on Human Rights (2011) *The Situation of People of African Descent in the Americas*. Consider the Peruvian, Honduran, Bolivian and Chilean cases respectively (State reporting).

[88]The Colombian and Bolivian cases may be particularly interesting to examine in terms of competing land claims, settlement practice and other questions of territorial nature.

[89]See, for instance, Venkateswar and Hughes (2013) and Ndahinda (2009).

[90]Rösch (2017) and Ndahinda (2011).

[91]See also the following work for more detailed discussions on the matter: Dersso (2006). See also: Baldwin and Morel (2009).

(1) & (3)), becoming an unavoidable reality, including persisting inequalities.[92] As an inevitable element of such debate, peoples' self-determination stands out as a precondition for other rights to be invoked, declared here as an "*unquestionable and inalienable right*" (art. 20(1)): interestingly, the equality principle is also invoked here, stating that "*all peoples shall be equal*", and more precisely, these are to enjoy "*the same respect (...) and have the same rights*". Any positive discriminatory approach seems to be left aside for a moment. The principle is invoked again in relation to peoples' economic, social and cultural development which is to be exercised "*in the equal enjoyment of the common heritage of mankind*" (art. 22 (1)). Again, the principle may establish important barriers to engaging in exploitative practice that could be played out to the detriment of indigenous peoples and them accessing, for instance, natural resources, while it clearly refrains from articulating any positive discriminatory treatment. Secondly, the term may allude to populations of States referring to themselves as 'peoples' (Banjul Charter, art. 23(2)(b)). Thirdly, the legal concept of peoples may be understood as the population of the African continent with the concept assuming a pan-African dimension, indicative being the instrument's preamble. Fourthly, States as such may consider themselves as peoples in the light of broader fostering efforts towards African unity and solidarity (art. 21 (4)). Fifthly, peoples as a legal construct may be applied to the individual, constituting communities of the State, including the different ethnic groups or inhabitants of a given territorial State unit; commonly, these base themselves on historical or cultural identity, or also discriminatory patterns.[93] It may be noteworthy to explore peoples' dedicated rights as spelt out by the Charter, including the right to dispose of their wealth and natural resources (art. 21); to their economic, social and cultural development, paying due consideration to their freedom and identity (art. 22(1)); to 'national' and international peace and security (art. 23(1)); and to a general satisfactory environment that proves favourable to their development (art. 24).

In relation to the particular situation of indigenous peoples, the Court has shown reluctant to relate indigenous peoples and their distinct rights to the 'peoples' definition presented above. Instead, the Court addresses these as 'indigenous populations' in the *Ogiek vs. Kenya* case, relying broadly on international human rights law, it is argued. It thereby relies on both subjective and objective criteria, with the latter category being highly disputed in current contexts: it principally draws on the work developed by the UN Sub-Commission on Prevention of Discrimination and Protection of Minorities drafted in the 1980s,[94] and a renown Advisory Opinion on the UN Declaration of Indigenous Peoples issued by the African Commission in 2007, adopted by its Working Group on Indigenous Populations/Communities. While the Working Group makes a point in including self-identification as one of

---

[92] Badie and Vidal (2017).

[93] Dersso (2006).

[94] See, for instance, UN Economic and Social Council (1996) *Standard-Setting Activities: Evolution of Standards Concerning the Rights of Indigenous People: Working Paper by the Chairperson-Rapporteur, Erica-Irene Daes, on the Concept of "Indigenous Peoples."*

the constitutive criteria, it also refers to "*the special attachment to and use of their traditional land*"[95] and a "*state of subjugation, marginalisation, dispossession, exclusion, or discrimination*",[96] forming part of the constitutive elements that lead to identifying indigenous populations. In turn, the Court establishes its own understanding of the concept of indigenous populations, by establishing what it calls "*relevant factors to consider*", notably

> the presence of priority in time with respect to the occupation and use of a specific territory; a voluntary perpetuation of cultural distinctiveness, which may include aspects of language, social organisation, religion and spiritual values, modes of production, laws and institutions; self-identification as well as the recognition by other groups, or by State authorities that they are a distinct collective; and an experience of subjugation, marginalisation, dispossession, exclusion or discrimination, whether or not these conditions persist.[97]

The Court also refers to empirical insights in that regard, reaffirming, for instance, the importance of indigenous peoples' "*strong attachment with nature, particularly, land and the natural environment*", representing the "*most salient feature of most indigenous populations*".[98] Possibly more far reaching, the African Commission had understood 'self-identification' as one of the most fundamental dimensions, alongside the relation between people, culture and land in the *Endorois vs. Kenya* decision.[99]

As it becomes apparent from the above, the Court seems reluctant to relate 'peoples' rights' to questions of definition (in the present case, 'indigenous populations'), and with it, questions of rights holdership. Interestingly, it approaches the same question, starting off however from the very rights attributed to indigenous peoples in a second step: the Court applies articles 21 and 22 on the right to development to the indigenous communities in question, building on a double rationale, that of adverse impacts caused by evictions without prior consultation, and of lacking active involvement in programmes affecting the communities.[100]

Let us return to the question of equality and non-discrimination as another venue from which to examine indigenous peoples' and minority rights in the African human rights system. Other than 'peoples' rights', non-discrimination and equality find expression in a rather ordinary fashion: accordingly, all rights and freedoms stipulated in the Charter are to be granted to individuals without distinction such as race or ethnic group affiliation (art. 2) while every individual is to be equal before the law and entitled equal protection of the law (art. 3). Importantly, said provisions refer to protective standards granted to individuals, principally, which may extend to individuals belonging to minority groups. More explicitly, the Charter relates the

[95] *Ogiek vs. Kenya*, African Court of Human and Peoples' Rights in 2017, para. 105.

[96] Ibid., para. 105.

[97] Ibid., para. 107.

[98] Ibid., para. 109.

[99] Rösch (2017).

[100] Claridge (2017).

equality principle to peoples in its article 19, stating that "*all peoples shall be equal; they shall enjoy the same respect and shall have the same rights*".

In fact, the provisions in question laid the normative grounds for a special mechanism to be established: in its Resolution on the Rights of Indigenous Peoples' Communities in Africa N° 51 adopted in 2000, the African Commission on Human and Peoples' Rights established the Working Group of Experts on the Rights of Indigenous or Ethnic Communities in Africa whose mandate was to study the implications of the Banjul Charter with particular regard to the right to equality—referring to articles 2 and 3 of the Charter—alongside other rights, namely dignity, protection against domination, self-determination and the promotion of cultural development and identity.[101] Equality in a collective sense has also come to be referred to in the case law of the African human rights system: in *Malawi African Association and Others vs. Mauritania*, the African Commission found that discrimination against black Mauritanians had to be attributed to negating the equality of peoples principle according to art. 19. At a broader level, the African Commission (in collaboration with the ILO and the Centre for Human Rights, University of Pretoria) has maintained in that regard, and as a consequence, that "*any law that discriminates against a people or an ethnic group would amount to a violation of Article 19*".[102] While conveying a clear positioning on the legal value of the collective right to be protected against discrimination, further reaching collective rights are viewed with suspicion as clearly defended by the African Commission in its Advisory Opinion on UNDRIPS:

> In Africa, the term indigenous populations or communities is not aimed at protecting the rights of a certain category of citizens over and above others. This notion does not also create a hierarchy between national communities, but rather tries to guarantee the equal enjoyment of the rights and freedoms on behalf of groups, which have been historically marginalised.[103]

We may be reminded of the classical distinction made between substantive and formal equality and in any case understand the present definitional endeavour as a way that principally excludes any proper group category of rights or specialised order for now.

---

[101] African Commission on Human and Peoples' Rights (2000) Resolution on the Rights of Indigenous Peoples' Communities in Africa N°51, para. 3(b).

[102] African Commission on Human and Peoples' Rights, Centre for Human Rights, University of Pretoria, International Labour Organization (2009) *Overview Report of the Research Project by the International Labour Organization and the African Commission on Human and Peoples' Rights on the constitutional and legislative protection of the rights of indigenous peoples in 24 African countries*, p. 30.

[103] African Commission on Human and Peoples' Rights (2007) *Advisory Opinion of the African Commission on Human and Peoples' Rights on the United Nations Declaration on the Rights of Indigenous Peoples*, para. 19.

## 6.3 Comparative Constitutional Perspectives on Equality and Group Rights

Regional human rights frameworks certainly prove flexible enough to live up to the ever changing landscape of equality law, more specifically, for new grounds to find recognition, or for intersectional grounds to be duly taken into account. Likewise, constitutional law has shown responsive to progressive societal trends, accommodating new gender identities in recent years[104] or intergenerational rights in relation to environmental protection,[105] for instance. More generically, it has been maintained though that discrimination law would find accommodation under employment and labour law rather than constitutional law, showing less at ease with the complexities inherent to respective concepts and institutions.[106] Elsewhere it was pointed to the historical legal origins of equality and non-discrimination, portraying these as principally drawn from US and UK law which would then be "*transplanted into European civil law jurisdictions 'from above' when the European Union issued its two famous directives on the matter to be transposed by all member states; however, it is product that does not align well with the legal architecture and culture of those systems*".[107] Another factor complicating the analysis concerns the value attributed to the different grounds in play with some enjoying more recognition than others, emblematic being gender discrimination provisions which have been found to lag behind, comparatively speaking, in jurisdictions like Czechia, Italy or Romania,[108] or is being attributed a proper term on its own such as feminist constitutionalism.[109] We may also relate back to the categorical division between formal and substantive equality with the latter having been endorsed by the Supreme Court of Canada and the South African Constitutional Court respectively.[110] Substantive forms of equality thereby materialised in a variety of ways, including "*indirect discrimination or disparate impact, reasonable accommodation, affirmative action, systemic discrimination, and unfair discrimination*" as illustrated by a few constitutions considered ground-breaking in developing the right to equality domestically, namely the US, Canada, South Africa and the UK.[111]

A final thought may indeed be devoted to the importance of group categories in the context at hand. Rather than being purely individualistic in orientation, anti-discrimination law has been described as "*promot[ing] and naturaliz[ing] a society*

[104] Goshal (2020) and Romana Ammaturo (2017).

[105] Tremmel (2017), González-Ricoy (2016) and Bustami (2022).

[106] Havelková and Möschel (2019).

[107] Pou Giménez (2020), p. 1056.

[108] Ibid.

[109] Atrey (2022).

[110] Fredman (2016).

[111] Ibid., p. 715.

*of groups*";[112] also elsewhere affiliation to a social group was regarded key for developing an understanding of equality principles.[113] We may relatedly consider group contexts as key, not only to deepen our conception of discrimination, inequalities or exclusion, but as a powerful claim in its own terms, furthering communitarian identities and collective agendas. Constitutional developments in South Africa and Canada reveal the importance of intersectional claims,[114] commonly carrying considerable weight for group-related grounds to become more accentuated. Conversely, group affiliation may operate as a valid indicator accommodating a variety of grounds and scales of discrimination, often much more strongly pronounced and systematic than it is the case individually.

### 6.3.1 'National' Minorities in European Constitutional Architectures

Comparatively speaking, so-called 'national minorities', that is, established categories of recognition, may enjoy wider acceptance in a given constitutional framework than migrant rights, especially in Europe: as a consequence, it has been maintained elsewhere that "*different degrees of harmony with antidiscrimination paradigms could be then associated not so much to the divide between European homogenous societies versus immigration and postcolonial ones, but to the sort of diversities, cleavages, and axes of belonging more prevalent in the different countries*".[115] Indeed, an exclusive focus placed on 'national minorities' discloses noticeable constraints regarding not only other minorities, but the complexity of group affiliation, identity categories and ultimately the panorama of violations.

'National minority' orders may, however, show considerable diversity as to the specific discriminatory grounds enjoying safeguarding and the varying scale(s) of protection. It may be broadly differentiated between orders that (1) establish special rights reserved for linguistic groups which may also extend to territorial autonomy, illustrative being the Belgian and Spanish contexts, (2) make explicit mentioning of 'national' or ethnic minorities who in turn enjoy specific rights, emblematically promoted by a few Central and Eastern European States, and (3) addressing dedicated ethnic groups enjoying special status as a result, as it is the case in the Slovenian, Italian, Hungarian, Cyprian, Finnish and Norwegian jurisdictions.[116] Two main categories result from this, notably those forms of constitutional recognition that identify distinct groups as rights holders, and those categories reserved for

[112]Pou Giménez (2020), p. 1062.
[113]Jovanović (2022).
[114]Atrey (2018).
[115]Pou Giménez (2020), p. 1062.
[116]Ringelheim (2008).

distinct rights.[117] It may also be noted here that international law has been considered key in triggering respective developments in European constitutional law, affecting cultural and ethnic minorities in particular.[118]

We may want to delve deeper into the meaning of equality and non-discrimination principles in such contexts, with a rich panorama of jurisprudence developed by the ECtHR which ought to inspire respective transformations domestically. Insights may be gained from the neighbouring regime of indigenous rights: in a partly dissenting opinion in the ECtHR case *Handölsdalen Sami Village and Others vs. Sweden*,[119] judge Ziemele refers, firstly, to a common standard according to which the parties are to be "*afforded a reasonable opportunity to present their case under conditions that do not place them at a substantial disadvantage with respect to the adversary*" (para. 10), and secondly, "*where one party by definition is disadvantaged, proper access to court is ensured by adopting such procedures and safeguards as indeed enable that party to enjoy the same opportunities*" (para. 10). In turn, this would require revising the "*entire approach to land disputes (...) to take account of the rights and particular circumstances of indigenous peoples*" (para. 10). Manifestly, a substantive equality approach is pursued here, referring to the particularity of not only the situation producing disadvantage but also indigenous peoples' special position. While less far reaching on the matter, the Court similarly holds that the parties are to present their case "*effectively before the court and that they are able to enjoy equality of arms with the opposing side*" (para. 51).[120] Similarly, the Court reiterates each side is to be "*afforded a reasonable opportunity to present their case under conditions that do not place them at a substantial disadvantage vis-à-vis the adversary*" (para. 51).[121]

Elsewhere, however, the Court clearly adopts a minority-prone approach, noting for there to be "*an emerging international consensus among the High Contracting States of the Council of Europe recognising the special needs of minorities and an obligation to protect their security, identity and lifestyle*".[122] In the case at hand, the ECtHR engages with the particular situation of the Roma, one of Europe's most prominent minority groups, stating that "*the vulnerable position of Roma means that special consideration should be given to their needs and their different lifestyles both in the relevant regulatory framework and in reaching decisions in particular cases*" (para. 181).[123] In fact, the Court very clearly adopts a positive discriminatory approach in relation to minorities, it holds that

[117] Eichler (2022).

[118] Ringelheim (2008).

[119] *Handölsdalen Sami Village and Others vs. Sweden*, European Court of Human Rights in 2010. See also: Klocker (2019).

[120] See also: Ganty (2022).

[121] See also: *Steel and Morris vs. the United Kingdom*, European Court of Human Rights in 2005, paras. 59–62.

[122] *Chapman vs. The United Kingdom*, European Court of Human Rights in 2001, para. 96.

[123] *D.H. and Others vs. The Czech Republic*, European Court of Human Rights in 2007.

> Article 14 does not prohibit a member State from treating groups differently in order to correct 'factual inequalities' between them; indeed in certain circumstances a failure to attempt to correct inequality through differential treatment may in itself give rise to a breach of the Article.[124]

An interesting observation may be made in relation to *de facto* and *de jure* forms of discrimination in that regard. Throughout its case-law, the Court explicitly

> accepted that a general policy or measure that has disproportionately prejudicial effects on a particular group may be considered discriminatory notwithstanding that it is not specifically aimed at that group (. . .) and that discrimination potentially contrary to the Convention may result from a de facto situation.[125]

This, in turn, carries important implications for the burden of proof when addressing unequal impacts relating to a specific rule in place:

> where an applicant is able to show, on the basis of undisputed official statistics, the existence of a prima facie indication that a specific rule – although formulated in a neutral manner - in fact affects a clearly higher percentage of women than men, it is for the respondent Government to show that this is the result of objective factors unrelated to any discrimination on grounds of sex[126]

With particular attention, we shall engage with a specific ground of discrimination meriting further observation: the Court unequivocally refers to ethnic origin as a form of racial discrimination that is described as "*a particularly invidious kind of discrimination and, in view of its perilous consequences, requires from the authorities special vigilance and a vigorous reactions*".[127] To be sure, the Court establishes respective high thresholds to be met in that regard, maintaining that

> no difference in treatment which is based exclusively or to a decisive extent on a person's ethnic origin is capable of being objectively justified in a contemporary democracy society built on the principles of pluralism and respect for different cultures.[128]

On a final note, we may get a sense of the politicised nature of the law and its institutions which becomes particularly accentuated in the case of (national) minorities, especially where these make claims challenging majority governance to the slightest extent. A few observations may be made in that regard. Predominating principles such as subsidiarity and, relatedly, the importance of the common legal traditions of CoE State Parties, clearly attribute discretionary powers to the Member

[124] Ibid., para. 175. *Case "relating to certain Aspects of the Laws on the Use of Languages in Education in Belgium" vs. Belgium*, European Court of Human Rights in 1968. *Thlimmenos vs. Greece*, European Court of Human Rights in 2000. *Stec and Others vs. the United Kingdom*, European Court of Human Rights in 2006.

[125] *D.H. and Others vs. The Czech Republic*, European Court of Human Rights in 2007, para. 175. *Hugh Jordan vs. the United Kingdom*, European Court of Human Rights in 2001. *Hoogendijk vs. the Netherlands*, European Court of Human Rights in 2005. *Zarb Adami vs. Malta*, European Court of Human Rights in 2006.

[126] *Hoogendijk vs. the Netherlands*, European Court of Human Rights in 2005, p. 21.

[127] *D.H. and Others vs. The Czech Republic*, European Court of Human Rights in 2007, para. 176.

[128] Ibid., para. 176.

States. It may be argued, minority rights find their most powerful expression where collectivity is being formalised, providing a forum for minority interests to be defended both internally and externally. The European Court of Human Rights remains hesitant to endorse a uniform view on the matter, probably also captured by its casuistic methodology which becomes manifested here, in relation to the freedom of assembly and association, as argued by judges Costa, Zupančič and Kovler in a joint concurring opinion in the *Gorzelik and Others vs. Poland* decision.[129] Indeed, the focal point of the Court's attention lies on the alleged dangers that association may bring to the public order or territorial integrity, both concepts having been exploited to justify a politics of exclusion. Adopting a progressive stance on the matter, the Court had found that the refusal to register a 'Macedonian association' under Greek law had violated article 11 of the Convention;[130] similar conclusions were reached where the Macedonian minority in Bulgaria had been banned from engaging in a peaceful assembly.[131] In the absence of dedicated minority rights under the Court's main legal instrument,[132] the European Convention on Human Rights and Fundamental Freedoms, the Court succeeded in deriving these from general constitutional principles: unequivocally, it maintained that "*although individual interests must on occasion be subordinated to those of a group, democracy does not simply mean that the views of the majority must always prevail: a balance must be achieved to ensure the fair and proper treatment of minorities and avoids any abuse of a dominant position*".[133]

The Court classically engages in a conflict of rights case which,[134] at the ending, is interpreted to the detriment of 'national' minorities in their exercise of special voting rights. On the one hand, the Court clearly advocates for implementing the principle of pluralism which in the Court's opinion "*is impossible without an association being able to express freely its ideas and opinions, the Court has also recognised that the protection of opinions and the freedom of expression within the meaning of Article 10 of the Convention is one of the objectives of the freedom of*

[129] *Gorzelik and Others vs. Poland*, European Court of Human Rights in 2004.

[130] *Sidiropoulos and Others vs. Greece*, European Court of Human Rights in 1998.

[131] *Stankov and the United Macedonian Organisation Ilinden vs. Bulgaria*, European Court of Human Rights in 2001.

[132] This surely opens a the floor for a debate on the sources of law, with minority regimes finding their roots in both domestic legal frameworks and the CoE's 'national minority' framework. In the case at hand, the Court maintains: "*that it is primarily for the national authorities, notably the courts, to resolve problems of interpretation of domestic legislation, the Court's role being confined to determining whether the effects of that interpretation are compatible with the Convention*" (para. 100)

[133] *Gorzelik and Others vs. Poland*, European Court of Human Rights in 2004, para. 90. *Young, James and Webster vs. the United Kingdom*, European Court of Human Rights in 1981. *Chassagnou and Others vs. France*, European Court of Human Rights in 1999.

[134] See also: Smet and Brems (2017).

*association*".[135] Pluralism, it is argued here, "*builds on the genuine recognition of, and respect for, diversity and the dynamics of cultural traditions, ethnic and cultural identities...*".[136] Importantly, the Court attributed particular value to freedom of association when exercised by 'national' and ethnic minorities as it considers "*forming an association in order to express and promote its identity may be instrumental in helping a minority to preserve and uphold its rights*".[137] While the Court clearly pronounced itself against any limitations on the freedom of association by the minority organisation and accordingly holds that "*exceptions to the freedom of association are to be construed strictly and only convincing and compelling reasons can justify restrictions on that freedom*",[138] it however referred, firstly, to the entitlement of a 'special status' under the Electoral Act in question and secondly, the proportionate nature of the interference that was deemed "*necessary in a democratic society*".[139] Critical voices may very well point to the double meaning attributed to democratic values[140] justifying, in the first place, exceptions to be granted to 'national minorities', and at the ending, serving an interpretation that conveys a clear majority orientation with the negation of special electoral rights 'in the name of equality' in the words of the concurring judges, or the prevalence of other societal interests outweighing minority rights.

### 6.3.2 *Multicultural and Plurinational Constitutional Frameworks in Latin America*

In recent decades we have come to witness a new wave of constitutional reforms in the Latin American Andes, Bolivia and Ecuador standing at the forefront of these transformations. As discussed earlier, these constitutional transformations initiated with a period of multicultural constitutionalism (1982–1988) in Canada, Guatemala, Nicaragua and Brazil, followed by a phase of pluricultural constitutionalism (1989–2005) in Colombia, Mexico, Paraguay, Peru, Bolivia, Argentina, Ecuador and Venezuela, and eventually embracing what has been termed plurinational constitutionalism (2006–2009) in Bolivia and Ecuador according to Yrigoyen Fajardo's panorama of pluralist constitutionalism.[141]

---

[135] *Gorzelik and Others vs. Poland*, European Court of Human Rights in 2004, para. 91. *Refah Partisi (the Welfare Party) and Others vs. Turkey*, European Court of Human Rights in 2003.

[136] *Gorzelik and Others vs. Poland*, European Court of Human Rights in 2004, para. 92.

[137] Ibid., para. 93.

[138] Ibid., para. 95.

[139] Ibid., para. 106.

[140] As noted earlier, the Court in fact very clearly pronounced itself in favour of a "*proper and fair treatment of minorities*" in the name of democracy with pluralism, tolerance and broadmindedness falling under the "*hallmarks of democratic society*" para. 90.

[141] Yrigoyen Fajardo (2016).

In essence, we are confronted with a wide landscape of legal amalgams and constructs that only recently came to assume the shape of entirely novel rights and principles. On numerous occasions constitutional principles, including entire structures have been transferred elsewhere, following the logics of legal transplants, illustrative being the block of constitutionality doctrine.[142] Similarly, it has been argued these would assume the shape of '*migrating constitutional ideas*', referring to the transformations and adaptations made to a given legal construct once it found accommodation in the new framework(s).[143] Indeed, the constitutional block doctrine (originally: *bloc de constitutionnalité*) may be illustrative of these transformations, especially in the light of post-authoritarian constitutional reform projects; the doctrine principally refers to a "*set of norms with constitutional rank in the domestic legal system*",[144] commonly important human rights norms to find firm establishment, including relevant international legal standards. Elsewhere it is distinguished between ideological, normative and political elements explored further in Latin American constitutional landscapes: especially the ideological dimension, it is argued, discloses considerable resemblances among European and Latin American frameworks, at least traditionally speaking; this may include a particular conception of the State rooted in 'democratic society' and its values and principles.[145] In terms of normative developments, what could be termed Latin American *Ius Commune* has shown receptible towards human rights, also alluding to notable developments in the Inter-American institutional scenery, including the expansion of its hard law but also relevant soft law such as the (Commission's) recommendations, resolutions, advisory opinions, or proceedings.[146] Finally, an important political element merits mentioning here: this concerns domestic structures such as the Defensoría del Pueblo (domestic Ombudsman's institution) but also the Inter-American system and its institutions,[147] with the Commission having played a key role carrying out field visits in crisis situations and extensive reporting on politically contentious issues.[148]

Now, constitutionalism is to be examined further when accommodating multicultural thinking, in terms of institutional transformation, rethinking of the State and distribution of power. Often considered as an outdated concept, multiculturalist thinking persists across many European constitutional frameworks, whereby multiculturalism may be understood as a political philosophy which approaches cultural diversity in contemporary societies, operating, at the same time, as a socio-political principle that strives to eliminate structural inequalities while aiming for substantive equality as far as marginalised groups are concerned.[149] Would we then deem

[142] Góngora-Mera (2017) and Hoyos (1992).

[143] Góngora-Mera (2017).

[144] Ibid., p. 240.

[145] García Ramírez (2017).

[146] Ibid.

[147] Ibid.

[148] Huneeus and Madsen (2018).

[149] Bernot (2015).

multicultural constitutionalism a particularly suitable answer to mitigate persisting inequalities? It may be critically noted from the start that the progressive constitutional moves in the field of constitutional rights have become blocked by how power was arranged but also by broader institutional deficiencies in the region.[150]

Indeed, we may depart from a legal pluralistic critique, returning to the question to what extent equality provisions would be sufficient to guarantee group rights or, instead, fall short of recognising indigenous justice systems, allowing for co-decision-making spaces or respecting territorial and political autonomies. Systemic questions indeed deserve to be further discussed here. Indeed, a persisting '*majority culture*' and an increasingly '*Eurocentric global society*' have gone hand in hand with the marginalisation of inter-alia "*feminists, minorities in multicultural societies, peoples struggling for national independence, and formerly colonised regions suing for equality of their cultures on the international stage*"[151] following a self-understanding of constitutionalism that manifestly builds on individual rights. The very orientation of human rights hence operates alongside a traditional, majority-driven framework of the State, relegating collective identities to the margins of the constitutional scope. A final remark relates to the specific grounds of discrimination finding accommodation under Latin American constitutional umbrellas: in fact, constitutions have come to embrace not only equality provisions, but

> order special affirmative action policies to make equality effective (...) in particular, several reforms explicitly set terms of equality and non-discrimination between men and women, meaning that Latin American constitutionalism authorises – or even requires – the adoption of certain gender approaches in public policy and legal developments.[152]

Integrated approaches are yet to see the light of the day, including, importantly, intersectional grounds of discrimination.

Answers may indeed be found in so-called '*plurinational constitutionalism*' which intends to formalise, ultimately codify long-established group claims. Somewhat in juxtaposition to the logics of equality principles, the new constitutional frameworks have been embracing a rationale that proves receptible towards different forms of plurality including its economic, social, judicial, political and cultural manifestations as shown in the Bolivian case. Among these forms of plurality, judicial pluralism[153] stands out as one of the most actively defended pluralisms in constitutional law while other forms such as economic pluralism[154] increasingly gain attention in the broader context of de-growth debates and *Buen Vivir/Vivir Bien*,[155] an emerging indigenous cosmovision that has found acceptation beyond indigenous communities. In fact, the new economic model promoted by the Political Constitution of the Bolivian State (Constitución Política del Estado) explicitly

---

150 Gargarella (2017).

151 Habermas (1992), p. 109.

152 Uprimny (2011), p. 1592.

153 Barrera (2012).

154 Acosta (2017) and Escobar (2014).

155 Solón (2017) and Gudynas (2011).

embraces a heterogenous economic system while regulating conditions of exchange between asymmetrical economic systems with the objective of diminishing social inequalities.[156] Seemingly, these latest constitutional reforms in the Andean region demonstrate a unique turn towards the multiplicity of rights, including an understanding of social justice reaching beyond the classical limited conception of equality and its focus on non-discrimination.

Other than their European counterparts, Latin American orders could be generally understood as favourable towards social constitutionalism: initiating with the Mexican Constitution in 1917, social rights became an accepted standard in constitutional reform processes from 1917 till the late 1980s.[157] More broadly, such reformist attitude would prove favourable to the declaration of rights across Latin America, marking a "*key moment of Latin American Constitutionalism*".[158] Albeit relatedly, it has been pointed to a "*region-wide tendency towards the juridification of social claims of all types*".[159] Similarly, it has been maintained that recent transformations in Latin American constitutionalism have been shaped by the recognition of collective, social, cultural and economic rights, hence contributing to higher levels of social equality and democratic transformation.[160] Such move may certainly be characteristic, distancing itself from the European origin of several Latin American constitutions,[161] contributing to a particular understanding of equality principles. A paradigm shift may indeed also be noted in terms of the theoretical rationale underlying such changes fitting into the categorical distinctions introduced by Fraser that highlight social equality and distributive justice, but equally justice of recognition as it may apply to indigenous peoples.[162] In a rather intense exchange with Honneth, Fraser in fact builds on the intrinsic relation between social justice and the politics of recognition with its difference-prone orientation.[163] If we were to derive larger conclusions on the matter as they relate to Latin American constitutionalism, equality principles have certainly been reinvented, by way of accommodating a multiplicity of pluralisms and collective rights, hence reflecting a positive discriminatory approach on the matter, and by including politically contentious social rights. These have become embedded in the social constitutionalism of the twentieth century, yet they have also proven influential more recently, notably throughout constitutional reform processes in Andean States leading to plurinational State designs.

---

[156] Romero Bonifaz (2009).

[157] Gargarella (2017).

[158] Ibid., para. 216.

[159] Sieder (2016), p. 144. Rodríguez-Garavito and Sousa Santos (2005) and Couso et al. (2010).

[160] Uprimny (2011).

[161] Góngora-Mera (2017).

[162] Uprimny (2011) and Fraser (1995).

[163] Fraser and Honneth (2003).

### *6.3.3 Peoples, Tribal and Nomadic Identities in Africa*

Comparative constitutional developments may provide yet another angle from which to appreciate the meaning of non-discrimination and equality principles in the different jurisdictions of the African continent. To be clear, a comparative study on the constitutional and legislative protection of the rights of indigenous peoples in 24 African States clearly demonstrates that only one State in the region established domestic legislation on 'indigenous populations' as such, being the Republic of the Congo that adopted a law to address the particular situation of the Pygmies by means of special measures, and Cameroon, which refers to indigenous populations in its constitution.[164] By contrast, the situation of minorities and that of ethnic groups is enjoying acceptance more widely, including the adoption of quota for ethnic groups in Burundi, also relevant being the criminalisation of incitement to ethnic hatred in the Congolese Constitution.[165] Noteworthy may also be the consideration of membership of a cultural or linguistic minority as a dedicated ground, complementary to race and ethnicity by the Democratic Republic of Congo, while also granting protection to vulnerable and minority groups.[166]

A rather fundamental component proving limiting to progressive laws may, however, lie with the colonial set-up in some constitutional frameworks, manifesting itself, for instance in the unequal treatment of chiefs, recognising some while not others in Botswana.[167] The Kenyan case similarly reveals tendencies towards treating different ethnic groups unequally, to be traced back to colonial times.[168] A final and related constraint to be considered concerns the assimilative design of some constitutions, illustrated indeed powerfully by the case of Rwanda that has been trying to strengthen unity with the objective of erasing ethnic divisions given its recent genocidal experience;[169] at the ending, this may be played out to the detriment of minority groups and their specific claims. In fact, the politics of recognition as

---

[164] African Commission on Human and Peoples' Rights, Centre for Human Rights, University of Pretoria, International Labour Organization (2009) *Overview Report of the Research Project by the International Labour Organization and the African Commission on Human and Peoples' Rights on the constitutional and legislative protection of the rights of indigenous peoples in 24 African countries.*

[165] Ibid.

[166] Ibid. See the following provisions in particular, arts. 11–13, 51 of the 2006 Constitution of the Democratic Republic of Congo.

[167] African Commission on Human and Peoples' Rights, Centre for Human Rights, University of Pretoria, International Labour Organization (2009) *Overview Report of the Research Project by the International Labour Organization and the African Commission on Human and Peoples' Rights on the constitutional and legislative protection of the rights of indigenous peoples in 24 African countries.* See also for an in-depth examination of indigenous peoples' situation in the region: Hitchcock et al. (2014).

[168] Ibid.

[169] African Commission on Human and Peoples' Rights, Centre for Human Rights, University of Pretoria, International Labour Organization (2009) *Overview Report of the Research Project by the International Labour Organization and the African Commission on Human and Peoples' Rights on*

these are promoted in different parts of the world enter into negotiation with conflict resolution and the fear related to ethnic dividing lines in Africa;[170] the Banjul Charter and its emphasis on decolonisation and non-domination of one people over another gives us a glance into the importance attributed to equality among peoples by African States.

In that sense, non-discrimination and equality principles assume a fundamental countervailing function, not least to prevent any legal gaps that would leave vulnerable groups completely unprotected. Interestingly, another twist is given to the debate, if we were to concern ourselves more profoundly with equality and non-discrimination principles: distinctions need to be made between different lists of grounds, those being exhaustive, others not necessarily being open-ended, and the related question of inclusive interpretation.[171] Courts may indeed play a considerable mediating role in that latter regard, in bridging the constitutional gaps in protecting indigenous peoples and distinct groups. Illustrative may be the Egyptian Constitutional Court maintaining that other "*equally serious forms of discrimination not explicitly referred to in the provision*" were to be considered which could also allow for "*indigenous status to be 'read into' the ambit of constitutional protection*".[172]

Yet another angle from which to look at equality principles concerns intersectionality with indigenous women's rights serving as a common reference: accordingly, indigenous Amazigh women in Algeria and Morocco have come to benefit from customary law 'Azref' recognising equality between women and men including individual freedoms while Algerian domestic laws have ignored the traditional Amazigh law and with it intersectional forms of discrimination; in Morocco, the effects of a relevant law are not perceived on the ground as far as Amazigh women are concerned.[173] This, it is argued, prevents a return to "*Amazigh values of equality and respect between the sexes*".[174] In neighbouring Tunisia, the Amazigh have come to face a related problem with standards not being implemented or regulated: while the Tunisian 2014 Constitution establishes gender equality, laws discriminating against women have been left in place, emblematic being the areas of marriage and inheritance.[175] Interestingly, these dynamics have been attributed to conflicts between (radical) Islamist movements and their gaining of political power

---

*the constitutional and legislative protection of the rights of indigenous peoples in 24 African countries.* See art. 54 of the Constitution of Rwanda for that matter.

[170] Jackson and Rosberg (1982).

[171] African Commission on Human and Peoples' Rights, Centre for Human Rights, University of Pretoria, International Labour Organization (2009) *Overview Report of the Research Project by the International Labour Organization and the African Commission on Human and Peoples' Rights on the constitutional and legislative protection of the rights of indigenous peoples in 24 African countries.*

[172] Ibid., p. 31. *Constitutional Case No. 17*, Egyptian Constitutional Court in 1995.

[173] Lounes (2022) and Amharech (2022).

[174] Amharech (2022), p. 97.

[175] Lounes (2022).

and the contrasting traditions of freedom and secularism promoted by the Amazigh.[176] Despite considerable progress to be noted in constitutional law in particular, enforcement remains a persisting challenge in the region, drawing our attention to the distinction between de jure and de facto equality, and its wide-reaching consequences for indigenous victims and Amazigh women to particularly visible extent.

## 6.4 Positive Discrimination and Equality Principles: Opportunities and Contradictions

To start with, we shall differentiate between different angles from which to examine positive discriminatory practice, more particularly, how the concept is being studied by different social scientific disciplines. For reasons of practicality, positive discrimination is not used interchangeably with the term '*affirmative action*' which may or may not coincide in terms of meaning: while some accounts clearly require positive steps to be taken for affirmative action to be called as such, others acknowledge the fact that affirmative action is to be regarded a form of discrimination which "*shares with discrimination some significant feature that has moral salience*".[177] Approaching positive discrimination from the perspective of the law, it implies "*actively favouring one category of people over others because they are considered to be disadvantaged and thereby discriminating against those others*".[178] The definition hence clearly builds on disadvantage and its mediation in a relative sense, establishing favourable treatment granted to one group to the exclusion of other groups. A similar conceptualisation is followed by international law, viewed transversally, considering positive discrimination "*a key instrument of a politics of catching up between different groups (...) striving to promote a greater de facto equality (...) and to guarantee members of disadvantaged groups genuine equality of opportunities*".[179] Indeed, disadvantages in practice or de facto inequalities stand at the forefront of what the law aims to address. Legal theorists too have found much worth in examining the concept in depth; of particular value here is the shifting focus, moving away from a (positivistic) account on what the law transmits on the case of differential treatment, and instead discussing what the law ought to express in moral or political terms.[180]

Similar to the juridical approaches on the matter, political accounts build on disadvantage as a reason for specific consideration and ultimately action; positive discrimination is broadly understood as "*an institutionalised way of enabling those*

[176] Ibid.

[177] Suk (2018), p. 394.

[178] Law (2018), para. 1.

[179] Calvès (2016), p. 8.

[180] Lippert-Rasmussen (2018).

*historically disadvantaged by a political system to participate in public life (...) [it] implies applying different criteria for selection to representatives of different groups as a way of addressing the existing social inequalities*".[181] Very manifestly, emphasis is placed on participation as well as questions of representation. Sociological account almost naturally engage further with both the situation of disadvantage and the specific objective to be addressed, tailored to the particularity of the group and its overall social context; it is understood as "*policies and practices that favour groups (mainly ethnic groups and women) who have historically experienced disadvantages (usually in the fields of employment and education) (...) given the existing structures of inequalities and stereotypes, the policy is necessary in order to create equality of opportunities with historically privileged groups*".[182] As it becomes apparent here, a contextual analysis may be relevant—as it is often neglected by the law—paying tribute to their very positioning in society at large while placing emphasis on the group nature of such position. Albeit relatedly, historical contexts have been commonly referred to as a decisive criterion from which to view discrimination against a group, emblematic being the "*separate but equal discrimination*" between US Blacks and Whites that would not allow for equal but inferior conditions for US Blacks.[183]

Attention may also be paid to relevant public debates. Positive discrimination has clearly developed a variety of meanings, ultimately depending on the functions it has been assuming in the daily reality of politics. In that sense, it may be distinguished between positive discrimination as a 'technique' such as quota, as a 'political objective' in the sense of positive promotion, integrating inter-alia women, faith groups or disabled people, and finally as a 'rule of selective application' that ought to differentiate, treating those differently who are different, considering their inequality of situation.[184] Different scales may similarly become apparent in that context, for instance, how equality of opportunity is spelt out in such situations, ranging, notably from mitigating social inequalities to "*requiring the neutralization of all sources of unchosen inequality*".[185] Again, a comprehensive, contextual perspective on the individual's and group's social environment seems inevitable if we wanted to get a sense of not only grounds and patterns of violations but also ways to take action in the form of positive discriminatory measures. Relatedly, a relevant policy dilemma concerns the sector the principle finds application in. As several accounts hint at, positive discrimination arguably remains limited in application to education admission processes, in the sense of admitting students from underrepresented groups.[186] Similar arguments have been made in relation to the neighbouring principle of affirmative action which has come to enjoy broad acceptance as 'justified

[181] Rai (2018), para. 1.

[182] Scott and Marshall (2015), para. 1.

[183] Thomsen (2018), p. 22.

[184] Calvès (2016).

[185] Moles (2018), p. 125. See also: Mason (2006) and Segall (2013).

[186] Elford (2018). See also: Guerrero (2002).

discrimination'[187] in some cases while remaining far from universally adopted throughout different policy sectors. Another final consideration concerns the very core of the action taken—legal action may differ in terms of its objective which could be '*forward-looking*' and in that sense "*invok[ing] the goal of achieving distributive justice in the future*"[188] or '*backward-looking*' which alludes to the "*necessity of rectificatory or compensatory justice*".[189] Especially the structural nature of most group rights violations renders a consideration of both rationales inevitable, namely paying due consideration of the historical context of marginalisation many minority groups are facing (backward-looking), and on the other hand, persisting challenges such as those arising with inter-generational claims, prominently defended by indigenous peoples.

### 6.4.1 Positive Discrimination as a Counterbalancing Right, Discourse and Policy

To start with, positive discrimination is commonly portrayed as a form of '*reverse discrimination*', intrinsically relating to discriminatory treatment that gives rise to respective responses by the law and beyond.[190] Similar conclusions may be drawn on its dealing with inequalities, their mediation constituting a key concern for positive discriminatory approaches and policies. Reverse discrimination indeed reflects a common approach taken. Conversely, one may argue there is "*hypocrisy in claiming a concern for social justice only when one becomes a potential victim of injustice*",[191] hence revealing the structural, long-lasting nature of violations which require a holistic approach on the matter. Interestingly, such reversal of discrimination is consciously placed into the surrounding societal context, that of the dominant majority whose "*primary concern [has been that of] accepting the privileges of their dominance*".[192] Very clearly then, policy decisions are made dependent on institutional logics and those actively employed by decision-makers benefitting from a privileged position and who show commonly at unease to amend the status quo in favour of differential treatment.

When taken seriously, reverse discrimination may give rise to respective obligations to adopt positive measures based on the principle of non-discrimination and the idea of equality.[193] More is said on such obligations as they have been interpreted by

[187] Suk (2018).

[188] Hull (2018), p. 414.

[189] Ibid., p. 414.

[190] Suk (2018).

[191] Noon (2010), p. 736.

[192] Ibid., p. 736.

[193] Inter-American Commission on Human Rights (2019) *Compendium on Equality and Non-Discrimination. Inter-American Standards*.

the Inter-American human rights system: affirmative action is explicitly solicitated to reverse discriminatory situations and relatedly, establishes important obligations towards third parties whose role in creating discriminatory situations is being tolerated or acquiesced.[194] What is more, the Inter-American Commission further elaborates on the point that any failure to take affirmative action with the objective of reversing discrimination gives rise to the State's international responsibility;[195] such obligation applies to *de jure* and *de facto* discriminatory practice respectively.[196] Conceptually, or more broadly speaking, reverse discrimination has been understood as falling under the umbrella of '*special measures*' according to IHRL terminology,[197] or, alternatively, as being tantamount to positive discrimination as catch-all categories considered "*necessary to guarantee the substantive equality and enjoyment of fundamental rights of historically disadvantaged persons and social groups or victims of ongoing prejudice*"[198] which has been embraced by international human rights bodies respectively.[199] Difficulties may however result from the technical nuances of the term: notably, is has been maintained that the expression 'positive discrimination' manifests a contradiction in terminis—"*if the difference is discrimination, it cannot be positive and, if it is justified, it cannot be discrimination*".[200]

In practice, the concept is rather commonly examined, contrasting its underlying rationale with meritocratic thought. This is the case for the education and labour sectors respectively, that is, those policy sectors most regulated in terms of non-discrimination.[201] In fact, positive discriminatory measures have been attacked for violating meritocratic norms, building on the premise or "*rhetorical framing of affirmative action as a form of discrimination*".[202] In most university contexts, for

[194] *V.R.P. and V.P.C. vs. Nicaragua*, Inter-American Court of Human Rights in 2016. *Advisory Opinion OC-18 Juridical Condition and Rights of the Undocumented Migrants*, Inter-American Court of Human Rights in 2003.

[195] *Wallace de Almeida vs. Brazil*, Inter-American Court of Human Rights in 2009. Inter-American Commission on Human Rights (2011) *Situation of Persons of African Descent in the Americas*; Inter-American Commission on Human Rights (2017) *Report on Poverty and Human Rights in the Americas.*

[196] *Wallace de Almeida vs. Brazil*, Inter-American Court of Human Rights in 2009.

[197] Inter-American Commission on Human Rights (2019) *Compendium on Equality and Non-Discrimination. Inter-American Standards.*

[198] Inter-American Commission on Human Rights (2011) *Situation of Persons of African Descent in the Americas*, para. 23.

[199] Committee on Economic, Social and Cultural Rights (2009) *General Comment N°20 Non-Discrimination in Economic, Social and Cultural Rights* (Article 2, para. 2). See also: Inter-American Commission on Human Rights (1999) *Annual Report Considerations regarding the Compatibility of Affirmative Action Measures Designed to Promote the Political Participation of Women with the Principles of Equality and Non-Discrimination.*

[200] Bossuyt (2016), p. 43.

[201] See e.g. Belavusau and Henrard (2018). See also Lippert-Rasmussen (2018). See also Bennett et al. (2005).

[202] Suk (2018), p. 394.

instance, discriminatory admission (selection) processes are governed by merit, depending on the "*broader justification for that criterion*".[203] In those cases, we get immersed into a complex debate on the entanglement and interplay of discrimination contexts such as socio-economic background and merit-based selection criteria and their different manifestations in the employment and education sectors:

> If part of the purpose of an education system is to develop merit, and if there are egalitarian reasons against allowing a child's social class to influence inequalities in that regard, then one might suppose that there are reasons that apply to an education system in particular to offset inequalities in merit, rather than take them as given. In this way the merit-developing purpose of education distinguishes it from other domains like employment, where it's not clear that any given employer has a particular responsibility to discount for background inequalities between candidates' ability to fulfil the selection criteria. In contrast, one might think of admissions processes in education as part of a wider education system which has a role responsibility for the allocation of educational resources, a part of which involves taking into consideration the desirability of ensuring that social class inequalities do not translate into differential opportunities provided by education. All of this falls far short of a case in favour of taking less meritorious students whose comparative lack of merit is partly a result of their social class.[204]

As it may easily become discernible from these accounts, background inequalities are counted as yet another core criterion that remains subject to evaluation, ultimately the subjective choice of taking or not socio-economic circumstances into account. The law remains short-sighted in that sense, failing to take account of a person's overall situation which remains intrinsically related to arising inequalities, a person's performance and (development of) capacities. Rather visibly, the quality inherent to positive discrimination as a specialised regime on its own falls far from being integrated into selection processes.

Relatedly, the meritocratic critique of the principle has been attributed to economic individualism.[205] As it becomes apparent from the above, we certainly witness a structural, group manifestation of the violations in place. Such line of reasoning inherently excludes any contextual perspective from being considered with economic individualism being understood as a value-free, neutral concept applicable to any individual forming part of society in one way or another. It is further aggregated that such view commonly attracts attention among proponents of "*non-interventionary approaches to securing equality*"[206] which may read like a contradiction from the perspective of substantive equality approaches and those considering *de jure* and *de facto* manifestations part of the same principle and ultimately obligation. Competing principles clearly stand in the way of any mainstreaming efforts towards positive discrimination as for discrimination to be reversed, it first needs to be acknowledged by policy makers, both as a phenomenon affecting individuals and groups at large.

---

[203] Elford (2018), p. 316.

[204] Ibid., p. 316.

[205] Noon (2010).

[206] Ibid., p. 733.

A reconciling position is assumed if we were to understand equal treatment as demanded by majority groups as not bringing about any absolute rights as the "*loss must be treated as a matter of concern, but that loss may be outweighed by benefit of the community as a whole*"[207] without refraining from treating such person with the same concern and respect. Ultimately, said loss would be outweighed by the interests of diversity and redressing the absence of minorities in senior positions such as in the case of the Black minority in US American universities.[208] Conversely, an absolute right could very well be seen from the perspective of minority groups countering the egalitarian priority of 'relativities', comparing different persons' levels for that matter: in that sense, we should be "*concerned only with people's absolute levels (...) [as] this approach makes equality redundant: what matters are people's absolute entitlements, rather than their entitlements relative to others*".[209] On the shadowy side, absolute entitlement may lead to settling at the minimum without engaging with any disparities above such levels, and in that sense, substantive equality is called for to at least "*reduce the gap between the more disadvantaged and the less disadvantaged*".[210]

### 6.4.2 *Levels of Positive Discrimination: Measuring and Examining Impact*

As the de facto—de jure divide demonstrates, positive discrimination may assume a multiplicity of forms and formats. Questions of implementation and monitoring remain an on-going challenge for the principle to bear fruit and to do justice to its premises and promises. As it is unequivocally maintained elsewhere, positive measures do not necessarily "*deny the successes of the existing law, but does show a frustration with the rate of change (...) therefore, there is a growing interest in the equality of results*".[211]

Some attempts have been made indeed with a view to implement positive discrimination which however, as would be expected, came to collide with classical legal principles such as 'proportionality' resulting in, for instance, the appointment of the best qualified person, presumably to "*promote fairness by regarding a candidate's sex as being just one of a number of characteristics that must be weighted up*".[212] Manifestly, a person's minority-specific background remains far from understood holistically, falling short of any structural, contextual examination

[207] Bennett et al. (2005), p. 224. Dworkin (1977).

[208] Dworkin (2000).

[209] Fredman (2016), p. 722.

[210] Ibid., p. 722.

[211] Bennett et al. (2005), p. 224.

[212] Ibid., p. 244. A similar reasoning becomes apparent in Dworkin's reasoning on positive discrimination, see Dworkin (2000).

of a person's circumstances which, in turn, could be understood as a conglomerate of individual discriminatory grounds.

Different scales that positive discrimination may assume have been discussed elsewhere, differentiating between '*affirmative mobilisation*' and '*affirmative fairness*' on one side of the spectrum and '*affirmative preference*' on the other side.[213] Affirmative mobilisation thereby refers to, for instance, affirmative recruitment, by incentivising relevant groups to apply for a specific social good such as a job or place at university while affirmative fairness could be seen as tantamount to "*a meticulous examination that takes place in order to make sure that members of target groups have been treated fairly in the attribution of social goods, such as entering an educational institution, receiving a job or promotion*".[214] When it comes to affirmative preference, discriminatory grounds are taken into account more directly, finding due consideration when certain social goods are either granted or withheld; it could be argued that such form of special consideration "*treats people as members of groups or categories without regard to individual merit*".[215]

Another attempt of scaling different forms of equality, albeit at a higher level, is made when distinguishing between '*substantive equality*' and '*transformative equality*': as explained earlier, substantive equality goes as far as offering opportunities to respond to disproportionate exclusion which has however been criticised due to its somewhat passive approach towards the "*underlying social framework that denies them genuine choice and generates inequitable outcomes*".[216] Transformative equality, instead, responds to systemic inequalities, demanding the removal of barriers or offering adequate resources, generally to be considered a reaction to systemic failings.[217] This indeed mirrors what has been understood as positive human rights obligations, the duty to fulfil, to be exact, requiring States to take action beyond mere non-interference that some proponents of classical equality principles would defend. Such analytical framework further stresses the need to alienate ourselves from the individualistic, case-oriented outlook, being emblematic of many legal accounts on the matter; again, proving largely ignorant of important contextual, systemic concerns.

A more technical division is made in an attempt of developing a taxonomy of positive discriminatory measures (here: presented as '*affirmative action*') including the following, namely "*positive measures to avoid unlawful discrimination; indirectly inclusionary measures; attracting qualified candidates using advertising and training targeting the underrepresented group; 'tie-break' policies, where individuals from underrepresented group are preferred where equally well qualified; and preferential treatment for members of the targeted group*".[218] While the first

[213] Bossuyt (2016).

[214] Ibid., p. 51.

[215] Ibid., p. 52.

[216] Hepple (2014), p. 28. Bossuyt (2016).

[217] Bossuyt (2016).

[218] McCrudden (2015), p. 248.

mentioned measures indeed imply a rather moderate dealing with discriminatory grounds, the last form would be considered as most controversial given the unpopularity of policies that prove to threaten meritocratic principles in favour of radical approaches towards positive discrimination. To start with, "*positive measures to avoid unlawful discrimination*" could be grouped around three types of action, namely "*(1) activity preventing and remedying direct discrimination; (2) activity taken proactively to remove indirect, systemic, and institutional discrimination; and (3) reasonable accommodation measures, taken to enable an individual from a particular group to gain access to particular employment or a particular service*".[219] Rather clearly, emphasis is placed on eliminating barriers which may however also include State action taken to prevent violations committed by the third sector. Albeit relatedly, '*indirectly inclusionary measures*' alludes to, for instance, government assistance in specific geographical areas, permitting minority groups to benefit disproportionately as these show disproportionately represented in a given region; it may also be noted that such measures at times prove more realisable given the unacceptability of other forms of affirmative action.[220] Thirdly, "*advertising and training targeting the underrepresented group*" commonly involves outreach programmes which are designed to informing members of such groups of employment positions, incentivising them to apply, and to prepare those members through capacity skills programmes in order to improve chances to be employed.[221] While this latter form is commonly termed as '*supply side-oriented*' (directed at underrepresented group members), so-called '*tie-break policies*' are meant to favour a member of an unrepresented group where candidates are equally well qualified, including identifying individuals for that matter, without however challenging the meritocratic foundations operating.[222] Finally, "*preferential treatment for members of the targeted group*" represent arguably a controversial form of positive discrimination, by offering an advantage to a 'less well-qualified' person being member of an underrepresented group to the detriment of a 'better qualified' person; different procedural nuances may coexist in that regard including preference for a specific candidate or quota favouring representatives from an underrepresented group.[223] Importantly, the concept of merit is either set aside granting preference to increasing participation; merit may also be reconceptualised by, for instance, amending admission procedures for relevant criteria to grant preference to members representing underrepresented groups.[224] As it becomes apparent from the above, policy measures in the field of positive discrimination commonly undergo sophisticated design processes in between the de jure and de facto logics of the principle,

[219] Ibid., p. 249.
[220] Ibid., p. 249.
[221] Ibid., p. 249.
[222] Ibid., p. 249.
[223] Ibid., p. 250.
[224] Ibid., p. 250.

negotiating ground between meritocracy and pure forms of minority representation, or shifting attention between majorities, minorities and the State.

More scales and levels of differentiation may become apparent from an integral reading of discrimination, for instance by putting an end to all kinds of discrimination,[225] including important intersectional questions of discrimination. This may be derived from the very rationale of intersectionality having "*primarily developed as a critique of equality and discrimination law*".[226] Intersectionality and its very legal expression could indeed be approached as adding another layer to special treatment, notably, as a response to discrimination law which has remained rather silent on the "*complexity of disadvantage associated with multiple grounds of identity and disadvantage*".[227] Another chronical ill lies in the common misconception founded in the belief that intersectionality is to be dealt with in isolation, as a 'specific intersectional problem' rather than "*problems of human rights law generally*"[228]—thereby demonstrating awareness of the complexity of the violation itself without however engaging further with underlying structural questions such as the positioning of IHRL on the question, let alone witnessing any emerging mainstreamed approach on the matter.

An interesting turn to the debate is given if we were to relate positive discrimination to the specific case of ethnic or cultural minority groups, meriting a debate on its own, and—it is being maintained here—would form a proper level of distinguished 'treatment'. Also elsewhere positive discrimination is understood in a particular group context, embracing inter-alia race or ethnic criteria which ultimately determine how rights are being guaranteed by the respective State.[229] Relatedly, positive discrimination is placed under the umbrella of multicultural policies or differential policy making.[230] It may similarly be argued that such targeting policies are not to be viewed in isolation but form part of a "*larger socio-political project that deals with diversity and equity*".[231]

### *6.4.3 Positive Discrimination: Towards an Inclusive Understanding of Recognition Through First, Second, and Third Generation Rights*

As the foregoing suggests, the sheer acknowledgement of difference may prove insufficient, especially structurally, in view of an integral protection of group rights.

225 Velasco Arroyo (2007). See also Dworkin (2000).

226 Atrey (2021), p. 2. Crenshaw (1989).

227 Atrey (2021), p. 2. Crenshaw (1989).

228 Atrey (2021), p. 3.

229 Velasco Arroyo (2007).

230 Wieviorka (2004).

231 Velasco Arroyo (2007), p. 3.

Instead, it is proposed here to engage more closely with the concept of positive discrimination as it materialises in diverging ways depending on the right at stake, it is hypothesised: first, second, and third generation rights engage in their own, particular way with positive obligations. Reflections of this kind may show facilitating in appreciating the extent or degree to which specific rights live up to the expectation of inclusiveness that is attributable to the question of recognition.

Some accounts portray the genealogy of human rights—initiating with first generation rights and finding their most recent form with third generation rights—as one that develops from negative to positive duties.[232] Debates on the nature of obligations in that regard appear endless among human rights scholars, broadly distinguishing between the aforediscussed triadic obligation to '*respect*', '*protect*' and '*fulfil*'[233]—and the right to '*promote*' as it is complemented by the African human rights system. Some attempts have been made as they relate to the different nature of positive obligations arising with the different generations of rights:

> It [right to promote] connotes a genuine legal obligation. But the drafters of the [C]ESCR were aware of the factual elements conditioning performance of the commitments undertaken by States. Economic and social rights are to a large degree context-dependent, more than civil liberties. They have as their backdrop a concept of the State as a potent provider, but with the proviso that the duties owed to citizens can never be set out in absolute terms, but must take into account the scarcity of resources which any human community has to reckon with. With a critical tone, economic and social rights have sometimes been called 'manifesto rights',[234] rights holding a promise but not yet actually in existence.[235]

Such legal historical account[236] gives us an idea of the political load inherent to the classification of human rights, influencing, in turn, the nature of obligations arising therewith.

Quite the opposite may be argued if we were to place a focus on the duty to fulfil in relation to ESC rights, finding indeed detailed articulation throughout international law.[237] In its General Comment on State obligations, the Committee on

[232] Tomuschat (2014).

[233] Ibid. See also: Shue (1996).

[234] Ibid. See also: Feinberg (1973).

[235] Tomuschat (2014), pp. 141–142.

[236] To be clear, the comment broadly alludes to obligations as spelt out in art. 2(1) of the covenant, establishing that "*each State Party (...) undertakes to stake steps, individually and through international assistance and co-operation, especially economic and technical, to the maximum of its available resources, with a view to achieving progressively the full realisation of the rights recognised in the present Covenant by all appropriate means, including particularly the adoption of legislative measures*".

[237] See e.g. Clapham (2015). In relation to the right to food in its General Comment N°12, for instance, the Committee clearly stipulates elements pertaining to the core content of the right to food, with the following elements that could also find application in relation to other rights, namely '*cultural or consumer acceptability*', '*availability*', and '*accessibility*'. The Committee further spells out obligations in its General Comment N°14 as they arise when implementing the right to the highest attainable standard of health; it stipulates the following "*interrelated and essential elements*", namely, '*availability*', '*accessibility*'—including '*non-discrimination*', '*physical*

Economic, Social and Cultural Rights takes a clear stance on the realisation of covenant rights, namely for "*steps towards that goal (must) be taken within a reasonable short time*" after ratifying the treaty and for such steps to be "*deliberate, concrete and targeted as clearly as possible towards meeting the obligations (recognised in the Covenant)*".[238] Relatedly, the Committee pronounces itself on the '*time criterion*', for rights to be supposedly realised over time:

> The fact that realisation over time, or in other words progressively, is foreseen under the Covenant should not be misinterpreted as depriving the obligation of all meaningful content. It is on the one hand a necessary flexibility device, reflecting the realities of the real world and the difficulties involved for any country in ensuring full realization of economic, social and cultural rights. On the other hand, the phrase must be read in the light of the overall objective, indeed the raison d'être, of the Covenant which is to establish clear obligations for States parties in respect of the full realization of the rights in question. It thus imposes an obligation to move as expeditiously and effectively as possible towards that goal.[239]

Also in terms of the relativising wording of art. 2(1) ICESCR, the Committee provides interpretative guidance as to the nature of obligations arising with the wording '*maximum of its [the State's] available resources*', an obligation that is often invoked, as a few extracts from its General Comment N° 3 clearly demonstrate:

> the Committee underlines the fact that even in times of severe resources constraints (...) the vulnerable members of society can and indeed must be protected by the adoption of relatively low-cost targeted programmes (...) international cooperation for development and thus for the realisation of economic, social and cultural rights is an obligation of all States. It is particularly incumbent upon those States which are in a position to assist others in this regard.[240]

Another key question spelling out positive discrimination concerns its '*appropriateness*'. The Committee retains important discretionary powers by stating that "*the ultimate determination as to whether all appropriate measures have been taken remains one for the Committee to make*".[241]

Curiously, the same Committee has engaged in comparative analysis, referring to civil and political rights (first generation rights), and in particular as to the specific obligations arising in that regard: rather than implying any '*progressive realisation*' of the rights at stake as it is the case for ESC rights, equivalent protection in the field of CP rights refers to an "*immediate obligation to respect and ensure all of the relevant rights*";[242] other than the ambiguous nature of ESC duties suggests, first

---

*accessibility*', '*economic accessibility (affordability)*', '*information accessibility*'—'*acceptability*', and '*quality*'. Similarly, the Committee uses the opportunity to spell out obligations as they relate to the right to education in its General Comment N°13, notably it reiterates the elements established in General Comment N°14 while it does add another element, namely '*adaptability*'.

[238] Committee on Economic, Social and Cultural Rights (1990) *General Comment No. 3. The Nature of States Parties' Obligations (Art. 2, Para. 1)*, para. 2.

[239] Ibid., para. 9.

[240] Ibid., paras. 12, 14.

[241] Ibid., para. 4.

[242] Ibid., para. 9.

generation rights appear more enforceable, more justiciable from the outset. It may however be observed that these very first generation rights show less at ease with positive obligations, broadly understood as '*defensive rights*' protecting against arbitrary interferences—reflecting a common opinion in the human rights literature.[243]

Categorical distinctions have been drawn in relation to first and second generation rights in the sense that they have been giving rise to remarkably distinct obligations. The difference in kind was concisely captured by the following account, bringing in different principles at work:

> *Civil rights require, in essence, an* abstention *of the State by imposing* negative *obligations, while social rights require an active* intervention *by imposing* positive *obligations. Consequently, the content of civil rights is* invariable, *regardless of the available resources, while social rights have* variable *content. (...) The recognition in international or domestic law of civil rights implies the respect of* all *those rights,* immediately *and for* everybody. *On the contrary, not all social rights of all persons can be implemented at once. (...) The function of a system of protection of civil rights is mainly* institutional *(setting up a mechanism of control), while for social rights its function is* normative *(providing new rights to the beneficiaries). In that sense, recognition of civil rights is* declaratory *in nature while the attribution of (new) social rights is* constitutive.[244]

In practice, boundaries may get blurred, demanding comprehensive protection frameworks for both generations under, most famously, the duty to fulfil. As alluded to earlier, a notable circle of scholars refers to the universal, indivisible, interdependent and interrelated nature of rights dating back to the Vienna Declaration and Programme of Action of 1993. Yet others have described the negative vs. positive rights distinction as "*occupy[ing] a rigid conceptual space*"[245] and prescribing the following, accordingly:

> Do not let any theorist tell you that the concrete reality of rights enforcement is so simple that all the implementation of any right can usefully be summed up either as positive or negative. The constructive point was: look what it actually takes to enable people to be secure against the standard, predictable threats to their rights – focus on the duties required to implement the rights.[246]

Despite its somewhat hostile stance towards theory, the account does seem to see some merit in the conceptual question of duties which is discussed here. At the end of the day, both first and second generation rights are constantly (re-)negotiated in practice, subject to a complex interplay of daily politics and prioritisations, and the multiplicity of actors involved when implementing positive duties. Not uncommonly, obligations beyond interference, that is, the taking of active steps is

---

[243] See e.g. Henrard (2020). See also van Boven (1982) and Bossuyt (2016).

[244] Bossuyt (2016), pp. 20–21.

[245] Koch (2005), p. 103.

[246] Ibid., p. 103.

associated with rights broadly speaking, without any further demarcation line drawn or taxonomies established.[247]

## References


Acosta A (2017) Posextractivismo: del Discurso a la Práctica—Reflexiones para la Acción. International Development Policy/Revue internationale de politique de développement 9

Alidadi K (2017) Religion, Equality and Employment in Europe: the Case for Reasonable Accommodation. Hart Publishing, Oxford

Alidadi K (2018) Cultural diversity in the workplace: personal autonomy as a pillar for the accommodation of employees' religious practices? In: Foblets M-C, Graziadei M, Dundes Renteln A (eds) Personal autonomy in plural societies: a principle and its paradoxes. Routledge, Abingdon

Amharech A (2022) Morocco. In: Mamo D (ed) The indigenous world 2022. The International Work Group for Indigenous Affairs, Copenhagen

Anaya J (2004) Indigenous peoples in international law. Oxford University Press, Oxford

Atrey S (2018) Comparison in intersectional discrimination. Leg Stud 38

Atrey S (2021) Introduction: intersectionality from equality to human rights. In: Atrey S, Dunne P (eds) Intersectionality and human rights law. Hart, Oxford

Atrey S (2022) Feminist constitutionalism: mapping a discourse in contestation. Int J Constitutional Law

Badie B, Vidal D (2017) Un Monde d'Inégalités. La Découverte, Paris

Baldwin C, Morel C (2009) Group rights. In: Evans M, Murray R (eds) The African Charter on Human and Peoples' Rights: the system in practice, 1986–2006. Cambridge University Press, Cambridge

Barrera A (2012) Turning legal pluralism into state-sanctioned law: assessing the implications of the new constitutions and laws in Bolivia and Ecuador. In: Schilling-Vacaflor A (ed) New constitutionalism in Latin America: promises and practices. Ashgate, Farnham

Baumgart N (2020) Alte und neue Minderheiten—Wahrung und Erhaltung der eigenständigen Identität durch das Recht. Minderheitenstudien: Sprache und Identität

Belavusau U, Henrard K (2018) EU anti-discrimination law beyond gender. Hart Publishing, Oxford

Belavusau U, Henrard K (2019) The impact of the 2000 equality directives on EU anti-discrimination law: achievements and pitfalls. In: Belavusau U, Henrard K (eds) EU anti-discrimination law beyond gender. Hart Publishing, Oxford

Bennett M, Roberts S, Davis H (2005) The way forward—positive discrimination or positive action? Int J Discrimination Law 6

Bernot S (2015) Die verfassungsrechtliche Anerkennung indigenen Rechts, Rechtspluralismus und Menschenrechte: Untersucht an den Beispielen Südafrika und Bolivien. Nomos, Baden-Baden

Bossuyt MJ (2016) International human rights protection: balanced, critical, realistic. Intersentia, Cambridge

Boulden J, Kymlicka W (2015) International Approaches to Governing Ethnic Diversity. Oxford University Press, Oxford


[247] Take, for instance, the following interpretation issued by the UK Joint Committee on Human Rights in its Sixth Report: "*This means that the obligation of States goes beyond mere non-interference with the rights. In some circumstances, they are obliged to take active steps to protect people's rights against interference by others, or to enhance people's capacity to take advantage of the rights*" (para. 6). For further details, see McCrudden (2004).

Boysen S (2011) Europäische Charta der Regional- oder Minderheitensprachen: Handkommentar. Dike, Zürich
Bustami A (2022) An intertemporal perspective on intergenerational equity. Verfassungsblog. https://verfassungsblog.de/an-intertemporal-perspective-on-intergenerational-equity/
Byrd DG (2015) The European Charter for Regional or Minority Languages: conflict, resistance and change. PhD dissertation, University of Utah, Faculty of Political Science
Calvès G (2016) La Discrimination Positive. Presses Universitaires de France, Paris
Caruso U, Malloy T, Hofmann M (2013) Introduction and acknowledgements. In: Malloy TH, Caruso U (eds) Minorities, their rights, and the monitoring of the European Framework Convention for the Protection of National Minorities: essays in honour of Rainer Hofmann. BRILL, Leiden
Cavallaro JL, Vargas C, Sandoval C, Duhaime B (2019) Doctrine, practice, and advocacy in the Inter-American human rights system. Oxford University Press, Oxford
Chakim ML (2019) The margin of appreciation and freedom of religion: assessing standards of the European Court of Human Rights. Int J Hum Rights 24(6)
Charters C, Stavenhagen R (2012) Making the declaration work: the United Nations Declaration on the Rights of Indigenous Peoples. IWGIA, Copenhagen
Clapham A (2015) Human rights: a very short introduction. Oxford University Press, Oxford
Claridge L (2017) Briefing: victory for Kenya's Ogiek as African Court sets major precedent for indigenous peoples' land rights. Minority Rights Group International, London
Couso J, Huneeus A, Sieder R (2010) Cultures of legality: judicialization and political activism in Latin America. Cambridge University Press, New York
Crenshaw KW (1989) Demarginalizing the intersection of race and sex: a black feminist critique of antidiscrimination doctrine, feminist theory and antiracist politics. University of Chicago Legal Forum 139
Davis KE (2021) Legal responses to black subordination, global perspectives. Harv Law Rev 134
De Schutter O (2005) Reasonable accommodations and positive obligations in the European Convention on Human Rights. In: Lawson A, Gooding C (eds) Disability rights in Europe: from theory to practice. Hart Publishing, Oxford
De Witte B (2000) Politics vs. law in the EU's approach to ethnic minorities. EUI working paper/ Robert Schumann Center 4
De Witte B (2008) Introduction: exploring a central pillar of the European minority rights system. In: Verstichel A, Andre A, de Witte B, Lemmens P (eds) The Framework Convention for the Protection of National Minorities: a useful pan-European instrument? Intersentia, Cambridge
De Witte B (2012) The worlds of European constitutionalism. Cambridge University Press, Cambridge
Dersso SA (2006) The jurisprudence of the African Commission on Human and Peoples' Rights with respect to peoples' rights. Afr Hum Rights Law J 6
Dworkin R (1977) Taking rights seriously. Duckworth, London
Dworkin R (2000) Sovereign virtue. Harvard University Press, Boston
Eichler J (2022) The transformative forces of international law? Questioning equality regimes from a multi-level perspective. Global Constitutionalism
Elford G (2018) Discrimination and education. In: Lippert-Rasmussen K (ed) The Routledge handbook of ethics of discrimination. Routledge, London
Escobar A (2014) Sentipensar con la Tierra: Nuevas Lecturas sobre Desarrollo, Territorio y Diferencia. Ediciones UNAULA, Medellín
Feinberg J (1973) Social philosophy. Prentice Hall, Englewood Cliffs
Foblets M-C (2017) Foreword. In: Alidadi K (ed) Religion, equality and employment in Europe: the case for reasonable accommodation. Hart Publishing, Abingdon
Foblets M-C, Bosset P (2010) Accommodating diversity in Québec and Europe: different legal concepts, similar results? In: Council of Europe (ed) Institutional accommodation and the

citizen: legal and political interaction in a pluralist society. Council of Europe Publishing, Strasbourg

Fraser N (1995) From redistribution to recognition? Dilemmas of justice in a "post-socialist" age. New Left Rev I(212)

Fraser N, Honneth A (2003) Redistribution or recognition? A political philosophical exchange. Verso, London

Fredman S (2016) Substantive equality revisited. Int J Constitutional Law 14(3)

Ganty S (2022) A right to the effective access to rights: a pleonasm? ICON•S annual conference, Wrocław

García Ramírez S (2017) The American human rights navigation: toward a Ius Commune. In: Bogdandy A, Ferrer MacGregor E, Morales Antoniazzi M, Piovesan F (eds) Transformative constitutionalism in Latin America: the emergence of a new Ius Commune. Oxford University Press, Oxford

Gargarella R (2017) The "new" Latin American constitutionalism: old wine in new skins. In: Bogdandy A, Ferrer MacGregor E, Morales Antoniazzi M, Piovesan F (eds) Transformative constitutionalism in Latin America: the emergence of a new Ius Commune. Oxford University Press, Oxford

Góngora-Mera ME (2017) The block of constitutionality as the doctrinal pivot of a Ius Commune. In: Bogdandy A, Ferrer MacGregor E, Morales Antoniazzi M, Piovesan F (eds) Transformative constitutionalism in Latin America: the emergence of a new Ius Commune. Oxford University Press, Oxford

González-Ricoy I (2016) Constitutionalizing intergenerational provisions. In: González-Ricoy I, Gosseries A (eds) Institutions for future generations. Oxford University Press, Oxford

Goshal N (2020) Transgender, third gender, no gender: rights perspectives on laws assigning gender part I. Opinio Juris. http://opiniojuris.org/2020/09/04/transgender-third-gender-no-gender-rights-perspectives-on-laws-assigning-gender-part-i/

Gover K (forthcoming) Article 33. In: Eichler J, Doyle C, Howard S (eds) United Nations Declaration on the Rights of Indigenous Peoples: article-by-article commentary. Beck/Hart/Nomos, München/Baden-Baden/Oxford

Gudynas E (2011) Buen Vivir: Today's tomorrow. Development 54(4)

Guerrero A (2002) Silence at Boalt Hall: the dismantling of affirmative action. University of California Press, Berkeley

Habermas J (1992) Struggles for recognition in the democratic constitutional state. In: Taylor C (ed) Multiculturalism and the 'politics of recognition'. Princeton University Press, Princeton

Halldenius L (2018) Discrimination and irrelevance. In: Lippert-Rasmussen K (ed) The Routledge handbook of ethics of discrimination. Routledge, London

Havelková B, Möschel M (2019) Anti-discrimination law in civil law jurisdictions. Oxford University Press, Oxford

Henrard K (2011) An EU perspective on new versus traditional minorities: on semi-inclusive socio-economic integration and expanding visions of "European" culture and identity. Colombia J Eur Law 17

Henrard K (2020) Positive state obligations regarding fundamental rights and 'changing the hearts and minds'. Erasmus Law Rev 3

Hepple B (2014) Equality: the legal framework. Hart Publishing, Oxford

Hitchcock RK, Sapignoli M, Babchuk WA (2014) Settler colonialism, conflicts, and genocide: interactions between hunter-gatherers and settlers in Kenya, and Zimbabwe and northern Botswana. Settler Colonial Stud 5(1)

Hofmann R (2004) The Framework Convention at the end of the first cycle of monitoring in filling the frame. In: Council of Europe (ed) Filling the frame: 5 years of monitoring the Framework Convention for the Protection of National Minorities. Council of Europe, Strasbourg

Hofmann R, Angst D, Lantschner E, Rautz G, Rein D (2015) Das Rahmenübereinkommen zum Schutz nationaler Minderheiten: Handkommentar. Nomos, Baden-Baden

Hoyos A (1992) El Control Judicial y el Bloque de Constitucionalidad en Panamá. Boletín Mexicano de Derecho Comparado 75

Hull G (2018) Discrimination and diversity. In: Lippert-Rasmussen K (ed) The Routledge handbook of ethics of discrimination. Routledge, London

Huneeus A, Madsen MR (2018) Between universalism and regional law and politics: a comparative history of the American, European, and African human rights systems. Int J Constitutional Law 16(1)

Imai S, Gunn K (2018) Indigenous belonging: membership and identity in the UNDRIP: Articles 9, 33, 35, and 36. In: Hohmann J, Weller M (eds) The UN Declaration on the Rights of Indigenous Peoples: a commentary. Oxford University Press, Oxford

Jackson RH, Rosberg CG (1982) Why Africa's weak states persist: the empirical and the juridical in statehood. World Polit 35(1)

Jovanović M (2012) Collective rights: a legal theory. Cambridge University Press, Cambridge

Jovanović M (2022) Making social groups visible to and in law—essentialisation and law's generality. In: Eichler J, Topidi K (eds) Minority recognition and the diversity deficit: comparative perspectives. Hart Publishing, Oxford

Klocker C (2019) Empowerment of indigenous and ethnic groups: comparing cases on land use under the ACHPR and ECHR. Völkerrechtsblog. https://voelkerrechtsblog.org/de/empowerment-of-indigenous-and-ethnic-groups/

Koch IE (2005) Dichotomies, trichotomies or waves of duties. Hum Rights Law Rev 5(1)

Kochenov D (2015) The European Union's troublesome minority protection: a bird's-eye view. In: Boulden J, Kymlicka W (eds) International approaches to governing ethnic diversity. Oxford University Press, Oxford

Kymlicka W (1995) Multicultural citizenship: a liberal theory of minority rights. Oxford University Press, Oxford

Larmore C (1990) Political liberalism. Polit Theory 18(3)

Law J (2018) Positive discrimination. In: Law J (ed) A dictionary of law. Oxford University Press, Oxford

Lebsanft F, Wingender M (2012) Einleitung: Zur Konzeption und Benutzung des Handbuchs. In: Lebsanft F, Wingender M (eds) Europäische Charta der Regional- oder Minderheitensprachen: Ein Handbuch zur Sprachpolitik des Europarats. Walter de Gruyter GmbH, Berlin

Lippert-Rasmussen K (2006) The badness of discrimination. Ethical Theory Moral Pract 9

Lippert-Rasmussen K (2018) The philosophy of discrimination: an introduction. In: Lippert-Rasmussen K (ed) The Routledge handbook of ethics of discrimination. Routledge, London

Lounes B (2022) Algeria. In: Mamo D (ed) The indigenous world 2022. The International Work Group for Indigenous Affairs, Copenhagen

Marko J (2013) Five years after: continuing reflections on the thematic commentary on effective participation. The interplay between equality and participation. In: Caruso U, Malloy TH, Hofmann M (eds) Minorities, their rights, and the monitoring of the European Framework Convention for the Protection of National Minorities: essays in honour of Rainer Hofmann. BRILL, Leiden

Marsal S, Palermo F (2018) Commentary of Article 3 of the Framework Convention for the Protection of National Minorities. In: Hofmann R, Malloy TH, Rein DB (eds) The Framework Convention for the Protection of National Minorities: a commentary. Brill/Nijhoff, Leiden/Boston

Martínez Cobo JR (1982) Study of the problem of discrimination against indigenous populations. Sub-Commission on Prevention of Discrimination and Protection of Minorities, New York

Mason A (2006) Levelling the playing field: the idea of equal opportunity and its place in egalitarian thought. Oxford University Press, Oxford

McCrudden C (2004) Mainstreaming human rights. Public law & legal theory research papers 47

McCrudden C (2015) Affirmative action: comparative policies and controversies. International encyclopedia of the social & behavioral sciences 1

Medda-Windischer R (2009) Old and new minorities: reconciling diversity and cohesion; a human rights model for minority integration. Nomos, Baden-Baden
Medda-Windischer R (2017) Old and new minorities: diversity governance and social cohesion from the perspective of minority rights. Acta Universitatis Sapientiae. Eur Reg Stud 11(1)
Moles A (2018) Discrimination and desert. In: Lippert-Rasmussen K (ed) The Routledge handbook of ethics of discrimination. Routledge, London
Mouffe C (1988) Radical democracy: modern or postmodern? In: Martin J (ed) Hegemony, radical democracy, and the political. Routledge, London
Ndahinda FM (2009) Indigenousness in Africa: a contested framework for empowerment of 'marginalised' ethno-cultural communities. PhD dissertation, University of Tilburg
Ndahinda FM (2011) Indigenousness in Africa: a contested framework for empowerment of "marginalized communities". Springer, Cham
Noon M (2010) The shackled runner: time to rethink positive discrimination? Work Employ Soc 24(4)
Palermo F (2013) Addressing contemporary stalemate in the advancement of minority rights: commentary on language rights of persons belonging to national minorities. In: Caruso U, Malloy TH, Hofmann M (eds) Minorities, their rights, and the monitoring of the European Framework Convention for the Protection of National Minorities: essays in honour of Rainer Hofmann. BRILL, Leiden
Phillips A (2018) Commentary of the preamble of the Framework Convention for the Protection of National Minorities. In: Hofmann R, Malloy TH, Rein DB (eds) The Framework Convention for the Protection of National Minorities: a commentary. Brill/Nijhoff, Leiden/Boston
Pou Giménez F (2020) Anti-discrimination law in civil law jurisdictions. Int J Constitutional Law 18(3)
Rai S (2018) Positive discrimination. In: Brown GW, McLean I, McMillan A (eds) A concise Oxford dictionary of politics and international relations. Oxford University Press, Oxford
Ringelheim J (2008) Minority protection and constitutional recognition of difference: reflections on the diversity of European approaches. In: Verstichel A, Andre A, de Witte B, Lemmens P (eds) The Framework Convention for the Protection of National Minorities: a useful pan-European instrument? Intersentia, Cambridge
Rodríguez-Garavito C, Sousa Santos B (2005) Law and globalization from below: towards a cosmopolitan legality. Cambridge University Press, New York
Rodríguez-Piñero L (2010) Indigenous peoples, postcolonialism, and international law: the ILO Regime (1919–1989). Oxford University Press, Oxford
Rodríguez-Piñero Royo L (2006) El Sistema Interamericano de Derechos Humanos y los Pueblos Indígenas. In: Berraondo M (ed) Pueblos Indígenas y Derechos Humanos. Instituto de Derechos Humanos, Universidad de Deusto, Bilbao
Romana Ammaturo F (2017) European sexual citizenship: human rights, bodies and identities. Palgrave Macmillan, Cham
Romero Bonifaz C (2009) Bolivia: De la Confrontación al Pacto Político. In: Romero C, Böhrt Irahola C, Peñaranda R (eds) Del Conflicto al Diálogo: Memorias del Acuerdo Constitucional. FES-ILDIS and fBDM, La Paz
Rösch R (2017) Indigenousness and peoples' rights in the African human rights system: situating the Ogiek judgement of the African Court on Human and Peoples' Rights. Verfassung und Recht in Übersee 50(3)
Scott J, Marshall G (2015) Positive discrimination. In: Scott J (ed) A dictionary of sociology. Oxford University Press, Oxford
Segall S (2013) Equality and opportunity. Oxford University Press, Oxford
Shachar A (2001) Multicultural jurisdictions: cultural differences and women's rights. Cambridge University Press, Cambridge
Shue H (1996) Basic rights: subsistence, affluence, and US foreign policy. Princeton University Press, Princeton

Sieder R (2016) Indigenous peoples' rights and the law in Latin America. In: Rodríguez-Garavito C (ed) Law and society in Latin America: a new map. Routledge, Abingdon
Smet S, Brems E (2017) When human rights clash at the European Court of Human Rights. Oxford University Press, Oxford
Solanke I (2017) Discrimination as stigma: a theory of anti-discrimination law. Hart Publishing, Oxford
Solón P (2017) Alternativas Sistémicas: Vivir Bien, Decrecimiento, Comunes, Ecofeminismo, Derechos de la Madre Tierra y Desglobalización. Fundación Solón, Focus on the Global South and Attac France, La Paz
Suk J (2018) Discrimination and affirmative action. In: Lippert-Rasmussen K (ed) The Routledge handbook of ethics of discrimination. Routledge, London
Swepston L (2015) The foundations of modern international law on indigenous and tribal peoples. BRILL, Leiden
Thomsen FK (2018) Direct discrimination. In: Lippert-Rasmussen K (ed) The Routledge handbook of ethics of discrimination. Routledge, London
Tomuschat C (2014) Human rights: between idealism and realism. Oxford University Press, Oxford
Tremmel J (2017) Constitutions as intergenerational contracts: flexible or fixed? Intergenerational Justice Rev 3(1)
Uprimny R (2011) The recent transformations of constitutional law in Latin America: trends and challenges. Tex Law Rev 89
van Boven T (1982) Distinguishing criteria of human rights. In: Vasak K, Alston P (eds) The international dimensions of human rights. Greenwood Press, Westport
Velasco Arroyo JC (2007) Discriminación Positiva, Diversidad Cultural y Justicia. Revista de Filosofía 41
Venkateswar S, Hughes E (2013) The politics of indigeneity: dialogues and reflections on indigenous activism. Zed Books, London
Verstichel A, Andre A, de Witte B, Lemmens P (eds) (2008) The Framework Convention for the Protection of National Minorities: a useful pan-European instrument? Intersentia, Cambridge
von Bogdandy A (2012) Founding principles. In: von Bogdandy A, Bast J (eds) Principles of European constitutional law. Hart/CH Beck/Nomos, Oxford/München/Baden-Baden
Wieviorka M (2004) La Discriminación Positiva. La Vanguardia
Wihtol de Wenden C (2022) Why do the old-established nation states fail to recognise minorities? Case studies from France. In: Eichler J, Topidi K (eds) Minority recognition and the diversity deficit: comparative perspectives. Hart Publishing, Oxford
Yañez N (forthcoming) Article 1. In: Eichler J, Doyle C, Howard S (eds) United Nations Declaration on the Rights of Indigenous Peoples: article-by-article commentary. Beck/Hart/Nomos, München/Baden-Baden/Oxford
Yrigoyen Fajardo R (2016) The panorama of pluralist constitutionalism: from multiculturalism to decolonisation. In: Rodríguez-Garavito C (ed) Law and society in Latin America: a new map. Routledge, Abingdon

# Chapter 7
# Collective Subject-Holdership, Processes and Scales of Collectivisation

## 7.1 Collectivising Human Rights: Collective Subject-Holdership

In the first place, we shall re-open the debate on subject-holdership for us to appreciate to what extent the dominant legal jargon proves apt and open enough to lend itself for collectivising the law. This may concern so-called processes of subjectivisation, a common terminology employed in that regard: accounts may differ, however, as to how subject holdership comes into being, an important question in any juridifying or constitutionalising endeavour. The subject, it is commonly argued, may not be considered as 'a priori subject', instead emphasis is placed on the process of constitution and socialisation following a Foucaultian (*assujjetissement*), Habermasian but also Kantian line of reasoning as suggested by Tully.[1] What stands at the centre of the argument is an intersubjective relation between the State and the individual, also to be found in Alexy's work.[2] The subject is formed through practice and dynamics between the actors, or as argued by Kant, "*subjects are constituted as individuals in the lifeworld*".[3] Also elsewhere it is maintained that those processes of subjectivisation entailing human rights safeguarding obligations do justice to the original sense of human rights which finds its roots in the individual rights tradition.[4]

Contrastingly, group and peoples' rights may require different legal constructs to be put in place, both substantively (what can be claimed? → typology of rights) and procedurally speaking (who can claim them? → standing). The individual legal tradition may also be criticised based on its clear demarcation line between but also

[1] Tully (2008).

[2] Alexy (2018).

[3] Tully (2008), p. 75.
Habermas (1995), p. 208.

[4] Alexy (2018).



J. Eichler, *An Interdisciplinary Journey from Non-Discrimination to Collective Rights*, https://doi.org/10.1007/978-3-031-54618-1_7

its focus placed on individual 'choice' and 'interest',[5] only difficult to be reconciled with collective interests, the collective good or collective self-determination,[6] some of the cornerstones of collective rights. Indeed, the right to collective self-determination is celebrated as one of the most influential and demanded rights among indigenous peoples,[7] opening, at the same time, the floor for other rights to find articulation; in other words, it may be understood from the perspective of inter-alia political rights, cultural development, socio-economically, legal pluralism etc. Given its considerable value and indispensability for indigenous peoples and other marginalised groups it has come to be recognised as being vested with *jus cogens* status,[8] that is, rendering said right non-derogable, not permitting exceptions to be granted. Other founding requirements may include for the group to possess a "*morally significant identity*" necessary for the group to be considered "*as an irreducible right-bearing entity*".[9] To be sure, a group right may be understood as such "*only if it is a right held by a group rather than by its members severally*".[10] In this context, we cannot possibly miss out on the meaning of subject holdership as a defining criterion for collective rights to be established to start with, as it is advocated elsewhere "*a group right is defined by its subject rather than its object: by who it is that holds the right rather than by what the right is a right to*".[11] In an attempt to further define collective rights, Jovanović draws our attention to the normative-moral stance of '*value collectivism*' to be distinguished from '*value individualism*',[12] alluding to the intrinsic value of groups while resembling the '*morally significant identity*' criterion established earlier. We may indeed provisionally conclude that collective rights find their roots, first and foremost, in the very subject(s) claiming them, and by that, bringing also procedural questions (locus standi) to the table.

In fact, challenges are to be located in the procedural dimension of the debate, but also in the ordinary balancing test when weighing collective rights against individual claims in the courts. Kymlicka seems to find an alternative conceptual venue, by establishing a new category on its own, that is, '*group-differentiated rights*' which may justify limits on the enjoyment of individual rights when conflicting with those

---

[5] Jovanović (2012).

[6] Ibid.

[7] Anaya (2004).
Tauli Corpuz, Victoria (2019) Report of the Special Rapporteur on the Rights of Indigenous Peoples, Autonomy and Self-Governance: Report.
Barelli (2011).

[8] Cassese (2012).

[9] Jovanović (2012), p. 103.
Jones (1999b).

[10] Jovanović (2012), p. 103.
Jones (1999a).

[11] Jovanović (2012), p. 103.
Jones (1999a).

[12] Jovanović (2012), pp. 105–108.

of the group ('*internal restrictions*') or, and importantly, by preventing the majority from imposing its will on the minority in question ('*external protections*').[13] The question of procedurally invoking collective rights remains a relevant concern, affecting 'national minority' rights in particular which are often seen as separate from collective rights and to be enjoyed individually (see next sub-chapter). One decisive criterion certainly lies in the so-called dual-standing dimension, allowing any member of a given group to wield a collective right "*either on his or her own behalf or on behalf of any member or members of the group, and the right may also be wielded by collective mechanism or by an agent or agents of the group*".[14] Again, we are to be reminded of distinguishing between the procedural and substantive dimensions of collective rights: as Jovanović rightly observes, collectively invoked rights such as collective bargaining rights (as in trade union rights) are not to be confused with group-specific rights, representing a common misunderstanding among theorists.[15] Emblematic may be the institutional dimension inherent to dual-standing rights, including but not limited to proper forms of organisational institutionality, governance and political autonomies as it becomes most visible in the case of indigenous peoples. Relatedly, it is referred to yet another demarcation criterion elsewhere, that is, for (group) rights holdership to be established, "*a plurality of persons must have a certain organisational structure (...) to be able to assert its rights, the group must be represented by legitimatised members that have been chosen as representative organs by the group*".[16] Again, we find ourselves wondering to what extent such group would rely on any value collectivism or collective identity that clearly distinguished itself from the aggregate individual interests of its members. French conceptualised such differentiation by contrasting '*aggregate collectivities*' that would indeed limit themselves to a collection of individual interests, and '*conglomerate collectivities*' referring to a unified being and its proper organisational structure.[17]

Indeed, theorists differ in the extent to which group rights are to be understood as rights shared and exercised jointly by group members, or, on the other side of the spectrum, for a group to be considered as a moral entity on its own terms, acquiring a status resembling that of an individual person.[18] The question of rights holdership, however, may open a different debate altogether, alienating itself from the idea of joint exercise; instead a group would need to meet a "*threshold of unity and*

---

[13] Kymlicka (1995).
Also see the following works heading into similar directions: Niezen (2003).
Mitnick (2006).
Sanders (1991).

[14] Buchanan (1993), p. 94.

[15] Jovanović (2012).

[16] Wenzel (2011), para. 3.

[17] Jones (2016).
French (1984).

[18] Jones (2016).

*identity*"[19] for it to exercise rights. For subject holdership to be established in the collective sense, we may want to revert back to Jovanović' value collectivism which is being observed in other accounts also, subsumed under the notion of subjectivity of a group—rather than objective features—or, similarly, taking the form of '*intra-group solidarity*' of a given constitutive community.[20] A group's moral status—for it to qualify as a rights holder group eventually—has been further disentangled, to include inter-alia the sharing of needs and possessing of interests, common benefits and harms, common obligations, and again a moral standing on its own.[21] Subject holdership may be further determined by the capacity of a given group to, for instance, sign international treaties or enter into judicial arrangements, in other words, for a group to acquire the judicial status of legal personality. In practice, such criterion may not be difficult to be met, basing itself on the organic statute and laws of the respective community—recognition as a State entity may be different, requiring the formal approval of other States which often pursue competing agendas. A final, related consideration concerns a group's agency, often based on its very decision-making capacities and internal structure[22] and the underlying principle of making choices.[23] Agency may be understood both internally and externally, notably, as a form of supervening on a community's members,[24] determining rights and responsibilities,[25] or, it may very well relate to a community's relations with other entities, also known as external self-determination.

Meticulous legal detail certainly enlightens us about the conditionalities and modus operandi inherent to group-specific rights, we tend however to forget about their positioning and embedment in the broader legal framework, and with it, their shaping socio-political environment. International legal developments prove illustrative in that regard; many States have voiced scepticism on the adoption of instruments protecting collective rights.[26] Such resistance may materialise in different ways, including opt outs from individual complaint procedures, reservations on progressive provisions or those standards threatening to limit State sovereignty or allowing territories to secede from States. Others may trace the origins of such undermining of collective rights back to the construction of the contemporary State and its theoretical basis, notably the principles of "*equal individual rights*

[19] Ibid.; p. 2.

[20] Ibid.

Galenkamp (1993).

[21] Jones (2016).

[22] Galenkamp (1993).

[23] Jones (2016).

[24] Ibid.

[25] See, for instance, Kirsty Gover's work.

See also the following case-law: *Sandra Lovelace vs. Canada*, UN Human Rights Committee in 1979; *Kitok vs. Sweden*, UN Human Rights Committee in 1988; Individual Opinion of Olivier de Frouville in *Sanila-Aikio vs. Finland*, UN Human Rights Committee in 2018; *Käkkäläjärvi vs. Finland*, UN Human Rights Committee in 2017.

[26] Wenzel (2011).

*and majority rule*",[27] hence presupposing the existence of a subordinate minority and their assimilation by the State. In other words, minority interests may be undermined by the majority given that "*the State and the cultural majority may form a hegemonic bloc (. . .) (while) the doctrine of equal and universal rights may support the hegemony of the majority culture over various subordinated cultures*".[28] Resultantly, it is those collectivities remaining "*systematically unrepresented by States that are anomalies in liberal-democratic theory*".[29] Exceptionalism thereby clearly assumes a value-loaded tone, for collective rights to be positioned in the majoritarian common-sensical rationale of the legal framework(s).

### *7.1.1 'National Minorities' and the Question of (Collective) Subject Holdership*

So-called 'national minorities' deserve special mentioning here, being emblematic of the State's very particular framework of recognition which remains exclusively reserved and accessible to constitutionally defined minority groups, other than '*new minorities*'[30] for instance, yet to be protected more specifically in the domestic realm. Let us initiate this reflection with an excursus on the question of subject holdership. It may legitimately be asked to what extent 'national minorities' would be considered different from other marginalised minorities, leaving aside the very evident issue of State recognition for a moment. While certainly fulfilling a clear purpose of dedicated protection, 'national minorities' and their very characteristics necessarily undergo a certain construction or put differently, these "*are necessarily superimposed, mutually diffused and profoundly intertwined in the world of overlapping identities*".[31] Others rely on a historical connection, referring to (national) minorities as "*long-settled historical groups*".[32] Some accounts make mentioning of ethnic, cultural, religious or linguistic group categories or grounds when referring to 'national minorities' which necessarily requires some level of contextualisation. The question has been approached differently at a governmental level, with diverging approaches adopted in Europe and the Americas:[33]

---

[27] Freeman (1995), p. 26.

[28] Ibid.; p. 26.

[29] Ibid.; p. 27.

[30] Kochenov (2015), p. 81.
Henrard (2011).

[31] Kochenov (2015), p. 82.
Kymlicka (1995).

[32] Kochenov (2015), p. 82.
Henrard (2011).
Eide (2004).

[33] Kymlicka (1995).

interestingly, multiethnicity was more eagerly acknowledged and accounted for in the Americas with multinationality and national minorities being less pronounced, if at all, whereas the latter groups succeeded in claiming cultural and self-government rights in Europe early on, with Belgium and Switzerland taking the lead.[34] Acknowledgement and explicit forms of recognition of both poliethnicity and multinationality may be witnessed in the Canadian context.[35] If we would relate this back to the question of subject-holdership, we could derive from the above, firstly, that poliethnicity would commonly not materialise as a dedicated subject category in the law—as in positive discrimination—and secondly, that multinationality including national minorities remained, similarly, subject to the legal conceptualisation established by the constitutional framework in question, and in turn, dependent on the State's discretion.

Despite the apparent merits attributable to such categorisation in protecting vulnerable groups, we shall critically engage with subject holdership, and the collective dimension in particular. Again, procedural detail appears to provide some answers on the locus standi issue where collective rights are to be invoked. Illustratively, Europe's national minority frameworks seem to establish clear stances on the matter, the Framework Convention for the Protection of National Minorities[36] in particular. While its article 3(2) enables persons belonging to national minorities to exercise the rights established therein "*individually as well as in community with others*", collective rights are explicitly excluded from its realm of protection following the Explanatory Report of the Convention.[37] What it does recognise concerns the "*possibility of joint exercise of those rights and freedoms*".[38] Jurisprudential developments seem to confirm such positioning. Indigenous organisations falling under the protective umbrella of the Convention are not granted special recognition as entities (legitimately) representing their peoples or in relation to responsibilities over territories, instead, these are being reserved to individual members.[39]

Procedural matters appear to be rather limiting than facilitating for national minorities to make collective claims. At the ending, the Council of Europe framework proves interwoven with political interests, as an intergovernmental organisation,[40] not least to mention State sovereignty or territorial concerns that States fear to be curtailed where national minorities gain in political weight and autonomy.

[34] Ibid.

[35] Ibid.

[36] See also Verstichel et al. (2008).
Hofmann et al. (2015).

[37] Council of Europe (1995) *Explanatory Report to the Framework Convention for the Protection of National Minorities,* para.37.
See also Jovanović (2012).

[38] Ibid.; para.37.

[39] Koivurova (2013).
*Könkämä and 38 other Sámi villages vs. Sweden*, European Court of Human Rights in 1996; *Johtti Sapmelaccat Ry. and others vs. Finland*, European Court of Human Rights in 2005.

[40] Forde (2022).

Attention may be paid to the nature of those organs in charge of offering interpretative guidance, emblematic being the Explanatory Report which was drawn up within the Council of Europe, more precisely by the Ad Hoc Committee for the Protection of National Minorities under the authority of the Committee of Ministers, ultimately constituted by political mandate-holders. This may concern different organs and mandates constituting the Council of Europe[41] such as the Secretary General whose diplomatic interventions seem to have slowed down or even reversed processes pursued by the Council's (other) institutions.[42] Most notable political influences may certainly be observed in the case of the Council's Parliamentary Assembly which showed rather reluctant to use sanctions, opting for opening monitoring procedures instead, which in itself has been leading to political controversies among members of the assembly, hence rendering it a highly political, also and politicised measure resulting in delays or evading of the procedure.[43]

Political reluctance may not only be felt systemically-institutionally speaking, it may also come to the surface when touching upon substantive issues. Illustrative may be the case of Sinti and Roma in European jurisdictions, also entering the jurisdictional realm of the ECtHR. While cultural rights and the particularities relating to the Romas' needs and ways of life[44] broadly find recognition in the case-law, concessions are made elsewhere, relating to housing rights and private life.[45] Very visibly, this may become manifested in the context of education systems, relegating Roma children to special education schools under the pretext of language-related criteria. Again, the Court appears to opt for a cautious approach, far from engaging with education policies directed at minority situations, and instead addresses the matter in the abstract, pronouncing itself in favour of pluralism in education and democratic society.[46] In that sense, we may certainly witness a growing awareness of the rights particular to national minorities amongst judicial instances presented here, which we may preliminarily understand as a trend towards establishing 'a sense of collective rights' in the Council of Europe framework. The ECtHR order falls short, however, of transversalising or systematising its case-law in that regard, owing, possibly, to a fragmented landscape produced by its very responsive role vis-à-vis a multiplicity of claims.

[41] For a comparative analysis on the matter, see: Çali and Demir-Gürsel (2021).

[42] Demir-Gürsel (2021).

[43] Donald and Speck (2021).

[44] *Oršuš and Others vs. Croatia*, European Court of Human Rights in 2010.

[45] *Chapman vs. the United Kingdom*, European Court of Human Rights in 2001.

[46] *Catan and Others vs. the Republic of Moldova and Russia*, European Court of Human Rights in 2012.

### 7.1.2 Intergenerational Rights, Their Relevance for Understanding Subject Holdership and Collective Rights

To start with, third generation rights, including the right to a safe environment, to peace or to development,[47] to communication or humanitarian assistance,[48] have given rise to complex duty-rights relations, owing to the difficulties associated with the attribution of damage, hence accountability, especially in environmental cases. To this we may add a vulnerability dimension, as a way to deal with difference and recognition thereof. More precisely, in the context of human environmental rights it could be distinguished between the public at large and the '*vulnerable public*', alluding to 'specific circumstances' and also 'personal conditions' encompassing, inter-alia, "*the social, economic, cultural, geographical, and gender characteristics of the public, and [give rise] to the following concrete barriers: lack of awareness of environmental rights, language, literacy, costs, physical location, cultural context, and fears of reprisal*".[49] Accordingly, we may easily think of these attributes as providing definitional grounds to possible group formations such as cultural discrimination or socio-economic background which seem to deserve a special place in human environmental rights regimes. Alongside these defining characteristics of vulnerability, and hence special consideration, the Escazú Agreement[50]—a wide-recognised judicial document in the field—attributes a state of vulnerability to specific communities which have proven, at the same time, relevant for the present (hypo)thesis, namely "*indigenous peoples, local communities, and human rights defenders*".[51] It needs to be noted though, these references have not entered the realm of justiciability in the Escazú Agreement, instead, it is referred to other domestic and international obligations applicable to these groups.[52] Another approach worth meriting further exploration concerns regional human rights jurisprudence, including the *Lhaka Honhat vs. Argentina* case but also the *SERAC* case before the African Human and Peoples' Rights Commission which conveys the view that "*environmental degradation does not affect the individual in isolation, rather the effects of environmental harm are felt across communities*".[53] Elsewhere such view has been termed a "*collective-social dimension of human rights affected by environmental degradation*".[54] This perspective is also supported technically, by the

[47] Tomuschat (2014).

[48] Jones (1999b).

[49] Aguilera Bravo (2023), p. 240.

[50] The Escazú Agreement carries the official name 'Regional Agreement on Access to Information, Public Participation and Access to Justice in Environmental Matters in Latin America and the Caribbean', adopted in Escazú, Costa Rica, in 2018.

[51] Ibid.; p. 240.

[52] Ibid.

[53] Buys and Lewis (2021), p. 963.

[54] Francioni (2010), p. 41.

provision in question (art.24, ACHPR), establishing a collective environmental right, and the Commission's *action popularis* approach which enables both individuals and groups to exercise standing.[55]

A crucial element concerns indeed the collective dimension intrinsic to third generation rights: one of the founding fathers of the taxonomy of human rights, Karel Vasak, referred to collective rights as forming the raison d'être of the third generation paradigm while terming the former '*solidarity rights*'.[56] Indeed, definitional concerns prove key to start with.[57] Oftentimes, the debate on third generation rights revolves around the question of rights holders benefiting from third generation rights in the collective sense. As maintained by Peter Jones,

> that the bearers of these rights (third generation rights) must be distinct groups of human beings, rather than individuals or mankind at large, is not readily obvious from the content of these rights.[58]

Relatedly, Jones distinguishes between those collective rights individuals may share without developing any collective, sociological and moral identity, in other words, collective rights do not give rise to claims beyond those constituted by individual interests.[59] Conversely, collective rights may also be understood as those attributable to groups as such, guided by a strong sense of group identity, and existing independently of individual, isolated claims.[60] Relatedly, this has motivated scholars such as Jovanović to address the special character of these rights as reflecting a "*genuine character of collective interests and the inherent value of certain groups*".[61] In that sense, these rights are referred to as group specific or group rights by Jones. We may be reminded of similar terminology introduced earlier, notably the concept of group-differentiated rights[62] that may serve as a useful working concept in view of the debate on the recognition of difference.

The question of recognition in the particular context of collective rights indeed merits some further thought, being an emblematic manifestation of the juridification of difference. Resembling the recognition of difference, Jovanović refers to a recognition of a group's uniqueness:

> The underlying normative assumption of the collective rights talk concerns the recognition of uniqueness of the group particularity, as opposed to the universality of 'sameness'. Accordingly, any attempt to draft a legal norm that will vest rights in a certain group is necessarily an instance of the legal recognition of that group's social distinctiveness.[63]

---

[55] Buys and Lewis (2021).

[56] Kiwanuka (1988).
See also: Vasak (1979).

[57] See, for instance, Alston (1982).

[58] Jones (1999b), p. 96.

[59] Ibid.

[60] Ibid.

[61] Jovanović (2012), p. 131.

[62] Kymlicka (1995).

[63] Jovanović (2012), p. 59.

From the foregoing it seems that the recognition of difference could be considered a not only necessary condition for collective rights—and analogically, third generation rights—to be codified by the law, but an absolute, constitutive premise, giving rise to (often) multivariate juridification processes in turn. The legal recognition of a group however demands further considerations which may be inspired by "*some conceptual schemes of the social sciences*"[64] as argued by Jovanović. He refers to Eric Heinze's and Kwame Anthony Appiah's work on the construction of difference.[65] Of relevance here are three steps to be taken in the context of such 'construction of difference', including

> recognition of other peoples or groups as such – as different from one's own, on the basis of, e.g., kinship, geography, language, anatomy, religion or custom (. . .) naming the difference [and] (. . .) evaluation of that difference through attribution of normative significance to it[66]

Despite the merits this bears in the move away from equality paradigms, we easily detect an external element to this, or what Jovanović calls "*artificial exogene group categorization*".[67] This would include firstly, the attributing element which, it could be argued, overrides any decision-making on group membership by the very collectivity concerned—indigenous rights to defining group membership in accordance with their procedures and customs may be emblematic here.[68] In fact, such rationale has been described as an '*intervention paradox*',[69] referring to the practice of intervening in the community space with the objective of identifying a community for the purpose of recognition on the part of the settler government, raising a couple of foundational questions:

> To what degree should a settler government dictate the human boundaries of a tribe as a condition of official recognition? Can a settler government legitimately act to prevent a tribe from transforming itself, post-recognition, into a 'different' community by changing membership rules?[70]

Secondly, this concerns the evaluation of difference including the setting up of different constituent features which may not reflect community realities, one of the burdens associated with so-called objective criteria as opposed to subjective criteria

---

[64] Ibid.; p. 59.

[65] Heinze (1999).
Appiah (2005).

[66] Ibid.; p. 60.
Heinze (1999), p. 34.

[67] Jovanović (2012), p. 62.

[68] See e.g. Gover (2016).
Gover (forthcoming).
See also Imai and Gunn (2018).

[69] Jovanović (2012), p. 129.

[70] Jovanović (2012), pp. 129–130.
For further details, see Gover (2011), p. 2.

in terms of the definition.[71] We may hence preliminarily conclude that the legal recognition side of the recognition of difference may prove facilitating when it comes to formalising and codifying difference or when ascribing legal personality to a group, it may however also give rise to patronising, neo-colonial ways of labelling groups by means of the law.

Delving deeper into the theoretical rationale of intergenerational thought in making sense of subject relations, we inevitably find ourselves confronted with the legal nexus between and the judicial implications arising with the multiplicity of subjects involved. Most visible this becomes where environmental goods are at stake, as articulated famously in intergenerational equity theory according to which

> every generation holds the earth in common with members of the present generation and with other generations, past and future. The principle articulates a concept of fairness among generations in the use and conservation of the environment and its natural resources.[72]

Indigenous peoples, it is argued widely, have come to develop a "*well-known sustainable relationship with nature, and (they) depict themselves as guardians*".[73] Yet more explicitly, we may witness a direct relation between future generations' rights in using natural resources and respective duties incurred on current generations, by understanding future generations as rights holders having dedicated interests, showing important enough to establish obligations on others: in other words,

> the claim X has interests which are sufficiently weighty to impose obligations on others – we can then claim, where X is future generations and weighty interests are things as life, health and subsistence, the living have obligations to protect future generations from environmental damage that threatens their weighty interests.[74]

In a way, this reverses the temporal rationale underlying the law, defending a perspective that considers the moral importance of these rights that wouldn't diminish over time.[75] Interestingly from a procedural perspective, these rights may hence be vindicated by future generations, doing justice to the preventive function of law.

A special case shall be made, however, as far as indigenous rights are concerned, demonstrating yet again a prominent situation in which not only environmental claims are to be considered special, but also proving pertinent when seen from a procedural and legal pluralistic perspective. To start with, indigenous weighty interests may importantly include, as suggested above, subsistence, health or physical integrity—alongside cultural integrity and survival and environmental rights as

---

[71] See, for instance, Marsal and Palermo (2018).
For an in-depth debate on the matter, also see Corntassel and Hopkins Primeau (1998).

[72] Brown Weiss (2021), para. 1.

[73] Fitzmaurice (2018), p. 208.
Hainämäki (2010).

[74] Winter (2022), p. 135.

[75] Ibid.

such[76]—yet, weighty interests may similarly amount to "*the right to maintain customs, spirituality, procedures, practices, and in the cases where they exist, juridical systems or customs*"[77] (also art.34, UNDRIPS), demonstrating some form of widening of classical justice theories. Cautious voices may however remind us of the rather traditional approach taken by the courts, building on classical procedural principles derived from international human rights law, as it is advanced, notably, '*access to information*', '*public participation*', and '*access to justice*'.[78] In that sense, indigenous conceptions of the law may remain at the periphery of intergenerational claims when confronted with State-centric justice institutions, or they may, following an optimistic reading of jurisprudence, inform procedural detail including respect for indigenous customary or traditional legal frameworks.

### *7.1.3 Intersectionality and Its Pertinence for Collective Contexts*

The panorama of distinct rights is a complex one, united by often shared manifestations of discrimination, targeting, arbitrariness, oppression, stereotypisation, unequal treatment, marginalisation and resulting forms of vulnerability among different rights holder groups. One field meriting particular attention in that regard concerns intersectional and cumulative grounds of discrimination giving rise to special claims. Just as the '*distinct rights approach*' outlined above, intersectional rights need to be contextualised against the background of equality principles.

To start with, let us briefly refer to the conceptual origin of intersectionality, broadly to be located in sociological thought as a term that

> was introduced in the late 1980s as a heuristic term to focus attention on the vexed dynamics of difference and the solidarities of sameness in the context of antidiscrimination and social movement politics. It exposed how single-axis thinking undermines legal thinking, disciplinary knowledge production, and struggles for social justice.[79]

In that sense, the term is certainly to be associated with broader social struggles whereas our current concern shall be limited to those rights interacting with the equality paradigm. Other attempts have been made ever since, understanding the new 'buzzword' as

---

[76] *Case of the Kichwa Indigenous People of Sarayaku vs. Ecuador*, Inter-American Court of Human Rights in 2012.

*Case of the Indigenous Communities of the Lhaka Honhat (Our Land) Association vs. Argentina*, Inter-American Court of Human Rights in 2020.

[77] Winter (2022), p. 139.

UN Declaration on the Rights of Indigenous Peoples, art.34.

[78] Inter-American Court of Human Rights (2017) *Advisory Opinion OC-23/17*; Inter-American Commission on Human Rights (1997) *Report on the Situation of Human Rights in Ecuador.*

[79] Cho et al. (2013), p. 787.

> the interaction between gender, race, and other categories of difference in individual lives, social practices, institutional arrangements, and cultural ideologies, and the outcomes of these interactions in terms of power.[80]

It may be highlighted here that despite the individual impact a specific treatment may exert, intersectionality proves rather receptive towards group demands and the systemic nature of discrimination. Such clearly systemic, group-based nature also shines through other accounts on the concept, holding that

> intersectionality conceives of 'disadvantage' broadly, including every kind of harm, oppression, powerlessness, subordination, marginalisation, deprivation, domination and violence. Moreover, the disadvantage is defined not by isolated or stray incidents but by systemic or structural nature. It represents a pattern of historic motifs of disadvantage which have been entrenched over time. Such disadvantage is also not personally towards random individuals but suffered by individuals because of their membership to a social group.[81]

Relatedly, we shall be reminded of the deeper asymmetries in play, allowing oppressive, subordinating patterns to affect the different lines of differentiation, ultimately discrimination to operate in people's daily lives[82]; (post)colonialism may be emblematic of such observation.[83]

In practice, such intersectional grounds may come to the fore in a variety of ways, including '*compounded discrimination*',[84] '*multiple forms of discrimination*'[85] or particularly '*severe forms of discrimination*';[86] any possible grounds and intersectionalities shall thereby be included.[87] Accounts vary to the extent to which these grounds would fall under or relate to intersectional forms of discrimination; some may advocate quite the opposite, maintaining that these were based on "*discrete, sequential and severable identity factors*" and hence qualify as "*cumulative, compound or multiple conceptions of discrimination*".[88] Considerable efforts have been spent on examining intersectionality as the concept gains consideration in

---

[80] Davis (2008), p. 68.

[81] Atrey (2019), p. 41.
See also: *Brink vs. Kitshoff NO*. Constitutional Court of South Africa in 1996.

[82] Krizsan et al. (2012a).
Borchorst and Teigen (2010).

[83] Hankivsky and Jordan-Zachery (2019).

[84] Committee on the Elimination of Discrimination against Women (2015) *General Comment N° 33 on Women's Access to Justice.*

[85] *Cecilia Kell vs. Canada*, UN Committee on the Elimination of Discrimination against Women in 2012.
UN Committee on the Elimination of Discrimination against Women (2013) *General Comment N°30 on Women in Conflict Prevention, Conflict and Post-Conflict Situations.*
UN Committee on the Rights of the Child (2006) *General Comment N°9: The Rights of Children with Disabilities.*

[86] UN Committee on the Rights of Persons with Disabilities (2016) *General Comment N°3 on Women and Girls with Disabilities.*

[87] UN Committee on the Rights of Persons with Disabilities (2018) *General Comment N°6 on Equality and Non-Discrimination.*

[88] Bourke Martignoni (2018), p. 143.

regional legal orders such as EU law[89] or the Inter-American human rights system,[90] yet, without enlightening us about the significance of intersectionality vis-à-vis (the) dominant equality order(s), structural questions or its relevance as a human rights category in its own terms.

First insights on the question may be gained when examining the institutional dimension(s) of intersectionality: what becomes apparent in European frameworks at least is a steady embracement of an '*integrated approach to multiple inequalities*' which becomes apparent in the way equality bodies addressing multiple inequalities have come to replace those institutions dealing with specific grounds,[91] or for States to amalgamate equality institutions. Generally, specialised equality ombudsmen would be merged into single equality bodies, illustrative being so-called 'national human rights institutions'.[92] Seemingly, an intersectional approach was not explicitly adopted but would rather result from these institutional changes, it would be regarded as "*more favourable to deal with multiple, intersecting inequalities and thus would better capture the social complexity of inequalities and disadvantages*",[93] hence replacing the single (ground) and multiple (yet isolated grounds) approaches with an integrated approach.[94] Interestingly, these institutionalising efforts have been criticised by feminists who pointed to the diminishing meaning of gender equality policies as a result.[95] Other challenges relate to the implications of such co-existing demands including while not limited to "*debate[s] about the relative merit of various equality demands and the tensions between these, with particular theoretical focus on the relation between feminism and multiculturalism*".[96]

In other words, internal or intra-group differences may distract from the broader collective struggle for substantive equality. We easily find ourselves trapped in the neo-colonial critique of, for instance, indigenous justice systems or other orders that may contradict our classical legal common sense and consensus. These may operate, it is alleged, to the detriment of groups within these communities. A few theoretical accounts however engage more closely with this form of critique by way of categorically separating internal rules, duties and responsibilities, from a collective position assumed vis-à-vis externals.[97] The focus of the present work will remain on

---

[89] Krizsan et al. (2012b).
Xenidis (2019).

[90] Góngora Mera (2020).

[91] Krizsan et al. (2012a).
Muir and de Witte (2017).

[92] Muir and de Witte (2017).

[93] Krizsan et al. (2012a), p. 1.

[94] Ibid.

[95] Ibid.
Squires (2008).

[96] Krizsan et al. (2012a), p. 6.

[97] See, for instance, Kymlicka's, Shachar's, Taylor's or Benhabib's work on the matter.

such external dimension, promising deeper insights into the collective position assumed (or attributed!) vis-à-vis equality frameworks that may materialise in the form of neo-colonial logics (e.g. in education and language policies), neo-liberal forces (e.g. in extractive projects), or simply a State-centric idea of the law and governance system (e.g. neglecting legal pluralism). Instead, it may be asked to what extent these external dimensions actually catalyse or perpetuate intersectional forms of discrimination. A prominent example may be the case of indigenous women when accessing justice institutions,[98] in the context of their struggle for self-determination,[99] or when relating violations to the colonial age, giving rise to gender-based discrimination to start with.[100] In that sense, equality frameworks by their very silence on the multiplicities of differentiation, operate to the detriment of groups' special protection, also owing to a general perception of equality as a sufficient condition for human rights to be upheld. Similar logics permeate constitutionally established rights that remain little susceptible to the cumulative impact of intersectional violations with few exceptions arising with progressive constitutional developments in inter-alia South African[101] or Canadian constitutional law.[102] Intersectionality probably remains one of the most unrecognised manifestations of discrimination under equality orders.

### *7.1.4 Democratic Thought and Equality as Safeguards for Group Rights*

It might not come as a surprise that classical democratic thought—in a strict, technical sense—proves somewhat ill-suited to meet the needs of underrepresented groups, given its procedural particularities including electoral rules, its decision-making procedures based on majorities, and also its orientation on particular constituencies (municipal, regional, federal etc.). And yet, participatory rights probably represent one of indigenous peoples' strongest and unheard claims, considering developments around the world.[103] Illustrative of the procedural particularities around voting rights and their salience for questions of indigenous representation

[98] Sieder and Sierra (2010).

[99] Kuokkanen (2012).

[100] Rivera Cusicanqui (2012).

[101] Wing (2008).

[102] Stoljar (2018).

[103] At relevant sessions convened by the Expert Mechanism on the Rights of Indigenous Peoples (EMRIP) and other international mechanisms, land, resource and participatory rights come to the fore on a very frequent basis, resulting in studies and other efforts to draw States' attention to the situation, see e.g. EMRIP's 2019 session "Indigenous peoples' rights in the context of borders, migration and displacement" or EMRIPs series of studies on participation and decision-making (issued in 2012).

proves to be the *YATAMA vs. Nicaragua* decision brought before the Inter-American Court on Human Rights.

Interestingly, the Court delves deeper into the indigenous cultural rights as being decisive, apparently, for justifying collective claims generally while it, importantly, uses the opportunity to rule on indigenous proper procedures and organisational structures to be considered, ultimately for indigenous peoples to enjoy voting rights at eye-level, that is, equally:

> YATAMA [indigenous regional political party] contributes to the consolidation and preservation of the cultural identity of the members of the indigenous and ethnic communities (. . .) Its structure and purposes are related to the practices, customs and forms of organisation of these communities. Consequently, the exclusion of the participation of the YATAMA candidates particularly affected the members of the indigenous and ethnic communities that were represented by this organisation in the general elections, by placing them in a situation of inequality as regards the options among which they could choose to vote, since those persons who, in principle, deserved their confidence because had been chosen directly in assemblies (according to the practices and customs of these communities) to represent the interests of their members, had been excluded from participating as candidates[104]

Importantly, the Court further specifies how such equal conditions could look like, considering the particularities of indigenous decision-making when taking part in the State's conduct of public affairs, it thus calls upon the State to:

> adopt all necessary measures to ensure that the members of the indigenous and ethnic communities (. . .) can participate, in equal conditions, in decision-making matters and policies that affect or could affect their rights (. . .) so that they can incorporate themselves into State institutions and bodies and participate directly and proportionately to their population in the conduct of public affairs and also do this from their own institutions and according to their values, practices, customs and forms of organisation. . .[105]

An even closer or more genuine approximation to indigenous own manifestations of participation is achieved by means of, albeit ad-hoc, procedures: consultation and free, prior and informed consent (FPIC)[106] have been developing into a common procedure whenever indigenous peoples would be affected by an external measure such as extractive operations, mega projects generally, infrastructure projects or the like. Partly attributable to the enormous scope of experience with prior consultation processes, indigenous peoples have been gaining more of a shaping role in recent years with an Inter-American Court developing sophisticated procedures on the matter throughout the years.

Let us more closely engage with the underlying rationale of democratic thought now. Indigenous decision-making processes have been described as largely consen-

[104] *YATAMA vs. Nicaragua*, Inter-American Court of Human Rights in 2005, para.227.

[105] Ibid.; para.225.

[106] Doyle (2015).
Wright and Tomaselli (2019).
Eichler (2019).

sual,[107] hence resisting any labelling as majoritarian, as it would be common in the Global North. Relatedly, decision-making has been described as largely direct with specific mandates created rather by sheer necessity. In fact, as anthropological accounts narrate, mandate holdership and other forms of organisational structuring were introduced during the colonial age[108] and would later be pushed for by external players to facilitate negotiation and inter-institutional decision-making.[109]

Interestingly, minorities have been facing similar difficulties in European contexts, with their organisational forms hardly fitting into the individualistic framework that would hardly permit any collective exercise of rights, in other words, the Court would prioritise general election rights, protecting the State's institutions and procedures while it would also defend basic freedoms of association at a general level.[110] Conversely, the Court seems to make commitments to group rights when clashing with majority views, demonstrating some sense or sensitivity for the matter:

> Although individual interests must on occasion be subordinated to those of a group, democracy does not simply mean that the views of the majority must always prevail: a balance must be achieved which ensures the fair and proper treatment of minorities and avoids any abuse of a dominant position[111]

Similar to the reasoning above, the European Court addresses the particular purpose common to minority associations, establishing a special status in that sense, while it relates such status to basic constitutional principles, highlighting the necessity of protecting collective identities and their organisational manifestations to guarantee democratic and pluralistic values at a broader level:

> . . . .associations formed for other purposes, including those protecting cultural or spiritual heritage, pursuing various socio-economic aims, proclaiming or teaching religion, seeking an ethnic identity or asserting a minority consciousness, are also important to the proper functioning of democracy. For pluralism is also built on the genuine recognition of, and respect for, diversity and the dynamics of cultural traditions, ethnic and cultural identities, religious beliefs, artistic, literary and socio-economic ideas and concepts.[112]

---

[107] Horn-Miller (2013).
García Linera et al. (2005).
Van Cott (2007).

[108] Postero (2007).
Melià (1989).

[109] Hirsch (1999).

[110] *Gorzelik and Others vs. Poland*, European Court of Human Rights in 2004.
see also *Sidiropoulos and Others vs. Greece*, European Court of Human Rights in 1998; *United Communist Party of Turkey and Others vs. Turkey*, European Court of Human Rights in 1998; *Socialist Party and Others vs. Turkey*, European Court of Human Rights in 1998; *Refah Partisi (the Welfare Party) and Others vs. Turkey*, European Court of Human Rights in 2003.

[111] *Gorzelik and Others vs. Poland*, European Court of Human Rights in 2004, para.90.
See also *Young, James and Webster vs. the United Kingdom*, European Court of Human Rights in 1982; *Chassagnou and Others vs. France*, European Court of Human Rights in 1999, para.112.

[112] *Gorzelik and Others vs. Poland*, European Court of Human Rights in 2004, para.92.

Yet more clearly, the Court develops an entire rationale bolstering a minority's right to form an association in its own terms, again, referring back to the specific collective cultural identity giving rise to such claim. It may be noted here that the Court remains rather silent on the question of invoking rights collectively, the status of such association and its powers vis-à-vis the institutions of the State, which does not rule out any prospective favourable interpretation on the issue, nor would this impose limits on current contexts:

> The Court recognises that freedom of association is particularly important for persons belonging to minorities, including national and ethnic minorities, and that, as laid down in the preamble to the Council of Europe Framework Convention, 'a pluralist and genuinely democratic society should not only respect the ethnic, cultural, linguistic and religious identity of each person belonging to a national minority, but also create appropriate conditions enabling them to express, preserve and develop this identity'. Indeed, forming an association in order to express and promote its identity may be instrumental in helping a minority to preserve and uphold its rights.[113]

Also in the case of Sami Parliaments in the European north, integrated decision-making bodies have fallen short of developing any effective powers domestically, and more importantly, as far as Sami's collective rights were concerned.[114] As it becomes apparent quite visibly, basic democratic rights have been following a rationale fitting with Europe's State-centric vision of equality that would not truly show apt to accommodating all those particularities—including dedicated powers—necessary to live up to minorities' realities, needs, and most fundamentally, self-determined agendas and decisions when it comes to vesting their organisational structures with any sovereign or co-governance virtues.

Democratic rights may be imagined differently though—varying degrees of specialisation have found their way into the procedures; this may include the establishing of dedicated ministries, sub-units, commissions, specific representatives or offices at domestic level, or also quota systems. While institution-building may open a worthwhile debate, there is an imminent risk for these debates to remain at the empirical level only. Our attention shall hence be devoted to the operating and above all theoretical implications of quota systems. The 2022 constitutive assembly (*Convención Constitucional*) in Chile gives us a first taste, drawing on an indigenous quota in the constituent assembly that is proportionate to the total number of indigenous peoples residing in Chile, that is 17 out of 155 seats in total.[115] The Ecuadorian and Bolivian constitutional frameworks similarly established quota systems, as concerning the judiciary,[116] for instance, or the '*conscripciones*', resembling a specialised electoral constituency system. Interestingly, minority quota may not only be understood as a proceduralised form of plural democracy, these have also

[113]Ibid.; para.93.

[114]Lawrence and Mörkenstam (2016).

[115]Eichler and Barnier-Khawam (2022).

[116]Barrera (2012).

been described as instrumental to enhancing diversity in institutions, and in turn, the quality of democracy.[117]

If we wanted to classify the concept further, we may want to relate it to the idea of representative democracy, constituting the overall framework in which quota may find (or not) due consideration. What is termed '*descriptive representation*' (*théorie mimétique*)[118] proves particularly relevant for our case, permitting minorities to be represented proportionately and for each parliamentarian to represent the interests of the group she/he/x is affiliated with.[119] Such reasoning may be contrasted with the school of thought that does not deem the relation between electorate and elected important enough (*théorie esthétique*) and instead engages with the principle of general interest or public good, juxtaposing the latter with the dedicated representation of group interests.[120] Indeed, equality orders depart from a similar view, establishing a one-size-fits-all approach in the name of the *demos* to the detriment of underrepresented groups. It is this gap which we have been trying to address here—a diversity deficit or pluralist critique—that equality principles generally do not show sensitive for, and in turn, necessarily require a more tailored difference-driven legal, institutional but also societal response (the latter not falling under the scope of the present work).

## 7.2 Processes and Scales of Collectivisation

When considering the triadic duties regime or also positive discrimination, we can think of an ad-hoc response to commonly individual(ised) contexts. Indeed, case-based logics rarely allow for more structural transformation which is, however, needed for minority and indigenous rights to be recognised in a collective sense. Indeed, group-specific rights and collective rights merit some thought in their own terms, as proper legal constructs carrying important implications for political theory, for instance, in the way these questions are inevitably to be related to the idea of the State, its functioning and ultimately space(s) of recognition provided (or not) for collective rights to become articulated.

In that sense, collective rights are not uncommonly juxtaposed with the State's emphasis on the individual as the main subject holder. Another common categorisation in that regard concerns human rights, both as an umbrella term and as a competing concept. Indeed, the doctrine of human rights itself has shown

---

[117] Stojanović (2013).

[118] Ibid., p. 126.

For an in-depth debate on the concept, feel free to revise Frank Ankersmit's work.

[119] Ibid.

[120] Ibid.; p. 129.

See also Soa Näsström's work on the 'non-ressemblance' aspect which guides the present theoretical approach on representative democracies.

affirmative of the principle according to which the "*human individual is the most fundamental moral unit*".[121] Some may speak in favour of '*collective human rights*'[122] which could, when conceptually correlating these with human rights, follow a similar universality claim.[123] To be sure, collective human rights would be referred to as to concern peoples and minorities,[124] hence serving the purpose of the present work and its emphasis. These groups might prove particularly affected by the doctrine of "*equal and universal rights (may) support[ing] the hegemony of the majority culture over various subordinated cultures*".[125] Returning to the structural nature of the claims made, we may be reminded that collectivities are not made up merely to confront 'external discrimination'—which they would share with individuals—but also distinguish themselves by 'internal cohesiveness', often to maintain or develop their proper cultural traits.[126] To this we may add those interests defended by 'outsiders' who could share an interest in the continued existence of a group,[127] which in fact represents a common terminology used in early international treaties that promoted a society's diversity as providing the rationale for establishing collective rights in a modest way (e.g. ILO Convention 107).

While manifesting itself as a sheer technicality at first view, we may be reminded of the differences between collective rights and positive discrimination here, also by way of introducing different scales of collectivisation as discussed later:

> These rights might be collective (for example, quotas in the political representation of women) but the claims of these groups can generally be met by implementation of the individual right to be free from arbitrary discrimination and appropriate measures of positive discrimination[128]

> To illustrate the difference in rights under this analysis, affirmative action programs involve individual and group rights, but not collective rights. Affirmative action programs are designed to redress the disadvantaged position of individual members of groups. When discrimination ends, the programs will end, and the particular group organization will cease to have a function[129]

Relatedly, this may carry implications for locus standi, and '*dual standing rights*'[130] in particular, which permits individuals or representative units to wield collective rights and, on the other hand, '*jointly exercised individual rights*',[131] such latter form

[121] Freeman (1995), p. 25.

[122] Dinstein (1976).

[123] Jovanović (2012).

[124] Dinstein (1976).

[125] Freeman (1995), p. 26.
See also: Van Dyke (1985).

[126] Sanders (1991).

[127] Jones (2016).

[128] Freeman (1995), p. 26.

[129] Sanders (1991), p. 370.

[130] Buchanan (1993).

[131] Jovanović (2012).

alluding to affirmative action which in principle does not amount to any collective claims as such.

Rather than placing the focus on group or collective rights per se here—as a satisfactory answer to majority-based frameworks, and ultimately to actually mitigate structural inequalities and injustices—we shall concern ourselves with its different underlying processes and scales. This, it is hoped for, will further assist us in making sense of collective rights in a conceptual sense, its different manifestations and related impacts this may have for the actual exercise of these rights. Again, we are confronted with a multivariate field of pro forma rights, formal equality on the one hand and substantive change, genuinely inclusive rights on the other. This may find accommodation under what we will term '*scales of collectivisation*'. It will further assist us in measuring the legal value of collective rights in contemporary frameworks comparatively. The following classification scheme shall help us in carving out in a systematic fashion both limits and opportunities for collective rights to materialise. Let us address each category in turn.

Firstly, we may want to compare and contrast *standardisation and mainstreaming processes* (I) that ultimately allow collective rights to become structurally embedded in a given framework, on the one hand, and ad hoc forms of collectivisation, on the other. Throughout the human rights decades that would follow the adoption of the Universal Declaration of Human Rights in 1948, collective rights have been witnessing—albeit at embryonic stage—repeated attempts of mainstreaming these rights across the international legal landscape of human rights. This became most pronounced in the case of the Convention on the Rights of the Child[132] which would not only understand indigenous origin as an important component of the spirit of understanding, peace, tolerance or life in a free society (art. 29), but it would also establish dedicated indigenous rights to enjoy culture, practice religion or use one's language (art. 30).[133] If we were to consider developments that could be located at the other side of the spectrum, this could include the somewhat isolated treatment of indigenous rights in the general comments and reporting framework of the main UN human rights treaties (ICCPR, ICESCR, CEDAW, CAT, ICERD, CRPD, CED, CMW): notably, indigenous rights may find mention in generic references to 'vulnerable groups' or groups needing special attention, commonly as these relate to specific issues such as physical violence against women or children.

Secondly, taking norms as a starting point, we may be able to observe the rise of collective regimes in their own terms, so-called *sui generis orders* (II). The latter term, however, seems to presuppose high thresholds to be met to qualify as such and it also strongly builds on institutionality: the European Union may be emblematic here, as a 'self-contained regime', a sui generis international organisation,[134] a legal

[132] See e.g. Rae (2006).

[133] See, for further debates, Schmahl (2021).

[134] Phelan (2012).

experiment with sui generis nature,[135] while others have understood its intermediate position between state and international organisation as being decisive for such status.[136] Similar terminology is to be found in human rights jargon. Notably, a proper *jus commune* has been attributed to international human rights treaties, again with a dedicated focus on relevant (interpretative) institutions.[137] Similar observations may be made in the case of collective rights, building on newly established orders including UNDRIPS and Convention No 169 as well as sporadic references elsewhere such as the Convention on Biodiversity (CBD) or the Convention on the Safeguarding of Intangible Cultural Heritage (CSICH), each building on proper forms of institutionality including monitoring systems. Returning to the other side of the spectrum, sui generis orders may be juxtaposed with other (possibly conflicting) legal regimes such as the intellectual property framework (WIPO), which require ways of integrating or accommodating collective rights into conflicting value systems. We may further feel compelled to draw lines of demarcation between hard-law and soft-law regimes, introducing yet another distinguishing factor which raises questions of legal leverage and enforcement. At domestic level this may take the shape of isolated policies, falling short of allowing for structural change, such as, for example, constitutional reforms with the potential to collectivise the law in a systematic and integrated manner.

Thirdly and relatedly, we may indeed seek answers in contemporary *constitutional orders* (III). Given the hierarchy of legal orders—especially as far as domestic law is concerned—constitutional orders offer valuable venues for collectivising the law. This may include, inter alia, provisions on indigenous self-determination, autonomies, self-governance, customary law, and historic or future treaty-making.[138] Conversely, isolated policies may hardly do justice to the promising institutional reinventions finding their origin in constitutional transformations such as constitutional reforms or processes leading to completely new constitutional frameworks, powerfully demonstrated by the Ecuadorian and Bolivian experiences.[139] In the case of indigenous peoples and traditionally left-out minorities, collectivisation processes naturally require systemic rethinking, including but not limited to applying novel legal principles, decolonising reforms, new participation schemes and mainstreaming efforts to enable those groups to find voice and due consideration throughout the constitutional framework concerned.

Fourthly, mainstreaming may not only concern jurisprudential developments, but can similarly be found across the expanding *institutional scenery of human rights*

[135] De Witte (2012).

[136] Boşilcă (2014).

[137] De Schutter (2018).

[138] Cats-Baril (2020).

[139] Barrios-Suvelza (2017).
Uprimny (2011).
Romero Bonifaz (2009).
Bernot (2015).

(IV), under the umbrella of the OHCHR in particular, and its ever more specialising institutional framework. What is meant here includes working groups, special rapporteurs and independent experts, sub-commissions or subcommittees.[140] Especially where collective rights remain far from being codified, specialised institutions demonstrably assume a leading role in developing jurisprudence, in monitoring state practice or offering complementary venues for individuals and groups to make claims. In the field of indigenous rights, considerable progress has been achieved under OHCHR special procedures, the Human Rights Council and ECOSOC, establishing the mandate of the Special Rapporteur on the Rights of Indigenous Peoples (SR), the Expert Mechanism on the Rights of Indigenous Peoples (EMRIP) and the Permanent Forum on Indigenous Issues (PFII), respectively.[141] These institutions and specialised agencies have come to play a leading role in interpreting and implementing relevant legal sources, UNDRIPS in particular (arts. 41 and 42).[142] Other collective regimes may remain far from enjoying institutional oversight, including peasants' rights—hence limiting collectivisation to the domestic realm or international non-governmental movements, as powerfully shown by Via Campesina.

Fifthly, collectivisation may take shape differently depending on a group's level of *autonomy and leverage* (V) relative to the State. Indeed, the indigenous right to autonomy remains one of the most vehemently demanded collective rights at global scale. Apart from its intrinsic value as a general principle, autonomy also materialises in the form of specific indicators. In that sense, a group's level of autonomy may depend on its voting procedures and respective quota regulations,[143] the establishment of dedicated mechanisms such as parliaments, sub-commissions or ministries,[144] particular mandates of representation to be created and assumed or political parties to arise,[145] or the extent to which pluralism is embraced by a given legal framework.[146] In other words, collectivisation is qualified by the State's eagerness to give up on its status quo, majority-oriented logics of daily operating. Institutional venues and procedures seemingly bear considerable potential in operationalising collective autonomy, allowing a State's institutions to open up towards pluralistic orders, and the diversity of subjects it pretends to represent.

---

[140] Charters and Stavenhagen (2012).
Youngblood Henderson (2008).

[141] Burger (2012).

[142] for further debates, see Clavero (2008) *Nota sobre el Alcance del Mandato Contenido en el Artículo 42 de la Declaración sobre los Derechos de los Pueblos Indígenas y el Mejor Modo de Satisfacerlo por Parte del Foro Permanente para las Cuestiones Indígenas.*

[143] Stojanović (2013).

[144] Expert Mechanism on the Rights of Indigenous Peoples (2011) *Final Study on Indigenous Peoples and the Right to Participate in Decision-Making.*

[145] Van Cott (2007).

[146] Barrera (2012).

Sixthly, collectivisation may be limited to certain rights only, proving ignorant of *human rights in their integrity* (VI), that is, the interrelated, indivisible, universal and interdependent nature of human rights (see the Vienna Declaration and Programme of Action and the 1993 World Conference on Human Rights). In short, the integrity of rights is to be transposed into legal orders if we wanted to approach collectivisation genuinely. International legal orders illustrate such shortcomings throughout the treaty-based framework. While economic, social and cultural rights remain limited to everyone's '*tak[ing] part in cultural life*' (ICESCR, art. 15),[147] civil and political rights similarly reveal a narrow focus, that is, minorities' right to '*enjoy their own culture, to profess and practice their own religion, or to use their own language*' (ICCPR, art. 27).[148] Regional frameworks, such as the 'national minorities' framework established by the Council of Europe, similarly approach collectivisation only hesitantly, leaving broader procedural matters, such as collective invoking of rights, untouched.[149] Yet, indigenous rights in particular reveal the urgent need to understand claims as interrelated given the shared holistic view on the environment or as intrinsic to their collective cosmovisions.[150] By way of collectivising minority rights, both substantive and procedural dimensions appear relevant in granting full access to any human right, including those rights particular to indigenous peoples and minorities.

## 7.3 Juridification Processes: Standardisation or Ad-Hoc Manifestations

Collectivisation processes—in the sense of juridifying collective rights—may take different forms and formats; this may vary from standardising processes put in place with the objective of embedding collective rights in a given framework on one side of the spectrum, to ad hoc forms of juridification on the other side, often being realised in relation to a specific human rights concern, isolated situations or cases. Little attention has been paid to collective rights in the human rights field, even less so to respective standardising or mainstreaming efforts unless discussed under the umbrella of specific regimes such as indigenous rights, environmental rights or peasants' rights. The following sub-chapters explore two main venues in that regard, firstly, classical individual rights orders as forums for standardisation practices and its critiques, and secondly, and more far-reaching, standardisation as it concerns collective rights, constituting a valuable venue for group-differentiated rights to find articulation.

[147] See also Yupsanis (2012).

[148] Yupsanis (2014).

[149] Jovanović (2012).

[150] *Case of the Kichwa Indigenous People of Sarayaku vs. Ecuador*, Inter-American Court of Human Rights in 2012.

Adding to the somewhat contentious nature of collective rights debates, juridification processes build on sophisticated negotiation practices, which are necessarily qualified by specific agendas driven by interest groups or specific governments in place. Especially human rights law commonly mirrors cultures of compromise, which finds articulation, very classically, in relation to gender and religious freedom or the upholding of human rights where the public interest is at stake to name a few. Conflicts of rights, constituting a traditional human rights concern, have also been addressed regionally, including the European Court on Human Rights portraying these as either a question of indeed conflict or, alternatively, understood as reflecting harmonious compatibility.[151] Juridification processes however also meet with strong neo-liberal lobbies and similar inimical movements to human rights agendas, hence further complicating the process of standardisation. This may be the case as far as extractivist or infrastructure developments are concerned or other global tendencies with their local detrimental impact. Juridification and also standardisation need to be understood against this background, with the obstacles not only attributable to complex on the ground realities but also structural questions at the very initial stage of the codifying process.

If we were to return to the origins of the term, we are undoubtedly confronted with a wide range of definitions: '*juridification*' in its essence has been described as a 'process of transformation', for something to become integrated into the law.[152] Most of the processes described here would live up to such expectations, appreciating to what extent legal orders provide spaces for alternative justice systems and legal constructs such as collective rights to ultimately become formalised, codified. Elsewhere, it is referred to the multiplicity of meanings, juridification has been assuming in the literature, comparing the concept with, inter-alia:

> 'the proliferation of law' or as 'the tendency towards an increase in formal (or positive, written) law, [...] as 'the monopolisation of the legal field by legal professionals', the 'construction of judicial power', 'the expansion of judicial power' [or] link juridification to the spread of rule-guided action or the expectation of lawful conduct.[153]

Elsewhere it is distinguished between three different manifestations of juridification, firstly, referring to what is termed '*legislative growth*' theory referring to an "*increased production of laws*" both in terms of the growth of legislation and regarding degree of specialisation; secondly, juridification is understood in terms of Weberian bureaucratisation in its administrative sense, that is resolutions or circulars; and thirdly, it assumes the form of judicialization, describing the "*production by the judiciary of norms with governing potential*".[154]

The present work takes up several dimensions, including the described tendency to increase the body of law without neglecting the importance attributable to judicial

---

[151] Smet (2017).

[152] Tavolari (2018).

For insights into several pertinent debates on juridification, see: Teubner (1987).

[153] Blichner and Molander (2008), p. 36.

[154] Papendorf (2018), p. 290.

power which distinguishes the law from other (social) rules but also in terms of the hierarchy attached to it, which becomes most visible in constitutional orders. Indeed, what lies at the heart of the chapter concerns an in-depth exploration of those processes resulting in codification in a last step, both referring to numerical aspects in terms of the sheer amount of references to hitherto unrecognised law(s), and in relation to specific weight given to such law(s) in consideration of legal hierarchies. By way of developing a yet more distinct assessment, it is evaluated to what extent these manifestations of juridification represent isolated or sporadic attempts resulting in a few provisions only, or prove to be more far-reaching, that is triggering changes in the State's architecture, introducing entire catalogues of rights, or by way of recognising legal pluralistic ideas and its materialisation, emblematic being collective rights.

We may however understand juridification also in a more overarching way, beyond the strict meaning attributable to codification processes. This is not to say that juridification assumes a meaning which has been propagated ever since Habermas' 'Theory of Communicative Action', that of considering juridification processes a way of colonising the lifeworld, referring to the law as assuming an external position that exerts assimilating powers on the lifeworld.[155] Somewhat relatedly, Habermas' approach developed in 'Between Facts and Norms' is referred elsewhere to what is described as "*implementing the wrong – that is, paternalistic – rules of law in the lifeworld*".[156] While such problematisation undoubtedly mirrors one of the most common struggles fought by indigenous peoples and minority groups alike, the emphasis is different here, examining the law in its preliminary stage, the very construction of the law in the way it proves receptible towards legal pluralistic ideas, including collective rights. In fact, a wide panoply of scholarly accounts assumes a less value-loaded position, portraying juridification as "*the process of the expansion of legal structures to areas of life that had not previously been regulated by law, or the intensification and increasingly detailed nature of existing law*".[157] In any case, we are witnessing an increasing proliferation of the law, its expansion on the ground to encompass virtually any aspect of social life. Relatedly, juridification has been associated with an "*increased concentration and/or extended social reach of rules, norms and procedures based in bureaucratic institutions and legislative enactment*".[158] The expansive scope of the law becomes visible here, encompassing considerable parts of the social world which is problematised here given its detrimental effects on indigenous, minorities and other groups in vulnerable positions. Accordingly, juridification has been described as "*the process of regulating social, economic, and political behaviour by creating*

[155] Loick (2019).

[156] Ibid.; p. 210.

[157] Hensel and Klippel (2015), p. 1.

[158] Niezen (2010), p. 218.

*norms and legislation*".[159] Again, the law and social reality are intimately linked, with the law exerting its powers on social life.

We may also witness a growing influence of the law in socio-economic activities that are gradually governed by legal rules which happens to the detriment of principles and values operating in the context of these activities;[160] in a way referring to an ever growing legal sphere. The law commonly assumes the role of an important safeguard, proving effective where conflicts with other logics or rules come to the fore. A particular accent is placed on those safeguards protecting vulnerable groups who commonly prove most affected by arbitrary social-economic realities which find expression where the protective umbrella of the law is missing. Indeed, these groups may be described as "*law-dissociated groups*" including "*their capacity to mobilise the law*", also finding accommodation by the term "*situation of double powerlessness*" which combines "*their lack of competence and economic opportunities*".[161]

What becomes a valuable starting point in these debates concerns what some may call the '*juridification of politics*' as it arises in indigenous contexts, very emblematically. Indeed, Sieder has referred to the '*juridification of indigenous politics*' which she distinguishes from generic processes of juridification with the former to be understood as "*the diffusion and vernacularization of state and international law, and the subjectivities generated by engagements with dominant norms and institutions*", and the latter being particular in terms of the "*complex dialectics involved*" when it comes to indigenous peoples' juridification of their own forms of law which becomes particularly salient where these are defended "*in the context of battles for state recognition of legal pluralism*".[162] These attempts of juridifying indigenous claims has not come without critique, with scholars being sceptical about the very frame of predominant legal orders being described as '*legal domination*', or the "*language of jurisprudence signal[ling] a consolidation of hegemony*" which may require an "*ideological critique of the institutions themselves*".[163] Not uncommonly though, scholars refer to the opportunities laying in international law in particular, in juridifying indigenous claims with the UN Declaration on the Rights of Indigenous Peoples constituting undoubtedly a widely recognised instrument building on indigenous proper voices throughout the process.[164] Indeed, indigenous movements and other forms of mobilisation have proven key in juridification processes at all levels, illustrative being the "*juridification of social protest signal[ling] the ways in which their contemporary forms of collective action draw on both local and transnational understandings of entitlements, obligations, and rights*".[165] Quite demonstrably,

[159] Ibid.; para.3.

[160] Cane and Conaghan (2009).

[161] Papendorf (2018), p. 287.

[162] Sieder (2020), p. 701.

[163] Kirsch (2012), p. 24.

[164] Charters and Stavenhagen (2012).

[165] Sieder (2010), p. 163.

different strategies become discernible when it comes to invoking rights stipulated in coexisting legal orders, rendering juridification a nuanced, multidimensional process. Let us examine in turn to what extent these forms of juridification assume an all-encompassing, holistic shape as in 'standardisation' or would be considered isolated, window-dressing attempts, as in 'ad hoc juridification'.

### 7.3.1 Individual Rights Orders as a Venue for Standardisation and Its Critiques

We may however derive some insights from related endeavours we are witnessing in the field of (individual) human rights at large. Such attempts of mainstreaming human rights have not remained without critique, pointing, for instance, at problems resulting from de-formalisation and bureaucratisation processes.[166] Relatedly, such processes need to be seen in view of the seizing of institutional power with its political significance,[167] in other words, human rights cannot be detached from the specific priorities or agendas under whose guise they are meant to become operationalised. This may further bring up questions related to the allocation of resources between different groups[168]—a classical concern for collective rights being largely undermined by individualised agendas, procedures and systemic ways of operating. Not uncommonly, those questions that are naturally raised in terms of intersecting or multiple identity affiliation[169] become relevant here: theoretical debates on the choice between '*diversity mainstreaming*' or '*gender mainstreaming*' have disapproved any preference on the matter, placing emphasis on practices and processes related to developing these approaches instead.[170] Given the predominance of a largely individual-steered human rights landscape (as an empirical basis to draw from), we might feel inclined to place our focus on individual rights regimes in the way these reveal accommodating potential for (mainstreaming) collective rights.

We may find some answers to this when examining art.30 (Convention on the Rights of the Child) on the rights of the indigenous child which stipulates: "*. . .a child belonging to such a minority or who is indigenous shall not be denied the right, in community with other members of his or her group, to enjoy his or her own culture, to profess and practice his or her own religion or to use his or her own language*". Interestingly, the exercising criterion is invoked here, adding a

[166] Koskenniemi (2007).
See also: McCrudden (2004).

[167] Koskenniemi (2010).

[168] Ibid.

[169] See also 'intersectionality' or 'intersectional discrimination' for further insights e.g. Atrey and Dunne (2019).

[170] Bacchi and Eveline (2010).

procedural dimension to the substantive right to practice culture, religion and language. Indeed, the Committee unequivocally maintains in its ground-breaking General Comment N° 11 on the matter that such right "*is conceived as being both individual and collective and is an important recognition of the collective traditions and values in indigenous cultures*".[171] Elsewhere it has been maintained that art.30 clearly establishes a collective dimension, even as a precondition for individual rights to be exercised and demanding positive measures to be adopted as defended by experts on the provision: "*significantly, if the exercise of an individual right under article 30 requires the existence of a group, taking protective measures for the benefit of the group as a whole may be justified*".[172] A conservative reading of the provision would focus on the individual as 'autonomous rights-holders' with art.30 "*not express[ing] true collective rights, but an individual right to the aspects of collective identity*".[173]

Yet more technically, the Committee engages in a detailed debate on the importance of '*collective cultural rights*' when applying the principle of the best interest of the child to indigenous children: this, it argues, "*requires consideration of how the right relates to collective cultural rights [as] indigenous children have not always received the distinct consideration they deserve*".[174] Indeed, art.3 under which such right is established gives rise to considerable implications for collective rights:

> it [the Committee] addressed the collective nature of indigenous children's rights more directly, but did so under article 3 rather than article 30, innovatively conceptualising the best interests principle as a collective and individual right and emphasising that the best interests of indigenous children cannot be considered in isolation from the interests of the group. The close relationship between children's best interests, their cultural rights, and the need to exercise those rights collectively with group members is again reiterated.[175]

Very importantly, indigenous peoples are to be consulted and participate in assessing a child's best interest: notably, where laws, policies or programmes threaten to affect indigenous children, the "*indigenous community should be consulted and given an opportunity to participate in the process on how the best interests of indigenous children in general can be decided in a culturally sensitive way. Such consultations should, to the extent possible, include meaningful participation of indigenous*

---

[171] Committee on the Rights of the Child (2009) *General Comment N° 11 Indigenous Children and their Rights under the Convention*, para.16.

[172] Harris-Short and Tobin (2019), p. 1171.

[173] Schmahl (2021), p. 414.

[174] Committee on the Rights of the Child (2009) *General Comment N° 11 Indigenous Children and their Rights under the Convention*, para.30.

More precisely, when assessing the best interests of an indigenous child, "they [State authorities] should consider the cultural rights of the indigenous child and his or her need to exercise such rights collectively with members of their group" (para.31).

[175] Harris-Short and Tobin (2019), p. 1171.

*children*."[176] Collective rights thereby find resonance as collective cultural expressions that are treated as demonstrably distinct from the generic public interest—when balancing individual and collective rights, for instance—and which are to be considered where individual rights are exercised; considerable procedural rights—consultation and participation in particular—carrying a collective dimension, have found their way into the standard-setting process.

## 7.3.2 Collective Rights and Their Potential for (Further) Standardisation

We may however also understand standardisation processes as viewed from the perspective of collective rights regimes, with albeit lower levels of judicial leverage given the predominance of soft law instruments dominating the scene in many collective frameworks.[177] Emblematic may be the case of indigenous rights emerging with the ILO Conventions N°107 in 1957 and N°169 in 1989[178] without however establishing as firmly the collective rights to self-determination, autonomies, pluralisms, participation and similar rights at eye level with the State as the UN Declaration on the Rights of Indigenous Peoples.[179] Collectivisation may take several shapes and formats in that context, including what we may term an '*integrationist approach'*, alluding to rights commonly juridified under human rights treaty bodies such as the right to vote, to health, education or language practice, or, alternatively, an '*autonomous approach*' resembling a '*lex specialis approach*'[180] which includes the right to free, prior and informed consultation and consent

---

[176] Committee on the Rights of the Child (2009) *General Comment N° 11 Indigenous Children and their Rights under the Convention*, para.31.

Where conflicts arise between the best interests of the child and the group, the "best interests of the specific child is the primary concern" (para.32)—however, the Committee also notes in that regard, "considering the collective cultural rights of the child is part of determining the child's best interests"(para.32).

[177] Consider, for instance, the following soft law instruments in the field of collective rights: the UN Declaration on the Rights of Indigenous Peoples (2007), the UN Declaration on the Rights of Persons Belonging to National or Ethnic, Religious and Linguistic Minorities (1992), the UN Declaration on the Rights of Peasants and Other People Working in Rural Areas (2018), the UN Declaration on the Right to Development (1986), the UN Declaration on the Right of Peoples to Peace (1984).

In relation to indigenous peoples, see the following work: Gómez Isa (2016).

[178] See, for instance, Rodríguez-Piñero Royo (2005).

Swepston (2015).

Yupsanis (2010).

[179] See, for instance, Charters and Stavenhagen (2012).

[180] Also known as 'lex specialis derogat legi generali' (special law repeals general laws), in other words, a "*principle according to which a rule of lex specialis is deemed to apply notwithstanding contrary general principles of international law*" Fellmeth and Horwitz (2009).

(FPIC)[181] but also those rights giving rise to indigenous proper procedures and customs, or those relating to repairing or generally remedying or mediating past (colonial) injustices. Key to such processes and particularly worthy to be mentioned are the specific working groups and caucus work,[182] allowing indigenous representatives to play an active part in the negotiation process of the Declaration,[183] making sure State sovereignty would not prevent larger indigenous autonomies to be excluded from the provisions. That way collectivisation would also take place procedurally, opening channels for indigenous peoples to negotiate according to their own customs and procedures while we may be reminded of the general intergovernmental nature of meetings, agendas and other constraining factors.[184] Standardisation processes would thereby depart from classical treaty making and other ordinary juridification processes, by appropriating international rules and procedures in a way that permitted collective rights holders to introduce—under the regular constraints imposed by State sovereignty—collective rights, following ordinary human rights language but also basing themselves on indigenous law and legal systems.

## 7.4 *Establishing* Sui Generis *Orders*

Not uncommonly, *sui generis* orders have been referred to in specific regional institutional contexts such as the European Union, denominated a '*sui generis* international organisation',[185] or called a 'legal experiment with *sui generis* nature'[186] by de Witte. Also elsewhere the EU is understood as a *sui generis* order, that is, "*a separate legal system with its own characteristics and specifics*".[187] Further conclusions have been reached on the concept by way of deriving core aspects from EU institutionalism, notably:

> the sui generis term represents a special organizational form with its own specific features. Since it contains characteristics that are specific and untypical, the concept of sui generis requires a thorough analysis to determine what it means. (. . .) The sui generis concept serves as a term to define a mixture of all features [federal, confederal and other elements],

---

[181] Doyle (2015).
Wright and Tomaselli (2019).
Rodríguez-Garavito (2011).
Fontana and Grugel (2016).
Szablowski (2010).

[182] Burger and Martín Castro (2006).

[183] See, for instance, Lightfoot (2016).

[184] For a critical reading of these international legal developments, see, for instance, Watson (2018a).

[185] Phelan (2012), p. 367.

[186] De Witte (2012), p. 20.

[187] Peročević (2017), p. 110.

> including those that are not characteristic of any of the foregoing systems (. . .) It represents a unique system that cannot be compared in its entirety with existing systems[188]

Again, the legal concept *sui generis* is invoked to refer to the special form of institutionality being at unease with existing organisational forms while establishing a new forum for hitherto non-existing institutional manifestations to find recognition. Elsewhere the EU's *sui generis* nature has been compared to it being unique.[189]

Alongside the undoubtedly unique nature of many of the present legal constructs including collective rights that would qualify to be termed *sui generis* order, the incompatibility with existing orders merits mentioning here, being a persisting aspect in a context of unequal positions of laws, principles, orders. Indeed, *sui generis* that way easily assumes a decolonising spirit, requiring recognition without being subjected to predominant legal language, institutionalism, core principles and the like. Relatedly, it has been maintained that *sui generis* regimes have been able to subvert existing orders,[190] a venue which shall be explored further in the following sub-chapters in relation to collective rights and their potential to provoke system change. More efforts are undertaken elsewhere to explore the nature of *sui generis* in the EU context, notably the term is considered

> a description 'without proper names', available for application to other international organisations, which does not in any way disguise what is extraordinary about the EU, but at the same time normalizes this distinction by demonstrating its wider relevance.[191]

Departing from the EU's unique nature then, it may set an example without establishing any dependencies on other international mechanisms with the exception of the ruling nature of international law where applicable. Conversely, the *sui generis* nature of the regime may create dependencies for conformity, understanding *sui generis* in its "*particularities of the proper constitutional system of the Union*".[192] Constitutionalisation processes (see following sub-chapter) indeed provide another venue to study further, by their very nature forming a proper order, that way resembling the *sui generis* construct.

A similar use of the term may be witnessed under African Union law, to which such term has been attributed, considering the steady transition from intergovernmentalism to supranationalism in the AU legal order.[193] Importantly, the "*strongest claim to a sui generis AU legal order*"[194] has been attributed to the field of human rights, given the unique emphasis placed on not only economic, social and cultural rights, but group and collective rights. A related relevant term may be the regional '*jus commune*' finding application in both EU and AU contexts

[188] Ibid.; p. 114.

[189] Phelan (2012).

[190] Martins and Tybusch (2016).

[191] Ibid.; p. 380.

[192] Rodríguez (2016), p. 206.

[193] Amao (2019).

[194] Home (2019), p. 320.

respectively. Interestingly, *sui generis* is contrasted with a construct which may similarly apply to the AU context, that of 'institutional isomorphism' defined as "*a similarity of processes or structure between organizations, as a result of independent development under similar constraints or imitation*".[195] Paradoxically, the two constructs may go hand in hand—without any concessions made to the unique organisational identity of the AU, the Union and other international organisations need to be understood as being "*constructed and propagated through global cultural and associational processes*".[196] What is more, international law is to be considered binding for its contracting parties, hence entering contentious debates on legal hierarchies.[197]

Beyond these regional manifestations of institutionalism, a so-called 'sui generis position' was identified in relation to the Federal Republic of Yugoslavia in the ICJ decision *Legality of Use of Force [Serbia and Montenegro vs. Belgium] [Preliminary Objections]* bolstered by the following curious explanation: "*in as much as the Court had spoken of a 'sui generis position' of the FRY, this was explained as not having been a prescriptive term conveying any particular legal consequences but rather as a phrase 'descriptive of the amorphous state of affairs'*".[198] Indeed, the concept *sui generis* largely lacks any widely recognised definition let alone constituent characteristics, turning the construct into an unspecific legal category without carrying any legal consequences with it. It shall however be employed here given its clear orientation towards a proper—possibly autonomous—legal order that merits an examination on its own account. In that sense, it vests collective rights or group-differentiated rights with a special character, an autonomous legal status, in a way gaining in recognition also in view of legal pluralistic ideas.

However—and by way of fulfilling the purpose of the present analysis of collective rights—the *sui generis* construct may also be understood beyond specific geographical-institutional formations. This is the case for the so-called '*human rights jus commune*' coined by de Schutter, defining such concept as "*one human rights body borrowing from the interpretation of human rights law by another body, in the absence of any formal link between the two bodies concerned*".[199] Such mutual borrowing has become manifest in a multiplicity of ways, which we could understand as defining criteria, namely a steadily growing accessibility of case law through e.g. NGO activism before the courts such as *amici curiae*, competition among human rights bodies in developing stronger protection compared to other institutions, and a rationale based on judicial economy that encapsulates the adoption

[195] Ibid.; pp. 319–320.

[196] Ibid.; p. 320.

[197] See, for instance, Búrca (2012).

[198] Thienel and Zimmermann (2019).
See also: Kamardi (2009).

[199] De Schutter (2018), p. 18.

of jurisprudence developed elsewhere.[200] Demonstrably, judicial dialogue and the engagement of civil society actors in judicial proceedings have been contributing to the fostering of a proper order. *Sui generis* has similarly found application in relation to very specific rights including the constitutional rights of Aboriginal peoples and also Aboriginal orders as such, in a similar vein as this would contribute to legal pluralism.[201] To be sure, *sui generis* indigenous orders need to be "*understood and interpreted as distinctive and integral to Aboriginal law and societies, rather than as part of European law and societies*"[202]—while we shall not forget about indigenous peoples in Europe, also falling under the frame of minority regimes. And, as argued earlier, these have demonstrably contributing to forming postcolonial and multicultural States as discussed in the Canadian case.[203] Yet another approach may be taken by understanding *sui generis* as a principle as it has been discussed in relation to human dignity, qualifying as *sui generis* due to the fact that it is to be considered a "*status principle whose function lies in unifying our normative orders*",[204] assuming important system integrating functions here. Indeed, *sui generis* exerts self-preserving functions, also protecting dedicated rights from the predominating order(s) in place. In that sense, constitutional orders similarly merit to be studied in their own terms, with both the dangers of perpetuating colonial logics and the opportunities for parallel justice systems and collective rights to gain recognition, as discussed in the following sub-chapter.

### *7.4.1* Sui Generis *Orders: Collective Rights and Definitional Attempts*

More broadly, *sui generis* has been defined as 'of its own kind' and refer to, for instance, legal rights that "*are unique and confined to their own facts, and therefore may not be of broader application*".[205] While collective rights would certainly qualify as particular or unique and follow their own rationale and characteristics, we shall be more wary as to the application of collective rights whose limits are to be defined not by legal technicalities but the political landscape permitting or not their widespread application. Indeed, *sui generis* lends itself for further exploration not only as to its 'inner life', but the relations a legal order maintains with institutions or

---

200 Ibid.

201 Sákéj and Henderson (2002), pp. 414–416.

202 Ibid.; p. 425.

203 Ibid.

204 Riley (2019), p. 439.

205 Practical Law - Westlaw (2023) Sui Generis. *Practical Law*, para.1. Retrieved from https://content.next.westlaw.com/practical-law/document/Ib2b7b8c69bb111e698dc8b09b4f043e0/Sui-Generis?viewType=FullText&transitionType=Default&contextData=(sc.Default)#:~:text=A%20Latin%20term%20meaning%20%22of,not%20be%20of%20broader%20application.

other legal systems. Indeed, the term has found application in indigenous contexts, such as in Canadian Aboriginal law which understands *sui generis* as a "*legal term describing the relationship between the Government (the Crown) and the Aboriginal peoples of Canada in relation to Aboriginal title, rights, and treaties*".[206] It is further advanced that "*these rights and relationships are 'unique', 'one of a kind', or 'in their own class'*",[207] referring to the particular place these rights and relationships occupy in Canadian law,[208] but also as a source of rights,[209] understood in the broader context of legal pluralism and legal history. Indigenous rights as *sui generis* constructs have also found expression in jurisprudential developments, both as a category of rights and indigenous land title in particular.[210] Others would however contend, indigenous rights would not qualify as carrying an absolute *sui generis* character given that they are not uncommonly "*claimed and justified on preconditions shared with other subjects*".[211] Instead, other vulnerable groups may equally make claims under such rights.

In that sense, collective rights may very well assume umbrella functions, accommodating a wide panoply of group rights which we may, in their entirety, cautiously term '*sui generis*' in kind. Similar arguments are made elsewhere, attributing to rights a facilitating function in their attempt to accommodate other collective claims, by addressing "*the formation of indigenous rights as a process (...) in which the allocation of rights to indigenous groups enables the national legal order to promote more even patterns of inclusion, generating rights that can be accessed by, and thus help to integrate, all collective actors*".[212] Indigenous rights in that sense exert some transformative powers in relation to the legal system embedding them, creating the space for collective rights at large to gain a proper sense and voice in State law.

### *7.4.2 Collective Rights and Dominant Legal Orders: Indigenous Sovereignty and Beyond*

Another approach on *sui generis* may lay in sovereignty conceptualisations as to the positioning of collective rights vis-à-vis the dominant legal order. Rather commonly, sovereignty is understood in a territorial sense or as referring to indigenous peoples

---

[206] Centre for Constitutional Studies / Centre d'études constitutionnelles (2019) *Sui Generis*. Retrieved from https://www.constitutionalstudies.ca/2019/07/sui-generis/ para.1.

[207] Borrows and Rotman (1997), p. 10.

[208] Centre for Constitutional Studies / Centre d'études constitutionnelles (2019) *Sui Generis*.

[209] Ibid.

[210] Bens (2020).
See e.g. *Delgamuukw vs. British Columbia*, Canadian Supreme Court in 1997.

[211] Thornhill et al. (2018), p. 8.

[212] Ibid.; p. 8.

as sovereign nations.[213] Also in international law more widely, the principle of sovereignty is largely being conceived as territorial, as "*of supreme authority within a territory*"[214] more precisely. Sovereignty easily assumes a relative nature when understood in the context of inter-State relations: equal rank among sovereign States would be considered an influential manifestation of sovereignty.[215] This necessarily gives rise to an institutional understanding (as in 'State') which would find application in the case of indigenous peoples and the nation-based idea of sovereignty discussed above. Cautious voices may, however, refer to '*indigenous sovereignty*' as a "*claim for autonomy and legitimacy as sovereign authority within the realm of the State*"[216] rather than representing any exclusive demands. This, it could be argued, may be understood as a weaker or ostensible form of legal pluralism, organised vertically. Indigenous sovereignty may be understood in various forms beyond the institutional dimension, embracing inter-alia traditional land ownership, identity and cultural facets, participation in decisions of concern to indigenous peoples and self-governance by means of customary laws.[217]

We may hence legitimately ask to what extent sovereignty could indeed become articulated as referring to legal orders on their own terms, and the position assumed by collective rights in particular. Oftentimes, legal order is being conceived as only one element alongside other forms of unity such as political order or supreme power embedded in such order.[218] Others have juxtaposed sovereign statehood with the idea of co-existing legal orders and respective mutual recognition[219]: without denying the importance and continued viability of State sovereignty, emphasis is placed on legal orders, as a category in constant negotiation with and—at least in current State-minority relations—as integrated into the umbrella of State sovereignty. It is this shared space having been termed '*inter-legality*' by Sousa Santos which shall enable State law to be decolonised while considering different scales, interactions and intersections among those spaces.[220] A similar paradigm finds its roots in the so-called '*jurisprudence of hybridity*' which requires three steps to be taken, namely to decolonise the mind, inspired by indigenous law, to destabilise colonial legal authority, and to transit from monist-pluralism to pluralist-pluralism.[221] Collective rights thereby gain a special place amongst (the) dominant individual rights order(s), promising transformative potential. It may be noted here this may require considerable epistemological but also ontological shifts to be realised: in other words,

---

[213] Bens (2020).

[214] Besson (2011), para.1.

[215] Ibid.
Roth (2011).

[216] Shrinkhal (2021), p. 74.

[217] Lenzerini (2006).

[218] MacCormick (1999).

[219] Lindahl (2001).

[220] Sousa Santos (1987).

[221] Nursoo (2018).

recognising collective rights as a proper legal order demands both questioning underlying assumptions defended by the dominant order,[222] and the reconstruction of the idea of the law to open up for diversity-oriented, pluralism-prone, group-minded, inequality-sensitive and communitarian thinking. In that sense, collective rights as an emerging *sui generis* order is preconditioned on transformations that concern the sources of knowledge and worldviews, ideological underpinnings, suitable political climate, constitutional and hence institutional openness as well as a transversal benevolence towards concessions to be made to the majority-oriented status quo.

## 7.5 Constitutionalising Collective Rights

Constitutionalization processes represent yet another important channel to elevate collective or group-specific rights to constitutional rank, thereby integrating difference-specific rights into a superior framework, and with it, higher levels of recognition, effectiveness and due regard to be paid in case of conflict with other norms. We shall understand constitutionalisation in a broad sense, beyond the restrictive framework of domestic constitutionalism, ultimately altering the status of human rights norms which in their majority and by their very nature benefit from some higher status already. To be sure, constitutionalisation does not refer to those processes that subject governmental action to the principles and structures of a domestic constitution,[223] rather constitutionalisation is meant in the juridifying sense, as an act of legal integration, at times harmonisation. Emblematic may be international legal developments witnessing a growing constitutionalisation, with international law reaching a level that may limit State sovereignty; more precisely, constitutionalisation proponents portray public international law as

> recognis[ing] a common interest of humanity transcending State interests, hierarchically supreme 'constitutional principles' set boundaries to the hitherto unlimited will of States, international organisation become relatively independent of their Member States, and States are no longer left with a genuine domaine réservé.[224]

While this certainly hints at the decay of domestic sovereignty and the new functionality of international law as yet another control instance, we shall focus on its substance, that is, such 'common interest' in the form of 'hierarchically supreme constitutional principles'. Also elsewhere it is maintained that constitutionalisation in international law reveals a shift in principles, notably from State sovereignty and territorial integrity to an appropriation and modification of constitutional principles and institutions in the international order.[225]

---

[222] See e.g. Smith (2012).
Watson (2018b).

[223] Loughlin (2010).

[224] Kleinlein (2012), p. 703.

[225] Peters (2019).

We shall however not limit ourselves to the ambit of international law here and rather see constitutionalisation as a general technical approach with its transformative potential which may concern sporadic provisions but also entire catalogues of rights or constitutional reform projects, allowing for ideological shifts through the law. Ultimately international legal developments similarly require respective adaptations at domestic levels despite the different forms it may take, following a monistic or dualistic approach. A number of scholars argues in fact international law proves interwoven by classical legal approaches predominant in the Global North, hence requiring decolonising efforts in their own terms.[226] Indeed, any legal process is shaped by those in negotiating positions which are either closed to or only allow for limited participation of those ultimately affected by the law. While the UN Declaration on the Rights of Indigenous Peoples seems to promise quite the contrary with considerable institutional efforts involved that would allow indigenous peoples to gain a shaping voice in the process,[227] references to State sovereignty and territorial conservatism continue shaping international law including the Declaration until today.

It seems evident then to voice criticism on constitutional frameworks as to their transformative potential irrespective of the level at which they are situated, including classical domestic constitutionalism, regional *ius commune* or global constitutionalism.[228] Appreciating the importance of each order may become important though if we were to consider the question of delegation of powers including the binding nature of international decisions and the forms of supranational decision-making becoming apparent in regional organisations such as the European Union. That way, regional constitutionalisation may not only lead to the recognition of progressive standards in its proper reach and scope of application, but also require respective steps to be taken domestically. The principles of '*supremacy*' and '*direct effect*' may be emblematic, referring to the authoritative nature of the law developed in the EU legal order.[229] Particularly emblematic may also be the '*constitutional block doctrine*' which refers to the granting of constitutional rank to international law. This may take different forms and formats with judges reinterpreting general declarations stipulated in the respective constitutions with the objective of introducing said doctrine, or by a conjunct reading of dedicated constitutional clauses and legislative reforms in the area of constitutional law or opening or primacy clauses.[230] Indeed, the constitutional block doctrine has been referred to as a '*legal transplant*' or '*migration of constitutional ideas*' where different legal orders would inspire each other.[231] With the democratic transition in Latin American States, the doctrine would

[226] See, for instance, Watson (2018a).

[227] See, for instance, Charters and Stavenhagen (2012).

[228] On global constitutionalism, see, for instance, Lang and Wiener (2017).

[229] Craig and de Búrca (2015).

[230] Góngora-Mera (2017), p. 240.

[231] Ibid.

See also: Hoyos (1992).

gain new meaning finding accommodation with due regard paid to the constitutional environment.[232] The doctrine indeed gains in significance where constitutions undergo substantial reform including amendment processes, creating a new place for international human rights law. What is quintessential here concerns the move towards progressive standards through processes of constitutionalisation which, as has been shown, may occur at various legal spheres. In turn, we shall concern ourselves with some of the most difficult endeavours in creating venues for rights to be enshrined in constitutionalism, that of collective rights and indigenous rights.

For collective rights to gain in enforcement powers, hence altering their legally binding value, constitutionalism provides a welcome avenue to explore. Examples are manifold, ranging from indigenous and Afro-descendant rights in Bolivia and Ecuador,[233] to the human right to a safe environment in Latin America,[234] or the right to development which has gained entrance into numerous constitutional orders. Our focus will remain on collective rights as important channels for indigenous peoples, ethnic, cultural, linguistic or religious minorities while, admittedly, processes of constitutionalisation commonly embrace labour rights at large as manifestations of collectivity.[235]

### *7.5.1 Dealing with Difference and Constitutionalising Collective Rights*

For the purpose of the present work, we shall primarily focus on the extent to which collective rights or a difference-oriented approach find entrance into constitutionalism. As alluded to earlier, human rights generally have largely benefited from juridification processes, sometimes dubbed '*dual positivisation*',[236] referring to their enshrinement in both international human rights law and constitutional law. It may be worth noting here that relevant constitutionalist debates on conflicts are commonly confined to the interaction of different legal orders, such as international and domestic law[237] or international law and regional *jus commune,*[238] rather than conflicting rights. Some idea bringing us closer to the subject under examination concerns the categorisation of rights which has famously been coined by Hannah

---

[232] Góngora-Mera (2017).

[233] Yrigoyen Fajardo (2016).

[234] See e.g. Aguilera Bravo (2021).

[235] See e.g. Vergis (2020).
See also Sabel and Gerstenberg (2010).

[236] Besson (2015), p. 279.
For a detailed discussion on this terminological addition, see: Neuman (2003).
See also: Garcia Alvarez (2022).

[237] Besson (2015).

[238] Búrca (2012).

Arendt who distinguished between moral and legal rights in a first instance, and domestic and international rights in a second step.[239] The question of collective rights encounters foundational problems in that regard, often not being properly stipulated in any legally binding order. Also other constitutional categorisations of human rights have demonstrated a certain unease or even ignorance in dealing with difference, at least explicitly: accordingly, constitutionalism, it has been argued, has settled for a preference system in dealing with different human rights norms, distinguishing between "*giving either* jus cogens *priority, or trade, or human rights, or* erga omnes *principles*".[240] As we learned earlier however, *jus cogens* duties may indeed provide a valuable venue to explore for some collective rights to find recognition—peoples' collective right to self-determination but also anti-slavery rights. Accordingly, *erga omnes* obligations have been described as a welcome legal category to protect collective interests, litigated by international tribunals or non-compliance procedures.[241] This however does not provide us with a fully satisfying answer, given its rather specific or ad-hoc application that remains far from mainstreaming collective rights in constitutional orders.

We are compelled to refer back to a largely individualised rationale that permeates and informs different legal orders. Classically, State-subjects relations are portrayed as those relating the State and the individual; this becomes apparent in ordinary human rights language that is used in constitutional law. Ordinary rights and freedoms are commonly phrased in individualistic terms, reaching back to the earliest human rights codes adopted in Europe and elsewhere. This also applies to international law; Kelsen, Lauterpacht and Scelle place emphasis on the individual as a subject of international law, reflecting indeed a position assumed by a great majority of international legal approaches on the matter.[242] Regional developments merit mentioning here as well, emblematic being a sort of precedent set by the African Charter on Human and Peoples' Rights declaring individual rights to coexist with group rights, enjoying resembling levels of recognition.[243] Indeed, similar observations can be made throughout constitutional developments in the region with several African States recognising cultural rights, for instance, at both individual and community levels respectively.[244] This concerns, inter-alia, measures to be adopted to protect the cultural patrimony of the Sao Tomean people as enshrined in the 1990 Political Constitution of São Tomé and Príncipe, or the Ugandan Constitution with its safeguards in relation to traditional and cultural chiefs, protecting their

[239] Besson (2015).

See for a more elaborated debate: Arendt (1951).

[240] Klabbers (2009), p. 18.

[241] Ulfstein (2009).

[242] Kleinlein (2012).

[243] Shyllon (2016).

[244] Ibid.

institutionality in particular and their proper culture, customs, traditions, wishes or aspirations ruling in that regard.[245]

Also in European contexts, collective rights assume a variety of shapes which becomes most visible in the minority context; freedom of religion, for instance, has been declared an individual and collective right serving religious minorities to "*claim autonomy from what they perceive as a highly securalized mainstream society*", hence vesting them with few opportunities to gain in visibility.[246] Related challenges concern the dividing lines between collective and individual rights where this requires ordinary weighing exercises: illustrative may be the US American jurisdiction where weight is placed on individual conscience rather than the protection of religious groups, based on the rationale that "*the basis of religious assembly is based on the individual act of conscience, rather than being a derivative of the special status of religious organisations*".[247] An interesting case concerns language policies as they become manifest in the Swiss case where territoriality policies establish collective language rights concerning, for instance, the "*prohibition of private German schools in the French-speaking district of the bilingual canton of Bern (...) echo[ing] the priority of inter-communal peace over individual freedoms (...) [and] more importantly, it testifies to a different nature of the relation between democracy and federalism. The availability of the referendum and initiative transformed an abstract principle of people's sovereignty into participatory democracy*".[248] Interestingly, the aforecited analysis does not address minority rights, but considers the question as being of individual nature, that is, individual language rights to be exercised; following the same line, democratic principles are understood in a majority sense in accordance with federal structures in place. Indeed, collective rights may be exercised in a territorial sense which could appear difficult to reconcile with classical minority perspectives on the matter. Interestingly, federalism may also be examined in the context of a more evident situation of collective rights, that of indigenous peoples, where federalism has been understood as tantamount to hostility towards the latter and as an '*antithesis of pluralist federalism*'.[249]

We would not expect collective rights to become constitutionalised to the extent to which entire ideological shifts would prevent individual rights from being codified or from remaining in the constitutional scenery. It may however be legitimately asked what role these would gain in the constitutionalisation process. As it was argued elsewhere the "*recognition of minority rights does not imply the communitarian logic that group rights take precedence over individual rights*";[250] in fact arguing that collective rights would place individual rights at risk would prove ignorant of conflicts of rights that concern individual rights (in relation to one

[245] Ibid.

[246] Zucca (2016), p. 40.

[247] Ibid.; p. 47.

[248] Basta Fleiner and Gaudreault-DesBiens (2013), p. 146.

[249] Ibid.; p. 153.

[250] Dersso and Palermo (2013), p. 171.

another)—recognising collective rights would not imply any preference afforded to these in relation to individual rights.[251]

### *7.5.2 Collectivising Rights: Domestic Constitutionalism Under Focus*

The present analysis attempts to trace collective rights more transversally, just as an 'ideological' constitutional reading would allow for. State architectures, it could be argued, need to demonstrate some proneness to accommodating collective rights, a general orientation towards decolonisation, and basic principles reflecting a collective sense. When discussing recent constitutional transformations in Latin America, a few remarks may be made in that regard: constitutional reforms and re-building show a lasting impact on the understanding of 'national' unity, as a '*pluralist idea (of national identity)*',[252] thereby departing from any '*homogenisation of cultural difference*'[253] originally embraced. Yet another dimension may be discernible in relation to the recognition of diversity as a constitutional principle, or '*diversity constitutionalism*'.[254] More specifically, constitutions have come to embrace forms of special rights as well as differentiated and multicultural citizenship.[255] Relatedly, transformations have become visible in what has been termed "*constitutionalising conceptions from indigenous traditions*",[256] opening up to new forms of pluralism including justice systems and forms of self-governance. Apart from autonomy rights, the underlying principle of self-determination has been described as a core principle to "*underpin the contemporary system of sovereign (. . .) States*".[257]

One distinguishing aspect which has become a reality in Andean constitutionalism concerns the legal construct "*convert[ing] indigenous peoples into subjects of rights*".[258] Domestic constitutional law has been formalising and codifying catalogues or lists of rights tailored to the specific group in question, commonly indigenous peoples. The Ecuadorian constitutional order demonstrates a progressive perspective in that regard, establishing collective rights as a proper category which it reserves to communes, communities, and indigenous peoples and nations (art.57) as well as afro-Ecuadorian people (art.58) while Montubio people also enjoy certain collective rights, established explicitly by the 2008 Ecuadorian Constitution. Without further defining the general nature of collective rights, the Constitution stipulates

[251] Spiliopoulou Åkermark (1996).

[252] Uprimny (2016), p. 95.

[253] Ibid.; p. 94.

[254] Ibid.; p. 94.

[255] Kymlicka and Norman (1994).

[256] Uprimny (2016), p. 95.

[257] Sieder (2016), p. 143.

[258] Ibid.; p. 143.

very specific rights falling under such category—collective rights, as they have become constitutionalised, appear to be defined by their specific group-specific orientation including the particular needs that shine through the provisions in question.[259]

Commonly framed under the indigenous rights umbrella, collective rights have come to assume a fundamental systemic function as it is narrated in the Ecuadorian constitutional context:

> . . .The only possibility for collective rights to be genuinely and effectively enforced lies with the new format of the State which the peoples and nations have denominated 'Plurinational State'. If this is so, then the struggle for collective rights needs to return to its origins, the movements of 1990, that is to say, collective rights are not the finish line but an indication of the way to go. The finish line would lie in the changes of relations of power, for these to decolonise democracy of its racists, excluding, discriminatory and violent premises, which do appear in liberal accounts. Collective rights are another manifestation of such political and historical struggle of the indigenous movement. They merely represent a moment in their millennial resistance. The indigenous movement, as a consequence, cannot fall into the trap of liberalism and to think that a law, a constitutional provision or a recognised right in their favour will fundamentally and automatically alter relations of power.[260]

A few premises stand out in that context, allowing us to derive some further reaching insights on the nature of collective rights in a highly relevant constitutional context: (1) (new) State design qualifies both nature and enforcement value of collective rights, (2) the State's underlying premises based on racist or discriminatory thought need to be eliminated in a first step alongside enacting broader collective rights, (3) collective rights may prove facilitating rather than representing end-results in the struggle for recognition, constituting only one component in such struggle, (4) collective rights are to be accompanied by other transformative action to confront power asymmetries including decolonising measures.

### *7.5.3 Constitutionalising Indigenous Rights*

Other than what might be expected from the foregoing, empirical observations suggest that traditional institutions and indigenous group rights have indeed found their way into constitutional frameworks, terming such developments a

[259] Respectively, collective rights include, to name a few, the right to maintain, develop and strengthen their identity, affiliation, ancestral traditions and forms of social organisation; the right not to be subjected to racism or any other form of discrimination based on their origin, ethnic or cultural identity; the recognition, reparation and redress granted to those communities that are affected by racism, xenophobia and other related forms of intolerance and discrimination. . .

[260] Grupo de trabajo sobre derechos humanos y derechos colectivos (CONAIE—Fundación Tukui Shimi) (2009) *Derechos Colectivos de los Pueblos y Nacionalidades: Evaluación de una Década 1998–2008*, p. 12.

'*constitutional resurgence*'.[261] A closer examination will be needed, however, in order to appreciate to what extent these represent mere isolated attempts, or alternatively, could qualify as a system change, enabling the entire range of difference-specific rights—also beyond specific groups—to be constitutionalised successfully eventually. Constitutionalisation processes may, as described above, be witnessed at different jurisprudential levels. The UN Declaration on the Rights of Indigenous Peoples represents one of the most far-reaching and successful attempts of juridifying collective rights, building both on indigenous peoples' wide-ranging support including global movements—hence vesting the Declaration with considerable legitimacy[262]—at the same time as it legalises a wide range of ground-breaking rights including collective self-determination and autonomies concerning virtually any aspect of life. Relatedly, much emphasis is placed on pluralisms as they concern justice systems, political institutions, education or other key dimensions of collective identity; in a similar vein, indigenous proper customs and procedures have come to be recognised, to be interpreted transversally, as an important constituent element of other collective claims indigenous peoples raise.

Constitutionalisation processes in the field of indigenous rights may similarly be observed regionally, the Latin American *jus commune* constituting a particularly receptible framework in that sense.[263] With its evolutionary interpretation of scarce, 'outdated' primary sources, the Inter-American Court of Human Rights has become a frontrunner in the field of indigenous rights as it becomes apparent in its interpretative efforts on land rights[264] or prior consultation and consent,[265] or the protection of human rights defenders[266] as well as its attempts in seeking appropriate remedies where authoritarian regimes of the recent past would systematically persecute indigenous leaders and their communities.

At domestic levels constitutionalisation processes promise far reaching owing to the systemic transformations we may witness in the domestic realm. Again, Latin America and Andean States in particular stand out given their recent attempts in re-building entire States, emblematic being '*plurinational constitutionalism*' in

---

[261] Holzinger et al. (2019), p. 1776.
See also: Aguilar et al. (2010).

[262] See, for instance, Charters and Stavenhagen (2012).
See also Centre for International Governance Innovation (2020).

[263] See, for instance, Sieder (2016).
See also Cavallaro et al. (2019).

[264] Monteiro de Matos (2020).

[265] Doyle (2015).
Rodríguez-Garavito (2011).
Fontana and Grugel (2016).

[266] See e.g. Inter-American Commission on Human Rights (2023) Personas defensoras del medio ambiente: Norte de Centroamérica; Inter-American Commission on Human Rights (2021) Basic Guidelines for Investigating Crimes against Human Rights Defenders in the Northern Triangle; Inter-American Commission on Human Rights (2017) Integral Protection Policies for Human Rights Defenders; Inter-American Commission on Human Rights (2015) Criminalization of Human Rights Defenders.

Bolivia and Ecuador.[267] A few observations are to be made in relation to the systemic, political game-changing character of these recent processes of constitutionalisation. A first observation certainly concerns the fact that indigenous rights are not relegated to specific, exhaustive catalogues of rights only, but find first mentioning in the preamble declaring the State's commitment to multiple forms of pluralism, notably in a decolonising spirit. Another indicator may lie in the fact that—alongside common human rights, usually taking an individual form—entire paradigms are transposed into the constitutional order, famously taking the shape of Mother Earth or *Buen Vivir/Vivir Bien* principles.[268] Relatedly, these cosmovisionist shifts are commonly accompanied by other systemic transformations, including a rethinking of economic forms of development, including so-called alternatives to development models.[269] Interestingly, collective rights are also introduced at a broader level, notably in the case of the rights of nature, pertinent questions of legal personality in that regard, and new forms of subject holdership, commonly gaining pertinence in the context of indigenous collective rights.[270] Finally, if we think of the juridification of indigenous collective rights in broader terms, we do need to contextualise these rights in the light of broader multicultural or plurinational turns—and resulting institutional transformations laying the ground for an institutional mirroring of the plurality of society while opening the space for co-governance and other forms of participation in the State's structures and public life.

By the very sense of the term, constitutionalisation processes fulfil the function of vesting rights with a particular rank in a given legal order, commonly a specific (territorial) jurisdiction. Resembling the aforediscussed idea of dedicated legal principles which may attribute to collective rights a particular legal strength, constitutionalisation would indeed assume a similar function. Similar conclusions may be reached on the specific context of indigenous rights, again, serving as an emblematic manifestation of collective rights. Importantly, indigenous rights are to be transposed into predominant orders, doing justice to their original framing and spelling out as these are to be found in indigenous proper orders or justice systems. It is indeed about the transfer of rights, principles, catalogues, entire orders into the predominant constitutional framework(s) that our focus shall be placed on. We thereby enter a rather complex sphere of not only judicial pluralism in which indigenous rights find their proper place,[271] but also more broadly, spaces of interaction and mutual encounter, negotiation and ultimately recognition.

---

[267] See, for instance, for a classification of recent forms of constitutionalism in Latin America: Yrigoyen Fajardo (2016).
See also: Sieder (2016).

[268] See, for instance, Solón (2017).
Gudynas (2011).

[269] Acosta (2017).

[270] See, for instance, Winter (2022).
See also: Rodríguez Caguana and Morales Naranjo (2020).
See also: Aguilera Bravo (2023).

[271] Gover (2020a).

Indeed, scholars have been studying these spheres in their own regard, often through proper terminology, shaped by decolonial thinking. Illustrative may be Sousa Santos' work which addresses the challenges attributable to the colonial origin of the law, with a proper body originally dealing with the law on the colonised which only used to consider indigenous law by terming the latter 'local customs' that would be "*selectively recognised as 'local customs', as the coloniser saw fit*",[272] and, in turn, represented its own manifestation of interlegality, while "*leading to complex legal assemblages with diverse political meanings*".[273] Interlegality—and judicial hybrids—assume yet another meaning, examining more closely, what is at stake here, namely indigenous proper justice ideas, principles and orders. Accordingly, '*interlegality*' is supposed to "*occur when different types of justice or legal systems are available in a given geopolitical time-space and individuals or social groups are allowed to choose between them, at least in certain circumstances*".[274] Elsewhere described as forum shopping, such manifestation of '*lived judicial pluralism*' could be considered as a first successful attempt of introducing indigenous justice while limited to the possibilities created by the predominant justice system. Judicial hybrids capture, what Sousa Santos, defines as "*composite legal constructs in which it is possible to identify the presence of various judicial cultures*".[275]

While undoubtedly serving as a practicable working definition, we may be left wondering what kind of place is reserved for indigenous laws (in relation to the predominant order), and the precise articulation of indigenous collective rights, placing a focus on the specific rights finding recognition eventually. We may similarly be wary of the flexible nature the law tends to adopt generally, with indigenous laws undergoing complex processes of mirroring, of shaping back or appropriating exogeneous manifestations, bits and pieces of law as it is established elsewhere. It is in this light that we may want to understand "*indigenous law (is) in itself a product of Interlegality, since the community actively engage with official legal documents in framing the indigenous law*".[276] What should stand in the focus however is the way indigenous law itself, in its purest form, including procedural particularities find due consideration in the predominant order or, alternatively, are vested with genuine autonomies as stand-alone orders.

Another question meriting further analysis concerns the 'peoples' definition as it has become articulated mostly in international legal accounts. To begin with, 'indigenous peoples' only found their way into legal vocabulary very late, having been denominated 'populations' at first, by the ILO Convention 107 'Indigenous and Tribal Populations Convention' in 1957, followed by considerable limitations

[272] Sousa Santos and Meneses (2023), p. 269.

[273] Ibid.; p. 269.

[274] Sousa Santos and Meneses (2023), p. 152.

[275] Ibid.; p. 522.

[276] Ibid.; p. 522.

See also Orellana (2004).

imposed by ILO Convention 169 'Indigenous and Tribal Peoples Convention' (1989) in its art.1(3) holding that:

> The use of the term peoples in this Convention shall not be construed as having any implications as regards the rights which may attach to the term under international law.

Indeed, human rights law has been establishing wide-ranging safeguards in that regard, including the collective right to self-determination beyond the political-territorial context, to give rise to important resource rights and the all-encompassing right to development as most famously articulated by art.1 (1) and art.1(2), ICCPR and ICESCR stating that

> All peoples have the right to self-determination. By virtue of that right they freely determine their political status and freely pursue their economic, social and cultural development. All peoples may, for their own ends, freely dispose of their natural wealth and resources without prejudice to any obligations arising out of international economic co-operation, based upon the principle of mutual benefit, and international law. In no case may a people be deprived of its own means of subsistence.

Long-lasting debates would follow the adoption of relevant legal instruments at international level, including those relating to the legitimate beneficiaries of such rights.[277]

While lacking any binding force, the UN Declaration on the Rights of Indigenous Peoples reverses the initial attempts made in the late 1980s to limit the application of specific rights reserved to 'peoples' to the detriment of indigenous groups: UNDRIPS not only invokes relevant sources such as the UN Charter, ICESCR, ICCPR and the Vienna Declaration and Programme of Action as they are to apply to indigenous peoples, but explicitly refers to the right to self-determination of 'all peoples' in that context and its corollary, the right to determine political status and to development.[278] Such developments undoubtedly entail important implications for the formalisation and codification of collective rights at large, with 'peoples' as powerful legal construct establishing an indispensable basis for collective claims.

---

[277] Fitzmaurice (2012).
Xanthaki (2007).
Gilbert (2006).

[278] More precisely, preambular paragraph 15, UNDRIPS, stipulates: "*Acknowledging that the Charter of the United Nations, the International Covenant on Economic, Social and Cultural Rights and the International Covenant on Civil and Political Rights, as well as the Vienna Declaration and Programme of Action, affirm the fundamental importance of the right to self-determination of all peoples, by virtue of which they freely determine their political status and freely pursue their economic, social and cultural development*".

## 7.6 Institutional Mainstreaming of Collective Rights

Codification and other juridification processes represent a considerable step towards the recognition of collective rights, if pursued as an integral endeavour rather than ad-hoc ways of considering collective rights, that is, through sporadic references in a given framework. More judicial strength is added however, where rights are submitted to thorough monitoring work, ensuring implementation of the law and supervision of State activities or of those realised by competent institutions. Collective rights rarely materialise in the form of treaty-making, being relegated to soft law instruments[279] instead, which commonly fall short of responding to implementation and supervision needs. Given the particularities of international law, we may witness institutional developments that show gradually increasing levels of specialisation through, e.g. special procedures in the case of indigenous peoples (e.g. Special Rapporteur on the Rights of Indigenous Peoples) or new institutions arising (e.g. Expert Mechanism on the Rights of Indigenous Peoples).[280] Since a codified text on indigenous rights was yet to be agreed on, different institutions were being established around the same time period, in the midst of negotiation on UNDRIPS, including the Permanent Forum on Indigenous Issues established in 2000 (ECOSOC resolution 2000/22), the creation of the mandate of the Special Rapporteur on the Rights of Indigenous Peoples in 2001 (Human Rights Commission resolution 2001/57), and the Expert Mechanism on the Rights of Indigenous Peoples in 2007 (Human Rights Council resolution 6/36). Such developments in the field of indigenous rights at international level have been described as a "*continuous and progressive process*" in which, importantly, indigenous communities and organisations have been playing a central role.[281] When further engaging with the organisational structures established internationally, we witness that indigenous collective rights tend to benefit from what we may term '*specialised institutionalism*' reflecting first attempts of mainstreaming collective rights institutionally, commonly on the basis of thematic studies or recommendations emerging from dedicated sessions. That way, however, collective rights remain in the limited spaces of expert institutions, hence falling short of any mainstreaming across institutional boundaries.

Let us return to the technicalities of mainstreaming rights for a moment to appreciate the opportunities that are provided for reinforcing rights at a broader scale institutionally. In broad terms, mainstreaming has been referred to as "*methods of integrating ideals considered disparate or bringing some value from the periphery to the centre*".[282] In even clearer institutional terms, mainstreaming is understood as "*conscious, systematic and concrete integration of certain values and standards*

[279] See, for instance, Gómez Isa (2016).

[280] E.g. Charters and Stavenhagen (2012).
Burger and Martín Castro (2006).
Burger (2012).

[281] Burger and Martín Castro (2006), p. 109.

[282] Alemahu Yeshanew (2014), p. 372.

*into policies, plans, programmes, priorities, processes and results of the work of an organisation*" while human rights mainstreaming more specifically is considered as the "*deliberate infusion of human rights standards into the work of organisations in areas such as development, emergencies and peace and security*".[283] For the purpose of the present work, we shall not limit ourselves to these fields but see mainstreaming of collective rights as an exercise of concern to human rights mechanisms also. Very commonly, human rights mainstreaming is placed in the context of so-called '*human rights-based approaches*' and the UN human rights institutional landscape in particular. In that sense, known international human rights practitioners such as Hunt argue human rights cannot possibly be implemented "*without mainstreaming them into law, policy and practice. Mainstreaming is the pre-condition of implementation*".[284] The origins of human rights mainstreaming may be traced back to the very founding document of the UN Human Rights Council, mandating the Council to "*promote the effective coordination and mainstreaming of human rights within the United Nations system*".[285] Importantly, the Rapporteur refers to several dimensions in that regard, emphasising the relevance of developing an understanding of mainstreaming in ministries competent in the specific field in question, hence introducing another hurdle into the process, being entirely intergovernmental.

Others derive the origins of such mainstreaming exercise from the UN's mandate at large, notably UN Secretary-General Annan's words in his report 'Renewing the United Nations: A Programme for Reform' in 1997 in which he calls upon the UN to not only "*enhance its human rights programme [but to] fully integrate it into the range of the Organisation's activities*",[286] in other words mainstreaming, which was however responded to to very varying degrees, ranging from priorities set in the field of development and humanitarian assistance to reluctance in treating human rights as a cross-cutting issue across UN organs.[287] Indeed, deficiencies were noted, becoming manifest in a lack of coherence and coordination in human rights matters but also sheer ignorance among the UN institutions.[288] A firm commitment was made as late as 2002 with the Secretary General's report 'Strengthening of the United Nations: An Agenda for Further Change', understanding the "*promotion and protection of human rights [as] as bedrock requirement for the realization of the Charter's vision of a just and peaceful world*".[289]

---

[283] Ibid.; p. 372.

[284] Hunt (2015), para.1.

Office of the High Commissioner for Human Rights (2023) *Mainstreaming human rights*. Retrieved from https://www.ohchr.org/en/mainstreaming-human-rights.

[285] Hunt (2015), para.2.

[286] Oberleitner (2008), p. 359.

[287] Ibid.

[288] Ibid.

[289] UN Secretary General (1997) Strengthening of the United Nations: An Agenda for Further Change, para.45.

An often discussed angle from which to mainstream human rights concerns the development agenda, not limited to the UN Common Understanding on a Human Rights-Based Approach to Development of 2003, but reflecting a practice adopted by many development organisations.[290] It may however be noted that development programmes in particular may face criticism voiced by recipient States as to the forms of conditionality related to the delivery of financial assistance but also as concerning possible conflicts between domestic policies and the exigencies of international human rights standards.[291] We shall however be mindful of the often universalising agenda of programmes that show ignorant of local manifestations of human rights, different priorities set, or rights remaining overlooked in classical legal orders and discourse.[292] Somewhat relatedly, human rights mainstreaming has been associated with other social justice matters such as gender, poverty, environment, health or refugee protection to name a few; in other words, human rights mainstreaming "*involves the integration of human rights norms and practices into social justice issues*",[293] thereby opening a wide field of application for human rights to be rendered effective.

Let us return to the underlying principles and logics of human rights mainstreaming. Relevant discourses are filled with buzzwords, being indicative of the broad, universal nature of the concept, lending itself however to be implemented beyond human rights institutions. In that sense, it was referred to a "*human rights culture in international, regional and national governance*",[294] referring to the consideration of human rights in any governmental decision to be adopted. In similar broad terms, mainstreaming has been regarded as being "*part of the rules of the game under which the system of politics and government is conducted*"[295]—as a guiding principle or core matter to consider in any policy issue. Also in legal theoretical terms, it has been argued human rights mainstreaming could be regarded as a response to the growing fragmentation of international law with its numerous treaties,[296] hence requiring an 'integrated approach' which finds materialisation with the mainstreaming of human rights, representing a "*shift from the 'one pipe-at-a-time' approach to a forward-looking, harmonised and holistic approach*".[297]

Critical voices may however draw our attention to the limits laying with the inherently political approach taken with the mainstreaming of rights, as it becomes apparent where individual rights conflict with collective interest demonstrating that mainstreaming ultimately depends on the political commitment of decision-makers

[290] Alemahu Yeshanew (2014).

[291] Ibid.

[292] See, for instance, Goodale and Engle Merry (2003).

[293] Olawuyi (2013), p. 216.

[294] Ibid.; p. 221.

[295] Ibid.; p. 220.
See also Blackburn (1999).

[296] see, for instance, McCrudden (2005).

[297] Olawuyi (2013), p. 224.

who may opt for security rights (collective interest) opposed to basic freedoms (individual rights).[298] Conversely, quite the opposite may be argued, portraying international human rights law in particular as a limit to "*bureaucratic discretion*", in response to what has been described as "*unfettered relativism and bureaucratic abuse (...) the language of 'rights' contrasts with that of 'management*'".[299] In other words, human rights mainstreaming would assist in creating an atmosphere which "*should leave no room to instrumental calculations*".[300] As a consequence, Koskenniemi understands mainstreaming as assuming important countervailing functions, notably the "*natural place (of rights) must be outside politics, yet constraining politics*".[301] Indeed, scholar accounts demonstrating critical attitude of human rights are manifold,[302] oftentimes rooted in the universality claim, its colonial heritage or as being interwoven with strategic priorities and agendas.

Another inherent problem arising with human rights mainstreaming undoubtedly lies with the impreciseness of what has generally been accommodated under '*human rights-based approaches*', embracing buzzwords such as 'poverty' or 'security and welfare' and the accompanying problem of "*render[ing] little administrative direction*".[303] Other problems may arise with such institutional failure in addressing human rights in a genuine way, that is paying tribute to underlying rationale or questions of effectiveness. One may be related to human rights experts being vested with institutional competence: owing to the alleged "*emptiness of rights*", these experts are placed into a situation of having to engage in "*increasingly detailed and technical analyses of economic efficiency, security, administrative appropriateness, and social causality*".[304] Secondly, the question is raised whether "*there is (or* can be*) any distinct commitment to* human rights *that would not be a commitment to a particular theory of economic development, security, or administrative appropriateness*".[305] The very exercise of human rights mainstreaming then takes our attention to also focus on questions of decision-makers, competent interpreters as well as overall institutional context including, importantly, the specific agendas and ideologies driving relevant sectors and organisations.

---

[298] Koskenniemi (2010).

[299] Ibid.; p. 48.

[300] Ibid.; p. 48.
see also Waldron (2005).

[301] Koskenniemi (2010), p. 48.

[302] See, for instance, Rajagopal (2003); Kennedy (2005); Schippers (2019).

[303] Koskenniemi (2010), p. 54.

[304] Ibid.; p. 54.

[305] Ibid.; p. 54.

### 7.6.1 *Placing the Focus on ('National') Minority Rights and the* Marge d'Appréciation

A particular view shall rest on 'national minority' orders as famously shown by the Council of Europe framework, with the Framework Convention for the Protection of National Minorities being monitored by the Committee of Ministers while advised by an Advisory Committee made up of independent experts. Based on its political role, the Committee of Ministers has been criticised, generally declared as a weakness in the monitoring arrangement.[306] Indeed, minority rights enjoy recognition under the umbrella of powerful committees whose politicised mandates and daily operating have faced criticism.[307] While benefiting from greater political leverage, such forms of institutionalism have shown susceptible to domestic priorities, especially where politically sensitive issues informed the debate such as religious matters, majority-minority relations or questions on territorial or political autonomies as well as minorities facing large-scale persecution in Europe such as the Roma or the Kurds. Until the current age, State legal orders have persistently maintained an institutional rationale based on principles that were supposedly violated by minority rights such as the "*basic liberal democratic principles of individual freedom and equality*".[308] Any respect for collective rights or positive discriminatory approaches were thereby clearly ruled out. The ECtHR itself has demonstrably struggled with such divide, being torn between what has been described as an individual rights approach underlying the European Convention and a multicultural perspective embraced by the Framework Convention.[309] Let's observe such positioning as part of a wider institutional approach.

Indicative may be the *marge d'appréciation* doctrine, allowing States to exercise broad discretionary powers when interpreting a norm, and hence align such interpretation with domestic agendas and priorities. In other words, room for manoeuvre is delegated to domestic authorities in compliance with their duties under the European Convention on Human Rights and Fundamental Freedoms.[310] Interestingly, the doctrine is widely attributed to the ECtHR which has indeed been reproached for its inflationary and inconsistent use of the doctrine.[311] In relation to minorities too, it has been pointed to the necessity for the Court to "*develop a consistent and rigorous methodology for the application of the doctrines in cases regarding minority rights*".[312] The principle has been described as dangerous in the minority context whenever its main rationale would be "*rooted principally in deference to legitimacy of democratic governments*",[313] hence leading to situations

---

306 Greer (2017).

307 See e.g. Çali, and Demir-Gürsel (2021).

308 Kymlicka (2012), p. 178.

309 Greer (2017).

310 Greer (2000).

311 Kratochvíl (2011).

312 Akerø-Stueland (2021), para.1.

313 Arai-Takahashi (2013), p. 96.

in which minority rights are eroded by the democratic majority, which, evidently, would "*be illegitimate because it being contrary to the foundational values of democracy itself*'[314] and also lead to an "*abandoning of the Court of its institutional role as the external guarantor against the 'tyranny of the majority'*".[315] Relatedly, democratic theory has been invoked elsewhere, highlighting the principles of '*pluralism, tolerance and broadmindedness*' being attributable to democratic society while holding that a balance is to be achieved that "*ensures the fair and proper treatment of minorities and avoids any abuse of a dominant position*".[316] Similarly, the principles of priority of Convention norms and democratic legitimacy on the other hand have been invoked in such context, clearly defining powers here, with democratic legitimacy "*maintain[ing] that democratically elected and accountable bodies should be primary sites of legally defined public policies and that their decisions should take precedence over both national and international judicial bodies*".[317] Indeed, the function of the Court in serving as a '*countermajoritarian check*' has been highlighted elsewhere, also when working against its own doctrines such as the European consensus (among State Parties)[318] which proves difficult to adhere to where the latter "*determines the rights of unpopular social groups and minorities*".[319] Another particularity lies with derogation cases, often declaring emergencies, resultantly, restricting freedoms including the use of excessive measures against minorities—hence calling for limitations on the margin of appreciation and stricter forms of judicial scrutiny.[320]

### 7.6.2 Institutionalism and Its Impact on Mainstreaming Human Rights

A final point shall be devoted to the question of institutionality as it shapes minority rights across different frameworks. The Framework Convention,[321] it has been

---

[314] Ibid., p. 96.
Brauch (2005).

[315] Arai-Takahashi (2013), p. 96.

[316] Greer (2000), p. 18.

[317] Přibáň (2017), p. 92.

[318] It has been maintained that in "*determining the margin of appreciation (...) the ECtHR may, if appropriate, have regard to any consensus and common values emerging from the state practices of the parties to the ECHR*".
McGoldrick (2017), p. 152.

[319] Akerø-Stueland (2021), para.5.

[320] Letsas (2006).

[321] See also: Verstichel et al. (2008).
Hofmann et al. (2018).
Weller (2006).
Hofmann et al. (2015).
Caruso and Malloy Tove (2013).

argued, seemingly attracted State Parties due to its vague, agreeable language,[322] possibly also given its hesitant attitude towards group rights.[323] Its legally binding nature certainly adds judicial weight to the institutionality question, rendering it a hard law norm that is to be invoked where appropriate. A different institutional context presents itself in international law with the soft law instrument, the UN Declaration on the Rights of Persons belonging to National or Ethnic, Religious and Linguistic Minorities adopted in 1992, following up on the rather one-time, sporadic mentioning of ethnic, cultural, linguistic and religious minorities in ICCPR, its article 27. Some attempts towards a 'system-wide approach' may be noted however, having emerged in a top-down way, steered notably by the UN Secretariat in convening a UN Network on Racial Discrimination and Minorites that would consider minority protection as part and parcel of the larger struggle in preventing conflicts, development agendas and environmental sustainability.[324] Also explicitly, the UN Secretary-General placed emphasis on the "*require[ment of] system wide, coordinated engagement*".[325] One of the crucial structural weaknesses was pointed out by the same mandate holder, drawing the world's attention to international engagement on the matter as being sporadic, considering minority rights only where extremely violent acts had been committed.[326] Indeed, the work developed by the UN High Commissioner on Human Rights discloses a similar rationale with its active engagement on the situation of the Rohingya minority in Myanmar or ethnic clashes in Kyrgyzstan, reflecting a certain urgency of the matter.[327] A similar scenario presents itself with several European States invoking international criminal law, notably declaring violent acts committed by the terrorist organisation IS a genocide against the Yazidi minority. In that light, we can certainly witness a growing awareness of the need to take multilateral action in post-conflict or transitionary justice contexts in support of minorities—in that sense, institutional mainstreaming has demonstrated some success. This is what we may term '*reparation-based institutionalism*', hence missing considerable preventive functions or any comprehensive approach that would deal with the daily and systematic exclusionary and discriminatory practice targeting minority groups, being relegated to sporadic soft law attempts.

[322] Greer (2017).

[323] Jovanović (2012).

[324] Korkeakivi (2018).

[325] Ibid.; p. 39.

[326] Ibid.

[327] Ibid.

## 7.7 Transposing and Integrating Collective Rights Into and Throughout Different Frameworks

It comes as no surprise that collective rights have remained rather absent from the technicalities of transposing international law into domestic law; as it becomes clear from the present processes and scales of collectivisation, this may require an initial acknowledgement and explicit recognition of collective rights. While enriched by empirical accounts, much of the following deals with these questions in theory, highlighting potential ways of judicializing (in a first step) collective or group rights, and also by uncovering different ways of rendering collective rights effective eventually, notably through different scales of collectivisation. Far from considering transposition processes as to concern the international-domestic legal nexus,[328] we shall embrace a broader understanding here, including the translation of indigenous justice conceptions and laws into international law but also the domestic legal realm.

Let us return to the transposing and integrating functions of legal frameworks to start with, and pay tribute to the particularities of collective rights in a second step. Some impetus was given as early as 1986 by the UN General Assembly in a resolution dedicated to "*Setting international standards in the field of human rights*"[329] in which it places emphasis on not only implementing existing international human rights standards and ratifying relevant treaties but also demands for States to consider the international framework when developing new human rights standards. A particular focus is further placed on the role of specialised institutionalism with the Commission on Human Rights vested with powers to develop relevant international instruments, and for Member States and UN bodies to pay due consideration to specific guidelines[330] when developing these. This may seem like a general call for actively engaging with international law, with implementation standing at the forefront of these endeavours, and for international mechanisms to play a key role in further developing international human rights law. At least in international law then, much value lies in international institutionalism in creating norms and exerting monitoring mandates with the potential to recognise newly arising rights.[331]

If we wanted to delve deeper into the technicalities of transposition processes, EU law provides for welcome venues to be explored further with directives and

[328] See, for instance, Tomuschat (2014).

[329] UN General Assembly (1986) *Resolution 41/120 Setting international standards in the field of human rights.*

[330] For such instruments to „*(a) be consistent with the existing body of international human rights law; (b) be of fundamental character and derive from the inherent dignity and worth of the human person; (c) be sufficiently precise to give rise to identifiable and practicable rights and obligations; (d) provide, where appropriate, realistic and effective implementation machinery, including reporting systems; (e) attract broad international support*".

[331] See also arts. 41 and 42 UNDRIPS and Bartolomé Clavero's work on the matter.

regulations providing diverging degrees of discretion exercised by the Member States.[332] The aforediscussed '*constitutional block*' doctrine finding vivid demonstration in contemporary Latin American developments may be emblematic of the technicalities associated with the judicial value of international human rights law in the domestic realm and constitutionalism in particular.[333] A known distinction is made where we refer to the applicability of international law in the domestic realm, commonly termed as monism vs. dualism. Dualism builds on the premise that "*the rules of the systems of international law and municipal law exist separately and cannot purport to have effect on, or overrule, the other*".[334] By and large, such theoretical orientation may be derived from the idea of the supremacy of the State and the persistence of differences between international and domestic orders respectively (Triepel's and Strupp's work).[335] Monism, by contrast, defends "*a unitary view of law as a whole and are opposed to the strict division posited by the positivists*".[336] This school of thought may either follow a pronounced ethical position with a focus on human rights (Lauterpacht's work) or by establishing a binding force with international law as a proper order which lays down a specific conduct for States to follow including respective sanctioning procedures (Kelsen's work).[337] Paradoxically, for the purpose of the present work, monist approaches may perpetuate a specific rationale including a strong emphasis placed on individual rights which may prove limiting in view of the recognition of collective rights and systemic transformations at large. At the end of day however both transposition procedures cannot be applied to the detriment of or diminish the value of international legal obligations, hence turning the debate on collective rights necessarily a question of international law.

We shall however not concern ourselves too much with technical detail here which may concern monist vs. dualist approaches in transposing international human rights law into domestic law,[338] and instead direct our view to the opportunities established within and throughout frameworks to accommodate collective or other group-specific rights. Viewed from a legal-historical perspective two main positions stand out, one declaring standard-setting forums and processes in the field of human rights to have come to an end, the other position maintaining these would have entered a new phase.[339] The debates on third generation rights may be

[332] See, for instance, Craig and de Búrca (2015).

[333] See, for instance, Góngora-Mera (2017).

[334] Shaw (2008), p. 131.

[335] Ibid.

[336] Ibid.; p. 131.

[337] Ibid.

[338] See, for instance, European Commission for Democracy through Law (Venice Commission) (2014) *Report on the Implementation of International Human Rights Treaties in Domestic Law and the Role of Courts.*

[339] Mutua (2016).

indicative of such latter developments[340] as they relate to human rights standardisation, giving rise to new discussions on attribution of damage, rights holder-duty bearing relations or the very substance of these rights. Also elsewhere human rights standardisation has been further defined, understanding norms as

> signposts for future behaviour, and standards (...) are meaningless if they remain abstract without a systemic structure for their implementation (...) Standard setting should therefore not be seen as an end in itself, but as a means to an unknown end – an end that is still in flux and in the process of definition.[341]

Especially the futuristic outlook and the fluidity of its conceptual dimension lend themselves for opening up to human rights categories not hitherto recognised such as collective rights yet to be adequately standardised. Further conceptual attempts have been made defining standard setting, namely by referring to the

> act of setting standards [as] signal[ing] that a matter of universal importance needs urgent attention and requires the international community to flesh out collectively a universally acceptable norm or standard around which consensus can be marshalled (...) Whatever the case, the elaboration of standards is a realization of the existence of a gap, a lacuna, that many, if not most, think must be filled.[342]

There would be no doubt about the urgency and pertinence of standardising collective rights, however, consensus remains far from being achieved, not least owing to the fact that collective claims are being perceived as a threat to a State's integrity and sovereignty.

This last thought merits some further elaboration given the systemic nature of the claim made. Its origins may be found in generic human rights critique which may concern the "*historical and ongoing exclusions wrought by 'universal' figurations of the human or to highlight the ways in which contemporary human rights practice silences or victimises particular subjects or communities*"[343]—in that sense, the very frame of the law constructed by a universalising common-sense, rooted in individualist approaches, may serve as a considerable obstacle in any integrating, standardising process as far as difference-based rights are concerned. As a response we may recall the 1990s 'alter-globalisation slogan': "*another human rights is possible*".[344] With developments in the field of disability rights or enforced disappearance, we may indeed witness a certain sensitivity towards novel categories of rights holdership. What may be termed a Butlerian politics of human rights could be helpful here, strongly building on 'subjectification', that is, the "*processes (linguistic, institutional, material and embodied) by which subjects are formed, created and hailed into being by the powers that they ostensibly oppose*".[345] Similar logics are

[340] Vasak (1977).

[341] Mutua (2016), p. 10.

[342] Ibid.; p. 11.

[343] Golder (2019), p. 28.

[344] Ibid.; p. 28.

[345] Ibid.; p. 33.
See also Butler (2004).

followed by the law—also commonly called '*subjectification*'—which ultimately decide upon questions of recognition in terms of subject-holdership. Not uncommonly, fundamental criteria including self-identification and self-determination fail to be respected where subjects are created by the law, resembling what was captured under subjectification discussed above, illustrative being indigenous peoples' rights having undergone considerable conceptual transformations throughout the second half of the twentieth century.

In a last attempt to approach standardisation from a difference-oriented perspective, we shall concern ourselves with integration processes, as a technical exercise that is not to be confused with integration as it is commonly invoked in migration discourses,[346] representing—undoubtedly—a regressive undertaking. These are frequently examined as human rights relate to development (e.g. human rights-based approach to development)[347] but also critical voices in that regard,[348] as relating to environmental questions or sustainable development,[349] or business operations, often finding articulation under social corporate responsibility.[350] An emerging group of scholars however engages explicitly with specific rights[351] that are to be integrated into human rights orders—which shall eventually assist us in identifying gaps and methods to pay due consideration to collective or related group-differentiated rights. Integrating processes may take a number of varying forms and formats. This may be the case for UNDRIPS as a prime example of integration based on the rationale that "*since as a specialised instrument it groups the most important principles and rights applying to indigenous peoples*"[352] and as it was created building on an inclusive participatory process while representing rights holders' views. In that sense, we may speak of a process much beyond integrating isolated rights into predominant legal orders, but instead, refer to integration in the *ius generis* sense. Interesting for the purpose of the present work is the fact that integration practices were observed in existing court practice in the sense of applying the law including quintessential principles to a specific group.[353]

---

[346] See, for instance, Xanthaki (2016).

[347] See e.g. Noh (2021).
Sano (2000).

[348] See e.g. Onazi (2022).
See also Alberto Acosta's, Edoardo Gudynas' and Pablo Solón's work on the matter.

[349] See, e.g., Bexell et al. (2023).

[350] See, e.g., Bilchitz and Deva (2013).

[351] See e.g. David (2018).

[352] Ouald-Chaib (2018), p. 7.
For more details, see: Inman et al. (2018).
Similar observations have been made in the case of the Yogyakarta Principles on the Application of Human Rights Law in Relation to Sexual Orientation and Gender Identity, see the following work for a detailed engagement: Bribosia and Rorive (2018).

[353] Ouald-Chaib (2018).

Another turn is taken with seeing integration as being realised in jurisprudence "*through cross-fertilisation between courts across the globe*";[354] indeed jurisprudence may give rise to standardisation and ultimately juridification processes resulting in the eventual adoption of legislation or inspiring constitutional reform processes. Elsewhere it was examined how human rights integration would gain meaning as far as constitutional reform processes were concerned, identifying two constitutional approaches with one taking an assimilationist stance vis-à-vis international human rights and hence for these norms to be directly applicable and a different approach that focusses on the protectionist nature of some constitutions, showing inimical to international and European judges.[355] Integration then would reflect a "*balanced conversation tak[ing] place between international human rights norms and the national constitutional tradition*",[356] also being captured by the term '*smart integration*'.[357] Important conclusions may be derived from this in an institutional sense, opening up the debate on judicial dialogue: rather than arguing that human rights monitoring mechanisms would develop identical reasoning, it is observed that "*each human rights implementation body shapes its specific function in a manner that shows awareness of it being a part of a project that transcends that particular body (...) hence, the goal of human rights integration is not uniformization, but rather conversation*".[358] Interesting for the purpose of the present work is the fact that integration practices were observed in existing court practice in the sense of applying the law including quintessential principles to a specific group.

In that sense, we may almost perceive integration processes as fulfilling some sort of ideological mandate: the law being largely fragmented despite the indivisible nature of human rights may virtually call for an '*Integrated Approach to Human Rights law*', especially in the implementation phase.[359] Elsewhere de Schutter relatedly comes up with a new legal construct, that of a '*Common Law of Human Rights*' or '*Human Rights Jus Commune*' as a proper ius generis order.[360] Integration processes may however differ in what is at stake with different agendas that may be followed, including critical debates reflecting internal disagreements on encounters between predominant and hitherto unrecognised laws. Accordingly, different models of human rights integration have been discerned, including '*hierarchical*

---

[354] Ibid.; p. 7.

[355] Van Drooghenbroeck and Van der Noot (2018).

[356] Ouald-Chaib (2018), p. 10.

[357] Brems (2018).

[358] Ouald-Chaib (2018), p. 11.

See, for more details, Brems (2018).

An interesting debate of judicial dialogue in the case of human rights integration in the European region is given by the following chapter: Krommendijk (2018).

Human rights integration similarly plays a role in the African human and peoples' rights order as explored in the following work: Rachovitsa (2018).

[359] Brems (2014).

[360] De Schutter (2018).

*integration*' to be found in global constitutionalism, '*coordinative integration*' becoming apparent in ordered legal pluralism or neo-institutionalism, and '*conflictual integration*' materialising with critical legal studies and Global South approaches.[361] We adopt a critical approach here, with a particular focus to be placed on victim groups and their specific collective demands which may be met through integration into predominant legal orders or in the form proper frameworks, that way acquiring *sui generis* status.

### *7.7.1 Integration and Standardisation Processes: Collective Human Rights Under Focus*

To start with, we shall return to a foundational problem related to the aforediscussed fragmentation of collective rights; indeed, it has been widely concluded that "*there are no binding instruments expressly intended to (...) ensure that basic collective human rights are protected and enforced globally*".[362] More generally, systemic observations have been made in relation to the position assumed by collective rights in the global sphere, notably by Cassese who notes:

> ...shift[ing] the world community from a reciprocity-based bundle of legal relations, geared to the 'private' pursuit of self-interest, and ultimately [ignorant] to collective needs, to a community hinging on a core of fundamental values strengthened by the emergence of community obligations and community rights and the gradual shaping of public interest[363]

In fact, rights have come to embrace broader interests, shared by the international community at large and appropriating public interest as a valid venue to claim rights, including intergenerational justice and environmental demands. In other words environmental standards may very well be considered "*the international community's first step toward the protection of the collective rights of humankind*".[364]

We may also defend the stance that collective human rights are only in a pre-state of being subjected to standardisation processes. It has been maintained elsewhere that collective rights reflect a position that "*indicates and details the parameters of the eventual goal of the long-anticipated 'development' of international law*".[365] Similarly, the related construct of '*third generation rights*'—encompassing, for instance the rights to peace, development and a clean (healthy) environment—has faced a similar positioning in the international community, defining them "*not as*

---

[361] Baumgärtel et al. (2014).
See also for a general view on the matter: Brems and Desmet (2014).

[362] Westra (2011), p. 207.

[363] Ibid. p. 56.
Cassese (2005).

[364] Westra (2011), p. 68.

[365] Westra (2011), p. 230.

*true rights, but rather as agreed objectives which the international community has pledged to pursue*".[366] Also more specifically, in relation to climate change, it has been argued that neither domestic nor treaty law has proven facilitating in relation to collective human rights, often conflicting with specific State interests.[367] Much weight may be attributed to the very nature of the rights (being far from a neutral drafting exercise), having remained ambiguous in terms of those claiming them (rights holders), those obliged to grant these rights (duty bearers), and ultimately their very substance, or put differently:

> It is even more difficult to gain a clear picture of the content of third generation rights. Generally, all of the rights under discussion [rights to peace, development and a clean (healthy) environment] are extremely wide in scope. They do not set out specific measures and steps to be taken by states or governments, but enunciate comprehensive goals (...) constitut[ing] an ideal situation that rests on a multitude of factual and legal elements, many of which are not under the control of governments alone.[368]

We may indeed find answers to the question on how collective rights are being standardised beyond the realm of the State which remains a key player in that regard. NGOs most notably have been described as "*those that support collective human rights*"[369] which has gone hand in hand with the decreasing importance of the State, also attributable to global trade developments.

### 7.7.2 Collective Environmental Rights and Their Standardising Role

Let us focus on a particular collective right for a moment, allowing us to gain a contextual view on its standardisation across coexisting frameworks. A right lending itself particularly well here includes the right to a safe and healthy environment, having gained an autonomous status[370] and rising recognition in recent years,[371] throughout different frameworks even. When placing such right, comparatively, into the European and African human rights frameworks, such right has primarily been denoted as a right "*securing optimal living conditions for humans*" only, disregarding broader environmental challenges or complex problems.[372] When framed in terms of human rights, however, its collective nature has been neglected

---

366 Tomuschat (2014), p. 154.
See also: Waldron (1993).

367 Westra (2011).

368 Tomuschat (2014), p. 153.

369 Westra (2011), p. 223.

370 *Case of the Indigenous Communities of the Lhaka Honhat (Our Land) Association vs. Argentina*, Inter-American Court of Human Rights in 2020.

371 See e.g. Aguilera Bravo (2023).

372 Buys and Lewis (2021), p. 966.

for a long time with courts placing emphasis on and also constructing an individualist view on human rights, being inconsistent with neither the "*inherent nature of the environment*" nor its meaning as a "*public good indispensable for the life and welfare of society as a whole*".[373]

Our focus shall remain on collective environmental rights and the increasing recognition thereof throughout legal systems. While developments may be noted in regional human rights systems principally, domestic constitutionalism too has paved the way for further standardisation, constitutionalism representing a particularly powerful way of codifying rights: accordingly, the South African constitution refers to such collective nature in two regards, firstly, by safeguarding the rights of present and future generations, and secondly, by alluding to the objective of economic and social development which carries important collective implications.[374] Similarly, the Dominican Republic stipulated, explicitly, the right to sustainable use and enjoyment of natural resources, health, environment in both individual and collective terms. Other constitutions have followed the lead, establishing either rights for future generations as in the case of Norway and Germany, for instance, or an '*indispensable collective solidarity*' according to the Spanish constitution adopted as early as 1978.[375] Yet other cases[376] such as French constitutional law have referred to the constitutional value of environmental protection, even declaring it a fundamental interest of the State alongside all other interests.[377]

Delicate attention is to be devoted to regional frameworks however, having contributed rather extensively to the standardisation of collective rights, the Inter-American and African human and peoples' rights mechanisms in particular. As the African Charter on Human and Peoples' Rights states in its article 24 on the right to a general satisfactory environment, 'all peoples' shall be in the position of exercising such right. Indeed, art.24 has been placed into the "*broader context of traditional African practices which saw the environment as central to religious and cultural lives*".[378] Relatedly, such argument was also invoked in the context of the right to development in art.22; in such context, the Court would maintain: "*access to the 'natural environment' has been 'inextricably linked' to religious and cultural practices for indigenous peoples*".[379] A collective dimension may be deduced here, relating environmental rights almost classically with group rights. A similar rationale underlies one of the landmark judgements on indigenous peoples, the

[373] Francioni (2010), p. 55.

[374] Lambert (2020).

[375] Ibid.

[376] For a comprehensive overview of environmental protection at constitutional level generally, see: Morand-Deviller (2014).

[377] *Décision N° 2022–843*, Conseil Constitutionnel in 2022.

[378] Murray (2019), p. 548.

See also the following work: Amechi (2009).

[379] Murray (2019), p. 554.

*African Commission on Human and Peoples' Rights vs. Republic of Kenya*, African Court on Human and Peoples' Rights in 2017.

*Endorois case* in which the African Commission referred to indigenous peoples' loss of lands, forests and natural resources.[380] Collective rights, it could be argued, become articulated rather implicitly, when relating environmental rights with other fundamental rights—following this line, the Commission associated art.24 with guarantees to "*ensure there is sufficient and safe water for present and future generations*".[381] Also more transversally speaking, the African Commission has demanded those Heads of State represented in the African Union Assembly to include 'special measures of protection' for vulnerable groups in their international agreements and negotiations,[382] hence standardising collective rights throughout relevant policy processes. Finally, the ECOWAS Court of Justice explicitly referred to collective rights in the context of reparations, understanding the latter as "*a collective benefit adequate to repair, as completely as possible, the collective harm that a violation of a collective right causes*".[383]

Also in a rather direct manner, the Inter-American human rights system has come to deal with environmental human rights, by specifying procedural obligations when claiming such rights collectively. Indeed, its *Advisory Opinion 23/17* on the matter has become an often referred jurisprudential source, to be considered as a form of standardising environmental human rights, and collective rights in the region. The right to "*have access to information, participation in relevant decision-making processes, and judicial recourse*"[384] were to be understood as conditions for preserving the environmental more generally, but also as establishing an important basis for indigenous collective rights. Also recently, in the case *Lhaka Honhat Association vs. Argentina*, the Court referred to said Advisory Opinion, establishing the right to a healthy environment as a "*fundamental right for the existence of humankind*",[385] hence clearly departing from the individualistic approach permeating human rights. Even more explicitly and powerfully, the Court famously derived collective land rights from a largely individualistic legal language promoted by the American Convention of Human Rights (Pact of San José) adopted in 1969, maintaining, firstly, that "*ownership of the land is not centred on the individual but rather on the group and its community*",[386] and secondly, the Commission establishes "*special protections for indigenous peoples may be required for them to exercise their rights fully and equally with the rest of the population, special*

[380] Murray (2019).

[381] Ibid.; p. 550.

[382] Ibid.; p. 555.

[383] Ibid.; p. 556.
*SERAP vs. Federal Republic of Nigeria*, ECOWAS Court of Justice in 2012.

[384] Inter-American Commission on Human Rights (2009) *Indigenous and Tribal Peoples' over their Ancestral Lands and Natural Resources*, para.197.

[385] *Advisory Opinion OC 23/17 requested by the Republic of Colombia*, Inter-American Court of Human Rights in 2017, para.203.

[386] *Mayagna (Sumo) Awas Tingni Community vs. Nicaragua*, Inter-American Court of Human Rights in 2001, para.149.

*protection may be required to ensure their physical and cultural survival*".[387] Through an evolutionary, systemic interpretative culture of the Court and the Commission, collective rights—initially in the land rights context[388]—would find an established place in its jurisprudence, become a common reference point for any emerging issue on indigenous peoples, and contribute to a paradigm shift in legal thinking, opening for a new collective rights dimension.

## 7.8 Levels of Autonomy and Leverage Vis-à-Vis the State

The right to collective autonomy necessarily requires us to view the matter from a pluralistic perspective. Certainly, the long-lasting demands for autonomy in the indigenous world(s) cannot be limited to struggles for territory and self-governance only, instead—for the sake of a holistic, and genuinely decolonising endeavour—autonomies similarly embrace educational sovereignty, language rights, religious freedoms or cultural practices.[389] While the right to collective autonomy represents a right in its own terms, it can hardly be viewed in separation from the principle of self-determination[390] and also self-determined development in its many senses as well as legal pluralism. For understandable reasons, each one of the rights have been viewed with scepticism by States committing to international treaty obligations, and as a result, produced limitation clauses that would curtail the scope of autonomy-based rights, reaffirming State sovereignty, and its corollary principles, territorial integrity or the predominance of certain laws and systems.[391]

We may want to distinguish between those manifestations of autonomy that materialise where collectives or groups exert forms of self-governance or retain exclusive decision-making powers, and those exercised in shared spaces of decision-making, classically being integrated into State structures. Self-exercised autonomies or 'autonomies in their most genuine form' only rarely enjoy acceptance from the start, usually looking back at lengthy struggles for recognition.[392] We may consider these endeavours part of a larger demand for decolonisation, initiating with the very State structures giving rise to and ultimately legitimising a certain status quo. This inevitably brings transformations with it at all levels, including important

[387] Inter-American Commission on Human Rights (2010) *Report on the Situation of Human Rights in Ecuador*, para. Fourth concluding paragraph.

[388] Monteiro de Matos (2020).

[389] See e.g. Tuhiwai Smith (2012).

[390] See e.g. Anaya (2004).
Barelli (2011).

[391] To get a more comprehensive view on these questions, see the travaux préparatoires of relevant treaties and declarations, most essentially ILO C107, ILO C169 and UNDRIPS.

[392] See, e.g., Van Cott (2007).
Postero (2007).

epistemological paradigm shifts.[393] Famously, this includes what has been termed an '*un-thinking*' and '*re-thinking*' (*des-pensar*) in relation to current logics of hegemony.[394] In turn, what is demanded includes a redistribution of language and novel approach towards the sense of life.[395] Emblematic are surely indigenous cosmovisions that have played a key role in such decolonising process,[396] establishing themselves as channels of legal pluralism and grassroots voices generally. Indeed, religious pluralism as such constitutes an important form of autonomy, not only in terms of its decolonising function. As it becomes easily discernible from the above, autonomy's ambits do not remain limited to territorial dimensions, let alone secessionist agendas. Instead, not uncommonly, autonomies serve as vehicles for neighbouring rights, assuming so-called umbrella functions.[397]

When understanding collective autonomy as an expression of institutional sovereignty exercised within classical State orders and State-centric constitutionalism, we necessarily need to examine organisational contexts particular to minority groups. Indeed, recognition processes granting indigenous autonomy and self-governance are necessarily conditioned upon their commensurability with not only existing structures but their positioning vis-à-vis State mechanisms.[398] Some would argue indigenous representative institutions came to the fore by the very necessity of negotiating with externals, such as the coloniser,[399] the State or, in current context, multinational companies. In the contemporary world, protecting institutional integrity has become one of the main concerns to guarantee collective rights.

Relatedly, indigenous institutionality could be considered as an important method to exert leverage vis-à-vis the State. Some autonomies have been secured by means of old treaty arrangements, making sure old established agreements on territorial and governance aspects would be paid due recognition in current contexts (e.g. art.37, UNDRIPS).[400] The Chilean case may be emblematic here, demonstrating how treaty law between Chile at the time of its independence in 1818 and the Mapuche would experience a form of '*legal regression*', especially under Pinochet's long-lasting dictatorial rule and the application of anti-terrorist legislation against the

[393] See. e.g. Sousa Santos (2017).
Sousa Santos (2013).
Fanon (2002).
Llanes Ortiz (2018).

[394] Sousa Santos (2013).

[395] Mbembe (2010).

[396] E.g. Escobar (2014).
Solón (2017).
Gudynas (2011).

[397] This is the case for procedural participatory rights in particular, including the right to prior consultation and free, prior and informed consent.

[398] Watson (2018a).

[399] Hirsch (2003).

[400] See e.g. Gover (2020b).

Mapuche.[401] With Pinochetian constitutionalism and its emphasis on neo-liberal values including its impacts on natural resource governance, indigenous peoples had come to face new pressures related to their land rights and titling processes.[402]

Considerable shortcomings may also be noted where old treaty rights find themselves in relations of dependence on the State's very structure: the concept of '*forced federalism*' has been used to describe the transfer of federal powers to State governments which, in turn, forced indigenous peoples into new arrangements, often to the detriment of their collective identity and status while overriding prior treaties that had established specific "*federal government-to-indigenous government relationships*".[403] Such shifts in the institutional scenery have been accompanied by underlying prejudice and patronising attitudes, serving to legitimise such positioning in relation to indigenous self-determination as the following demonstrates:

> . . .First, policymakers invoking rich Indian racist attitudes contend that indigenous peoples do not need what they used to (. . .) Second, rich Indian racist attitudes invoked by state policymakers require indigenous peoples to demonstrate that they deserve self-determination and a distinct nationhood status[404]

The above reveals rather illustratively how indigenous self-determination had been re-interpreted to mean quite the opposite, absolving indigenous peoples from any self-defining powers on forms of governance and returning to the basic rationale of defining themselves as indigenous peoples, lying at the heard of indigenous peoples' struggle for recognition. Elsewhere such denial of indigenous 'peoplehood' and self-determination would disclose the following strategies:

> . . .by insisting tribes prove that they still need sovereign rights to be self-sufficient and by invoking the notion that gaming tribes are less authentically Indian, diminishing their claims to political independence[405]

This raises important identity issues, questioning key principles that lay the foundations of collective self-identification and its corollary, collective institutional independence.

Entering the debates on co-governance demands a more detailed examination of the procedures giving rise to autonomies under the State umbrella. Classically, this may include the influence of indigenous organisations on policy processes or, alternatively, affiliation with larger political parties advocating for indigenous rights or accommodating indigenous agendas.[406] Indeed, electoral procedures have proven

[401] Clavero (2010).
Huilcamán Paillama (2014).

[402] Eichler and Barnier-Khawam (2022).

[403] Corntassel and Witmer (2008), p. 5.

[404] Ibid.; p. 4.

[405] Ibid, p. 4.
See more particularly: Spilde (1999).

[406] See e.g. Yashar (2005).
Warren and Jackson (2003).
Becker (2011).
Miranda Torres (2020).

crucial for indigenous organisations to gain a voice in the State's governance processes, its functioning and forms of institutionalism. Very emblematically, the Inter-American Court of Human Rights referred to the importance of active and passive electoral rights to be granted to indigenous organisations (YATAMA in this case) and the larger implications this may have for indigenous peoples to exercise participatory rights in accordance with their own procedures:

> YATAMA contributes to the consolidation and preservation of the cultural identity of the members of the indigenous and ethnic communities (...) Its structure and purposes are related to the practices, customs and forms of organisation of these communities. Consequently, the exclusion of the participation of the YATAMA candidates particularly affected the members of the indigenous and ethnic communities that were represented by this organisation in the general elections, by placing them in a situation of inequality as regards the options which they could choose to vote, since those persons who, in principle, deserved their confidence because they had been chosen directly in assemblies (according to the practices and customs of these communities) to represent the interests of their members, had been excluded from participating as candidates.[407]

Based on the foregoing, the Court then specified those rights and obligations particular to indigenous peoples in the context of (and in contrast to) basic voting rights:

> [the State is called upon to] adopt all necessary measures to ensure that the members of the indigenous and ethnic communities (...) can participate, in equal conditions, in decision-making matters and policies that affect or could affect their rights (...) so that they can incorporate themselves into State institutions and bodies and participate directly and proportionately to their population in the conduct of public affairs and also do this from their own institutions and according to their values, practices and forms of organisation[408]

Autonomies may also find expression through specific procedural arrangements to guarantee indigenous representation in the executive, legislative or judiciary bodies respectively. This may materialise in the form of reforms in the dominant justice system to include indigenous judges on the bench or to introduce indigenous laws as valid legal sources,[409] it may include specific quota[410] or establishing specialised mechanisms such as entire ministries or departments as it is the case in Andean States. Despite the merits laying with these procedural special rights, not enough thought is devoted to indigenous proper customs and procedures that would need to find due consideration if we were to take a genuine stance towards institutional reforms, or proceduralising the law to include participatory group rights. This may, in turn, qualify the level of autonomy granted to collective rights holders. At the end of the day, both manifestations of autonomy, that is, self-governance forms and those decision-making powers shared with the State, depend on a variety of factors in order for these to take effect, essentially political will to reform the State, a specific political climate receptible towards these transformations, and ultimately the

[407] *Case of YATAMA vs. Nicaragua*, Inter-American Court of Human Rights in 2005, para.227.

[408] Ibid.; para.225.

[409] Barrera (2012).

[410] Stojanović (2013).

willingness to establish procedures that take account of indigenous self-determined forms and formats of autonomy, including their proper customs and procedures.

## 7.9 Dealing with the Integrity of Human Rights

A final point of reference, whilst scale of measurement, lies in the comprehensiveness, scope and integrity of rights dealt with. As an emerging legal regime, collective rights are yet to be articulated further in jurisprudence and beyond, including questions related to their integrity. Broadly, human rights have been understood as '*interrelated*', '*indivisible*', '*universal*' and '*interdependent*' as proclaimed by the *World Conference on Human Rights* of 1993 in the *Vienna Declaration and Programme of Action*.

Especially the claim for universality represents an often debated phenomenon in human rights debates, considering how "*Western imperialist or ex-colonial powers try to pass off their own, very specific and localised, idea of what 'rights' should be as universal*".[411] Conversely, some merit has been attributed to what is condemned as '*Eurocentric universalism*', referring to its potential for a form of "*genuine universalism that permits cultural pluralism*",[412] notably, by combining Enlightenment philosophies without ignoring the "*brutal legacy of colonialism or minimising the contributions of non-Western peoples [as in 'colonised peoples'] to subsequent human rights thinking*".[413] Relatedly, claims to universalism have been criticised based on the fact that human rights policies would miss out on considering local realities, and would threaten cultural diversity more broadly.[414] Nevertheless, 'universally valid principles' permeate many classical legal codes including the ancient Babylonian Hammurabi Code, or natural law traditions based on Roman law, as in '*law for all peoples*' (*jus gentium*), or referring to the Greek Stoics.[415] Indeed, the claims for universality could be portrayed as a virtually universally supported theoretical premise to build from, being embraced by considerable numbers of scholars and practitioners since time immemorial, understanding human rights as "*colour [ignorant] and direction [ignorant], as knowing neither right nor left but only human*".[416] Critical voices may very well criticise such portrayal given the importance of socio-economic inequalities persisting until today.[417] Indeed, Marxist

---

[411] Clapham (2015), p. 12.

[412] Frezzo (2019), pp. 181–182.

[413] Ibid.; p. 182.
For more details, see Ishay (2008).

[414] Wahl (2019).

[415] Ibid.; p. 5.

[416] Tomuschat (2014), p. 48.
Agarwal (1983).

[417] Hoover (2019).

theory of law has been one of the schools showing sceptical of the universality claim while one of its founding arguments—its orientation towards the State—no longer finds sufficient support to be upheld.[418] Some may argue collective rights and the often-associated communitarian idea have filled such gap in human rights practice. One way out of the dilemma has often been described as a '*process of universalisation*' which rejects the static claim of human rights universalism and instead places emphasis on the political-legal dealing with human rights.[419] This is not to reject a localised, contextual understanding of human rights. Instead, as argued by Judith Butler, "*...no assertion [of universality] can be made without at once requiring a cultural translation. (...) Without translation, the only way the assertion of universality can cross a border is through a colonial and expansionist logic*".[420] Indeed, the 'shaping-back' power of human rights becomes a sheer necessity, as famously discussed by Sally Engle Merry when proposing the concept of '*vernacularisation*', or localisation and appropriation of a norm.[421]

Merit also lies in the fact that collective rights manifestly respond to persisting (e.g. ethnic, cultural, linguistic, religious) inequalities going unperceived by most legal orders and their ignorance towards difference. Universalising such claims and presenting them as the only truth hence perpetuates existing vulnerabilities. Conversely, it has been maintained elsewhere that universal rights would demand 'universal coverage', ensuring every person is covered by its protection.[422] Again, we shall be reminded of the differentiated approach needed to allow vulnerable groups to exercise special rights, or as argued here, collective rights. Lastly, we may understand '*universality*' in the way the law finds application, technically, returning to basic State responsibilities that are commonly understood as being confined to a State's territory[423]—hence escaping any extraterritorial responsibilities which prove key in the case of corporate violations of indigenous peoples' rights to territories and resources.

Another common approximation concerns the '*interrelatedness*' claim of human rights. If we were to consider collective rights as part of the wide scenery of human rights, this would carry considerable implications in terms of their justiciability and also the value attributed by the international community in terms of recognition. Originally, the '*interrelated*', '*indivisible*' and '*interdependent*' nature of human rights was categorised in the context of the first two main human rights covenants, ICCPR and ICESCR, in consideration of "*the status, importance, or equality of*

[418] Tomuschat (2014).
[419] Golder (2019).
[420] Butler (2000), p. 35.
[421] Merry (2006).
[422] Gibney (2016).
Shue (1988).
[423] Gibney (2016).

*economic and social rights vis-à-vis civil and political rights*".[424] Indeed, interrelated rights—as in 'interconnected'—have become more closely associated with connecting '*broader categories or families of rights*' rather associating particular rights which '*interdependency*' tries to pursue.[425]

Evidently, collective rights benefit from such categorisation, gaining a space of articulation in broader human rights debates. Another characterising trait in defining such interrelatedness lies in the "*shar[ing of] common characteristics*".[426] If applied to collective rights, this might cause some problems of incommensurability at first view, given their distinct rationale and the particularities of both individual and collective rights regimes. However, focussing on one of the most fundamental collective claims, we easily find common origins, such as self-determination, being largely derived from basic autonomies, freedoms and decision-making capacities. Another defining facet includes what has been termed "*equality of importance or legitimacy*",[427] again representing a scenario yet to be established for collective rights in an individualistic human rights framework. A final component finding mentioning concerns '*institutional interrelatedness*', alluding to respective monitoring mechanisms.[428] Quite visibly, individual rights have been benefiting from stronger monitoring in terms of individual complaints or comprehensive supervision of State activities. Despite its legally non-binding nature, the UN Declaration on the Rights of Indigenous Peoples deserves some thought though, establishing, rather innovatively, new competences for a multiplicity of specialised entities to monitor implementation and application.[429]

Let us now turn to the '*interdependency*' claim. Often portrayed as an undisputed attribute, interdependent rights create conditionalities among different rights and in that sense divisions and categorisations are accepted without further critical engagement.[430] Not uncommonly, collective rights serve as quintessential umbrella claims for other rights to be exercised: this is the case where indigenous participatory rights such as prior consultation safeguard or are considered even existential for other rights such as cultural identity, physical integrity, food or health.[431] Given the complexities arising with the approach when pairing different rights, and in the light of the multiplicity of human rights embedded in a specific framework,

---

[424] Whelan (2010), p. 2.
See also: Neves-Silva et al. (2019).

[425] Whelan (2010), p. 4.

[426] Ibid.; p. 4.

[427] Ibid.; p. 5.

[428] Ibid.; p. 6.

[429] Clavero (2008) *Nota sobre el Alcance del Mandato Contenido en el Artículo 42 de la Declaración sobre los Derechos de los Pueblos Indígenas.*
See also: Roy (forthcoming).

[430] Whelan (2010).

[431] See, e.g., Doyle (2015).
Wright and Tomaselli (2019).
Rodríguez-Garavito (2011).

interdependencies have been discussed by focussing on families of rights instead of individual rights.[432] Again, such categorisation would work to the benefit of collective rights, usually to be considered as an entire regime of rights that are commonly attributed to specific groups of individuals. Indeed, it is maintained elsewhere that human rights' interdependency can only be ensured where those most vulnerably and marginalised are included.[433] As a corollary, in view of building a more egalitarian society, important ESC rights shall mitigate persisting inequalities affecting those groups to particularly alarming degrees, and hence demonstrating the importance of such rights without which other rights may hardly be exercised.[434]

Finally, the '*indivisible*' character of human rights deserves some historical contextualisation, also pursuing the objective of appreciating the potential lying in the concept for collective rights. In times of the drafting process around the Universal Declaration, indivisibility became a '*rhetoric for postcolonial aspirations*', later to re-appear as a '*revisionist view of human rights*' which would prioritise ESC rights over CP rights as it was demanded by the 'developing world' back then.[435] Further developments around the concept would follow in the 1990s in the form of a "*rhetoric of restoration of the spirit of the fundamental unity of the rights contained in the 1948 Universal Declaration of Human Rights*".[436] As it becomes manifest here, the term serves as an important tool for determining the (political) direction it may take, as an emancipatory tool for those traditionally left out in world politics, and in that sense, allowing to re-set human rights priorities with promising potential for collective rights.

## References

Acosta A (2017) Posextractivismo: del Discurso a la Práctica – Reflexiones para la Acción. International Development Policy/Revue internationale de politique de développement 9

Agarwal HO (1983) Implementation of human rights covenants with special reference to India. Kitab Mahal, Allahabad

Aguilar G, Lafosse S, Rojas H, Steward R (2010) The constitutional recognition of indigenous peoples in Latin America. Pace Int Law Rev 2

Aguilera Bravo MG (2021) Human rights and the environment in Latin America and the Caribbean: environmental human rights under the American convention on human rights and the Escazú agreement on access rights. Georg-August Universität Göttingen, Göttingen

Aguilera Bravo MG (2023) Environmental human rights in Latin America and the Caribbean: a regional contribution to sustainable development. Brill, Leiden

[432] Whelan (2010).

[433] Neves-Silva et al. (2019).

[434] Ibid.

[435] Whelan (2010), p. 2.

[436] Ibid.; p. 2.
See also Morsink (1999).

Akerø-Stueland KV (2021) The European Court of Human Rights, the margin of appreciation and European Consensus: strengthening or diluting minority rights. LSE Law Review Blog. Retrieved from https://blog.lselawreview.com/2021/03/european-court-of-human-rights-the-margin-of-appreciation

Alemahu Yeshanew S (2014) Mainstreaming human rights in development programmes and projects: experience form the work of a United Nations Agency. Nordic J Human Rights 32(4)

Alexy R (2018) Theorie der Grundrechte. Suhrkamp Taschenbuch Verlag, Frankfurt a.M

Alston P (1982) A third generation of solidarity rights: progressive development or obfuscation of international human rights law? Neth Int Law Rev 29

Amao O (2019) African union law: the emergence of a sui generis legal order. Routledge, Abingdon

Amechi EP (2009) Enhancing environmental protection and socio economic development in Africa: a fresh look at the right to a general satisfactory environment under the African charter on human and peoples' rights. Law Env Dev J 5(1)

Anaya J (2004) Indigenous peoples in international law. Oxford University Press, Oxford

Appiah KA (2005) The ethics of identity. Princeton University Press, New Jersey

Arai-Takahashi Y (2013) The margin of appreciation doctrine: a theoretical analysis of Strasbourg's variable geometry. In: Føllesdal A, Peters B, Ulfstein G (eds) Constituting Europe: the European court of human rights in a national, European and global context. Cambridge University Press, Cambridge

Arendt H (1951) The origins of totalitarianism. Penguin Books, London

Atrey S (2019) Intersectional discrimination. Oxford University Press, Oxford

Atrey S, Dunne P (eds) (2019) Intersectionality and human rights law. Hart, Oxford

Bacchi C, Eveline J (2010) Gender mainstreaming or diversity mainstreaming? The politics of 'doing'. In: Bacchi C, Eveline J (eds) Mainstreaming politics: gendering practices and feminist theory. University of Adelaide Press, Adelaide

Barelli M (2011) Shaping indigenous self-determination: promising or unsatisfactory solutions? Int Commun Law Rev 13(4)

Barrera A (2012) Turning legal pluralism into state-sanctioned law: assessing the implications of the new constitutions and laws in Bolivia and Ecuador. In: Schilling-Vacaflor A (ed) New constitutionalism in Latin America: promises and practices. Ashgate, Farnham

Barrios-Suvelza F (2017) El Impacto de las Recientes Reformas de Regionalización en Colombia, Ecuador, Perú y Bolivia: Conceptos y Procesos. Revista de Estudios sobre Espacio y Poder 1(8)

Basta Fleiner LR, Gaudreault-DesBiens J-F (2013) Federalism and autonomy. In: Tushnet M, Fleiner T, Saunders C (eds) Routledge handbook of constitutional law. Routledge, Abingdon

Baumgärtel M, Staes D, Mena Parras FJ (2014) Hierarchy, coordination, or conflict. Global law theories and the question of human rights integration. Eur J Human Rights 3

Becker M (2011) Pachakutik: indigenous movements and electoral politics in Ecuador. Rowman & Littlefield, Lanham

Bens J (2020) The indigenous paradox: rights, sovereignty, and culture in the Americas. University of Pennsylvania Press, Pennsylvania

Bernot S (2015) Die verfassungsrechtliche Anerkennung indigenen Rechts, Rechtspluralismus und Menschenrechte: Untersucht an den Beispielen Südafrika und Bolivien. Nomos, Baden-Baden

Besson S (2011) Sovereignty. Max Planck Encyclopedias of International Law. Retrieved from https://opil.ouplaw.com/display/10.1093/law:epil/9780199231690/law-9780199231690-e1472

Besson S (2015) Human rights and constitutional law: patterns of mutual validation and legitimation. In: Cruft R, Liao SM, Renzo M (eds) Philosophical foundations of human rights. Oxford University Press, Oxford

Bexell M, Hickmann T, Schapper A (2023) Strengthening the sustainable development goals through integration with human rights. Int Environ Agreem: Politics Law Econ 23(2)

Bilchitz D, Deva S (2013) Human rights obligations of business: beyond the corporate responsibility to respect? Cambridge University Press, Cambridge

Blackburn R (1999) Towards a constitutional bill of rights for the United Kingdom. Frances Pinter Publishers Ltd, London

Blichner LC, Molander A (2008) Mapping juridification. Eur Law J 14(1)
Borchorst A, Teigen M (2010) Political intersectionality—tackling inequalities in public policies in Scandinavia. Kvinder Køb & Forskning 19:2–3
Borrows J, Rotman L (1997) The sui generis nature of aboriginal rights: does it make a difference. Alberta Law Rev 36(5)
Boşilcă RL (2014) The European Union – A "Sui Generis" international diplomatic actor: challenges posed to the international diplomatic law. Romanian J Eur Aff 1(14)
Bourke Martignoni J (2018) Sexual and reproductive rights at the crossroads: intersectionality and the UN treaty monitoring bodies. In: Bribosia E, Rorive I (eds) Human rights tectonics: global dynamics of integration and fragmentation. Intersentia, Cambridge
Brauch JA (2005) The margin of appreciation and the jurisprudence of the European court of human rights: threat to the rule of law. Columbia J Eur Law 11
Brems E (2014) Should pluriform human rights become one? Exploring the benefits of human rights integration. Eur J Human Rights 4
Brems E (2018) Smart human rights integration. In: Brems E, Ouald-Chaib S (eds) Fragmentation and integration in human rights law: users' perspectives. Edward Elgar Publishing, Cheltenham
Brems E, Desmet E (2014) Introduction: theorizing the multi-layered nature of human rights law. Eur J Human Rights 3
Bribosia E, Rorive I (2018) Human rights integration in action: making equality law work for trans people in Belgium. In: Brems E, Ouald-Chaib S (eds) Fragmentation and integration in human rights law: users' perspectives. Edward Elgar Publishing, Cheltenham
Brown Weiss E (2021) Intergenerational Equity. Max Planck Encyclopedia of Public International Law. Retrieved from https://opil.ouplaw.com/view/10.1093/law:epil/9780199231690/law-9780199231690-e1421
Buchanan A (1993) The role of collective rights in the theory of indigenous peoples' rights. Transnl Law Contemp Probl 3(1)
Búrca G d (2012) The ECJ and the international legal order: a re-evaluation. In: Búrca G d (ed) The worlds of European constitutionalism. Cambridge University Press, Cambridge
Burger J (2012) Making the declaration work for human rights in the UN system. In: Charters C, Stavenhagen R (eds) Making the declaration work: the United Nations declaration on the rights of indigenous peoples. IWGIA, Copenhagen
Burger J, Martín Castro D (2006) Pueblos Indígenas en Naciones Unidas. Mecanismos de Protección, Agencias e Instancias. In: Berraondo M (ed) Pueblos Indígenas y Derechos Humanos. Universidad de Deusto, Bilbao
Butler J (2000) Restaging the universal: hegemony and the limits of formalism. In: Butler J, Laclau E, Žižek S (eds) Contingency, hegemony, universality: contemporary dialogues on the left. Verso, London
Butler J (2004) Undoing gender. Routledge, London
Buys E, Lewis B (2021) Environmental protection through European and African human rights frameworks. Int J Human Rights 26(6)
Cane P, Conaghan J (2009) Juridification. The New Oxford Companion to Law. https://www.oxfordreference.com/display/10.1093/acref/9780199290543.001.0001/acref-9780199290543-e-1239
Çali B, Demir-Gürsel E (2021) The Council of Europe's reponses to the decay of the rule of law and human rights protections: a comparative appraisal. Eur Conv Human Rights Law Rev 2
Caruso U, Malloy Tove H (2013) Minorities, their rights, and the monitoring of the European framework convention for the protection of national minorities: essays in honour of Rainer Hofmann. BRILL, Leiden
Cassese A (2005) International law. Oxford University Press, Oxford
Cassese A (2012) Realizing utopia: the future of international law. Oxford University Press, Oxford
Cats-Baril A (2020) Indigenous peoples' rights in constitutions Assessment tool. International Institute for Democracy and Electoral Assistance, Stockholm

Cavallaro JL, Vargas C, Sandoval C, Duhaime B (2019) Indigenous and tribal peoples' rights and the inter-American system. In: Cavallaro JL, Vargas C, Sandoval C, Duhaime B (eds) Doctrine, practice, and advocacy in the inter-American human rights system. Oxford University Press, Oxford

Centre for International Governance Innovation (2020) UNDRIP implementation: comparative approaches, indigenous voices from CANZUS, special report. Centre for International Governance Innovation, Waterloo

Charters C, Stavenhagen R (2012) Making the declaration work: the United Nations declaration on the rights of indigenous peoples. International Work Group for Indigenous Affairs, Copenhagen

Cho S, Crenshaw KW, McCall L (2013) Toward a field of intersectionality studies: theory, applications, and praxis. Signs J Women Cult Soc 38(4)

Clapham A (2015) Human rights: a very short introduction. Oxford University Press, Oxford

Clavero B (2010) Reconocimiento Mapu-Che de Chile: Tratado Ante Constitución. Derecho y Humanidades 13

Corntassel JJ, Hopkins Primeau T (1998) The paradox of indigenous identity: a levels-of-analysis approach. Glob Gov 4

Corntassel J, Witmer RC (2008) Forced federalism: contemporary challenges to indigenous nationhood. University of Oklahoma Press, Norman

Craig PP, de Búrca G (2015) EU law: text, cases, and materials. Oxford University Press, Oxford

David V (2018) The integration of cultural and economic rights by human rights courts. In: Bribosia E, Rorive I (eds) Human rights tectonics: global dynamics of integration and fragmentation. Intersentia, Cambridge, Antwerp and Chicago

Davis K (2008) Intersectionality as buzzword. A sociology of science perspective on what makes a feminist theory successful. Fem Theory 9(1)

De Schutter O (2018) The formation of a common law of human rights. In: Bribosia E, Rorive I (eds) Human rights tectonics: global dynamics of integration and fragmentation. Intersentia, Cambridge, Antwerp & Chicago

De Witte B (2012) The European Union as an international legal experiment. In: Búrca G d (ed) The worlds of European constitutionalism. Cambridge University Press, Cambridge

Demir-Gürsel E (2021) The former secretary general of the Council of Europe Confronting Russia's annexation of the Crimea and Turkey's state of emergency. Eur Conv Human Rights Law 2

Dersso S, Palermo F (2013) Minority rights. In: Tushnet M, Fleiner T, Saunders C (eds) Routledge handbook of constitutional law. Routledge, Abingdon

Dinstein Y (1976) The collective human rights of peoples and minorities. Int Comp Law Q 1(25)

Donald A, Speck A-K (2021) Time for the gloves to come off? The response by the parliamentary assembly of the Council of Europe to rule of law backsliding. Eur Conv Human Rights Law Rev 2

Doyle CM (2015) Indigenous peoples, title to territory, rights and resources: the transformative role of free prior and informed consent. Routledge, Abingdon

Eichler J (2019) Reconciling indigenous peoples' individual and collective rights: participation, prior consultation and self-determination in Latin America. Routledge, Abingdon

Eichler J, Barnier-Khawam P (2022) Criminalization, securitization and other forms of illegalizing indigenous contestations in Chile: responses from constitutional law and inter-American jurisprudence on Mapuche People's rights. J Human Rights Pract

Eide A (2004) The rights of "old" versus "new" minorities. Eur Yearb Minor Iss 2(3)

Escobar A (2014) Sentipensar con la Tierra: Nuevas Lecturas sobre Desarrollo, Territorio y Diferencia. Ediciones UNAULA, Medellín

Fanon F (2002) Les Damnés de la Terre. La Découverte, Paris

Fellmeth AX, Horwitz M (2009) Guide to Latin in international law. Oxford University Press, Oxford

Fitzmaurice M (2012) Tensions between States and Indigenous People over Natural Resources in light of the 1989 ILO Convention No.169 concerning Indigenous and Tribal Peoples in

Independent Countries and the 2007 UN Declaration on the Rights of Indigenous Peoples (including relevant national legislation and case-law). The Yearbook of Polar Law IV
Fitzmaurice M (2018) Indigenous peoples and intergenerational equity as an emerging aspect of Ethno-cultural diversity in international law. In: Pentassuglia G (ed) Ethno-cultural diversity and human rights: challenges and critiques. BRILL I Nijhoff, Leiden
Fontana LB, Grugel J (2016) The politics of indigenous participation through "free, prior informed consent": reflections from the Bolivian case. World Dev 77
Forde A (2022) Political Salvation of Europe's Human Rights System? The Case for a Fourth Council of Europe Summit. ECHR Blog. Retrieved from https://www.echrblog.com/2022/03/political-salvation-of-europes-human.html
Francioni F (2010) International human rights in an environmental horizon. Eur J Int Law 21(1)
Freeman M (1995) Are there collective human rights? Polit Stud XLIII
French P (1984) Collective and corporate responsibility. Columbia University Press, New York
Frezzo M (2019) Critical theory, sociology and human rights. In: Schippers B (ed) Critical perspectives on human rights. Rowman & Littlefield International, London/New York
Galenkamp M (1993) Individualism and collectivism: the concept of collective rights. Rotterdamse Filosofische Studies, Rotterdam
Garcia Alvarez J (2022) The Processes of Constitutionalization and Internationalization of Human Rights. European Student Think Tank 14. Retrieved from https://esthinktank.com/2022/02/14/the-processes-of-constitutionalization-and-internationalization-of-human-rights/
García Linera Á, Chávez León M, Costas Monje P (2005) Sociología de los Movimientos Sociales en Bolivia: Estructuras de Movilización, Repertorios Culturales y Acción Política. Plural Editores, La Paz
Gibney M (2016) International human rights law: returning to universal principles. Rowman & Littlefield, Lanham
Gilbert J (2006) Indigenous peoples' land rights under international law. From victims to actors. Transnational Publishers, Ashley Park
Golder B (2019) Human rights trouble? Judith Butler and the performative refusal of human rights. In: Schippers B (ed) Critical perspectives on human rights. Rowman & Littlefield, London and New York
Gómez Isa F (2016) The role of soft law in the progressive development of indigenous peoples' rights. In: Lagoutte S, Gammeltoft-Hansen T, Cerone J (eds) Tracing the roles of soft law in human rights. Oxford University Press, Oxford
Góngora Mera M (2020) Discriminación en clave interseccional: tendencias recientes en la jurisprudencia de la Corte Interamericana de Derechos Humanos. In: Morales Antoniazzi M, Ronconi L, Clérico L (eds) Interamericanización de los DESCA. El caso Cuscul Pivaral de la Corte IDH, Querétaro, Instituto de Estudios Constitucionales del Estado de Querétaro
Góngora-Mera ME (2017) The block of constitutionality as the Doctrinal Pivot of a Ius Commune. In: Bogdandy A, Ferrer MacGregor E, Morales Antoniazzi M, Piovesan F (eds) Transformative constitutionalism in Latin America: the emergence of a New Ius Commune. Oxford University Press, Oxford
Goodale M, Engle Merry S (2003) The practice of human rights: tracking law between the global and the local. Cambridge University Press, Cambridge
Gover K (forthcoming) Article 33. In: Eichler J, Doyle C, Howard S (eds) United Nations declaration on the rights of Indigenous Peoples: Article-by-Article commentary. München, Baden-Baden, Oxford: Beck, Hart, Nomos
Gover K (2011) Tribal constitutionalism—states, tribes and the governance of membership. Oxford University Press, Oxford
Gover K (2016) Indigenous membership and human rights: when self identification meets self-constitution. In: Lennox C, Short D (eds) Handbook of indigenous peoples' rights. Routledge, Abingdon
Gover K (2020a) Legal pluralism and indigenous legal traditions. In: Schiff Berman P (ed) The Oxford handbook of global legal pluralism. Oxford University Press, Oxford

Gover K (2020b) Treaties and the UN declaration on the rights of indigenous peoples: the significance of article 37. In: Centre for international governance innovation. 2020. UNDRIP implementation: comparative approaches, indigenous voices from CANZUS, special report. Centre for International Governance Innovation, Waterloo

Greer S (2000) The margin of appreciation: interpretation and discretion under the European convention on human rights. Council of Europe Publishing, Human Rights files N°17

Greer S (2017) Universalism and relativism in the protection of human rights in Europe: politics, law and culture. In: Agha P (ed) Human rights between law and politics: the margin of appreciation in post-National Contexts. Hart Publishing, Oxford

Gudynas E (2011) Buen Vivir: Today's tomorrow. Development 54(4)

Habermas J (1995) Moral consciousness and communicative action. MIT Press, Cambridge

Hainämäki L (2010) The right to be a part of nature: indigenous peoples and the environment. Academic Dissertation. University of Lapland, Faculty of Law

Hankivsky O, Jordan-Zachery JS (2019) The Palgrave handbook of intersectionality in public policy. Palgrave Macmillan, Cham

Harris-Short S, Tobin J (2019) Article 30 cultural, linguistic, and religious rights of minorities and indigenous children. In: Tobin J (ed) The UN convention on the rights of the child: a commentary. Oxford University Press, Oxford

Heinze E (1999) The construction and contingency of the minority concept. In: Fottrell D, Bowring B (eds) Minority and group rights in the new millennium. Martinus Nijhoff Publishers, The Hague

Henrard K (2011) An EU perspective on new versus traditional minorities: on semi-inclusive socio-economic integration and expanding visions of "European" culture and identity. Colombia J Eur Law 17

Hensel R, Klippel D (2015) Juridification. Encyclopedia of Early Modern History Online. https://doi.org/10.1163/2352-0272_emho_COM_029645

Hirsch SM (1999) The Capitanía of the Izozo: the struggle for political autonomy among the Guaraní Indians of Eastern Bolivia. In: Miller ES (ed) Peoples of the Gran Chaco. Greenwood Publishing Group, Westport

Hirsch SM (2003) The emergence of political organisations among the Guaraní Indians of Bolivia and Argentina: a comparative perspective. In: Detlef E, Muñoz E (eds) Contemporary indigenous movements in Latin America. Rowman & Littlefield Publishers, Lanham

Hofmann R, Angst D, Lantschner E, Rautz G, Rein D (2015) Das Rahmenübereinkommen zum Schutz nationaler Minderheiten: Handkommentar. Nomos, Baden-Baden

Hofmann R, Malloy TH, Rein DB (2018) The framework convention for the protection of national minorities: a commentary. Brill Nijhoff, Leiden/Boston

Holzinger K, Haer R, Bayer A, Behr DM, Neupert-Wentz C (2019) The constitutionalization of indigenous group rights, traditional political institutions, and customary law. Comp Pol Stud 52(12)

Home R (2019) Book review: African union law: the emergence of a sui generis legal order. J Sustain Dev Law Policy 10:1–2

Hoover J (2019) The political movement for a human right to the City. In: Schippers B (ed) Critical perspectives on human rights. Rowman & Littlefield International, London/New York

Horn-Miller K (2013) What does indigenous participatory democracy look like? Kahnawà:ke's community decision making process. Rev Const Stud/Revue d'études constitutionnelles 18(1)

Hoyos A (1992) El Control Judicial y el Bloque de Constitucionalidad en Panamá. Boletín Mexicano de Derecho Comparado 75

Huilcamán Paillama A (2014) El Respeto a los Tratados Internacionales y el Falo de La Haya. Wallmapu Futa Trawun Blogspot. Retrieved from http://futatrawun.blogspot.com/2014/01/el-respeto-los-tratados-internacionales.html

Hunt P (2015) Is the UN Human Rights Council delivering on its mandate to mainstream human rights? Universal Rights Group (blog). Retrieved from https://www.universal-rights.org/un-human-rights-council-delivering-mandate-mainstream-human-rights/

Imai S, Gunn K (2018) Indigenous Belonging: Membership and Identity in the UNDRIP: Articles 9, 33, 35, and 36. In: Hohmann J, Weller M (eds) The UN declaration on the rights of indigenous peoples: a commentary. Oxford University Press, Oxford

Inman D, Smis S, de Andrade D, Edson 'Krenak'. (2018) Fragmentation, harmonization and the users' perspective: the Munduruku peoples' view on land and the developing standards on indigenous peoples' land rights. In: Brems E, Ouald-Chaib S (eds) Fragmentation and integration in human rights law: users' perspectives. Edward Elgar Publishing, Cheltenham

Ishay M (2008) The history of human rights: from ancient times to the globalization era. University of California Press, Berkeley

Jones P (1999a) Group rights and group oppression. J Polit Philos 4(7)

Jones P (1999b) Human rights, group rights, and peoples' rights. Hum Rights Q 1(21)

Jones P (2016) Group Rights. The Stanford Encyclopedia of Philosophy. Retrieved from https://plato.stanford.edu/entries/rights-group/

Jovanović M (2012) Collective rights: a legal theory. Cambridge University Press, Cambridge

Kamardi C (2009) Die Ausformung einer Prozessordnung sui generis durch das ICTY unter Berücksichtigung des Fair-Trial-Prinzips. Springer, Heidelberg

Kennedy D (2005) The dark side of virtue: reassessing international humanitarianism. Am J Int Law 99

Kirsch S (2012) Juridification of indigenous politics. In: Eckert J (ed) Law against the state: ethnographic forays into law's transformations. Cambridge University Press, Cambridge

Kiwanuka RN (1988) The meaning of "people" in the African charter on human and peoples' rights. Am J Int Law 82(1)

Klabbers J (2009) Setting the scene. In: Klabbers J, Peters A, Ulfstein G (eds) The constitutionalization of international law. Oxford University Press, Oxford

Kleinlein T (2012) Constitutionalization in International Law. Beiträge zum ausländischen öffentlichen Recht und Völkerrecht, 231

Kochenov D (2015) The European Union's troublesome minority protection: a Bird's-eye view. In: Boulden J, Kymlicka W (eds) International approaches to governing ethnic diversity. Oxford University Press, Oxford

Koivurova T (2013) Jurisprudence of the European court of human rights regarding indigenous peoples: retrospect and prospects. In: Fitzmaurice M, Merkouris P, Okowa P (eds) The interpretation and application of the European convention of human rights: legal and practical implications. Martinus Nijhoff Publishers, Leiden and Boston

Korkeakivi A (2018) Beyond Adhocism—advancing minority rights through the United Nations. In: Hofmann R, Malloy TH, Rein DB (eds) The framework convention for the protection of national minorities: a commentary. Brill Nijhoff, Leiden/Boston

Koskenniemi M (2007) The fate of public international law: between technique and politics. Mod Law Rev 70(1)

Koskenniemi M (2010) Human rights mainstreaming as a strategy for institutional power. Human Int J Human Rights Humanit Dev 1(1)

Kratochvíl J (2011) The inflation of the margin of appreciation by the European court of human rights. Neth Q Human Rights 29(3)

Krizsan A, Skjeie H, Squires J (2012a) Institutionalizing intersectionality: a theoretical framework. In: Krizsan A, Skjeie H, Squires J (eds) Institutionalizing intersectionality: the changing nature of European equality regimes. Palgrave Macmillan London, London

Krizsan A, Skjeie H, Squires J (2012b) Institutionalizing intersectionality: the changing nature of European equality regimes. Palgrave Macmillan London, London

Krommendijk J (2018) Opinion 2/13 as a game changer in the dialogue between the European courts? In: Bribosia E, Rorive I (eds) Human rights tectonics: global dynamics of integration and fragmentation. Intersentia, Cambridge, Antwerp and Chicago

Kuokkanen R (2012) Self-determination and indigenous women's rights at the intersection of international human rights. Hum Rights Q 34(1)

Kymlicka W (1995) Multicultural citizenship: a Liberal theory of minority rights. Oxford University Press, Oxford
Kymlicka W (2012) Ethnocultural minority groups, status and treatment of. Encyclopedia of Applied Ethics
Kymlicka W, Norman W (1994) Return of the citizen: a survey of recent work on citizenship theory. Ethics 104
Lambert E (2020) The environment and human rights: introductory report to the high-level conference 'environmental protection and human rights'. Steering Committee for Human Rights, Strasbourg
Lang AF, Wiener A (2017) Handbook on global constitutionalism. Edward Elgar Publishing, Cheltenham
Lawrence R, Mörkenstam U (2016) Indigenous self-determination through a government agency? The impossible task of the Swedish Sámediggi. Int J Minor Group Rights 23
Lenzerini F (2006) Sovereignty revisited: international law and parallel sovereignty of indigenous peoples. Tex J Int Law 42(1)
Letsas G (2006) Two concepts of the margin of appreciation. Oxf J Leg Stud 26(4)
Lightfoot SR (2016) Indigenous mobilization and activism in the UN system. In: Lennox C, Short D (eds) Handbook of indigenous peoples' rights. Routledge, Abingdon
Lindahl H (2001) Sovereignty and the institutionalization of normative order. Oxf J Leg Stud 21(1)
Llanes Ortiz G (2018) Keynote 'La Academia como un Territorio: Epistemologías Indígenas en la Investigación'. University College Middelburg, 9th Multidisciplinary Meeting on Indigenous Peoples 'Territories in Dispute: Epistemologies, Resistances, Spiritualities and Rights'
Loick D (2019) Juridification. In: Allen A, Mendieta E (eds) The Cambridge Habermas Lexicon. Cambridge University Press, Cambridge
Loughlin M (2010) What is constitutionalisation? In: Dobner P, Loughlin M (eds) The twilight of constitutionalism? Oxford University Press, Oxford
MacCormick N (1999) Questioning sovereignty. Oxford University Press, Oxford
Marsal S, Palermo F (2018) Commentary of Article 3 of the framework convention for the protection of national minorities. In: Hofmann R, Malloy TH, Rein DB (eds) The framework convention for the protection of national minorities: a commentary. Brill Nijhoff, Leiden/Boston
Martins EJ, Tybusch JS (2016) Apropriação e Exploração enquanto Faces da Nova Colonialidade Latino-Americana: Limites e Possibilidades para a Construção de um Regime Sui Generis. Revista de Direito Ambiental e Socioambientalismo 2(2)
Mbembe A (2010) Sortir de la Grande Nuit: Essai sur l'Afrique Décolonisée. La Découverte, Paris
McCrudden C (2004) Mainstreaming human rights. Public Law Legal Theory Res Pap 47
McCrudden CJ (2005) Mainstreaming and human rights. In: Harvey C (ed) Human rights in the community: rights as agents for change. Hart, Oxford
McGoldrick D (2017) Religious rights and the margin of appreciation. In: Agha P (ed) Human rights between law and politics: the margin of appreciation in post-national contexts. Hart Publishing, Oxford
Melià B (1989) Ñande Reko, Nuestro Modo de Ser. Vol I, Los Guaraní-Chiriguano. CIPCA, La Paz
Merry SE (2006) Transnational human rights and local activism: mapping the middle. Am Anthropol 108(1)
Miranda Torres RP (2020) La Justicia Electoral para los Pueblos Indígenas en México (A Tres Décadas de su Reconocimiento en la Constitución). Derecho Global. Estudios sobre Derecho y Justicia 5(15)
Mitnick EJ (2006) Rights, groups and self-invention: group-differentiated rights in liberal theory. Ashgate, Aldershot
Monteiro de Matos M (2020) Indigenous land rights in the inter-American system: substantive and procedural law. Brill Nijhoff, Leiden & Boston
Morand-Deviller J (2014) L'Environnement dans les Constitutions Étrangères. Les Nouveaux Cahiers du Conseil Constitutionnel 2(43)

Morsink J (1999) The universal declaration of human rights: origins, drafting, and intent. University of Pennsylvania Press, Philadelphia
Muir E, de Witte B (2017) The procedural and institutional dimension of anti-discrimination law. In: Rossi LS, Casolari F (eds) The principles of equality in EU law. Springer International Publishing, Cham
Murray R (2019) The African Charter on human and peoples rights: a commentary. Oxford University Press, Oxford
Mutua M (2016) Human rights standards: hegemony, law, and politics. State University of New York Press, New York
Neuman G (2003) Human rights and constitutional rights. Stanford Law Rev 55(5)
Neves-Silva P, Martins GI, Heller L (2019) Human rights' interdependence and indivisibility: a glance over the human rights to water and sanitation. BMC Int Health Hum Rights 19(14)
Niezen R (2003) The origins of indigenism: human rights and the politics of identity. University of California Press, Berkeley
Niezen R (2010) Public justice and the anthropology of law. Cambridge University Press, Cambridge
Noh J-E (2021) Review of human rights-based approaches to development: empirical evidence from developing countries. Int J Human Rights 26(5)
Nursoo I (2018) Indigenous law, colonial injustice and jurisprudence of hybridity. J Legal Plur Unoff Law 50(1)
Oberleitner G (2008) A decade of mainstreaming human rights in the UN: achievements, failures, challenges. Neth Q Human Rights 26(3)
Olawuyi DS (2013) Mainstreaming human rights under national and international law: legal and epistemic question. Indonesia Law Rev 3(3)
Onazi O (2022) Human rights from community: a rights-based approach to development. Edinburgh University Press, Edinburgh
Orellana R (2004) Interlegalidad y Campos Jurídicos. Discurso y Derecho en la Configuración de Órdenes Semiautónomos en Comunidades Quechuas de Bolivia. Huella Editores, Cochabamba
Ouald-Chaib S (2018) Introduction. In: Brems E, Ouald-Chaib S (eds) Fragmentation and integration in human rights law: users' perspectives. Edward Elgar Publishing, Cheltenham
Papendorf K (2018) Juridification, marginalised persons and competence to mobilise the law. In: Hammerslev O, Hakvorsen Rønning O (eds) Outsourcing legal aid in the Nordic states. Springer, Heidelberg
Peročević K (2017) European Union legal nature: EU as Sui Generis – A Platypus-like society. InterEULawEast 4(2)
Peters A (2019) Constitutionalisation. In: d'Aspremont J, Singh S (eds) Concepts for international law: contributions to disciplinary thought. Edward Elgar Publishing, Cheltenham
Phelan W (2012) What is sui generis about the European Union? Costly international cooperation in a self-contained regime. Int Stud Rev 3(14)
Postero N (2007) Now we are citizens: indigenous politics in postmulticultural Bolivia. Stanford University Press, Stanford
Přibáň J (2017) Anything to appreciate?: A sociological view of the margin of rights and the persuasive force of their doctrines. In: Agha P (ed) Human rights between law and politics: the margin of appreciation in post-national contexts. Hart Publishing, Oxford
Rachovitsa A (2018) The African Court on human and peoples' rights: a uniquely equipped testbed for (the limits of) human rights integration? In: Bribosia E, Rorive I (eds) Human rights tectonics: global dynamics of integration and fragmentation. Intersentia, Cambridge, Antwerp and Chicago
Rae J (2006) Indigenous children: rights and reality. A report on indigenous children and the UN convention on the rights of the child. First Nations Child and Family Caring Society of Canada, Ottawa
Rajagopal B (2003) International law from below: development, social movements, and third world resistance. Cambridge University Press, Cambridge

Riley S (2019) Human dignity as a sui generis principle. Ratio Juris 32(4)
Rivera Cusicanqui S (2012) Violencias (Re)Encubiertas en Bolivia. Otramérica, Santander
Rodríguez Á (2016) El Régimen Constitucional de los Partidos Políticos en el Derecho de la Unión Europea: Un Equilibrio Sui Generis. Teoría y Realidad Constitucional 38
Rodríguez Caguana A, Morales Naranjo V (2020) Los derechos de la naturaleza en diálogo intercultural: una mirada a la jurisprudencia sobre los páramos andinos y los glaciares indios. Deusto J Human Rights 6
Rodríguez-Garavito C (2011) Ethnicity.gov: global governance, indigenous peoples, and the right to prior consultation in social minefields. Indiana J Glob Legal Stud 18(1)
Rodríguez-Piñero Royo L (2005) Indigenous peoples, postcolonialism, and international law: the ILO regime (1919–1989). Oxford University Press, Oxford
Romero Bonifaz C (2009) Bolivia: De la Confrontación al Pacto Político. In: Romero C, Böhrt Irahola C, Peñaranda R (eds) Del Conflicto al Diálogo: Memorias del Acuerdo Constitucional. FES-ILDIS and fBDM, La Paz
Roth BR (2011) Sovereign equality and moral disagreement: premises of a pluralist international legal order. Oxford University Press, Oxford
Roy C (forthcoming) Articles 41 and 42. In: Eichler J, Doyle C, Howard S (eds) United Nations declaration on the rights of indigenous peoples: article-by-article commentary. Beck, Hart, Nomos, München, Baden-Baden & Oxford
Sabel CF, Gerstenberg OH (2010) Constitutionalising an overlapping consensus: the ECJ and the emergence of a coordinate constitutional order. Eur Law J 16(5)
Sákéj J, Henderson Y (2002) Sui generis and treaty citizenship. Citizsh Stud 6(4)
Sanders D (1991) Collective rights. Hum Rights Q 13(3)
Sano H-O (2000) Development and human rights: the necessary, but partial integration of human rights and development. Hum Rights Q 22
Schippers B (ed) (2019) Critical perspectives on human rights. Rowman & Littlefield International, London/New York
Schmahl S (2021) United Nations convention on the rights of the child: article by article commentary. Nomos/Hart, London/Baden-Baden
Shaw MN (2008) International law, 6th edn. Cambridge University Press, Cambridge
Shrinkhal R (2021) "Indigenous sovereignty" and right to self-determination in international law: a critical appraisal. AlterNative 17(1)
Shue H (1988) Mediating duties. Ethics 98
Shyllon F (2016) Collective cultural rights as human rights simpliciter: the African and African charter example. In: Jakubowski A (ed) Cultural rights as collective rights: an international law perspective. BRILL, Leiden & Boston
Sieder R (2010) Legal cultures in the (un)rule of law: indigenous rights and Juridification in Guatemala. In: Couso J, Huneeus A, Sieder R (eds) Cultures of legality: judicialization and political activism in Latin America. Cambridge University Press, Cambridge
Sieder R (2016) Indigenous peoples' rights and the law in Latin America. In: Rodríguez-Garavito C (ed) Law and society in Latin America: a new map. Routledge, Abingdon
Sieder R (2020) The Juridification of politics. In: Foblets M-C (ed) The Oxford handbook of law & anthropology. Oxford University Press, Oxford
Sieder R, Sierra MT (2010) Indigenous Women's Access to Justice in Latin America. CMI Working Paper 2
Smet S (2017) Introduction—conflicts of rights in theoretical and comparative perspective. In: Smet, Brems E (eds) When human rights clash at the European court of human rights. Oxford University Press, Oxford
Smith LT (2012) Decolonizing methodologies. Zed Books, London
Solón P (2017) Alternativas Sistémicas: Vivir Bien, Decrecimiento, Comunes, Ecofeminismo, Derechos de la Madre Tierra y Desglobalización. Fundación Solón, Focus on the Global South and Attac France, La Paz
Santos B d S (1987) Law: a map of misreading. Toward a postmodern conception of law. J Law Soc 14(3)

Santos B d S (2017) Épistémologies du Sud et militantisme académique. Entretien avec Boaventura de Sousa Santos, réalisé par Baptiste Godrie. Sociologie et sociétés 49(1)

Santos B d S, Meneses MP (2023) Colonial legal duality: the creation of legal codes for indigenous populations. In: Santos BS (ed) Law and the epistemologies of the south. Cambridge University Press, Cambridge

Santos DS, Boaventura (2013) Descolonizar el saber, reinventar el poder. LOM ediciones, Santiago de Chile

Spilde KA (1999) 'Rich Indian' Racism is a Direct Attack on Tribal Sovereignty. Hocak Worak: A Publication of the Ho-Chunk Nation p 5

Spiliopoulou Åkermark A (1996) Justification of minority protection in international law. Nijhoff, The Hague

Squires J (2008) Intersecting inequalities: reflecting on the subjects and objects of equality. Polit Q 79

Stojanović N (2013) Dialogue sur les quotas: Penser la représentation dans une démocratie multiculturelle. Presses de Sciences Po, Paris

Stoljar N (2018) Discrimination and intersectionality. In: Lippert-Rasmussen K (ed) The Routledge handbook of ethics of discrimination. Routledge, London and New York

Swepston L (2015) The foundations of modern international law on indigenous and tribal peoples. BRILL, Leiden

Szablowski D (2010) Operationalizing free, prior, and informed consent in the extractive industry sector? Examining the challenges of a negotiated model of justice. Canadian J Dev Stud/Revue Canadienne d'études du développement 30(1–2)

Tavolari B (2018) Juridification. Krisis J Contemp Philos 2

Teubner G (ed) (1987) Juridification of social spheres: a comparative analysis in the areas of labor, corporate, antitrust and social welfare law. Walter de Gruyter, Berlin and New York

Thienel T, Zimmermann A (2019) Yugoslavia, Cases and Proceedings before the ICJ. Max Planck Encyclopedias of International Law. https://opil.ouplaw.com/display/10.1093/law:epil/9780199231690/law-9780199231690-e235?rskey=muUJni&result=2&prd=MPIL

Thornhill C, Calabria C, Céspedes R, Dagbanja D, O'Loughlin E (2018) Legal pluralism? Indigenous rights as legal constructs. Univ Toronto Law J 68(3)

Tomuschat C (2014) Human rights: between idealism and realism. Oxford University Press, Oxford

Tully J (2008) Public philosophy in a new key: volume I democracy and civic freedom. Cambridge University Press, Cambridge

Ulfstein G (2009) The international judiciary. In: Klabbers J, Peters A, Ulfstein G (eds) The Constitutionalization of international law. Oxford University Press, Oxford

Uprimny R (2016) The recent transformation of constitutional law in Latin America: trends and challenges. In: Rodríguez-Garavito C (ed) Law and society in Latin America: a new map. Routledge, Abingdon

Uprimny R (2011) The recent transformations of constitutional law in Latin America: trends and challenges. Tex Law Rev 89

Van Cott D (2007) From movements to parties in Latin America: the evolution of ethnic politics. Cambridge University Press, Cambridge

Van Drooghenbroeck S, Van der Noot O (2018) Between assimilation and exclusion: is there room for an 'integrated' approach towards constitutional and international protection of human rights? In: Brems E, Ouald-Chaib S (eds) Fragmentation and integration in human rights law: users' perspectives. Edward Elgar Publishing, Cheltenham

Van Dyke V (1985) Human rights, ethnicity, and discrimination. Greenwood, Westport

Vasak K (1979) For the third generation of human rights: the rights of solidarity. Inaugural lecture. In: 10th study session of the International Institute of Human Rights, Strasbourg

Vasak K (1977) A 30 year struggle: the sustained effort to give the force of law to the universal declaration of human rights. The UNESCO Courir 3

Vergis F (2020) Collective labour rights as an element of the substantive constitutionalisation of EU law after the treaty of Lisbon. University of Cambridge, Cambridge

Verstichel A, Andre A, de Witte B, Lemmens P (2008) The framework convention for the protection of national minorities: a useful pan-European instrument? Intersentia, Cambridge
Wahl R (2019) Language and freedom in critiques of human rights. In: Schippers B (ed) Critical perspectives on human rights. Rowman & Littlefield International, London/New York
Waldron J (1993) Liberal rights. Collected papers 1981–1991. Cambridge University Press, Cambridge
Waldron J (2005) Torture and positive law: jurisprudence for the white house. Columbia Law Rev 105(6)
Warren KB, Jackson JE (2003) Indigenous movements, self-representation, and the state in Latin America. University of Texas Press, Austin
Watson I (2018a) Indigenous peoples as subjects of international law. Routledge, Abingdon
Watson I (2018b) Introduction. In: Watson I (ed) Indigenous peoples as subjects of international law. Routledge, Abingdon
Weller M (2006) The rights of minorities in Europe: a commentary on the European framework convention for the protection of national minorities. Oxford University Press, Oxford
Wenzel N (2011) Group Rights. Max Planck Encyclopedias of International Law. Retrieved from https://opil.ouplaw.com/view/10.1093/law:epil/9780199231690/law-9780199231690-e805?prd=EPIL
Westra LS (2011) Human rights: the commons and the collective. University of British Columbia Press, Vancouver
Whelan DJ (2010) Indivisible human rights: a history. University of Pennsylvania Press, Philadelphia
Wing AK (2008) The South African constitution as a role model for the United States. Harv Black Lett Law J 24
Winter CJ (2022) Subjects of intergenerational justice: indigenous philosophy, the environment and relationships. Routledge, Abington
Wright C, Tomaselli A (2019) The prior consultation of indigenous peoples in Latin America: inside the implementation gap. Routledge, Abingdon
Xanthaki A (2007) Indigenous rights and United Nations standards: self determination, culture and land. Cambridge University Press, Cambridge
Xanthaki A (2016) Against integration, for human rights. Int J Human Rights 20(6)
Xenidis R (2019) Multiple discrimination in EU anti-discrimination law: towards redressing complex inequality? In: Belavusau U, Henrard K (eds) EU anti-discrimination law beyond gender. Hart Publishing, Oxford
Yashar DJ (2005) Contesting citizenship in Latin America: the rise of indigenous movements and the postliberal challenge. Cambridge University Press, Cambridge
Youngblood Henderson J (S'k'j) (2008) Indigenous diplomacy and the rights of peoples: achieving UN recognition. University of British Columbia Press, Vancouver
Yrigoyen Fajardo R (2016) The panorama of pluralist constitutionalism: from multiculturalism to decolonisation. In: Rodríguez-Garavito C (ed) Law and society in Latin America: a new map. Routledge, Abingdon
Yupsanis A (2010) ILO convention no.169 concerning indigenous and tribal peoples in independent countries 1989-2009: an overview. Nordic J Int Law 79
Yupsanis A (2012) The meaning of "Culture" in Article 15 (1) (a) of the ICESCR – positive aspects of CESCR's general comment no. 21 for the safeguarding of minority cultures. German Yearb Int Law 55
Yupsanis A (2014) Article 27 of the ICCPR revisited – the right to culture as a normative source for Minority/Indigenous participatory claims in the case law of the human rights committee. In: Lavranos N, Kok R (eds) Annuaire de la Haye de Droit International/Hague Yearbook of International Law, p 26
Zucca L (2016) The cultural contingency of the human right to freedom of religion. In: Jakubowski A (ed) Cultural rights as collective rights: an international law perspective. BRILL, Leiden & Boston

# Chapter 8
# Concluding Thoughts

The book strives to develop a critical approach on the equality principle, undoubtedly being one of the most influential and ground-setting legal principles we know. More specifically, it examines to what extent a de facto meaning is envisaged throughout the multiplicity of legal orders, and how these would satisfy or not the demands of vulnerable groups, in other words, to what extent this would live up to the expectations underlying positive discriminatory approaches or collective rights. Through theorising exercise, a couple of processes and principles are proposed that shall guide or serve as indicators of how the collectivisation of human rights might be operating or not throughout institutions, the law itself, or society. Thereby different schools of thought and paradigms are brought together which commonly find themselves operating in isolation from one another.

Notably, in its essence, the piece brings distinct principles, rights and other constructs together, connecting equality and non-discrimination principles; indigenous peoples', ethnic/cultural/religious/linguistic minority and peoples' rights; positive discrimination, positive measures and affirmative action approaches; collective rights and collectivisation; as well as recognition and politics of difference. Being grounded in different social scientific disciplines including the law, these conceptual paradigms hardly enter into negotiation with each other. Anti-discrimination law, for instance, usually remains confined to purely juridical inquiries without seeking any socio-political contextualisation which would prove necessary for understanding its broader impacts on inequality situations. Questions on recognition and the politics of difference commonly remain within the realm of political theory without being translated into positive measures or other technical legal outcomes. Now, the present work attempts to situate these principles, rights and constructs along a spectrum, departing from equality and non-discrimination law to finally redefine recognition by establishing a set of constituent principles, and to introduce collective rights, by further defining the latter, by identifying processes and scales.

If we now return to the '*equality critique*', of it embodying not only an established principle and right but constituting an entire regime or paradigm (as we term it here) laying at the core of legal orders, we soon become aware of the necessity to examine

 
J. Eichler, *An Interdisciplinary Journey from Non-Discrimination to Collective Rights*, https://doi.org/10.1007/978-3-031-54618-1_8

its underlying premises, respective majority-minority relations, its surrounding contexts or the institutional approval thereof. As it easily becomes apparent, an interdisciplinary exploration becomes a sheer necessity without devaluing the juridical salience of the question. What is more, a purely positivistic approach on the matter may not suffice which would, admittedly, provide promising insights on the precise articulation of equality throughout the multiplicity of (legal) orders: instead, what is primarily sought is a critical engagement with equality, its distinct meaning (s), challenges and especially pitfalls when it comes to recognising difference. Such difference is not solely approached in the abstract, but assumes a real shape—notably, indigenous peoples as well as cultural, ethnic, religious and linguistic minorities, 'national' minorities, and recognised vs. unrecognised minority groups are taken as leading examples throughout the entire piece. Despite the merits lying with such in-depth exploration of equality principles, the work also examines alternative orders, particularly those establishing valuable human rights protection in the group-differentiated sense. A notable focus lies with collective rights, not only motivated by the prospect of granting genuine protection for (minority) groups, but also given their system-transforming nature, that is, offering a valuable alternative to or by complementing individual rights, and also bearing the potential of introducing co-governance and other co-shaping possibilities, including pluralisms, into the predominant order. The book hopes to produce thought-provoking re-conceptualisations, possibly new principles, that could contribute to a rethinking of current equality paradigms and their persistence throughout the multiplicity of legal orders.

## 8.1 Studying Equality Throughout Different Normative Frameworks: Commensurability and Conflicts

Other than what our understanding of legal orders would suggest, these may not only differ horizontally, that is, considering their distinct jurisprudential traditions, but also internally, with group rights usually assuming a separate position, being articulated in a separate legal framework than ordinary equality provisions. As a general trend we may witness a strong orientation on 'conservative or cautious equality approaches' in European frameworks including the EU and Council of Europe mechanisms respectively, and rather 'progressive trends' in the Inter-American and African human and peoples' rights systems. This may not solely be attributed to their founding documents which certainly embrace elements that can be traced back to the earliest human rights codes such as the *Déclaration des Droits de l'Homme et du Citoyen* of 1789 or the *Virginia Declaration of Rights* of 1776, but also the relative power or negotiating potential of relevant rights holder groups. Not insignificantly, rights need to be read in the particular context in which they arise which becomes especially relevant in Latin America where indigenous communities and representatives have been forming the world's most powerful movements, or on the African continent where the decolonial struggle has been leading to debates on indigeneity[1] and peoples' definition[2] seen in relation to not only the population at large, but also vis-à-vis former colonial powers.[3] Following basic legal principles, equality that has found its way into these two latter regional instruments needs to be read in conjunction with provisions establishing peoples' or collective rights, or alternatively, other forms of positive discrimination. In that sense, we may naturally derive a de facto meaning from ordinary equality and non-discrimination provisions being articulated in the regional *Ius Commune*, and provide safeguards where groups do not fall under the scope of protection offered by peoples' or collective rights respectively.

When engaging with international legal frameworks, we are confronted with a similar scenario where civil and political rights, emblematically, fall under the protective scope of art. 2 of the Covenant which ensures that all individuals without '*distinction of any kind*' benefit from the protection established therewith, and art. 26 providing '*equal protection without discrimination*' (art. 26); by contrast, art. 27 of the same instrument guarantees minority rights which are however largely framed in individual terms.[4] It is to be distinguished between arts. 2 and 26 in the sense that the former serves as an '*accessory prohibition*' or '*subordinate norm*' in terms of its application in conjunction with other provisions, and the latter being largely autonomous, with a generic '*equality before the law*' and '*equal protection of the law*' safeguard coexisting alongside the condition that discrimination is prohibited and equal and effective protection against discrimination is protected against.[5] Equality is further specified in the context of women's rights (art. 3) while discrimination is understood very overarchingly to encompass any forms of distinction, exclusion, limitation or preference on the basis of the grounds[6] established in art. 2.[7]

The equality principle is however also approached more generically, developing important safeguards through positive discrimination without necessarily qualifying for and meeting the high threshold established with collective rights. In its General Comment N° 18 on Non-Discrimination, the Committee appears to apply a positive discriminatory approach, pronouncing itself in favour of preferential treatment for specific parts of the population which would constitute a legitimate ground of distinction.[8] On an interesting note we may also refer to the jurisprudential particularity of declaring indigenous minority background alongside racial and ethnic

[1] See also on the concept and African experiences: Venkateswar and Hughes (2013).

[2] Dersso (2006). See also Ashamu (2011). See also: Baldwin and Morel (2009).

[3] Huneeus and Madsen (2018).

[4] For further in-depth debate on these provisions, see Taylor (2020), Nowak (2005) and Schabas (2019).

[5] Taylor (2020).

[6] This includes "*ethnic background, colour, sex, language, religion, political or other opinion, nation/citizen-based or social origin, property, birth or other status*" (art. 2, see also art. 26).

[7] Human Rights Committee (1989) *General Comment N°18: Non-Discrimination.*

[8] Ibid.

minorities one of the most common forms of discrimination falling under the safeguard of art. 26:[9] on one occasion, the Committee stated that indigenous peoples were "*entitled to special rights and protection*".[10] In fact, the Committee has been introducing legal language which permits reading equality, rather clearly, in a *de facto* sense, namely by employing terms such as '*special measures*', '*affirmative action*', '*positive action*', '*positive measures*', '*reverse discrimination*' and '*positive discrimination*'.[11] Specifically in the equality context, the Committee used the chance to make further sense of the affirmative action doctrine, notably it calls upon States to

> take measures to diminish or eliminate conditions which cause or help to perpetuate discrimination prohibited by the Covenant. The purpose is to achieve substantive equality by correcting the conditions affecting a certain part of the population which prevent or impair their enjoyment of human rights. The State should take specific action to correct those conditions. Affirmative action may address historic, national or cultural prejudice, and may involve granting preferential treatment for a time in specific matters[12]

A very distinguishable de facto meaning of equality is embraced here while the Committee hesitates to establish safeguards more systematically, on a permanent basis or as applying to any human rights matter. Group-differentiated rights would indeed cure this systemic ill, with their overarching thematic scope that is commonly embraced (applying to a wide panoply of rights) and their solid enshrinement in constitutional chapters or by forming entire orders such as the UN Declaration on the Rights of Indigenous Peoples.

The book takes as one of its primary objectives a contextual examination of equality throughout coexisting, vertically or horizontally, legal frameworks which all share the common classical legal heritage of equality. Only few founding documents go as far as codifying positive discriminatory approaches or group-differentiated rights, that is, collective rights which are used as a working category in this piece, undoubtedly constituting one of the most progressive legal expressions of minority and group rights. Instead group-differentiation has been introduced, firstly, rather sporadically with relevant cases being submitted to monitoring instances, and secondly, referring to particular groups only and remaining far from establishing any integrated, comprehensive legal regimes. With the growing inter-institutional dialogue connecting the main three regional human rights systems and with more constitutional courts seeking advisory opinions issued by regional and international courts, we may witness a growing awareness, ultimately recognition of group differentiation and collective rights. As a matter of illustration, Inter-American Human Rights mechanisms have become known for their evolutionary interpretation of an outdated legal foundational document which also came to benefit indigenous rights, especially in the field of land, resources and participatory rights. In European

[9] Taylor (2020).
[10] Schabas (2019), p. 802.
[11] Ibid.
[12] Ibid., p. 742.

institutional spheres, we may note an interesting interplay of indigenous and minority rights, constituting a completely new experience in the EU legal order and hence requiring some creative exercise of interpreting human rights in a group-oriented manner. The African human and peoples'(!) rights experience similarly stands out given its open dealing with largely undefined legal categories, starting with peoples' rights and the embracement of indigenous rights being recognised as 'distinct' in that context (*Endorois vs. Kenya* case), or definitional attempts around tribal and other collective identity (*Ogiek vs. Kenya case*).

Equality has commonly been employed as an underlying premise or principle from which to derive group rights, albeit in an ad-hoc way, being constraint to very specific communities, groups or collective identity. It has certainly been assuming a *de facto* meaning throughout judicial orders without however clearly establishing collective rights, remaining—while far-reachingly—limited to positive discriminatory approaches. In this light, the present contribution attempts to further articulate, identify and construct venues that could serve such endeavours, namely the question of collectivising human rights.

## 8.2 Equality, Anti-Discrimination Law, Positive Discrimination and Collective Rights: Bringing Fields Together

One major contribution certainly lies with the interdisciplinary journey that takes the reader from equality and non-discrimination principles to positive discrimination and collective rights. When viewed from a strict reading of equality, group-differentiated rights approaches may seem far-fetched indeed. In other words, the universalising difference-ignorant understanding of rights hardly invites for a group-prone interpretation of the existing law, remaining largely conservative in its application. One of the key objectives of the present work does in fact lie with examining the capacities and adequateness of applying foundational legal principles—equality and non-discrimination in particular—to group-differentiated contexts beyond the individual impacts of a violation. A critique on the conventional use of the principle of equality shall be developed with the dedicated purpose of pluralising perspectives in academic debates but also, essentially, in societal discourse. This inevitably goes hand in hand with a rethinking of rights in collective terms, coming, naturally, with procedural and substantive reconsiderations of the law.

It is conveyed to us a fragmented impression when studying equality and non-discrimination law in detail, given the exclusive focus on specific grounds of discrimination. Institutionalising endeavours under the EU umbrella have started mediating the effects of such isolated treatment through an integrated approach, also known as '*judicialised equality approach*',[13] that is also supposed to tackle

[13]Krizsan et al. (2012), p. 210.

intersectional forms of violations through what has been termed a "*cross-national trend to amalgamate equality institutions*".[14] Other than initial trends would suggest, initiating with 'gender' and 'citizenship' with the adoption of the EEC Treaty (1958), we may speak of widening scope of equality throughout Europe.[15] A few observations may however be made in relation to ongoing challenges anti-discrimination law is facing, especially as these relate to the inherent (in)capacities of anti-discrimination law in dealing with group differentiation. Some of this may be attributed to the somewhat broad nature of many anti-discrimination regimes requiring further spelling out as it was the case for the Racial Equality Directive being complemented by Council Framework Decision 2008/913/JHA on combating certain forms and expressions of racism and xenophobia by means of criminal law. It could be argued that the systemic nature of many such violations only uneasily fits with the protection granted by anti-discrimination law—not necessarily owing to the ground(s) established, but given its unresponsiveness to interrelated violations or the scale of the infringement.

Other related difficulties may be attributed to the particular forms of EU institutionalism, including the delegation of competences to Member States in relation to minority rights,[16] or the general market-driven rationale that shines through EU jurisprudence.[17] We may indeed want to refer to sovereignty issues, also beyond the EU context, that explains for States generally committed to anti-discrimination law to take any further reaching steps towards minority recognition. This becomes particularly visible in the field of 'national' minority rights undergoing monitoring on the part of Council of Europe institutions,[18] thereby allowing us to gain insights into relevant inter-institutional dynamics at Council of Europe—Member States level: often under the guise of diversity arguments, that is, paying due regard to the constitutional traditions of the State parties, States retain considerable powers to address 'national' minority questions.[19] Similar observations may be made in relation to international law where ethnic, cultural, religious and linguistic minorities have only found consideration under individual rights provisions, establishing group-differentiated rights in a very ad-hoc manner. Renegotiating minority rights at domestic constitutional level thereby becomes a sheer necessity, often requiring constitutional reform processes to be initiated, as shown famously in the Andes where new constitutions were built on the idea of '*plurinationality*'[20] or the Corsican minority situation in France more recently. We could hence conclude—or rather

[14] Muir and de Witte (2017), p. 142. On multiple discrimination in EU Anti-Discrimination Law, see Xinidis (2019).

[15] Krizsan et al. (2014).

[16] Kochenov (2018).

[17] Ibid.

[18] See, for instance, Forde (2022). For a comparative analysis on the matter, see: Çali and Demir-Gürsel (2021) and Demir-Gürsel (2021).

[19] Kochenov (2018). See also: Arai-Takahashi (2013) and Born et al. (2020).

[20] Yrigoyen Fajardo (2016).

hypothesise—based on the foregoing analysis on the positioning of equality throughout a multiplicity of legal orders that processes of politicisation predominate in the field of minority rights whereas equality is commonly accepted as a minimum standard, easier to commit to.

We hence preliminarily conclude from the foregoing reflection on anti-discrimination and equality law that these legal safeguards hardly live up to the expectations, needs and dedicated demands of vulnerable groups. Conversely, positive discrimination and collective rights, being situated on the other side of the spectrum, prove more promising in providing sensitive responses to groups and their very specific situation which is largely unforeseen, hence unaddressed, by equality and non-discrimination law. Positive discrimination, by contrast, clearly conveys an outcome-oriented approach on equality, by "*actively favouring one category of people over others*",[21] hence being also specific in the method to be adopted to achieve true equality. Equality principles may indeed be considered empty legal constructs, lacking any precise idea of what objectives could be set, what measures to be adopted, hence leaving States with considerable discretionary powers as to how to (further) regulate anti-discrimination and equality law. A closer idea to what positive discrimination attempts to achieve in that regard, that is, its mitigating potential, is reflected in what has been termed a '*politics of catching up*'[22] between different groups, carrying with it the dedicated purpose of "*promot[ing] a greater de facto equality among those groups or at least to guarantee those members of disadvantaged groups a real equality of opportunities*".[23] As it becomes apparent here, positive discrimination as a policy may wary in terms of its ambition, an often quoted example being university admission processes which also gained attention in the context of affirmative action approaches,[24] promoted in the 1990s. Positive discrimination in that sense serves as a useful starting point for discriminated groups to find due consideration, constituting the first step towards recognition, equality of outcome and special rights to be granted.

In a last step, we shall devote ourselves to these special rights as a particularly noteworthy category, proving not only pivotal in achieving true equality, but giving rise to an entire legal regime that finds its roots in the very situation groups are facing, but also their self-defined demands. Indeed, collective rights show at its finest how minorities' self-defined demands have been absorbed through processes of juridification and codification, it is hence collective self-determination which assumes a steering role in these processes and for rights to become receptive towards proper justice systems, entire new legal constructs and principles. Collective rights do indeed play a very particular role in mediating inequalities, providing a systemic response to systemic violations, in most cases departing from the ad-hoc—often sector-specific—nature of anti-discrimination law, and instead developing entire

[21] Law (2018), para. 1.

[22] Calvès (2010), p. 8.

[23] Ibid., p. 8.

[24] Elford (2018). See also: Guerrero (2002).

sections or chapters of rights. Indeed, collective rights give rise to a paradigm shift in the law and legal orders, what resembles the kind of *despensar* (‘*unthinking*’/ ‘*rethinking*’) in decolonial studies approaches,[25] constituting in fact a crucial dimension in decolonising the law, liberating the latter from its individualistic property-oriented vision. In fact, self-determination may be thought of in a multidimensional sense here, referring both to the way rights holders themselves having been shaping an entire legal regime, that of collective rights, and in the way predominant orders (domestic, regional, international) have been approached by, inter-alia, indigenous and civil society movements and scholarship, the Global South, Third World Approaches to International Law (TWAIL) or other decolonising thinking.[26]

Other than equality and anti-discrimination law, collective rights do not merely require systemic shifts at an ideological level, but call upon us to rethink procedural requirements, surrounding legal structures, entire frameworks. This may concern procedural options for rights to be claimed by the group or representative members; a dedicated openness to legal pluralism[27] opening up for new procedures, judges and jurisdictions;[28] for preambular and other foundational parts of a constitution to undergo reforms, indeed, for collective rights to serve as a transversal rationale permeating entire orders. As it easily becomes apparent here, collective rights and other forms of positive discrimination build much less on existing forms of constitutionalism or other classical legal heritage compared to the somewhat sporadic attempts of equality and non-discrimination to mitigate inequalities, injustices, and vulnerabilities, and in that sense, require fundamental rethinking of legal constructs, processes, principles and structures.

## 8.3 The Merits of Interdisciplinary Work when Studying Equality: Insights from Judicial Studies, Theory, Political Science, and Socio-Legal Inquiry

The field of equality and non-discrimination law but also extending to collective rights and positive discrimination is certainly to be rooted in the legal discipline and legal theory in particular. What is described here as a systemic malaise of the concept of equality has to do with the realm of the law and the specifics of litigation processes. As it has become apparent throughout the book—and this is non-exhaustive—we would have to engage more closely with the complexity of vulnerability, with the systemic nature of human rights violations, with group context, with the socio-political dynamics in place, with rights holder perspectives,

[25] de Sousa Santos (2013).

[26] See, for instance, Smith (2012), Watson (2018) and Adébísí (2023).

[27] On legal pluralism, especially indigenous position, see Gover (2020). See also, essentially: von Benda-Beckmann and Turner (2020).

[28] Barrera (2012). See also Rachel Sieder’s work.

and with the systematic and large scale nature of many violations that are specific to minority groups or groups in minoritized situations. This is where observations beyond the law are necessarily required, ultimately to consider aspects not playing immediately into a violation (at least following a strict reading of the facts) or crucial components of a group-specific violation that are not deemed relevant enough by the bench, again, being intrinsic to the individualistic outlook of the law, including legal codes, jurisprudence or other manifestations of the law.

Group contexts necessarily give rise to very specific procedural and substantive considerations, a context which is commonly to be related to past injustices, complex majority-minority relations, nuanced identity questions or the need for pluralisms to be paid due consideration to at all levels, including political, legal, social, cultural and economic pluralisms. As it may easily become apparent, the legal discipline may not provide adequate methodological tools to explore these pertinent questions that necessarily arise where groups are affected by a violation, commonly further perpetuated by the foundational equality doctrine. In that sense, past injustices, for instance, would require us to engage in legal historical analysis including perspectives introduced by colonial studies to make sense of intergenerational issues, constituting a key concern for indigenous peoples, at times also 'national' minorities. Another relevant question remaining largely unexplored by the law concerns majority-minority relations that may be addressed by means of quota or specialised institutionalism, but would still require further appreciations of asymmetries and power relations in place, or questions of agency to be examined further. Insights from political science thereby become a sheer necessity, examining the actors including rights holders more closely, understanding their relations and dynamics but also as relating to questions of recognition. Identity questions also naturally come up where identity is relegated to the individual and her/his/x respective rights, hence undermining the sheer relevance of group identity construction which is commonly viewed from a sociological or socio-legal approach respectively as far as rights based on identity/ies are concerned. Finally, the question of pluralisms is commonly addressed by legal anthropological work, by working on rights holder or community perspectives, often to translate these into predominant orders, including transnational legal debates or global law. Fundamentally, these perspectives allow translating indigenous interests, including proper procedures and customs into predominant orders, for autonomies and demands for self-determination to be heard and recognised.

Special attention shall also be devoted to the interdisciplinary contribution of the book. As it may easily become apparent, legal positivistic approaches may not suffice when suggesting new legal processes and principles. The same could be said about scales of collectivisation which build on both legal premises as to the nature and operating of rights, and on indicators and ways of measuring processes of collectivisation, the latter being necessarily a social science endeavour. This also concerns the equality principle which allows us to delve into theoretical debates on its underlying premises, its objectives including mitigating inequalities, or its differential application to individuals and groups. As alluded to earlier, socio-political context becomes apparent starting with a multidimensional perspective on inequalities beyond the immediate violations perpetrated and instead to include, emblematically, a social justice dimension. The law enters into dialogue with other disciplines, enabling us to explore surrounding contexts in depth and also, particularly, to get familiar with the specifics of collective rights, and especially the nature of the violations incurred, the specific detrimental impact exerted by equality principles. At the heart of the social scientific inquiry certainly lies a blend of political and legal theory that tries to take the reader from equality and non-discrimination to recognition, positive discrimination and collective rights, often basing itself on principles and imagined constructs. Another interdisciplinary element is introduced with the empirical dimension of the law which, in that sense, departs from the purely normative contribution the book makes while the empirical component remains marginal. Studying equality as it becomes articulated throughout the multiplicity of legal orders demands a closer dealing with a wide variety of legal data, also emblematic case studies and key developments. In fact, the piece is enriched with data taken from indigenous studies and the field of minority studies, providing an important empirical input to the debates, beyond mere illustrative purposes. The book hence combines normative and deeply theoretical work (legal and political theoretical) with empirical inquiry, by making sense of, by constructing and deconstructing legal categories with the help of the legal discipline, but also by contextualising the findings by means of socio-political approaches.

## 8.4 Towards a Paradigm Shift in Equality Law? Systemic Reflections

To start with, equality principles are to be understood in a multidimensional sense for the purpose of the present work, that is, following a narrow approach that considers equality as an isolated equality and non-discrimination provision enshrined in constitutional or other orders, or in a wide sense, embedding equality throughout legal orders, as a founding principle, preambular premise, and as defining the direction of human rights stipulated in a given framework. As it may become apparent quite easily, ad-hoc reforms enacted through regular legislative changes may not suffice to transform our vision on the treatment of minorities through the law. What is indeed needed, concerns a changed societal mindset, assuming a critical view on what is presented to us as '*(European) heritage of fundamental rights*', as '*human rights universalism*'[29] or the safeguards of domestic constitutional law. Indeed, classical equality provisions are taken at face value, as a necessarily 'good thing', as a fundamental starting point for any human rights endeavour. Any ideological orientation is thereby failed to be acknowledged, that is, its focus on

[29] See, for instance, Donnelly (2003). See also different international human rights law documents, starting with the *Universal Declaration of Human Rights* (1948) or the *Vienna Declaration and Programme of Action* (1993).

the individual, liberal theory or possible corollaries of these premises, such as the idea of property. As a result collective identities are commonly constructed around the logics permeating individual rights, in exercising these rights (procedurally) and in terms of the needs that arise in group contexts (substantively). It is indeed the generality and common sense of the individualising forces of equality law that proves most difficult for minority-sensitive agendas to be considered by predominant legal orders.

Now, if we were to go back to the fundamentals of Kuhnian paradigm shifts in science,[30] we need to show awareness of a certain common sense or ruling rationale that is being adhered to by a majority of relevant scholars, further supported by a protective belt[31] of auxiliary hypotheses and conditions that protect the hard core from Popperian falsification.[32] We may easily consider persisting classical legal constructs such as property and its derivatives such as land or natural resources as further undergirding conditions for individual rights to remain at the heard of human rights codes, orders or constitutional chapters. A different vision is defended by communitarian approaches in the collective rights sense, considering natural resources or lands as common public goods or sources of subsistence. The self-fulfilling prophecy rationale promoted by a considerable number of contemporary legal orders thereby assumes a function resembling that of a protective belt in defence of existing human rights definitions, their positioning in legal orders, hierarchies among principles, legal-epistemological sources, majority-minority relations but also a certain proneness to adhere to '*human rights protectionism*' in the sense of developing resistance towards, for instance, (international) human rights review procedures. The inherently politicised nature of international decision-making bodies opens yet another important debate on the actual existence of a concession-free human rights paradigm in practice. It may be legitimately asked to what extent we shall measure human rights in practice, how to monitor and reinforce them or to establish thresholds such as following and implementing genuine, decolonised or gendered approaches. This is also of considerable relevance to the equality principle that is being promoted by a considerable number of States, both domestically and globally.

One of the answers may indeed be sought in the origins of collective rights as promoted by global movements principally. The most prominent regime, that of indigenous rights, has largely been attributed to the Global South with agendas driven by a general decolonising and democratising trend following authoritarian periods of governance in the second half of the twentieth century, most notably in Latin America.[33] Social movements, Cocalero and peasant agendas became fused indigenous rights, leading to the rebuilding of entire States.[34] Especially at global

[30]Kuhn (1962).

[31]Lakatos (1974).

[32]Popper (1959).

[33]Bogdandy et al. (2017).

[34]Yashar (2012), Van Cott (2005) and Postero (2017).

institutional levels, relevant human rights mechanisms had to open up to allow for indigenous representation,[35] notably by reforming decision-making procedures such as the consultative status with ECOSOC or the putting in place of entirely new institutions such as the Expert Mechanism on the Rights of Indigenous Peoples. We may very well imagine that juridification or codification processes would only prove successful where international mechanisms would demonstrate a certain openness to negotiations beyond classical inter-governmentalism. Very prominently, indigenous representation has almost initiated a new era in human rights law in the sense that indigenous organisations and other representative instances have become actively involved in the drafting and other negotiations related to the eventual adoption of the UN Declaration on the Rights of Indigenous Peoples.[36]

Indeed, we may witness progressive trends at international level, for collective rights to have increasingly entered treaty law which concerns indigenous rights but also the right to development[37] or developments on the right to self-determination,[38] carrying considerable implications for rights to be claimed, for rights holder groups including legal personality issues, and also for entirely new rights to enter official legal vocabulary. Similarly, Inter-American[39] and African[40] regional protection standards have shown a certain proneness towards collective rights approaches; in the latter case, novel categories including ‘peoples’ rights’ would be introduced. With sovereignty remaining a key concern in the process of making achievements in international human rights law, the same could be said about the domestic level, being interwoven with majority interests and a clearly pronounced idea of the individual as subject holder. The Council of Europe framework takes an intermediate stance with a dedicated ‘national minority’ convention which however conveys an individual-oriented view on rights, owing, at least in part, to the political nature of the organisation and relevant decision-making instances.[41] Given the lack of relevant legal sources at EU level, it is largely for European States to decide on collective rights matters. Equality principles clearly remain the dominant frame of reference and of (high) legal authority, requiring systemic rethinking to turn towards an active engagement with minority rights—through specific provisions, entire human rights chapters, preambular paragraphs or as a transcending rationale of domestic constitutionalism. In that sense, it is argued throughout the book, dedicated ‘*processes of collectivisation*’ need to be put in place, for achieving systemic transformations,

---

[35] Charters and Stavenhagen (2012).

[36] Ibid.

[37] See, for instance, Marks (2004). For its application to indigenous peoples, see Claridge (2017). See also on its meaning in the African human and peoples’ rights framework: Murray (2019).

[38] See, for instance, Saul (2011).

[39] Inter-American Commission on Human Rights (2009) *Indigenous and Tribal Peoples’ over their Ancestral Lands and Natural Resources: Norms and Jurisprudence of the Inter-American Human Rights System.* See also Sauca and Wences (2016) and see: Talbot (2018).

[40] Baldwin and Morel (2009). Also check: Talbot (2018) and Murray and Wheatley (2003).

[41] See, for instance, Forde (2022). See also: Demir-Gürsel (2021).

including *'juridification'/'standardisation'*, *'establishing sui generis orders'*, *'constitutionalising processes'*, *'institutional mainstreaming'*, and *'transposing/ integrating processes'* as well as these should address autonomy and leverage vis-à-vis the State, and deal with the integrity of human rights.

## References


Adébísí FI (2023) Decolonisation and legal knowledge: reflections on power and possibility. Bristol University Press, Bristol

Arai-Takahashi Y (2013) The margin of appreciation doctrine: a theoretical analysis of Strasbourg's variable geometry. In: Føllesdal A, Peters B, Ulfstein G (eds) Constituting Europe: the European Court of Human Rights in a national, European and global context. Cambridge University Press, Cambridge

Ashamu E (2011) Centre for Minority Rights Development (Kenya) and Minority Rights Group International on behalf of Endorois Welfare Council vs. Kenya: a landmark decision from the African Commission. J Afr Law 55(2)

Baldwin C, Morel C (2009) Group rights. In: Evans M, Murray R (eds) The African Charter on Human and Peoples' Rights: the system in practice, 1986–2006. Cambridge University Press, Cambridge

Barrera A (2012) Turning legal pluralism into state-sanctioned law: assessing the implications of the new constitutions and laws in Bolivia and Ecuador. In: Schilling-Vacaflor A (ed) New constitutionalism in Latin America: promises and practices. Ashgate, Farnham

Bogdandy A, Ferrer MacGregor E, Morales Antoniazzi M, Piovesan F (2017) Transformative constitutionalism in Latin America: the emergence of a new Ius Commune. Oxford University Press, Oxford

Born G, Morris D, Forrest S (2020) "A margin of appreciation": appreciating its irrelevance in international law. Harv Int Law J 61(1)

Çali B, Demir-Gürsel E (2021) The Council of Europe's responses to the decay of the rule of Law and human rights protections: a comparative appraisal. Eur Convention Hum Rights Law Rev 2

Calvès G (2010) La Discrimination Positive. Presses Universitaires de France, Paris

Charters C, Stavenhagen R (2012) Making the declaration work: the United Nations Declaration on the Rights of Indigenous Peoples. International Work Group for Indigenous Affairs, Copenhagen

Claridge L (2017) Briefing: victory for Kenya's Ogiek as African Court sets major precedent for indigenous peoples' land rights. Minority Rights Group International, London

de Sousa Santos B (2013) Descolonizar el saber, reinventar el poder. LOM ediciones, Santiago de Chile

Demir-Gürsel E (2021) The Former Secretary General of the Council of Europe confronting Russia's annexation of the Crimea and Turkey's State of Emergency. Eur Convention Hum Rights Law 2

Dersso SA (2006) The jurisprudence of the African Commission on Human and Peoples' Rights with respect to peoples' rights. Afr Hum Rights Law J 6

Donnelly J (2003) Universal human rights in theory and practice. Cornell University Press, Ithaca

Elford G (2018) Discrimination and education. In: Lippert-Rasmussen K (ed) The Routledge handbook of ethics of discrimination. Routledge, London

Forde A (2022) Political salvation of Europe's human rights system? The case for a Fourth Council of Europe Summit. ECHR Blog. https://www.echrblog.com/2022/03/political-salvation-of-europes-human.html

Gover K (2020) Legal pluralism and indigenous legal traditions. In: Schiff Berman P (ed) The Oxford handbook of global legal pluralism. Oxford University Press, Oxford

Guerrero A (2002) Silence at Boalt Hall: the dismantling of affirmative action. University of California Press, Berkeley
Huneeus A, Madsen MR (2018) Between universalism and regional law and politics: a comparative history of the American, European, and African human rights systems. Int J Constitutional Law 16(1)
Kochenov D (2018) When equality directives are not enough: taking issue with the missing minority rights policy in the EU. In: Belavusau U, Henrard K (eds) EU anti-discrimination law beyond gender. Hart, Oxford
Krizsan A, Skjeie H, Squires J (2012) European equality regimes: institutional change and political intersectionality. In: Krizsan A, Skjeie H, Squires J (eds) Institutionalising intersectionality: the changing nature of European regimes. Palgrave Macmillan, London
Krizsan A, Skjeie H, Squires J (2014) The changing nature of European equality regimes: explaining convergence and variation. J Int Comp Soc Policy 53(30)
Kuhn T (1962) The structure of scientific revolutions. University of Chicago Press, Chicago
Lakatos I (1974) Falsification and the methodology of scientific research. In: Lakatos I, Musgrave A (eds) Criticism and growth of knowledge. Cambridge University Press, Cambridge
Law J (2018) Positive discrimination. A dictionary of law. Oxford University Press, Oxford
Marks S (2004) The human right to development: between rhetoric and reality. Harv Hum Rights J 17
Muir E, de Witte B (2017) The procedural and institutional dimension of anti-discrimination Law. In: Rossi LS, Casolari F (eds) The principles of equality in EU law. Springer International Publishing, Cham
Murray R, Wheatley S (2003) Groups and the African Charter on Human and Peoples' Rights. Hum Rights Q 25(1)
Murray R (2019) The African Charter on Human and Peoples' Rights: a commentary. Oxford University Press, Oxford
Nowak M (2005) U.N. Covenant on Civil and Political Rights: CCPR commentary. Engel Publisher, Kehl
Popper K (1959) The logic of scientific discovery. Routledge, London
Postero N (2017) The indigenous state: race, politics, and performance in plurinational Bolivia. University of California Press, Oakland
Sauca JM, Wences I (2016) Derechos colectivos (en la doctrina de la Corte Interamericana de Derechos Humanos). Eunomía. Revista en Cultura de la Legalidad 9
Saul M (2011) The normative status of self-determination in international law: a formula for uncertainty in the scope and content of the right? Hum Rights Law Rev 11(4)
Schabas WA (2019) U.N. International Covenant on Civil and Political Rights: Nowak's CCPR commentary. N.P. Engel Publisher
Smith LT (2012) Decolonizing methodologies. Zed Books, London
Talbot M (2018) Collective rights in the inter-American and African human rights systems. Georgetown J Int Law 49
Taylor PM (2020) A commentary on the International Covenant on Civil and Political Rights: the human rights monitoring of ICCPR rights. Cambridge University Press, Cambridge
Van Cott DL (2005) From movements to parties in Latin America: the evolution of ethnic politics. Cambridge University Press, New York
Venkateswar S, Hughes E (2013) The politics of indigeneity: dialogues and reflections on indigenous activism. Zed Books, London
von Benda-Beckmann K, Turner B (2020) Anthropological roots of global legal pluralism. In: Schiff Berman P (ed) The Oxford handbook of global legal pluralism. Oxford University Press, Oxford
Watson I (2018) Indigenous peoples as subjects of international law. Routledge, Abingdon
Xinidis R (2019) Multiple discrimination in EU anti-discrimination law: towards redressing complex inequality? In: Belavusau U, Henrard K (eds) EU anti-discrimination law beyond gender. Hart Publishing, Oxford

Yashar DJ (2012) Contesting citizenship in Latin America: the rise of indigenous movements and the postliberal challenge. Cambridge University Press, Cambridge

Yrigoyen Fajardo R (2016) The panorama of pluralist constitutionalism: from multiculturalism to decolonisation. In: Rodríguez-Garavito C (ed) Law and society in Latin America: a new map. Routledge, Abingdon

MIX
Papier aus verantwortungsvollen Quellen
Paper from responsible sources
FSC® C105338

If you have any concerns about our products, you can contact us on
**ProductSafety@springernature.com**

In case Publisher is established outside the EU, the EU authorized representative is:
**Springer Nature Customer Service Center GmbH**
**Europaplatz 3, 69115 Heidelberg, Germany**

Printed by Libri Plureos GmbH
in Hamburg, Germany